GEORGE MACKAY BROWN is remembered for his poetry, novels, plays and short stories. Much of his fiction and verse was based on his life in Orkney, especially his childhood. He was born in Stromness, Orkney, in 1921. He was at Newbattle Abbey College when Edwin Muir was Warden. He read English at Edinburgh University and did postgraduate work on Gerard Manley Hopkins.

He was awarded an Arts Council grant for poetry in 1965, The Society of Authors' Travel Award in 1968, The Scottish Arts Council Literature Prize in 1969 for *A Time to Keep*, and the Katherine Mansfield Menton Short Story Prize in 1971. He was awarded the OBE in January 1974.

He received honorary degrees from the Open University (MA), Dundee University (LLD), Glasgow University (DLitt) and he was a fellow of the Royal Society of Literature. In 1987 his novel *The Golden Bird* won the James Tait Black prize. George Mackay Brown died in 1996.

ROCKPOOLS AND DAFFODILS

'Each essay is coloured by the "sounds and delicate pulsating of nature", the "astonishing weather", the "horizon hazy with haar", the autumn on a "wild raging slut of a day". Read this book and discover the poet, his sources and his muse. You won't be disappointed.'

—*The Scots Magazine*

Rockpools and Daffodils

George Mackay Brown

Steve Savage
LONDON AND EDINBURGH

Steve Savage Publishers Ltd
The Old Truman Brewery
91 Brick Lane
LONDON
E1 6QL

www.savagepublishers.com

Published in Great Britain by Steve Savage Publishers Ltd 2017

First published in hardback by Gordon Wright Publishing Ltd 1992
Copyright © George Mackay Brown 1992

ISBN 978-1-904246-43-5

Typeset by Steve Savage Publishers Ltd
Printed and bound by SRP Ltd, Exeter

FSC
www.fsc.org
MIX
Paper from
responsible sources
FSC® C014540

Contents

Introduction 9

Dounby Show 11

The Month of 'Thunder Spoots' 12

Stromness Shifts its Centre of Gravity 13

Into the Dark of Winter 14

A Desolation of a Day 15

Is Stromness Sinking? 16

Folk-Lore 17

St Columba 18

Bottles 19

Margaret Tait's Films 20

Let the Wind Burst its Cheeks! 22

A Treaty with the Earth 23

Early Souvenir for Tourists 24

Delight of Ordnance Survey Maps 25

Closes 26

Gray's Pier 27

Keeping a Diary 28

Palm Sunday Walk 29

Sean O'Casey 30

St Magnus Relics 31

Winters of War 32

Themes for Orkney Writers 33

The Enchanting Chariot 34

Up Brinkie's Brae 35

Thor the Thunderer 36

Corrigall Farm Museum 38

Images from Arran 38

Music of Old Place Names 39

Torn from their Surroundings 40

Cruise on the *Marques* 41

Royal Visitors 42

Summer Is Winding Down 43

Hundi's Butterfly Dance 44

Redressing the Balance 45

The Small Darkling Masquers 46

The Laconic Orcadians 47

Words Gone into the Silence 48

Sweeties 49

A Poet in Stone 50

A Christmas Story 51

Retrospect of 1980 53

'Quiet Orkney'? 54

The Orkney Book 55

Brendan's Voyage 56

The 'Lang Reed' of March 57

Riddles of the Universe 58

Rescue from Bleak Ox-Pastures 59

View from Kirkwall 60

St Magnus Day 60

No More Pipes 62

Time's Dark Stainings Removed 63

'Bloomsday' 64

Mysterious Island 65

Ordeal by Filming 65

Speak Softly, or Not at All 67

Orkney's Part in the Royal Wedding 68

Three Giant Strides 69

Pastoral Emptiness to Growth Area 70

Don Quixote 71

A Truncated Meal 72

The Golden Age 73

A Great Stromnessian 74

The Old Grey Man of Langskaill 75

The Red-Cheeked Ghost 76

Punch and Judy 77

Vandalism 78

The Kirkyard 79

Month of the Equinox 80

The Mill of Eyreland 81

A New Folk Tale 82
The Work Ethic 83
Summer Flowers 84
The Bay of Skaill 85
Johnsmas 86
Under Moorfea 87
Lure of the Tall Ships 88
The *Fortune* 89
Equinoctial Gales 91
Mr Bluebottle 92
Conversation of the Seasons 92
Childhood Reading 93
A Few Bright Snapshots 94
The Story of Burnt Njal 95
Christmas in the Heroic Age 96
St Lucy's Day 97
New Year Wishes 98
The Ferocious Month 99
Breakfast TV 100
A Strangely-Patterned Winter 101
Grumbling and Gratitude 102
Orkney Ministers 102
'A Little of What You Fancy' 104
Aberdeen's European Triumph 104
'Whales!' 105
The First Turf Fire 106
A Mysterious Stranger 107
A Dead Gull 108
Black Bags 109
Filipino Feast 110
A Literary Coincidence 111
Braal in Strathy 112
Kirsty Watt 113
Praise and Prizes for Writers 114
Gypsy 115
Daily Newspapers 116
The Witch of Leafea 117
Crusaders 118
Christmas, Ahoy! 119

Short Story Writing 120
Christmas Cards 121
George Orwell 122
A Pair of Kippers 123
Football Heroes 124
Vanished from the Street 124
'Comparative' Safety 125
Solzhenitsyn 126
A Seat at the Pierhead 127
Latin Disappears 128
Laureate Memories 129
Housman and the End of May 130
The Masked Fisherman 131
Loss of the *Marques* 132
The Noust at Sandy Geo 133
An Enchanted Week 134
Summers at the West Shore 135
Believe it if You Like 136
Park where Three Parishes Meet 137
Tastes Vanished and Acquired 137
Bygone Brands 138
Look for 'the Peedie Summer' 139
TV Finds its Level 140
Sleeping Habits 141
Santa in 1934 142
The End of 1984 143
Twelfth Night 143
The Faithful Power Supply 144
The Blank Screen 145
Sillocks 146
Rent Increase! 147
A New Art Gallery 148
Psychology in Numbers 149
April Foolery 150
Cosmic Drama 151
The End of World War II 151
A New Ice Age Begins 152
Penguins Are 50 153
Poetry of Western Mountains 154

Summer Insects	155	Persons from St Andrews	192
No News	156	Frayings and Wearings-Out	193
Visitors from Abroad	157	An Iron Discipline	193
Gale Warnings	158	Edwin Muir Centenary	194
Stromness Street Names	159	The End of a Toaster	195
Mealtimes	159	Colditz on the Heights	196
The Open Window	160	Pilgrimage to Wyre	197
The Price of 'Civilisation'	161	Macbeth Country	198
Christmas in Hamnavoe, 1085	162	Midsummer Myths	199
Bygone Hogmanay	163	Rackwick Rain	200
Why Come to Orkney in Winter?	164	The Stromness Correspondent	201
A Fall of Snow	165	Convalescence in Kirbister	201
Demanding Gypsy	166	Three Empty Spaces	202
Origins: Nothing for our Comfort	167	The Free Kirk	203
Assiepattle and the Stoor-Worm	168	Orkneymen in the Nor'-Wast	204
The Child, the Eagle and the Mother	169	Windmills on Burgar Hill	205
Caged Dragons	170	Eye Trouble	206
Never Cast a Cloot	171	Christmas Decorations	207
World Cup Football	172	Soup	208
Festival-Time	173	Short-Lived Daughter of Winter	209
Rackwick Holiday (1)	174	Spring-Cleaning	209
Rackwick Holiday (2)	175	Equinoctial Blues	210
Giant Hogweed	176	Interfering with 'God's Time'	211
To Yesnaby as Evenings Draw in	177	Novels on Film	212
The Gairsay Viking	178	Flowers Spun from Light	213
Starting Secondary School	179	New Glasses	214
Mapmakers' Mess	180	The First Morning of May	215
The Eventide Club	181	The Gab o' May	216
Flying to Turnhouse	182	Orkney Churches	217
Return to Rose Street	183	Holiday in Shetland (1)	218
Midwinter Festival Revived	183	Holiday in Shetland (2)	219
Disaster at Hogmanay	184	Holiday in Shetland (3)	220
Sledging	185	Holiday in Shetland (4)	222
The Poets on Winter	186	Holiday in Shetland (5)	223
Firelighting	187	Highland Park Distillery	224
From Orkney to New Zealand	188	Icelandic Sagas	225
'Spike'	189	Early Tourists	226
Wedded to the Sea	190	Isabel Gunn	227
Water Supply	191	Discovery of a Poet	228

Labyrinth of Books	229	Poet in the Prison-House	276
The Street-Devouring Dragon	230	Home Thoughts from Hospital	278
No Praise for the Dog	231	The Sunday School Picnic	279
Christmas in Literature	232	Festival Poets	280
Game at the Year's End	234	'Wet' and 'Dry' Times	281
The Ozone Layer	235	The Putting Green	282
The Master of the *George*	236	A Wilderness of Paper	283
Local Traditions	238	Poets of the Sagas	284
The 'Quiet South End'?	239	Remembered Autumns	285
Candlemas Day	240	Strategy for the Fire	287
'Inspiration' and Work	241	Recollections on Radio Orkney	288
A Drive to Birsay	242	Tales of the Black Craig	289
The Lady Nicotine	243	*Vinland*: the Birth of a Novel	290
Sailors in the White-House	245	Return of the Light	292
Academy Library—Old and New	246	Flavour of the Week	293
Bessie Millie	247	House Interiors	294
A Golden Summer	249	The South Orkneys	295
Gerard Manley Hopkins	250	The Real Earl Hakon	296
Ecclesiastes	251	Work-Place and Dining-Room	298
Orkney Tatties	253	The Sounds of 'Music'	299
The First Shopping Week	254	A Sad Story	300
The May Burn	255	Sea-Haar	301
Origin of the Dounby Show	256	The Craft of Verse-Writing	303
Hamnavoe Market	258	Midsummer Sunset	304
Robert Rendall	259	The Day of Freedom	305
Lyrics	260	Summer Is Here	306
Largesse	262	Gavin Muir	307
All Saints' Day	263	Town and Parish: the Beginnings	309
Return of the Rats	264	One of Those Days	310
The Telephone	265	A Shadow on the Mind	311
Preparing for Christmas: 1920s	266	Letter from Foresterhill	312
Impressions of 1989	267	Shut up in Vulcan's Smithy	313
'Chief o' Scotia's Food'	268	Seventy Today	314
Burns' Day	269	Menace from the May Burn	315
Stromness v Kirkwall	271	A Precarious Verge	317
'The Cup that Cheers'	272	'The Quirks of Blazoning Pens'	318
Rev William Clouston	273		
Women in *The Orkneyinga Saga*	274		
The Unfolding Drama of War	275		

Introduction

Writers that have been born and nurtured in a small community invariably want to break the circle and to reach a wider audience. It is not necessary, to try to achieve 'universality' (though that is too grand a phrase for the work of writers), to break away from the native roots and sources. Thomas Hardy wrote about Wessex, and William Faulkner about one small county in the Deep South of the USA.

But there is always the danger that at last a writer might, without wishing to do so, appeal to the wider anonymous readership and forget, to some extent, the reader by lamplight in Hamnavoe or Hoy.

That would be to impoverish both the reading and the writing.

I have long thought it a good thing to keep in touch with my fellow islanders by means of a small weekly essay in *The Orcadian*. There are treasures enough to rummage among, childhood memories and contemporary happenings and, as well, the turning wheel of the seasons and the astonishing weather in the north that can wear four different coats in a single day.

So, most Thursday mornings I write 'Under Brinkie's Brae' on the kitchen table, after the tea cups and the marmalade pot have been cleared away. And every Thursday morning Orkney folk who are interested can read in *The Orcadian* the 'Under Brinkie's Brae' that was written the Thursday before.

If the article is any good, both readers and author can expect to be mildly pleased.

The first of these articles was published on 18 February 1971 under the heading 'Letter From Hamnavoe' and a collection covering the period to 27 March 1975 was published in book form in November 1975 with the title *Letters From Hamnavoe*. Following a short gap in publication I resumed this column in 1976 with the new title 'Under Brinkie's Brae' and a further collection was published in 1979 covering the period from 5 February 1976 until 19 July 1979. This third collection continues from almost where we left off.

Thanks to the editor of *The Orcadian*. And thanks especially to Brian Murray who originally proposed the idea of the first volume to the publisher and did so much work editing and correcting the newspaper originals in order to make this third volume possible. Brian in turn, wishes to acknowledge the help he received from Marion Corsie and Lenise Philp in Stromness Public Library and Alison Fraser, the Archivist at the Orkney Library, Kirkwall.

George Mackay Brown
Stromness 1992.

To the Folk of Hamnavoe

Dounby Show

16.8.1979

We went to the Dounby Show yesterday in a fine new big car, seven of us, including two children.

Everything turned out fine. It was an afternoon of the utmost clarity. The sun had shone brightly about noon, while I sat in a store yard above the harbour and tried to sketch out an introduction to a book. Two cats devoured—one of them at first with curiosity, then with great intensity—separate parts of a trout's head... Young folk fished for sillocks[1] from the neighbouring pier.

The fried trout in the sun-bright yard, with new tatties, was, of course, delicious.

There were dark bars of rain-bearing cloud south over Scapa Flow, but they hardly moved in the still, lucent air.

The harbour brimmed with light, like a new mirror.

* * *

I have known Dounby Shows that wept with rain and blew out the canvas of the beer-tent like a galleon in distress. These were bitter occasions.

There was one Dounby Show steeped in Mediterranean heat. One could hardly drag—sweating—around the pens of the marvellous beasts. Outside the beer-tent folk sat, bemused with heat, and drank lager from cans.

The best Dounby Shows of all were, I think, small bits of dialogue with farmers from this parish and that; then with students not seen, perhaps, for a year or two; then with strangers who have been friends ever since.

The Dounby Show breaks down barriers. It is a foretaste of harvest and the year's plenitude. All men exist by the fruits of the earth. Here the creatures of the earth—animals, fowls, and folk—appear at their most splendid and festive.

It was a near-perfect day for the Show.

The sun shone, but it was not too hot, for a cool wind blew across the mid-Mainland plain. One cloud, indeed, threatened rain; which is why I made the circuit of the show-park clutching a plastic mac... But

---

1. coalfish, kind of coley

11

the cloud moved on, like a high grey battleship, and the sun—a golden barque—had the sky to itself again.

Beside the huge black bulls at the wall, beside the pens of tinted sheep, and the goats and the carolling cockerels and the patient horses, we lingered out the afternoon talking to this friend and that. And I ended, as always, among a throng of friends at the mouth of the beer-tent, relishing malt, that rare ancient earth-fruit.

The Month of 'Thunder-Spoots'

23.8.1979

The rain is nagging at the skylights, an insistent throb and patter. It makes a not unpleasant background to the writing of letters.

August is the month of 'thunder-spoots', as the old folk called them. The rain makes only a quiet music on the glass now. An hour ago, for five intense minutes, it fairly throbbed against the skylights. The glass surged with sweet sudden waters.

* * *

I thought, after breakfast, of the backlog of letters I had to write.

Outside, in the sun, was the place to write them. The day brimmed with sunlight. The harbour water was blue tremulous silk. A flock of white clouds drifted high, northwards.

Drag a weathered hundred-year-old chair into the yard. Beg for a few sheets of paper. Rest feet on the sea wall. Any letter, thus written, is bound to be touched with August ripeness, and with the fullness of the sea inching its way up the pier stones.

I looked up from the opening paragraph of the second fluent sun-splashed letter, and saw an immense blue-grey-black cloud over Hoy. I wrote to my friend in St Albans: '...seems I might have to finish the letter indoors.' ... My friend knows Orkney; he knows all the varied wardrobe of our weather; in fact, in the letter I got from him yesterday, he is actually hoping to visit the islands in December. 'It is brave of you' (I wrote) 'to think of visiting Orkney in December. But winter here can be very beautiful, with stars and storms, lamps and leaping fires.'...

Three paragraphs later and the first raindrops hit my writing hand. In order not to have the letter reduced to a wet pulp, I carried the comfortable old chair inside. Whether you think winter beautiful or not, summer (especially August) can be disconcertingly dramatic. Here was a swift change in the wardrobe from blue-and-gold to sackcloth.

The rain intensified, as I wrote the fourth and the fifth letters.

* * *

Now, outside, the rain has stopped. There are great swatches of blue in the sky. Could a sixth letter be written in the yard, in mellow afternoon sun? Maybe—but the great August thunderheads are still over Hoy, like black bulls ready to shatter the idyll with sudden hooves and horns.

I think, however, I will risk it. There has not been that much sun this summer, and the swans are out, a brilliant pair, riding the flood waters.

Stromness Shifts its Centre of Gravity

13.9.1979

Two friends from Edinburgh have come to spend a fortnight at the Glebe in Innertown situated on the green brae that looks onto Hoy and the open Atlantic.

Was the Glebe Farm in every period the minister's acres, either to work himself or to glean the crops from? This farm must be very old, if it dates from the time when the parish church stood in the kirkyard. There is a ruined wall in the oldest 'God's-acre' of the three. Possibly that was part of the parish church of Stromness.

The name Monkerhouse has come down through the centuries; is marked, indeed, on some maps. There was very likely a little monastery in the vicinity, though now all traces of it have vanished. The sea has eaten deeply into this part of the coast. The circling magnificence of the ocean—its boundlessness—seems always to have had symbolical appeal to those interested in the things of time and eternity.

There, where the kirkyard is, was once the centre of Stromness parish. It is fascinating to speculate that in those days, perhaps 400 years ago, there was no burgh of Stromness. At best, under Brinkie's Brae might be a little group of fishing bothies. But here and there must have been a merchant or a skipper with an eye for safe harbourage. What better haven for stormbound ships than the little blue tongue of water between the granite hill and the Holms? The first-comers from the east had done well to call the place Hamnavoe: 'haven-bay'.

But it seems that Innertoon had risen a bit in the world. The original centre of the parish was in Cairston, at the far side of Stromness. Two brochs have lately been excavated there. The Bu' Farm is in Cairston, and the Bu' Farm belonged to the local Norse chieftain. It was here—possibly at Congesquoy—that the pre-Reformation priest had his church and vicarage.

* * *

For some reason, the centre of gravity of the parish tilted first to Innertoon. For a century or two the minister and Breckness, the chief landowner, lived and worked here.

Then the merchants began to dig into the side of Brinkie's Brae; they began to build stone piers above the shifting harbour water. There was a ringing of gold and silver coins on counters.

It was time soon for minister and kirk to move to this busy place.

* * *

But four or five generations of ministers must have stood, on summer evenings, and seen, over the ripening oatfield, the magnificent meeting of sun and sea.

Into the Dark of Winter

4.10.1979

Tomorrow (as I write this) it will be the 1st of October.

October is the month of increasing shadows. The equinox is behind us. We go into the dark of winter.

Time to think about thick coats, and articles made of wool. Time to turn from the salads and fruits of summer and to think of the foods that put thick marrow in the bones—broth, clapshot. (It is almost worth having winter for those thick hot bowls of soup, the buttered and well-peppered tangle of mashed tatties and neeps.) Time to put on a darker richer brew.

If you think winter is still a fair time away, there comes some day in early October a rattle of hail-stones on the window; the outriders of ice having a small preliminary skirmish in the empyrean, shaking our panes with a fusillade before retiring to link up with the main army— the columns and divisions that will assault and possess our fields in December and January. General Winter is probing, delicately, our defences.

Witches are out, under the new moon or the full moon, gathering for the great witch-coven of Hallow-E'en. While they journey among the stars, the children hunt nuts and apples, in circling enchantments of water, beside the early winter fires.

October used to be the first month of story and song. The old malt-tongued story-teller at the fire, telling about seal-men and croft-maidens, and Assiepattle's deadly fire-battle with the world-destroying Stoor-Worm, or the raven banner of the Orkney Earl at Clontarf. Then, the tongue being too heavy with its weight of words, the fiddle would be taken down from the wall. Winter was worth waiting for, for such delights. (But now we turn a switch, and a box in a corner of the room brims with shadows and echoes.)

It often happens that October has a sequence of sweet mild sunny days: as many as seven or twelve in a row. If ever we needed such a 'peedie[1] summer', it is this year, when the big summer was a wet nondescript lout with little or nothing to be said for it; it is out of the story; let it go.

This October the burns are full: they go down, making their small fresh chuckling music, into the loch or the sea. The sea gathers that sweetness into the hush before it unleashes its great winter symphony over darkling piers and fields.

A Desolation of a Day

11.10.1979

Even in this abnormally wet year of 1979, I had not imagined such a desolation of a day as Thursday, October 4.

The continuous downpour seemed to gnaw into nerves and blood and brain-cells. At any rate, I made no progress on the piece of work I was trying to do. (To be truthful, I made an utter mess of it.) It was the rain to blame, I consoled myself.

* * *

We were to go, in the early evening, to a house in Birsay, to a birthday dinner. The car went the fifteen miles through a huge grey earth-draggled weeping cloud.

Over the steak, the trifle, the red wine, the talk, it was possible to forget about the nag of the rain outside. Over a whisky and a large cigar, later, the incessant drumming of the rain at the windows could be said to add, by contrast, to the euphoria.

A sudden blinding flash!—the house was whelmed in darkness!—a prolonged peal of thunder trundled across the north... Then, thankfully, the power returned, the lamp, fire, TV resumed where they had been so rudely interrupted.

The rain kept crashing down.

* * *

Ten o'clock, and time to be going home. Rain, or a piece of wind-whipped Boardhouse Loch, lay inside the back lobby.

Rain slanted in dark diagonals across the headlamps of the car. More than once the car crashed through a pool, with a mighty cleaving of the waters. I think we met only one other car all the way back to Stromness.

1. little (but *see* 27.11.1980 on p49)

It should have been a night with the moon near its full, a night of 'peedie summer' with a maze of mild stars. But earth and sea and sky were wrapped in that one seeping cloud.

It seemed, in Stromness, that the violence of the rain was tempered a little, sheltering us. For, when we came within sight of Mayburn Court, an astonishing sight met our eyes. A great river of water flowed down the Distillery Close, crashed over the steps at the foot, and swerved past the telephone box and the Museum wall! I have never seen anything like that before. The wetness of 1979 was saying, in effect, 'What are all you Orcadians grousing about? Look at what I can do, if I really want to ...'

When I went to bed, after midnight, the rain had moderated a little.

Is Stromness Sinking?

18.10.1979

Certain houses on the seaward side of Stromness are apprehensive nowadays when the moon is rounding out to the full. The full moon for a day or two brings big flood-tides, and if the tides are augmented by following wind, the cellars and kitchens of certain Stromness houses are liable to be inundated to the depth of a foot or two.

For some reason these floodings are much commoner now than formerly. Is the tide-level higher? Is Stromness, like Venice, very slowly sinking? Can it be—as some think—that the Churchill Barriers have affected the behaviour of the sea by blocking three natural outlets on the south-east?

Whatever the reason, a stormy Saturday night in September 1978 flooded a few Stromness apartments with dark cold frightening surges.

* * *

Last Saturday evening, the moon was full. It summoned a brimming glittering sea into the harbour. Quickly the water inched up the piers, obliterated slipways, laid siege to the ancient stones of the town. The sea, being far more ancient than the town, was trying to reclaim some of the realm filched from it by generations of Stromness fishermen, builders, merchants. If it floated a few rugs and chairs, and put a few fires out, and poked salt fingers into electric cookers and fridges, what was that to the strictures and bounds that men have been putting on the sea from time's beginning?

But for those Stromnessians who actually have cellars and kitchens in the disputed territory, it is no fun when the moon, the sea, and the south-west wind conspire together.

16

Fortunately, it was a calm weekend, with only a ruffle on the waters. The wind was having no part in the conspiracy this time. But it was a near thing all the same. Inexorably the flood rose about the threatened piers round 10.30pm. It hung and lingered there for a half-hour or so. Torches were flashed at certain key stones; if the flood rose above them, then it was time to put on rubber boots and retire upstairs.

The sea yielded, at the very last moment.

The next night, Sunday, was very beautiful. The moon—the enemy—could not have thrown a more tranquil image in the looking-glass of the sea.

The tide lapped in, it laved (brimming and bright) the stone feet of Hamnavoe. It rose higher even than the night before. Then stone and sea hung in perilous balance for twenty minutes or so, before the sea withdrew.

A dozen or a score of Stromness rooms would be dry for another twenty-eight days or so.

But I tremble to think what would have happened if a gale had whipped a host of grey horses in through Hoy Sound that night.

Folk-Lore

8.11.1979

October ended with a beautiful day. The morning was so bright and calm that I decided to abandon paper and pens and do some shopping.

There was the pleasure of meeting some friends from distant places in the street.

I returned to the sheets of paper and the pens in the afternoon. But nothing exciting happened at last. Indeed, the dreary waste of words on the pages was depressing. Could order and beauty ever be salvaged from this chaos?

* * *

Since Sunday, darkness is upon us in late afternoon in one black stride.

But this is the season when the moon begins to be in her glory. The moon in the south-east was rounding out to the full; the harbour was full of rough silver.

Going north along the street, Stromness seemed to be possessed by witches and warlocks, some of them very tiny. The Hallow-E'en revellers had been busy already; hardly a window that wasn't daubed with white paint or treacle.

Was the ghost of Bessie Millie moving somewhere along the side of Brinkie's Brae?

Our destination was the Pier Arts Centre, where a talk was to be given by Howie Firth on a subject most appropriate for the season: 'Folk-Lore'.

I'm certainly glad I went. The lecturer was in brilliant form; he led us through the labyrinthine subject with style and a wealth of new information. The great three-fold mother goddess that the first Orcadians celebrated—the potent symbols, deep-rooted in the ancestral memory, of mill and whirlpool and cauldron—the houses built in the shape of woman (one of them very possibly at Skara Brae)—the tree alphabet and how it threw light on the Sanday legend of Arthur Deerness and his mermaid lover, as told by Walter Traill Dennison. And much more.

I am grateful to Howie Firth for those first points of his researches. I hope he will publish something on the subject soon.

* * *

The late evening was very cold. The young witches and warlocks had all gone home. A few householders and shopkeepers were purging walls and windows of treacle and white paint.

I wondered if my hand would get all sticky from opening the door. But no: the handle hadn't been touched.

The moon was hid. In half an hour it would be November. Parkinson (on TV) was talking to Mortimer and Levin[1].

St Columba

15.11.1979

It was good that the play *Columba* drew a decent-sized audience on Thursday evening. (One remembers with a tingle of shame the handful that once turned up to see the 7:84 group in *The Cheviot, the Stag, and the Black, Black Oil.*)

It was good also to see a play that compelled us to use our imagination. When we were young playgoers, realism was all; even to the extent of having a flickering fire and a calendar hung on the hessian. But that kind of verisimilitude is an aberration. The Greeks had few or no props—the Elizabethans made do with a balcony and an inner curtain and a trapdoor... It was good to see Columba and his monks rowing to Iona with no boat visible under them; but the surge and exhilaration of the sea were splendidly suggested by the rhythm of the bodies in unison and the chorus in their mouths. One could almost taste the spindrift.

1. Michael Parkinson talking to John Mortimer and Bernard Levin

The music was particularly fine. Here again the Adamnan Players were in the true tradition. Drama and Music have always delighted in each other.

The only touches of the 20th century were the few back-projections of forest and of the beautiful island where Columba at last settled.

* * *

How a high-born Irish prince in the 6th century, who bid fair to become the High Lord, deliberately turned his back on that barbarous splendour, and instead sought solitude and poverty on a bleak Atlantic-beaten rock, is the theme of the play. It is performed in a series of swift fragments; in the end the imagination delights to put them together in a harmonious whole.

Whether life is better now than it was in the 6th century is a highly debatable question. We have better food and clothes and houses, we live longer, we can read newspapers and watch TV. But that might be the extent of the improvement, and on the way we might have lost deep communal wisdom and intuitions.

For a few men, then as now, there are more precious things in life than gold or power: the contemplation, among other things, of the marvellous web of creation of which man is himself a part. The end of such contemplation is praise of a birdlike purity and a restless desire to share the marvels of existence with other men, high and low, whose actions and words, generation by generation, wrung the sad cry from one ancient writer—the life of man is 'brief, brutish, and wretched...'

So Columba and his monks took their poetry and prayers into savage places. And they didn't forget to send a man to Orkney. A first candle was lit on a stone.

Bottles

22.11.1979

We take the simplest things so much for granted. Bottles, for example. How did people store their liquors and waters and cures in the days before bottles? Only the rich, one supposes, had jars, pitchers, pots, amphorae in their cool cellars.

For the rest, there was some kind of cured animal skin hung on a hook or nail. Not very satisfactory.

Then one of the big discoveries was made, glass. The curious mind of man was soon blowing the transparent stuff into bubble shapes: the first bottles. For the first time, you could see how the new wine was clearing, how the draught taken from the medicinal spring sparkled in the sun.

It was such a good invention, it is still with us.

* * *

These reflections rise from a visit to the Museum, to see the exhibition called, simply, 'BOTTLES'.

In the last half-century, bottles have changed a good deal. I remember early picnics to West Shore or Warbeth. Gowans' lemonade bottles came out of the basket with 'swing stoppers'. You applied thumbs to the stoppers—out came the lemonade in a gassy exclamation! With the sandwiches and the apples it made a merry meal, between the breakers of Hoy Sound and the Innertoon larks.

I also remember the stone bottles of ginger beer. Did the stone keep the liquor cool? Or would the transparency of glass, letting in light, destroy that unique ginger tang?

And I remember big black bottles of stout with handsome corks in them. The corks have gone into the silence, vanquished by tin and the synthetic ugly stuff that 'screw-tops' are made of.

* * *

There is a rich bewildering variety of bottles in this exhibition.

There are bottles huge as motherhood itself for preserves. There are small sinister tinted bottles for poisons.

There are the large square bottles that held pirates' gin—they were square the better to fit into Gow's sea chest.

The 'Old Orkney' distillery—on the site of which I am writing this—was no slouch when it came to bottles. They had handsome plain bottles for their normal whisky. They had coloured dimpled ornate bottles for some 'de luxe' brand or other. They were even, it seems, in the vanguard of 'the miniature'. (It was good for slipping into the jacket pocket when you were invited out to some excessively boring afternoon tea.)

What does a man—a sailor, say—do with a bottle emptied of its rum? He carves a small boat with sails and rigging; across the bottle the ship of his heart's desire sails its blue plaster curling waves forever... (There is a ship-in-a-bottle in the exhibition also.)

Margaret Tait's Films

13.12.1979

I was glad to be able to see some of Margaret Tait's films at last.

A quartet of them was shown at the Pier Arts Centre one evening last week.

The first was an entrancing 'translation' into film of a poem by Gerard Manley Hopkins. The theme is a common one in this most difficult and yet most transparently simple of all poets: all things lovely and young are doomed inevitably to decay and death—nothing can keep them away. Yet (comes back the golden echo from the greyness of the lamentation) having once existed they can never pass away; beauty is gathered and stored in granaries beyond corruption...

Every film artist who attempts to interpret such a poem will do it in her own different way. I found Margaret Tait's choice of individual images extraordinarily moving and evocative: the flowers, the children, the wrinkles in the mirror.

I am sure Hopkins, who died just before cinema was invented, would have clapped his hands with delight.

* * *

Margaret Tait went on to interpret the work of a very different poet, Hugh MacDiarmid. She gave the subject a bold original treatment. Why does she have the ageing Scottish poet walk teeteringly atop a wall, and throw stones across a burn? It may be to demonstrate how poised and perilous and daring is the art of this poet, who dealt in homely things as well as in vast cosmic themes.

It was an original kind of tribute, and yet I felt that the interpretation of the poetry was not as precise and illuminating as her Hopkins piece.

* * *

The longest and most ambitious film was a kind of threnody for a house long lived in and loved, in the few summer and autumn months before it was finally vacated. The shade of another poet intruded as I watched—T. S. Eliot and his poem, 'Burnt Norton'.

Garden and house, a small enclave in time where gracious and lovely and stirring things have happened—love and birth and death. The lyricism is evoked again and again in the garden shots—bird and bee and flower—as the year mellows and thins out. Is there a hint of menace as the Siamese cat eyes the throbbing blackbird?

The brash modern world is intruding as the film unfolds, with pneumatic drills and modern council schemes. In the old house itself, only half-audible voices are heard, and shadow movements, as if already it is possessed only of kindly ghosts.

It is a beautiful film, half-way to music, that pure 'condition towards which all the arts aspire'.

I hope we may soon have the pleasure of seeing more Margaret Tait films.

Let the Wind Burst its Cheeks!

20.12.1979

Never, I think, can the islands have been so sodden and squelchy as this winter. We expect rain in winter, but summer and autumn were a 'wash-out' too, literally.

The wells ought to be brimming.

There was one night in early October when 'South-Enders' saw an astonishing sight—a river cascading down the Distillery Close and flowing on past the telephone kiosk and the Museum door.

If we were more poetically-minded, we might remember 1979 as The Year of the Rain-Drop.

* * *

Yesterday morning there was that rare sight; a splash of sun on the bedroom wall. The occasion was too precious to be wasted. I breakfasted quickly and took some Christmas mail to the Post Office.

After two days of rain, it was one of those beautiful winter mornings of crisp air and a pale gold sun.

In the street cheerfulness reigned. Dankness and wetness were forgotten. A few folk, it's true, complained of the cold.

But it was a beautiful morning.

How dare we have thought it might last, the tranquil blue and gold? As I walked home, there was a ruffle on the harbour water, there was a silent piling up of grey cloud in the south and west.

The wind sounded a first trumpet.

I was so busy all afternoon that I had no time to spare for the weather. Urgent happy things had to be done, the writing of a few Christmas pieces in prose to be given to certain people.

Also, there was a pot of thick ham broth in the cupboard. There were a few bottles of ale in the ale-store. The pen was going as serenely as a swan over the page.

Let the wind burst its cheeks!

When work stops and the mind is a blank, one can see how a rich day had become a beggar and a bankrupt. The storm beat about the house. Rain surged and throbbed on the windows. The flagstones outside were like ink-bottles. Draughts sieved through every crack in the house. I sat in the rocking-chair with two jerseys on, and a jacket.

The ale in the mug seemed to say, 'I always taste best on a night like this.'

The dark tempest howled heroically over Orkney.

One by one the TV channels bowed out. It was time to go to bed.

* * *

22

Next morning, the gable-ends of a hundred Stromness houses had survived another battering; though the incessant driving rain had penetrated thick walls and chimney-heads here and there.

Snow—as one gets older, the thought of snow makes the spirit wince. You can tell how essentially old a person is—no matter the number of his or her years—by the attitude to snow.

But a few flurries of snow—the real beautiful flocculent 'silver moths', millions of them—would make a brave sight between now and Christmas. Provided always, of course, the fall behaved itself and took a swift clean sudden departure.

A Treaty with the Earth

17.1.1980

Think how desolate the islands must have been for the first-comers (whoever they were). Above the shore, wherever they landed, bog and stone and moor.

Yet those Stone Age people had stuff of heroism in them. They lived in caves (perhaps) or in little stone huts, and they fished and they hunted rabbits and birds.

They must have known, all the same, that in the end they must make a treaty with the earth. It was the soil of 'the whale islands' that would eventually nourish their descendants.

So they drained and they dug the obdurate earth and they covered up the precious seed.

And while the unheard mysterious pulse of fruition beat—if it beat at all—they fished at the edge of the tide in their little skin boats. Their hands took blue lobsters from under the rocks. Their dogs fell on the hares that hurtled along the hill.

The first few cornstalks appeared!

The earth had kept its part of the treaty. That first 'harvest home' must have been a time of great rejoicing in the village.

Now a great hazard had been removed from their days. They would never again be so dependent on the savagery and unpredictability of the sea.

The tribe was safe within the limit of its few fields. The earth had declared itself their friend.

Next spring they drained and dug out a few more squares.

* * *

That is, essentially, the history of Orkney from then till now.

We are still breaking out new areas of tilth from the hillside; but perhaps now not with the same mysterious sense of kinship with the earth. Cold statistics are no substitute for the ancient treaty, the ancient peace.

And perhaps we are encroaching too deeply into the wildness.

* * *

These thoughts were prompted by a beautiful gift that arrived before Christmas. It is a wall-hanging, a piece of exquisite embroidery, with words by my favourite poet Gerard Manley Hopkins stitched on it:

'What would the world be, once bereft / Of wet and of wildness? Let them be left, / O let them be left, wildness and wet; / Long live the weeds and the wilderness yet.'

Hopkins loved cornfields and pasture; but he knew that in our dealings with Nature a balance must be struck and kept.

Early Souvenir for Tourists

24.1.1980

Some time ago a friend gave me one of the long-vanished Valentine series called 'Collotype View Books'—the one entitled *Stromness and Vicinity*.

I suppose it was one of the earliest attempts to cater for tourists and their desire to have a souvenir of the places they had been to.

There is no date on the book, which is a pity—but there is some indication from the fact that St Magnus Cathedral has its squat spire, and the ships in Stromness harbour are sailing ships.

The book consists simply of sixteen full-page photographs, without any text.

There are several intriguing things in the collection: for example, the sailing boat lying at what must have been Copland's yard, for careening or repairs.

There has been an alteration in the way we spell places. What is now Stenness was then 'Stennis'. The picture in question shows the Stones at Brodgar, probably one of the earliest photos of that famous monument. There is an early appearance too of the Old Man of Hoy. Millions of pictures must have been taken of those places since; in fact, it could be said that the camera has tamed the savagery and the ceremony of those places for us.

The little book is much taken up with rocks and cliffs. There is North Gaulton Castle, with wild white seas gnawing at its thin base, and on the adjacent cliff, right on the very verge, is a minute upraised insect figure—a man.

By the time this souvenir book appeared Skara Brae had been partly excavated. The caption says: 'Weem of Skara Brae, Skail', which is something new and surprising; and when I say 'new' I mean it is very old, a name half-sunk in oblivion. What does it mean, 'Weem'?[1]

We are well into the time, with this book, when Progress was creating a certain kind of snobbery. Here, for example, is the famous photo-joke, 'The Hoy Express'—an ox and cart, with a young man, and a covered load and a very wet swamp indeed, all around. The tableau has paused, patiently and courteously, for the camera to record them... But this is the age of trains, maybe the first motor-cars—what a laughable relic of antiquity, this 'Hoy Express'!... Yet there is something in the soil-rooted patience and forbearance of ox and driver that is more impressive than the first marvels of progress.

In an old Orkney croft-house the crofter and his wife sit at opposite sides of the hearth—and she is at her spinning-wheel, as if the wheel and the shawled woman had been made for each other, almost from the beginning... But hints of progress are intruding: the goodman is reading a book, and the wall behind him is covered with pictures that look as if they might have been cut out of some magazine of the day.

The story is no longer being taken in at the ear, but through the eye, silently. And that was a significant revolution, in its way.

Delight of Ordnance Survey Maps
7.2.1980

Glancing through the Ordnance Survey maps of Orkney is a never-failing source of delight, and sometimes of awe. It is the place names I am thinking of, our main link now with the Norse past of the islands.

The men from east-over-sea must have been impressed with Hoy, so different in its starkness and grandeur from the gently contoured islands to the east and north.

They bestowed resounding names on this part of Hoy and that: The Too, The Sneuk, Black Nev are the names of some of the cliffs in that magnificent line of cliffs that is Hoy's Atlantic rampart.

One wonders what the Norsemen called The Old Man? And the tallest crag of all, St John's Head—is that a more recent name? I seem to remember that in the Blaeu map of 1654 the main cliff marked thereabout is called Braebrough. Or could it be the Old Man—'most magnificant natural forte', it is called.

---

1. Weem means cave, and the word has also been used to
   mean an iron age underground store house

Of course Hoy is not all grandeur and starkness. It is splashed all over with beautiful glens and waters and houses, and some of the names are like lyrics in the great drama of the island: Moss of the Whitestones, Melsetter, Summer of Hoy, Kame, Lyra Geo, Burn of the White House.

There are enchanted areas—the Dwarfie Stone and the Trowie Glen are near neighbours. Many a Hoy man needed all his courage to walk near these places in the first darkness of night.

Hoy itself is a marvellous name, 'the high island'. It is the briefest of all the island names and yet (after Mainland, or Pomona, or Hrossey) it is the largest of the Orkneys. Economy is often a virtue in the naming of places.

We do wrong, perhaps, to think that the first-comers chose names for their sound. The hard-headed Norsemen were untroubled by lyricism. The names they gave to places were in large part, cold factual descriptions.

Yet, a thousand years later, the names—whatever the original meaning—have 'weathered' to grandeur or beauty. Candle of Sneuk, Glifters of Pegal, Nowt Bield (a spur of the Ward Hill) are resounding names.

Did some early Thorfinn or Harald smile when he called a headland Nose of the Bring? It sounds comical to us, but 'nose' and 'ness' have the same derivation. Here is a mystery of language: why is 'nose' regarded as slightly funny, but 'ness' has music in it, suggestions of landfall, welcome, home, safety?

If some day you have a half-hour to spare, have a look at the map of your own island or parish.

Closes

14.2.1980

There's an interesting article in the current Newsletter of the Heritage Society about the closes of Kirkwall and how parts of them are threatened by time and 'progress'.

In Stromness it is the main street that has suffered most, with concrete squares replacing here and there over the years lovely old flagstones. What will happen when at last the flagstones are worn and broken beyond repair? (I remember, in the 1920s and 30s, masons seemingly always busy somewhere on the street, lifting and replacing flagstones.)

Where the closes of Stromness differ from Kirkwall closes is in 'steepness'. The score of them go swarming up the side of Brinkie's

Brae, flanked with houses and gardens. (I will mention the sea-closes in another article.[1])

Some of them are beautiful. I'm thinking of the close that begins at the men's hairdresser's and ends near the entrance to the Braes Hotel. Khyber Pass itself is a delightful place to linger in, with the tumult of roofs to the north and, in summer, a bush of white roses spilling petals over the stones.

Long ago, in childhood, I used to love the little by-pass that skirted the front portal of the Free Kirk, now the Academy Hall. And there was that other close that climbed up from where the fish-and-chip shop now is, stone-stepping to the houses and gardens above. That close has a little secret endearing side-branch that leads out to Church Road, just beside the Episcopal Church.

The Boys' Lane was not an enchanted place for my generation, whatever it is now. The Boys' Lane led to the School and we must have been hundreds of times in the middle of the Boys' Lane when the School bell rang! We were late, we were in trouble...

Part of my childhood was spent in a beautiful close called Melvin Place. (Of course in those days we never thought of Stromness, or any part of it, as beautiful. I used to wonder why lady tourists would set up their easels on the street and, all a summer morning, paint Melvin Place. I don't wonder any more.)

Broad steps go up from the street. The close suddenly narrows, climbing still. I remember a little hidden garden on one side, full of dew and flowers. Further up, the close opened onto vegetable allotments. The Smithy, Town Hall, Temperance Hall (used by the Salvation Army), Cliff Cottage, The Braes; and above the Temperance Hall, on a small level green rectangle in the tilt of the hill, a little hard rubber ball and a few boys at football or cricket there, all summer long.

Gray's Pier
21.2.1980

There was an old couple with kind faces at the top of the pier. They had a line of fishes drying on the wall outside. He was Coxswain Johnston of the lifeboat, hero of at least one great drama of Hoy Sound and the Kirk Rocks—the wreck of the trawler *Carmenia* in the 1920s.

Gray's Pier no longer exists; it has been blocked in by the council housing scheme Gray's Noust. But it was wide open in my young days. We seemed to spend much of our summer holidays there. Catching

1. But *see* the end (p28) of the next article

sillocks was a favourite sport. Most boys had hooks baited with limpet pieces. The hooks were bought from George Linklater's shop across the street from the Union Bank. The shop is part of a house now; the bank is the Bank of Scotland. The hooks cost something like five for a penny.

More ambitious and ingenious boys fished with 'rippers'—lead slugs with a triangle of hooks fixed in them. The 'rippers' flashed viciously through the water. Whether they were more efficient at catching sillocks I don't remember.

Sometimes a crab came oscillating up from the harbour floor, and was manœuvred onto the pier. Sometimes the crab went scuttling back to the pier-edge and home.

Sometimes—such are innocence and ferocity mingled in boys—a boy would jump close-footed on the crab. All that was left of it was a vivid yellow splash on a flagstone, and pieces of shell.

If the harbour was lavish with sillocks, the fishing boys called at houses where cats lived. The going rate of exchange was about five sillocks for a penny. Cats cried plaintively on the doorstep, eyeing the slim grey silver shapes.

Late in the afternoon the *St Ola* arrived from Scrabster. There was a great stir among the boys then, to get the loan of a dinghy or a flattie[1]. We rowed towards the curving bow wave of the little black mailboat. All at once our serene harbour progress was in ruins. We fell into gulfs of sea—up and down, up and down and over!

It was over too soon, the adventure of 'the *St Ola*'s waves', deliciously frightening.

I had meant to write about many of the seaward closes. But Gray's Pier has taken all the space; and I haven't even mentioned lifeboat launchings and the delectable warren that was once Gray's Inn.

Keeping a Diary

6.3.1980

The keeping of a diary becomes, at last, an obsession: like drink or drug-taking. If the diary hasn't been written up, what an ache there is in one's day. The ache will not be cured until the events of the day before have been recorded. It doesn't matter that what is put down on the page of the Collins diary is a record of the most trivial happenings; it must be pinned to the page like a butterfly...

A year or two later, reading the record, you realise what a gossamer-thin web your life is.

1. small rowing boat traditional to Stromness

28

The great novelist E. M. Forster says somewhere that, even in the most exciting day, there are times when the experiencing person would say (if he was honest with himself), 'How bored I am!...'

That is a way of looking at it. On the other hand, it could be argued that if we were perfectly attuned to nature and time and the universe, we would be overwhelmed with a rush of treasures. There is so much to know and experience. 'The world is so full of a number of things, / I'm sure we should all be as happy as kings,' wrote R. L. Stevenson. Seventy years is all too brief a span. Another writer, Bernard Shaw, argued that at the age of seventy a man is only beginning to know himself, and to comprehend (however dimly) the manifold significances all around him. To realise himself fully, to do something of real value in the world, he would have to live to be about three hundred... That is the theme of Shaw's greatest play, *Back to Methuselah*...

In spite of the treasure houses all around, most of what I record in the diary is, for example, that I had cold ham for breakfast instead of an egg; or that I had to take off my long Norwegian scarf, it was so mild on the street...

* * *

One possible virtue of diary-keeping is that it helps to get you started of a morning. The mere movement of ballpoint across paper establishes a rhythm. The engine gets heated slowly and gently.

Then you do not have to stare in bafflement and frustration at the blank sheet of paper that has, in the next hour or two, to be filled with a piece of narrative or verse, or a fragment of dialogue. The diary has overcome 'initial inertia'. The proper business of the day can begin, smoothly and painlessly.

Palm Sunday Walk

10.4.1980

Palm Sunday, and a fine spring sun over the awakening fields and the tranquil waters.

Last weekend's snow had gone, except for a band or two of white on the upper slopes of Hoy.

Here they were, under dykes and in ditches, the first dandelions and daisies. They will march across summer in hordes and tumults and legions, and so we are apt to despise them; but the first-comers are beautiful—the little star, the small shaggy torch of flame.

A cold air still from the north, whenever you stood in the shade.

But, sitting at the pier without a coat, there was kindness and kindling in the Palm Sunday sun.

Ropes here and there in the town fluttered with washing. Gardeners were turning the earth, to let sun and black soil greet each other, before tatties are set.

* * *

Quite a few folk were out walking on the old shore road that leads to the Kirkyard, Warbeth, and Breckness. The tide was far, far out; it left acres of rock, pool, and seaweed uncovered.

A serious question is, how much longer will we be able to walk along this beautiful road? In one section, just beyond the burn of Nethertoon, erosion has eaten to within a foot or eighteen inches of the wall that separates road and field. In one or two other adjacent places the slow silent destruction of the road is going on. How this decay is to be arrested I confess I don't know, for the erosion is eating into our west coasts, sometimes slowly, sometimes spectacularly.

* * *

The turning of the tide is no precise event in the sea-quartered day. A swirl here, an eddy there, Atlantic-drawn, turns back on itself, yearns for the quieter waters of bay and harbour. The mighty outpouring sea slowly slackens its impetus; hangs undecided for as long perhaps as it takes a gull to wing from Breckness to the Kame; and then, little by little (and with a perceptible change in the sea music, a distant echo, a boom and thunder) the flood begins to seek Hamnavoe, Clestrain Bay, Scapa Flow: at last it is a brimming, irresistible, hushed river.

Time for us too, to be turning home, for the Atlantic air, enriched now and again with decaying seaweed and cattle ordure, was putting a fine edge to our appetites. (Also I was tired, not having walked so far for weeks.)

* * *

In the evening the moon, mistress of the tides, rose full and daffodil-bright over Orphir, and spangled the brimming harbour water.

Sean O'Casey

17.4.1980

The battery wireless of pre-war days: sometimes it brought magic into the living-room. Teenagers, we listened to the dance orchestras: Henry Hall, Joe Loss, etc. We began to quicken with interest at the News, because politics was becoming a part of our lives. Burns' Nights, in the depths of winter, I always enjoyed: the inevitable spate of poetry and song. Nowadays, Burns gets brusque treatment in comparison.

But the programme that stands out in my mind like a star was an Irish play called *Juno and the Paycock*, by a dramatist called Sean O'Casey. That mingling of tragedy and comedy was purest magic—the heroic mother, the death-doomed son, the idle drunken pair, Captain Boyle and Joxer Daly: their dialogue entered deeply into us and became a part of our conversation for months to come. *Juno and the Paycock* was set in Dublin during the civil war in Ireland in the 1920s.

This dramatist, Sean O'Casey, seemed to touch the deeper sources of life and society; and he did it with poetry and passion, rather than with the analytical word-probings of his compatriot Bernard Shaw.

The play was a glorious rhapsody, threaded through and through with drollery and pain.

Later, I read other books by O'Casey, the plays *Shadow of a Gunman* and *The Plough and the Stars*, and his marvellous autobiographical sequence, beginning with *I Knock at the Door*.

The two plays were unmistakably the work of the same genius. But somehow the characters did not breathe and move in *Juno*'s atmosphere of utter magic.

Once, in Edinburgh, I bought a copy of *Juno* from a bookstall. On the flyleaf the name 'Sean O'Casey' was written. It might have been— I fondly think—the author's own copy. It is one of the most cherished books in my collection.

Last night, on TV, one of O'Casey's later plays was screened, *The Silver Tassie*. It seems to me an inferior work in every way to the masterpieces that preceded it. It may be that O'Casey had become too much the preacher, with hardened attitudes to society.

It's said that when O'Casey brought the manuscript of *The Silver Tassie* to the Abbey Theatre in Dublin, the poet W. B. Yeats, an Abbey director, refused to put it on. And naturally, the author was hurt.

But, looking coldly at last night's play of the 1914–18 war, it was possible to agree, after a fashion, with Yeats.

St Magnus Relics

24.4.1980

April the 16th today—St Magnus Day. Two visitors arrived in Orkney last Friday, with a fine big car. Where ought they to go, for a start? Where other than Orkney's heart-land, Birsay?

At the Brough, the tide, seemingly far out still, was coming in fast. My friends walked across to the steep green island and the Norse remains. Was Magnus buried here, after his removal from Egilsay, or in some other part of Birsay? There seems to be confusion. I still like to think that Bishop William had his cathedral on the Brough; and that it was to the Brough that all the blind and halt came for cures, hirpling and groping across the seaweed and the pools until the harps of the sea began to sing again the turning of the waters.

It was a bright breezy day. We had a picnic in the lee of a ruined croft on the north side of Birsay: delicious cheese rolls and ham rolls, and a bottle of red wine and a bottle of white wine.

Later, with Harray Loch beyond a window, we spoke about books and literature.

* * *

Yesterday, I had to go to Kirkwall about some business. Later, with the same two visitors, we were conducted round St Magnus by the genial and informative Custodian, Mr Windwick.

At last we stood beside the very pillar where the bones of Magnus are immured. There, half-way up, behind the loose stone, eight and a half centuries of our dark history are touched with light and fragrance.

After many bright April days, today a thin haar covered Orkney. We went from the Cathedral to Tankerness House Museum, where the whole story of man's occupation of Orkney is arranged in beautiful patterns. And here, in a glass case, is the very box that held the relics of St Magnus. And, beside the box, a photograph of the bones, including the skull with the cleft in it: '"...Stand in front of me and strike me hard on the head," said Magnus, "it's not fitting for a chieftain to be beheaded like a thief. Take heart, poor fellow, I've prayed that God grant you his mercy." With that he crossed himself and stooped to receive the blow...'

* * *

Rain spotted the windscreen as we drove westward.

Winters of War

15.5.1980

The eighth day of May, 1980.

I had forgotten, till somebody reminded me on the street, that thirty-five years ago the war against Germany ended.

Four and a half years of darkness and austerity. The dramatic things happened early, in Orkney—the Royal Oak, the air raid one March evening and the first civilian casualty at Brig-o-Waithe.

Stromness was a garrison town, occupied by friendly forces. The town was ringed with Army camps; the familiar fields were given strange names. The Market Green became Craigmillar Camp—what is now Hoymansquoy was called by the soldiers Castlegate. Perhaps names more familiar to the first khaki-clad comers reminded them of home.

Stromness in the early 1940s was a hive of khaki.

What is surprising, looking back, is the accord that existed between the military and the townsfolk. It was an artificial situation that could have made for upsets of all kinds—young men, many of them from cities, suddenly set down in a few austere islands where there weren't enough girls to go round, for one thing.

But in fact my memory is of a mutual courtesy and kindness. The Stromnessians opened their doors in welcome. The soldiers gave the townsfolk the benefit of their musical evenings and concerts and canteens and debating society and their Garrison Theatre (now the Swimming Pool) where great artistes performed: Gracie Fields, Goossens, Sybil Thorndike, Nat Gonella, and scores of others.

The early days, as I said, were the times of drama. After about 1941 the air raids petered out. The last four years, when little happened, must have been unutterably boring to the island-based troops that outnumbered the Orcadians three to one.

Yet the military–civilian accord held to the end.

* * *

For the Orcadians, the winters of war were the worst. There was a strict black-out. Black drapes shrouded every window after sunset. One had to grope and guess one's way along the winter streets by night. Torches were allowed at last, but only a feeble pencil of light fell on the flagstones.

So it was the wild relief of lighting the gas lamps—for Stromness had no electricity until 1947—and letting them blaze out on a Europe at peace, that is my chief memory of the war's ending.

Themes for Orkney Writers
29.5.1980

A pleasant and intelligent Swedish lady asked me yesterday, 'Are there young writers at work in Orkney?'

It is a question I have pondered sometimes. The answer seems, unfortunately, to be 'No'. There ought to be young men and women in their twenties and thirties exploring in words and images the rich lore of Orkney. For the mine is well-nigh inexhaustible, and only a first few probings have been made.

What (some people might well ask) is there to write about in a small insignificant place like Orkney? The modern heroes of the craft of literature, like Joyce and Lawrence, have shown us that there are no places or people too insignificant and small to write about. Every human life is fascinating—even the two boring aimless hopeless tramps in *Waiting for Godot*.

This discovery of the marvellousness of the ordinary is modern writing's greatest contribution to the sum of literature.

* * *

But supposing, like me, you do not feel entirely at ease in modern progressive Orkney, a look into the past reveals heaped troves and treasures. Here are a few themes waiting to be worked on: Earl Rognvald's pilgrimage between 1151 and 1154; the hectic and boisterous life of Sweyn Asleifson; the sad epic of Sir John Franklin and Dr John Rae; the extraordinary story of that other John, the pirate Gow (who seems to me to be a more interesting character by far than other more celebrated pirates); and the adventures of another Hamnavoe John—the John Renton who lived among Malaitan cannibals, after a terrible Pacific journey in an open boat...

How fascinating it would be to follow a typical Orkney 19th-century family out to Australia or Canada or South Africa; or to trace the graph of a press-ganged man, from the furrow where he was seized through Trafalgar to his last days over a storied peat-fire... There is the agriculture epic that spans centuries. A woman author might consider doing an imaginary biography of the sea-witch Bessie Millie, beginning with her childhood.

Perhaps—for all I know—at this very moment, in some Orkney attic or cellar, an eager pen is scurrying across a white page, for the enrichment of our island literature.

The Enchanting Chariot

5.6.1980

There was never, to small boys, such an enchanting chariot.

We read, much later, about the caravans that made the golden journey to Samarkand; but these Arab camel-trains were only a shadow of the magic we waited for, with bare feet perhaps, in the rain-pearled grass of an Orkney roadside.

And there, further on a bit, waited the women with baskets over their arms: some with farm produce to barter—butter, eggs, cheese—a much more pleasant transaction than cash.

And the bees staggered, heavy-hoarded, among the clover and the lupins. The sun flashed bright looks from burn or pool. The women gossiped and laughed. A blackbird was beside himself with joy.

There was a distant rattle, growing louder. The women looked up. A dog barked in this farm, or that. Round a bend of the road it came, in a cloud of summer dust, with smoke and fumes and an engine that coughed.

The grocery van had arrived. Treasures from Fez or the Yukon are not to be compared to the goodness the van carried.

* * *

Sometimes, half a century ago, we stayed in the country for a few summer weeks.

It's strange how, in a small place like Orkney, a few miles can transport a child into an entirely different world. I won't say that the green world of the country enchanted me utterly, as Fern Hill in Wales did Dylan Thomas.

There were frightening things in the fields—swift angry barking collies, ponderous bulls breathing fire (the stories I heard about the savagery and ferocity of bulls), horses with square teeth and black writhing lips that leaned over walls, and wanted only—innocent creatures—a handful of fresh grass.

I missed the streets and the people, the piers and the closes.

But I never experienced such kindness as the country folk showed—such gentleness and courtesy, to the children especially.

What could you do with a penny, among hills and fields?

'The van—it comes on such-and-such a day...' I was up and out early, waiting for the van, a brown disc of copper clutched in my fist.

The van stopped. Very beautiful transactions began.

Up Brinkie's Brae

12.6.1980

The golden weather of May has spilled over into June.

Last evening was Sunday. There wasn't a shred of cloud, and the air was tranquil; after a day spent in gardens in pleasant conversation.

It was certainly too fine a night to sit and watch the telly, no matter what masterpieces were flowing out of it; too fine even to waste the precious time with a book.

It is best, perhaps, never to plan a walk; let it come of itself, like an impromptu.

At Graham Place we turned up one of the beautiful Stromness closes, with steps and gardens. Here, hidden, runs the burn that traditionally divides Stromness into North End and South End.

Beyond the top of that close, where in my childhood there was only a house here and there, some of the Stromness housing schemes are massed; the most recent of which, Grieveship, occupies one entire flank of Brinkie's Brae.

Our feet drifted on, without goal or purpose. We climbed up what is now called 'Christie's Brae', and found ourselves on the steep surge of road that ends at the old house of Grieveship itself.

About here the landscape begins to unfold dramatically: Graemsay, Hoy, the powerful dark-blue thrust of the Sound; and, faint etchings on the horizon, the mountains of Sutherlandshire.

Having got thus far, there seemed to be little point in returning before the summit of Brinkie's Brae. (Indeed, when one uses the name week after week, it seemed a positive duty to pay it a visit.) Last June, when we trod this path, there were pools and runnels and soggy patches everywhere. On Sunday evening, it was as dry as it will ever be.

Cows watched us stumbling up, among outcrops of granite, to the top. The whole South End of Stromness lies at one's feet, a doll's village, and the Holms, like two green leaves, and north-east the narrow gleams of the lochs. To the north, the western parishes ending abruptly in high unseen cliffs. But the music of the sea against that superb buttress drifted, a powerful sonorous pulse, across the moorland in between.

One field below was overflowing with wild flowers.

The same small bird that had been singing his heart out as we ascended was still at his chimney-head, chortling into the sunset.

The street lamps of 'new Stromness' (Grieveship) were lit.

Later the moon, two days past the full, cleared, silently and magnificently, a hill near Houton, and put a silver causeway on the sea.

Thor the Thunderer

19.6.1980

I think we have never had a thunderstorm like it this generation in Orkney.

We had almost forgotten what a thunderstorm was. A few warnings lingered in the memory. 'Cover the mirrors'... 'Don't take shelter under a tree'... Someone had said to us, as children, 'The lightning won't strike you if you wear rubber boots'... (Old wives' mutterings beside the fire, half-forgotten.)

I suppose we ought to have been prepared for thunder—day after day of sunshine, a still brooding loaded atmosphere, no rain for weeks. We were so thankful for early tokens of a good summer, no one was complaining.

It came with dramatic suddenness, between breakfast and lunch. The darkening sky, the first few raindrops heavy as coins, a low growl across the sky (as if Thor wasn't in the sweetest of tempers). But Thor, in the last two or three decades, has occasionally given a growl or two on a summer day, and turned over to sleep again.

Thor the Thunderer had urgent things to do today, it soon became obvious. He had business on his hands. His mighty hammer thudded on the hills, amid flashings.

The clouds were torn apart. Black bags of water, they emptied themselves upon the town. The gardens, at least, must have loved it, after the long drought. One could sense the roots gorging themselves.

The stones of Stromness could do nothing with the sudden weight of water. The gutters gushed and spluttered. Down the Distillery close came a river of water, and swung south.

The lightning was mostly vivid blinks, followed at once by peal upon peal. Hundreds of tons of coal were being shifted along the horizon. There was a mighty furniture removal in the sky: grand pianos and huge Victorian sideboards. And sometimes it was as if a cannon had exploded by accident in a close or down a pier, a hideous ripping of hot metal.

The cosmic electricity had quelled the little expensive electricity that man makes. I switched on a light in the eerie darkling room—nothing doing.

A candle responded with a tranquil flame.

A golden fork stabbed down and singed Hoy Sound!

After a time it seemed that Thor had finished his mighty labours for the day. The sky brightened, the thunder grumbled under the horizon.

But Thor must have forgotten some tool in his sky-smithy. Back he came and blew up his forge and struck the anvil a few more mighty blows: while we nervous earthlings below trembled.

By early afternoon it was all over. We looked at each other in the cleansed air, we spoke to each other, like folk who had had some wonderful, frightening new experience.

Corrigall Farm Museum

26.6.1980

The road strikes due north from just before Binscarth and Finstown, and then a smaller road turns right and meanders into the heart of Orkney (which Harray may well be, in every sense).

We feared that we might get lost, in this unfamiliar territory. But no: a signpost appeared, then another. The car stopped at last beside a cluster of little low buildings among the fields.

Here is quintessential Orkney. This is the source of Orkney life and the meaning of its history. After *The Orkneyinga Saga*, perhaps the most meaningful of Orkney books is John Firth's *Reminiscences of an Orkney Parish*, a plain and beautiful account of Orkney rural life in the mid-19th century—how the people lived and worked and enjoyed themselves, what customs were grained into them, how they faced the great mysteries of birth and love and death... Life, in the physical and economic sense, was much harder then for the common folk of Orkney, but, girt around with the age-old rituals of agriculture and with simple sure beliefs, it was more meaningful also.

Here, at Corrigall Farm Museum, is John Firth's account translated into solid stone, vivid to all our senses. The byre for the cattle, the horse's stable, the barn and the kiln where the harvested crops were brought, the but-and-ben where the people lived generation by generation—these are more than rather simple country buildings; they are symbols of an austere and beautiful way of life that had its beginnings, perhaps, in tribes whose language and names are lost, the builders of Skara Brae and Brodgar and Gurness.

The opening of Corrigall Farm Museum is an important event. There has been saved, before it was too late, the true meaning of Orkney, in stone that will take a long time to erode. And inside the stone complex are the symbols, plough and harrows and scythe and flail and winnowing doors and quern and loom: the complete cycle of life.

While we wandered gratefully from place to place, a peedie black kitten with enormous ears flowed around us, and seemed to be very much at home in this piece of old early-rooted Orkney.

Images from Arran

10.7.1980

What a splendid gift to Orkney is the set of panels depicting St Magnus and the building of the Cathedral in Kirkwall. The artists are all in their teens, and they and their art teacher Mrs Farquharson came to Orkney to hand over the gift in person; and they came appropriately, at midsummer and during the St Magnus Festival.

There is a splendid strength and energy in the fourteen pictures, which one gets from so-called 'primitive' art more than from the products of a suaver age. One trembles, for example, to imagine what conventional Victorian artists would have made of Magnus and his story. Here, out of the imagination of these young artists, is much of the direct strength of the saga itself.

Weaving through all is a charm and innocence that belongs to youth; the dew is still on the grass, the first birds are still singing. So, two distinct events fuse in the same picture. Blind Mary goes on the road with her dead dangling white chicken; then, the miracle of seeing having been restored to her, there is the chicken alive and perky among her rags! It is a small triumph of the imagination.

It's marvellous that children from another quite far-away island should have been fired by this Orkney story. It proves, for one thing, that it is not just a story of local and limited appeal. It proves, too, that eight and a half centuries on it is still valid and potent, and not just a weave of medieval miracle and fantasy. The brute power of 'real politics' has never succeeded in choking the pure spring of the spirit, however often it has seemed to. (Read Edwin Muir's great poem on the subject, 'The Combat'.)

But how comes it that this flock of images has flown all the way from Arran to Orkney, across the Grampians and the grey Pentland whirls?

Magnus Erlendson, trencher-bearer to the King of Norway, must have set eyes on an island in the Firth of Clyde as the great Norse fleet sailed southward to Wales and the Scillies. Who lived in Arran then?— a few embattled original Celts, a few bright-haired incomers?

We can't tell. But, for every island, there is need for the dove to fall some time or other.

And the hawk-ships, with Magnus the great king and Magnus the server at the king's table, sailed on south: and the island faded behind them.

Music of Old Place Names

17.7.1980

I was thinking for some reason about Skeabrae the other day, when it struck me (not for the first time) what an ugly name it is—that is, as it's pronounced nowadays, something like 'Skee-bray'. That's how the servicemen of 1939–45 pronounced it. But I seem to remember that the Orkney folk had from time immemorial called it 'Skay-bra', or something similar: an altogether more beautiful sound. Why should we be saddled forever with a war-time improvisation? (But the place is so scabbed still with the ruins of RAF huts and hangars, that perhaps only when they are erased will the old music of the name flow sweetly back.)

It seems more than likely that once Birsay and Harray were pronounced 'Birsa' and 'Harra'. Here again we have meekly accepted a change imposed maybe by dominies or officials. But the islands—Rousay, Westray, Ronaldsay, Stronsay—were possibly pronounced as they were written.

The towns have offered more resistance. The posh way is to say Kirk*wall* and Strom*ness*, but the locals continue to lay the stress on the first syllable, in each case. Phonetically, Orcadians call the western burgh something like 'Strum-niss'. Better if old names—Kirkvoe and Hamnavoe—had been tenaciously held to; but that music has gone for good.

Tourists are puzzled by a name like Holm, pronounced 'Ham'. What geographer or map-maker committed the weird blunder? (A holm is a little off-shore islet where a man might keep a few sheep.) Originally, the name was 'Havn', a sheltered bay. Language is always a prey for laziness; it is easier for the tongue to say 'Ham' than 'Havn'—easier but uglier.

The name Hoy has a varying pronunciation. In some mouths the curt monosyllable has little music. The Orkneyman who knows his place names and their ancient power gives to 'Hoy' a deep dark purple sound, as if he was bodying forth the landscape itself, with its hills and cliffs, moors and valleys.

Torn from their Surroundings

21.8.1980

I try sometimes to imagine what it must have been like, two centuries ago, for a young Orkneyman to be seized suddenly by the officers of the Press Gang and thrust on board a British man-o'-war. Everything was new and frightening—the size of the ship, a kind of food and drink he had never tasted, the new deep ocean-rhythms, duties and tasks he was unpractised in, the draconian discipline, even the speech and behaviour of his shipmates.

Life on the croft at home had been simple and meaningful. He had caught trout in the burn, he had snared rabbits on the hill, he was part of the slow wheel of birth and flourishing and death that never failed about him.

Always, on the horizon, he could see the lovely shape of Hoy.

But this world into which he had been suddenly hurled was without beauty or meaning. (Now, having been torn from his surroundings, he was aware for the first time that beauty and meaning existed.)

And then, a new terror: the thunder and flash of the guns, the splintering timbers...

Likewise for the boys who signed on as whalers or as employees of the Hudson Bay Company. They went of their own free will (though, in many cases, to stay at home would have been to starve slowly). But ice-packs, wolves, caribou, Indians and Eskimos—they were so utterly different to the little green world that they had left. Life was suddenly 'out of joint'—it called for bravery and imagination to endure this new world, and at last master it.

Something similar happened to Edwin Muir when his family left Orkney for Glasgow eighty years ago. It was such a shattering experience—this head-on encounter between two civilisations, the pastoral and the industrial—that four of the Muir family died in a short time; and Edwin Muir himself barely escaped. Yet without that terrifying change and that clash of opposites, the poetry of Muir might never have been ground out.

It is good to see that *An Autobiography*, by Edwin Muir, has just been reprinted. There the whole story, and much more besides, is told in the lucent beautiful prose of a master.

Cruise on the *Marques*

28.8.1980

7am, and the sky to the west like stained glass. The harbour water barely moved.

The crew and passengers on board the *Marques* were beginning to stir. There, waiting at the South Pier, lingered a group of us, invited to sail on the *Marques* as far as Rousay.

There was hardly enough wind to flutter a feather. The *Marques* chugged out of harbour and plunged a little in the swell of Hoy Sound. Hoy shifted around us; soon we were right under St John's Head; almost at the Old Man's feet the boat turned around. The young sailors, as well as some of the 'paying guests' aboard, stirred and climbed to shake the sails free. The engine shut off.

Here there was a wind, and it was freshening all the time. The *Marques* moved to a new free, delicate rhythm, like an open-pinioned bird, northwards.

But the wind, alas, did not bring bright weather, as it often does. Instead, it blew thin grey clouds over Orkney. Occasionally a haar descended on the urgent ship, and left the deck wet.

The *Marques* had this fine free motion that is possibly never experienced on a steamer or an oil-driven ship: as if the wind and sea and sails were in a sweet conspiracy to bring the ship to her bourne with some good message...

There loomed Black Craig, to the right, and Yesnaby half-dissolved in haar, and the indistinct crescent of Skaill. The wind freshened, and ravelled more greyness along Orkney's west coast. The *Marques* winged on, scattering cold sea. Marwick Head was there, superbly, and the Brough; but all indistinct in the haar.

Plates of corned beef and tatties and bread were brought up from the galley and passed around, and eaten to the music of the wind in the rigging.

Ahead loomed the cliffs of Rousay. It would be dicey in this tide, we were told, to slip between Eynhallow and the other shore-line studded with brochs. The 'roost'[1] sent its whirls around us. The ship seemed headed straight for a cliff-pillar in Rousay; but at the last minute swerved away, and plunged delicately between 'Rolf's island' and the little 'island of the saints'.

The weather was deteriorating all the time. At the Rousay pier a few folk lingered in the rain and wind; for, said one elderly islander, it was the first time for sixty-eight years that such a ship had sailed through Eynhallow Sound.

At Rousay, in mid-afternoon, we said farewell to the *Marques* and her young laughter-loving crew.

Royal Visitors

11.9.1980

Prime Ministers in Orkney—Kings and Queens in Orkney. Certainly more monarchs have stepped ashore in the islands than heads-of-government.

The present monarch and her three immediate predecessors have been here; at least, I think Edward VIII was here as Prince of Wales.

But I think that neither Queen Victoria nor Edward VII saw Hoy or St Magnus Cathedral. Queen Victoria's uncle, William IV, visited Kirkwall Bay as a naval officer.

But, reaching back into time, the Hanoverian kings did not think Orkney worth a glance, nor did the later Stuarts. What were a few bare

1. tidal race

rocks in the North Atlantic compared to London, 'the flower of cities all', or Edinburgh, 'Athens of the North'?

But Mary Queen of Scots' father, James V, came with gracious soothing words to Orkney after the Orkney rebels had defeated his punitive force at Summerdale in 1529. And perhaps, if legend is true, the same king had visited Orkney in disguise, many years earlier. He worked for a time as an ordinary farm worker at the farm of Stove in Sandwick, and won the heart of the farmer's daughter. It was a little adventure, perhaps to see how things really were with his subjects. (This was not the only time King James moved among his people in disguise.) On the eve of his departure, on a stone somewhere on the farm, he knighted the farmer. For many a year thereafter they were called 'the belted knights of Stove'.

Some say that King Robert the Bruce sought sanctuary in Orkney for time to plan his campaign against the English that reached its triumphant climax at Bannockburn, at midsummer 1314. It must have been in an Orkney cave, then, that Bruce was taught by a spider to try and try again.

But Orkney, in Bruce's time, was still part of the Kingdom of Norway. It was in Orkney that King Hakon assembled his great fleet to reassert his sovereignty over all the islands of Scotland. He returned, a broken king, to die in the Bishop's Palace, Kirkwall.

A century and a half earlier another great Norwegian king, Magnus Bare-legs, had a more spectacular triumph, as he swept through the Hebrides and beyond with fire and steel and set a conqueror's eye on Man and Anglesey. Everything fell before King Magnus. The only thing that troubled him on that famous voyage was that his trencher-bearer and namesake, Magnus, son of Earl Erlend of Orkney, sat in the prow all through the terrible battle in Menai, and sang psalms.

What had that shining thread to do in the immemorial red weave of battle? It was a thing not known before.

Summer Is Winding Down

25.9.1980

Summer winds down. I have never known a summer pass so quickly. But as one gets older the wheel turns faster. A single day is timeless to a child in summer, with sun, insects, birds, sea and stones and sky. To the ageing, years merge together in a grey blur.

Every summer has its different pattern. May was a good month this year; so was June till that black thunderstorm shattered the idyll. After that, the weather was no longer a bale of blue silk unrolling—it was an indifferent patchwork of good days and stormy days and intermediate grey days.

September has brought us far more sunshine than that drab August. The September sun always has a different quality—a sweetness and mellowness. The yard above the sea lay open to the sun, whenever it shone, from May to August. One could sit and drink wine and write letters among congregations of gulls, while three black cats came and lingered and went, softly.

But now, of a bright afternoon, the houses to the west cut shadows into the yard. By four o'clock there is only one bright segment next the sea. The sun goes behind a high chimney-head; the yard is a well of shadows. So the sweet mellow sun of September is touched with melancholy. Summer is over. Ahead lie the darkness and the snow.

We have few trees to make autumn vivid and gorgeous. But there's no mistaking the feel of rain that no other season knows. One night I lay awake in the early hours. Outside, the rain surged darkly down, shower after shower with hardly a pause between. The world was being well-scoured of the dust and sweat of summer.

Some creatures at this time of year rouse themselves to last hectic life. Whether the bluebottles are in an agony or an ecstasy, it's difficult to know. But there they are, day after day, bouncing on the windows. ('The blue fly sung in the pane,' wrote Tennyson; and notice how happily he broke the rules of grammar with 'sung' rather than 'sang'.) A fine fortnight or so they have of it, the bluebottles, a hectic feast and a revel before the cold kills them off. Even at night they won't let you read in peace under the lamp: they crash into the bulb, again and again, frenzied with light.

All Nature knows when summer is winding down.

Hundi's Butterfly Dance

2.10.1980

Among the tall death-scorning men and the proud arrogant mischief-making women who play such a large part in the Saga, there are a few gentle innocent characters who appear briefly and then are 'out of the story'—a butterfly dance in a bright wind then they are gone.

Such a one is the boy Hundi, son of Earl Sigurd.

Hundi was in his father's ships lying off Osmundwall, Hoy: the ships were ready to sail out on a Viking cruise.

A stronger fleet came out of the Pentland Firth. The captain was the Norwegian Olaf Tryggvason, bright from his conversion to Christianity in the Scilly Isles. He offered the Orkney Earl two alternatives—death or conversion. Earl Sigurd was baptised on the spot.

Olaf took the boy Hundi into his own ship and sailed east to Norway. The small hostage looked back. There lay the quiet familiar islands; ahead lay a grey waste of sea.

* * *

The sagamen can never be accused of sentimentality. Think of what Dickens or Barrie would have done with the boy Hundi. The sagaman says coldly—'He didn't live long and after his death Sigurd refused to pay homage to King Olaf'...

We would like to know a lot more about little Hundi. Did he die of grief in his place of exile? Did he miss his hawk and his horse in Birsay, and the women who teased him and spoiled him alternately, and the chess game and the stories beside the winter fires?

Or did he die, like so many other children, of an infection or a sickness?

The sagaman is not interested in such things. Hundi died—there's an end of it. The only consequence of the death was that Earl Sigurd disowned his allegiance to the King of Norway and reverted to the pagan faith of his fathers.

* * *

And if Hundi had lived, what then? He would certainly have been embroiled in the violent arguments that broke out among the sons of Sigurd after Sigurd's spectacular death on the battlefield of Clontarf outside Dublin in 1014.

Hundi might have come into his inheritance, one of the great Orkney Earls. Or he might have grown into a violent brutal man like his ancestor Torf-Einar (who also had the gift of poetry). Or he might have gone the way of quietude and silence, an old wise man beside the candles...

For Hundi there were no such destinies. Young, he turned his back on the sun. The earth of Norway covered his innocence.

Redressing the Balance

16.10.1980

What cruel and pitiful things happen in the world! We would hardly know about them but for TV.

The other night there was a programme from Merseyside. One by one a succession of old ladies appeared on the screen. What they had in common was that their houses, where they lived alone, had been broken into by young thieves. If the intruders had left it at robbery, that would have been bad enough. But, to add sauce to their night's criminality, they proceeded in each case to beat up the householder. Inset, on the screen, were pictures of the bruises, lacerations, and black eyes.

The sad thing is that those young thugs are hardly ever caught.

But they leave dire misery behind. People who might expect to end their days in some kind of serenity, have this brutality put upon them as a final bonus from life...

It was the kind of programme that leaves one in a state of impotent rage; and what is worse, a kind of despair of humanity.

One person redeemed the darkness. Quite independently, and with no official backing to begin with, this woman sought out all those old ones who had been robbed and battered; her comfort and practical help must have been of incalculable value to them.

* * *

Then, yesterday morning *The Orcadian* arrived. Who could fail to read with astonished admiration the main story: that storm off the west of Orkney, the Swedish freighter *Finneagle* burning, the dangerous cargo, her crew and passengers in desperate peril. Then out of the lurid darkness the helicopter stooping and plucking them two by two to safety. It is a story of immense endurance and courage, enacted while we 18,000 Orcadians (or most of us) were sleeping comfortably in our beds.

It is a story, too, that redresses the balance a little. Human beings can inflict mean and cruel hurts on each other. And yet they can rise to this pinnacle of altruistic heroism. Most of us range in the grey territory in between—sometimes unwittingly cruel, sometimes generous; but mostly glad to get the day's tasks over with as little fuss or unpleasantness as we can.

* * *

Without TV and newspapers, would we know that such things happened in the world? Our ancestors, I suppose, received the essence of such deeds by means of sagas and ballads.

The Small Darkling Masquers

13.11.1980

November is the month that puts a first dark shiver over the year. Little wonder that it is the month of graveyards, month of souls.

It was on a November day that the field-mouse broke from Burns the poet's plough and went, homeless, into winter.

In America this November they sent a President out into the winter of politics. (Still, retired or dismissed politicians need never starve— one thick book of reminiscence and they are set up in comfort for life.)

* * *

Where were the Guy Fawkes children this year?—I asked myself at lunchtime on Wednesday. For usually there is a troupe with carved and painted turnips at the door between 1 and 2pm. Nothing—silence. There is a brass bowl in the house that stands all the year round full of copper coins, mostly twopences. Until recently you could make a local phone call for 2p. No more, it's 5p now... So the brass bowl brimming with coppers was all for the turnip paraders.

It happened that I was out visiting till after 5 o'clock. As I went home, there were the small darkling masquers drifting from door to door with their fantastic carvings. One of them held me to ransom; I told him to knock at my door on his way home.

I had no sooner switched the house light on than I was under siege. The door knocker fell on the letter-box loudly, erratically, imperiously. I despaired of watching the News on TV—Reagan's triumph, Carter's rejection—for I had to beat a constant path from the brass bowl to the quivering door panels. There was quite an ebb of twopences from the brass bowl.

After a time there were longer intervals between summonses. They were dispersing to spend the loot on chocolate or fireworks or chips; or perhaps to the parade of turnip sculptures to be held—and a good idea too—in Marwick Playing Field.

Almost last of all, when I was settling for the night into the rocking chair, a very small blond boy came. 'I was here before,' said he. 'I was out,' said I, and gave him 3p. He considered for a while, gravely. 'So you can't have been in,' said he, 'last time I was at your door.'

Having worked out the logic of the situation to both our satis-factions, he went away and I returned to my book and the images on the screen.

Winter has come.

The Laconic Orcadians

20.11.1980

It is always said that Orcadians are given to understatement, and I suppose that compared with certain classes further to the south, they are. 'Simply wonderful' ... 'How gorgeous' ... 'Super-duper'... No

Orcadian worth his salt would indulge in such spurious ecstasies, even if he was truly half out of his wits with delight.

'No bad,' he says: meaning that his health, or the weather, or the Dounby Show, is in excellent shape... 'We're in wur usual,' a man will reply guardedly, when asked how his family does. Nothing is given away; the 'usual' may mean anything, but in general it signifies something between fair and good.

No doubt this parsimony with words is rooted deeply in our nature and history. *The Orkneyinga Saga* is a mine of understatement. This carefulness about words has, of course, nothing to do with other kinds of meanness. If it did, we would not have descriptions of the bounteous feasts of Viking times; nor, indeed, would we be able to enjoy the splendid hospitality of modern Orkney houses.

It is rather the ingrained knowledge that (paradoxically) more can be said by means of understatement than by laying words on with a lavish trowel. The bare phrase is nearer the truth, always.

There is one strange Orkney phrase, to do again with health or estate. 'Ower-weel'—this seems to contradict everything that has been argued hitherto. 'Ower-weel'—better than well—surely this is to fly in the face of fortune, invite sickness and disaster. (Perhaps someone will be able to unravel this knot.)

It is all based, perhaps, on the medieval idea of the wheel of fortune. Never claim to be 'on top of the world', 'the best ever'; for after that, the only way for the wheel to move is downwards. And if a man admits that himself and family and affairs are 'no bad', there is a chance still for the wheel to take another upward turn.

The old Orcadians never praised a baby, no matter how much they loved it and admired it. There were dark jealous influences abroad in the world that might do the child harm, if they heard it unduly praised.

Round most cradles was a prudent silence brimming with love.

Words Gone into the Silence

27.11.1980

My friend in Norway, Liv Schei, has sent me a list of marked words from the 'Old Orkney Words' section of John Firth's *Reminiscences of an Orkney Parish*. Liv Schei is doing some study in language; and, as she says in her letter, 'I've marked the words that to me are strikingly Norwegian and familiar'...

I spent part of this morning going over the list. Sadly, I've had to tell my friend that some of the words I've never heard. Others were familiar in my childhood, when the old folk used them with style and relish. But now you hear them only very occasionally. As for the new generation, these are words from beyond a great divide. More and more our speech is approximating to Standard English; with, it's true, the music of the islands in it still.

* * *

What lovely words have gone into the silence! 'Voar', the springtime, for example. Another is 'ice-lowsing', meaning the thaw—a marvellous word that. When a child was born, there was 'blide-mate', defined by Firth as blithe-meat, a joy feast after a birth... 'Party' is a poor thin word in comparison.

Still, in lonely crofts, there is the 'sae-bink', a stone shelf for water vessels to be set. There is excuse for the vanishing of such a fine word, for now there is little need of the 'sae-bink'; just as there is a fading need for a word like 'taik' (thatch).

Will there come a day, maybe in the last years of the century, when the most tenacious Norn word of all, 'peedie' or 'peerie', is a ghost— when we will all purse our lips and say 'little' or 'small', which doesn't mean the same as 'peedie', with its undertones of joy and affection?

'Rive' (tear), 'rime' (frosty haze), 'speer' (to ask), 'swee' (to smart with pain), 'haas' (inside of throat), 'host' (to cough), 'gapus' (a blockhead), 'cloor' (to scratch)—all these were common enough when I was young, and some of them we young ones spoke ourselves, though others we felt to be archaic and 'uneducated'.

This is how the rot sets in; though it had begun long before. It is only when you see such a word-list that you realise what a treasure has been lost.

Sweeties
11.12.1980

The shops are beginning to fill up with sweetmeats for Yule— handsome boxes filled with every variety. You pause and think, 'How fortunate children are nowadays, compared to their grandparents of fifty winters ago.'

But then, on reflection, we didn't do so badly for sweets, though there was a lot less sophistication in the way of packaging, etc. The Saturday penny went a long way. Even a ha'penny would keep you chewing and licking for an hour or so.

The old folk had pokes of sweeties beside their rocking chairs and they favoured a very ancient brand called 'Scotch Mixture', some of which had cloves in the centre. And other old folk liked peppermints, or 'pan drops', because they were good for wind on the stomach.

Slightly grander were 'butter-nuts', a yellow hard sweet with a toffee centre.

Then there were the sticky sweeties, black-striped balls and brandy balls, deliciously flavoured as if they had been brought from Arabian confectioners in some desert oasis.

How the ladies in the close laughed when they picked a 'conversation sweetie' out of a paper bag and read some legend like, 'How beautiful you are!' or, 'Can I meet you tonight?'

Bon-bons—what genius of a confectioner first thought of them? They were little spheres of toffee lightly coated with a kind of sweet flour, and as they melted in the mouth the throat was a long column of joy!

Liquorice came in many shapes. There were liquorice straps reminiscent of the strap in Teacher's desk, but much more delectable. There were liquorice pipes. There were little triangular bags of sherbet with a hollow liquorice tube.

For a ha'penny you could choose among all those dainties and many more. For twopence—an opulent sum—you could buy a bar of Cadbury's Milk Chocolate and eating that was to languish for half an hour or so in pure sensuous delight.

One Saturday in Melvin Place a boy unwrapped a new twopenny sweetmeat—a Mars bar, the first I had ever seen. Another confectionery genius had been at work! For a while after that, every twopence I could scrape together went on Mars bars, with their indescribably rich interiors. I see, in the sweetie shops, they are still on the go.

A Poet in Stone

18.12.1980

Winter came, the sun went in a narrower arc across the sky. There were days of wind and rain, and for two days the hills were blanched with snow.

But the people who lived then in the largest of 'the whale islands' were comfortable enough in their houses of stone and whalebone and turf, though some evenings when the stories and poems were recited, they could hardly see each other for the smoke from the fire. And the old ones coughed and coughed.

There was a melancholy man in one of the villages. He foresaw a time when the year, having spilled the last of its light, would not renew itself. Then instead of the growing light and springing grass and blue opening skies, there would be ever-deepening winter, in which a few last men moved like shadows in the ice of the end.

But no, argued the wise ones. Winter has its time, then gives way to spring with the new grass and lambs, then to the corn-patches of summer, at last to the harvest feast by torchlight. Thus it had been, always. The year was marvellously and precisely balanced. So indeed was human life: the old ones died but new children were there, always. So it was too with the life of tribes. Their great-grandfathers, young and strong, had come and uprooted an earlier people. Some day, from some airt, a tribe of strangers would fall on the villages and destroy them and till the fields in a new better way. Thus it had always been: a growing, flourishing, fading. But life went on.

But the melancholy man upset many of the people with his vision of eternal winter.

* * *

There grew up among the folk a young man, who considered long, and drew lines and circles on the sand with a stick, and looked often and earnestly at the great wheel of the sun at all seasons of the year. And he visited often the quarries, and probed the stones, and looked again from a certain flat field at the midwinter sun going down over one of Hoy's blue hills.

This man was a builder, a poet in stone.

He considered the seasons, and life and death and renewal. At last he built in the field near the loch a great stone dome, with chambers for the bones of the great ones to lie.

From such mighty hewings and settings of stone, from such delicacies of observation and calculation, a 'primitive mind' established the visible symbol of light's victory over darkness. It ought to make us pause a little and think.

A Christmas Story

25.12.1980

Rolf Scroogeson was the meanest man in Orkney. If somebody sent him a Christmas card, he would say 'Bah!' and throw it in the fire. Then he would quickly retrieve it, all scorched and smoky as it was—for it might come handy to write a note on.

His fire was two peats that licked each other half-heartedly with small red tongues. That fire would not have kept a cat warm.

A peedie boy stood in the snow and called, 'A Merry Christmas, Mr Scroogeson, when it comes.'... Rolf Scroogeson put such a blue cold look on the boy that might have stricken him on the spot, there and then, but the boy ran red-cheeked through the fields to share his winter merriment with farms and crofts near and far.

Rolf Scroogeson looked into his wretchedly bare cupboard and saw that he had only a crust left and half a spoon of tea and no sugar. Grumbling about the expense of everything, he set out in the late afternoon to the village shop. It was Christmas Eve.

He saw a snowman in a field smoking a cold pipe upside-down. Rolf was so mean he stole the pipe from the snowman's mouth and put it in his pocket.

'Merry Christmas,' said Bella Muir who kept the village shop... 'Your goods get dearer and dearer,' was all the reply she got, plus a barbed look.

A blizzard came on as Mr Scroogeson walked home with his few errands. The snow came thicker and faster, it whirled round and round, a dense ravelment and confused Rolf Scroogeson entirely.

At last he saw a wall and a spectral building, and was glad, because the drifting snow had half-choked him. He would shelter here till the storm passed. He went through a gate.

He discovered, to his surprise, that he was in the kirkyard. He crouched down behind a stone. The blizzard lasted a long time. Also the darkness was coming down. Rolf snoozed for a time. Then, when he woke up, the snowstorm had passed. The moon shone on the white-heaped kirkyard. The moon lay bright on the tombstone in front of Rolf Scroogeson. He read: ROLF SCROOGESON on the cracked neglected face of the stone.

* * *

We all know the rest of the story: how he went home and opened the kist under his bed and brought out heaps of mouldy ten-pound notes and little tarnished tinkling rivers of sovereigns. And how he distributed that hoard to all the poor and infirm of the island. And how he greeted the red-faced peedie boy next morning and gave him 50p; so that in utter surprise, the peedie boy fell into a snowdrift.

And how Rolf passed away at last, a merry old man full of years and friendship, and lies in the summertime kirkyard.

Retrospect of 1980

1.1.1981

1980 has been one of those grey uneventful years that one doesn't particularly want to remember—unlike 1947 with its long marvellous summer and 1963 with its suppressed air of excitement everywhere (as if something marvellous was about to happen in the world).

The weather was indifferent, as usual. We have become used to drab summers. There was a beautiful patch at the end of May. There was one warm delightful afternoon at Warbeth, soaking up sunshine and eating pâté rolls and drinking wine and listening to the larks.

After another fine St Magnus Festival, a boat-load of us went to Hoy. A heavy saturating cloud descended on Rackwick and lifted occasionally, letting through wan light. The visitors sheltered in ruins from the wetter cloud descents. Finally we all arrived, rather wet and breathless, at Bunertoon; where all miseries were quickly forgotten with food, conversation and 'good red wine'.

* * *

Going into shops in 1980 one was constantly surprised at the startling increase in the prices of everything. What, 25p for *The Observer*, that used to cost six old pence! What, 5p for a roll, that used to be one old ha'penny! What, £1 for a prescription, that used to be free!... But most of us have grown resigned to such economics, as we are to the law of gravity...

* * *

There were a few pleasant evenings, sitting with visitors at the balcony of the Braes, with its marvellous outlook—a better place for the entertainment of guests than my cold book-littered house.

But I think there weren't so many tourists around this summer.

I don't remember all that much about Shopping Week or the Dounby Show—but that is only to confess that one is growing old, and that life in general gets greyer.

* * *

There was one quite extraordinary day in August. I got up out of bed at the extraordinarily early time of 7.30am, hastened along the street to the pier and there, with a dozen other Orkney folk boarded the sailing barque *Marques*. Under the Old Man of Hoy she shook out sails and with a beautiful lithe airy rhythm leaned along Orkney's west coast, which, alas, was mostly shrouded in a fine mist. The wind was freshening. The guests were put ashore in Rousay, in cold rain. But for part of one day we were in the 18th century.

'Quiet Orkney'?

5.2.1981

We ought to be thankful that we are living in one of the quiet places of the world.

This thought comes when you think of Rhodesia, Afghanistan, Iran, Chile, the little hot states of Central America, the Basque territories; but especially after watching the two television serials on Ireland. Last night it was Ulster between 1968 and the present; all flames, bombs, bullets, and demagogues, and the anguished faces of women. How awful, to live in the midst of such dangers! Here, we have nothing to complain about except the weather and the non-arrival, some winter days, of mail and newspapers.

And yet it wasn't always so. The places we think of as settled and peaceful—Iceland, France, Tasmania, Norway—were once wrung with fire and steel. And once, turbulent Ireland was a land of scholars and poets and sent out enlightened missionaries to the skin-clad tribes of Europe.

And what about our quiet Orkney? So many generations have passed since the peace of Orkney was threatened that we think sometimes dangerous days could never have been... Perhaps the dark-haired people who lived round the half-ruined brochs thought the same; then one day they looked up and tall blond men with bright axes were standing in their doorways, and great dragon-ships were anchored out in the bay. It was the end of an old song.

It was the beginning of a new song of rage and cunning and fire, made splendid, to be sure, with heroism and stoicism and gaiety. It is all contained within the pages of *The Orkneyinga Saga*. You could not tell, in those times, whether you would ever take a sickle to the corn you sowed. You could not even tell, when you opened your door in the morning, whether before night the whole house would be a red smouldering ruin.

So, it's no use sitting back smugly and congratulating ourselves that we don't live in Ulster or the west bank of the Jordan. As the poet John Donne said more than three centuries ago, we are all involved with each other, we share in each other's calamities and triumphs. What has been may come again, when it is least expected; for I suppose the woes and triumphs of mankind are more or less equally divided among the tribes of the earth over the generations and centuries.

But now we are so closely involved with each other that one mistake might, in Shakespeare's words, dissolve the great globe itself.

The Orkney Book

12.2.1981

Huge prices are being paid for Orkney books now, according to a report of a sale in today's Orcadian.

I didn't see the original (1909) *The Orkney Book* in the sale. Goodness knows what that valuable compilation might have gone for. I think I paid four and six for my copy (i.e. 22½p) away back in 1944.

The Orkney Book can be one of those rare volumes that change the whole course of one's thinking, and nourish the imagination mightily.

I remember with what delight I read the chapters on the history of Orkney, that included large sections of Dasent's translation of *The Orkneyinga Saga*. It was in truth, a very Victorian translation, but still the great gale blew through it and waves crashed on the shore.

There are exquisite nature essays in *The Orkney Book*, two in particular by Duncan J. Robertson: 'A Road in Orcady' and 'A Loch in Orcady'.

The section on imaginative writing is not so good, but here too by Duncan J. Robertson is the haunting legend of Eynhallow, 'A Vanishing Island', and the macabre and powerful tale of Helen Waters, whose bridegroom went to Suleskerry to shoot birds and was carried back to the festive bridal barn with bird-scars on him.

* * *

In Stromness Primary, there was a cupboard in the classroom crammed with copies of *The Orkney Book*. But for some reason they were only brought out on rare occasions, when some kind of relaxation was due, either because of diligence or because holiday time was near. Perhaps we were too young then to be properly nourished by *The Orkney Book*, but I remember with what pleasure we turned the pages. I thought, 'How amazing, that there should ever have been a book written about Orkney!'

And yet the editor, Dr John Gunn, says in the preface that the book was 'for use in the schools of Orkney'... And later he writes: 'Educationalists now recognise that knowledge ought, like charity, to begin at home ... history, geography, literature and the rest'...

The educationalists in authority two decades later had done a complete U-turn. It was the great outside world that we had to turn our attention to.

Brendan's Voyage

26.2.1981

It's fairly certain now that it wasn't Columbus who discovered America. More than two centuries earlier an Icelander called Leif Ericson sailed west and found an unknown shore. Wild grapes were growing. They were attacked by people whom they called 'skraelings', who must have been American Indians. They stayed awhile, then sailed off home. It was a heroic voyage, commemorated in two sagas.

But, maybe four centuries before Leif and his Icelanders, an abbot in the west of Ireland, called Brendan or Brendon, ordered a ship to be built; the material was mostly ox-hide. Then Abbot Brendan and a company of his monks sailed west in search of the Earthly Paradise. On the way there they encountered as many adventures as Odysseus; from the pen of the 9th-century scribe every league of the Atlantic is full of wonder and awe and dread. The voyagers breakfasted one morning on the back of a huge fish, Jascoyne. They were courteously received on another shore by a dog, who led them to a fine empty hall where delicious food and drink had been set out for them, and unseen musical instruments played for their delight...

On a cliff-face they beheld Judas Iscariot, lashed with spray and wind.

As a recent sea experiment has shown, it is possible in a boat such as Brendan had to traverse the Atlantic. Certainly the medieval mariners got as far as Iceland—the volcanoes are vividly described, it seemed like the hell-portal. And further north and west, they sailed among icebergs—'crystal pillars'... Probably there were Irish monks in Iceland already.

It is delightful to let the imagination play upon Brendan and his voyage. Years ago, I began to write a long play about it, that I hope to finish quite soon. It seemed, when I began, that it was quite impossible in the 8th or 9th century that a leather boat could sail as far as America; and I imagined the ship coasting among the islands of Scotland—Barra, St Kilda, Skye, Hoy—then on as far as Faroe, Iceland, Rockall... Does it matter, after all? The marvellous tale is everything.

And, when we talk of the discoverers of America, what about the people who were there before Columbus, or Leif Ericson, or Brendan: the so-called Indians who perhaps crossed the Bering Strait from Siberia? The name of the first man to set foot in Alaska will never be known.

The 'Lang Reed' of March

12.3.1981

I happened to look through the harbour-facing window two evenings ago, and saw scars of crimson on the Orphir Hills. Muirburn: that is a sure sign that spring is on the way.

March is always an impressive month, for one reason or another—perhaps, chiefly, because it contains one of the four cardinal points of the year: the vernal equinox. A door opens and beyond lies summer.

It used to be said that ale brewed in March was the best ale of the year, perhaps because the temperature was exactly right for the yeast to sing and to woo and transmute the malt.

Here and there a spindly lamb is seen, blinking at an earth and sky new-minted. The crocuses are here, and soon it will be time for daffodils to 'take the winds of March with beauty'.

For senior school pupils, March used to be an awesome time, for it was the month of the Highers. If you could clear that grim hurdle, the whole world was yours for the taking; at least, you could go to college or university, and 'get on in the world', which was the ambition of every Scottish parent for his/her offspring. One must strive to rise a rung on the social ladder, the old ones ardently believed. Experience has taught me that those near the foot of the ladder are every bit as happy and wise as those a step or two up... But, on a certain Monday morning in March, the great ordeal of the Highers loomed. We lifted pens and the English exam began: 'Composition'...

The year that I left school, one week-end in March occurred the most dramatic and world-shattering event we Orcadians had experienced: the German air raid that caused the first civilian casualties of the war at Brig-o-Waithe. The hillsides of Orkney roared red against the invaders; as twilight came searchlights scythed the sky, silently... the Luftwaffe never appeared so formidably over Scapa Flow again.

March, to our ancestors, was a hard time: was this the period called 'the lang reed'? The winter stocks of food were wearing done; oatmeal was low in the girnal and the smoked ham was sliced almost to the bone. It may have been at this time of year that a group of Harraymen, going for seafood to the Evie shore, was caught in a freak blizzard on that bleak high moor between the two parishes. A March blizzard can be beautiful viewed from the security of a warm well-stocked cottage; but for those Harraymen of two centuries ago, it spelt death.

Riddles of the Universe

26.3.1981

To think, even for a moment, about 'the infinite regions of starry space', is to be struck through with awe. The glittering majesty of the night sky in winter! And yet our frail human eyes can only see the barest scattering. Beyond are galaxies and star-systems of unapprehended grandeur and mysterious complexity. There are collapsed stars and exploding stars. There is the sinister phenomenon of 'the black hole', so dense that not even light can escape its gravity.

To think that earth-dwellers might be existing entirely alone in the universe is such a chilling thought—like a mouse or a spider lonely forever in the Empire State Building or the Palace of Versailles—that we cannot bring ourselves to credit it. For our comfort, there are the people who believe in 'unidentified flying objects'—more, they claim to have had actual contact with the beings who visit earth in them. But the serious sky-scientists pay little credence to them. Instead, they have constructed vast radio systems that can probe outwards almost to the limits of space, in case somewhere there are sentient beings listening. So far, only one uncertain wavering response has come back from the depths of space. But the astro-scientists keep on trying.

The above notes are prompted by a *Horizon* programme—'Hello, Universe!'—that I watched on TV the other night. I only partially understood it. But it seems the scientists are as keen as everyone else to be assured that we are not alone on our little planet.

An astonishing thing transpired. Even supposing our message got through to a very distant planet, its journey there would take 40,000 years. The planet's reply would take a further 40,000 years. At the end of that time we of 1981 would long have been kirkyard dust, and the earth itself perhaps a cinder.

Other mysteries crowd in. The galaxies are receding from each other at ever-increasing speeds. Therefore, it is argued, in the beginning there was an enormous explosion of primordial matter. But where, in the first place, did the dense original stuff come from? There are many riddles to be answered.

Sitting lonely, late at night, in a council house in Orkney—as one shuts off the TV and, beyond the window, the innumerable star-systems wheel—one realises that one is not lonely at all. However isolated, in a croft above the seashore or on a hillside, we are involved with *homo sapiens*, we live on a teeming ant-hill of a planet, between skulls and seeds.

Rescue from Bleak Ox-Pastures

2.4.1981

To ride all the black night hours after sleep on the broken labouring ox of the breath—I'm sure it happens to everyone, some time or other.

But then to try to get out of bed in the morning becomes, yet once more, an act of small heroism: helped, in my case, by a sip or two of gin—one is forced to realise that there is a morbid imbalance somewhere in the body. The shadow communicates itself to mind and spirit—you know, without a possibility of doubt or contradiction, that nothing good or wise or pleasant or joyful will ever happen in the world again, as far as you personally are concerned.

And strangely, you accept it all, dumb as an ox. It is probably an inheritance from our fate-fraught ancestors.

* * *

Anyway, I was soon rescued from the bleak ox-pastures by our two doctors—one of whom suggested that I would be the better of a few days' rest and treatment in hospital and half an hour later the other doctor was driving me through a fine brisk spring morning to Kirkwall.

* * *

In case you are feared of ever having to go into hospital, let me assure you that you will be entering a place of the greatest kindness and patience. Certainly the old stubborn ox-rhythm of your days is broken— an excellent and highly-to-be-recommended change.

You are woken up about 6am, and breakfasted and cleaned up soon after. You have curtain-drawn rest-hours in the middle of the day; and temperature-takings; and, if necessary, probes to test the wholesomeness of the heartbeat; and tablets of various sizes and hues to swallow. There are delicious meals. There are two visiting times in the day, with news and sometimes flowers and chocolate and fruit, but the visitors themselves are what matter. Then last drinks, and the curtains drawn upon early sleep.

There is no such thing as tedium, for those regular little rituals of healing break up the day into acceptable fragments; and the cure is made fragrant by those who minister to you with such cheerful efficiency.

* * *

You are as safe as our threatened ancestors of 200 years ago were inside their broch—where even the ox, maybe, was kept from foreign axes, and the well of healing water never failed.

View from Kirkwall

9.4.1981

No Brinkie's Brae in sight, or its presence felt, as I sit writing this in a Kirkwall house.

Instead the gentle wedge of Wideford Hill, with its frail metal artefacts, thrust into the western sky; and to the left, a smaller squatter cone still, Keelylang, with its needle-thin television mast, and its ancient peat-banks.

The roof and spire of St Magnus are in the window-frame, the spire-tip just piercing the sky between Wideford and Keelylang.

And those three shapes have stood there, unchanged, for eight and a half centuries; but the hills much longer, so long that they remember the ice and the ice's withdrawal.

I doubt whether the builders of the Cathedral sited it where it is, so that it forms from this particular place on the outskirts of Kirkwall a fine juxtaposition with the two hills. It was probably a pure accident. But, as it is, they come together beautifully.

But men have been at work on the ancient hills too, apart from the TV and telecommunication structures (if that is what they are). Very dark, barren, and austere Wideford Hill must have seemed to the first Orcadians and to the Picts and the Norsemen after them, bleaker still, perhaps, Keelylang.

Soon enough the precious peat would have been divined on the bleak slope of Keelylang, and men would have made the first trenches, digging out their fire against the snows and gales of winter—woundings that, over the centuries, hardened to scars.

And a century ago, or more, the green fields and pastures would have begun to eat into the barren heather of Wideford; until today, seen from this window, there is only a dark brown strip athwart the summit. There, at the summit, technological man has arrived before agricultural man.

A beautiful view altogether. And there, somewhere beyond Wideford, hidden and under the horizon is Stromness's hill, Brinkie's Brae, with its outcrops of granite and intricacies of dry-stone dyke— Stromness's guardian, as Wideford is Kirkwall's and Keelylang is Finstown's and other places around.

St Magnus Day

23.4.1981

Today, as I write this, is St Magnus Day, 16 April.

60

I wonder sometimes what was happening in Orkney on that long-ago 16 April, 1117. Was it such a beautiful day as this, I wonder; with daisies beginning to star the grass and dandelions blazing out like little suns—and the sun itself having the whole blue sky for its summer-ward journey?...

Well, on 15 April, 1117, the peasants and fisherfolk of the inner North Isles would have noticed that something strange was about. What was happening—what was going to happen—in Egilsay? they must have wondered. Two fine ships, well-manned with rowers, had crossed the Sound to Egilsay in the middle of the day, and the crews and passengers had gone ashore. They were no ordinary passengers either, they had stylish coats and footgear on them; no doubt they were important folk.

It may be that a few of the men in the islands roundabout—Rousay, Wyre, Eday, Gairsay, Evie—had dark talk among themselves about the great ones of Orkney and what was liable to be discussed when they collogued together: higher taxes, more compulsory harvest sweat.

And the women at well and fish-pool would have been agog with gossip.

But there was the spring work to be done—the plough and the ox, baiting the haddock lines.

The day's drama, however, was not over by a long chalk. From the North Isles (possibly) or from Kirkwall, more ships headed for Egilsay. This time it was a little fleet of eight ships; and, again, the ships were crowded with the gentry of Orkney. Here and there, on these ships, axes gleamed.

Once more, passengers and crews went ashore on Egilsay.

The watchers on other islands—those with good eyesight—could see that now there was commotion on Egilsay, a running of men here and there, stretched mouths and shaking of fists, a prying with axe behind every rock, and into the gloom of every cave. Men with messages went here and there.

The Egilsay folk themselves had long since closed and barred their doors.

Then the sun went down, and the April stars came out in serene clusters.

In the crofts, lit with feeble fish-oil lamps, wonderment grew on their tongues, till it was time for them to lay their ox-weary and fish-weary bones down.

* * *

Perhaps in the early light of next morning, the first risers in Rousay, Wyre, Gairsay, Eday, Evie, saw what appeared to be a kind of tableau in the centre of Egilsay: a man kneeling beside a rock, and a ring of men round him like a chorus, and another man walking up from the cooking fire at the shore.

The chorus made utterance. The man in the centre replied. This exchange went on for a while. Then, in the light of the new day, 16 April (Easter Monday) there was a blinding flash of metal in the sun.

No More Pipes

7.5.1981

It's amazing, how easily a habit that you thought too deeply-ingrained ever to be broken, can be discarded with hardly a pang.

I had some affection for my collection of pipes that had accumulated through the years—the Petersons and the cherry-woods and those with the steel shanks; and perhaps the best one of all, an American corn-cob (lost, alas, long ago).

I liked smoking one of those pipes in the evening, late, with a drink. Then recent manuscripts were brought out, and the rocking-chair rocked and the pipe reeked and the manuscripts often seemed to be better than they were in the light of common day... Another 'pop' of an ale bottle, more kindlings of flame and new-filled pipe, more testing of words for sound and meaning; and outside, midnight and silence and the stars.

Then, about the middle of March, I had to go quite quickly into hospital. I didn't take my pipes with me; it wouldn't have done me an iota of good to take them, for in the first place there was a huge cylinder of oxygen beside my bed.

How could one possibly get through an evening without tobacco? in the old days, even in Lent, I used to wonder; and the Lady Nicotine (as J. M. Barrie called tobacco) had me in her power again.

But in that comfortable hospital bed, lying in luxury against a heap of white pillows, I never gave a single thought to the Lady Nicotine. I found that I could exist quite well without pipe and matches and tobacco pouch... Indeed, as the days passed, I thought of my smoking paraphernalia with a touch of disgust—all that filthy tar that had to be mopped up with a pipe-cleaner every day—all that ingrained carbon that had to be scraped from the bowl with a knife—all those ashes everywhere in the fireplace.

One day, soon after getting home, I gathered all my pipes together and threw them in the kitchen bin.

'There's an end of that!' I said, perhaps too complacently.

For still, in the deep midnight with a mug of ale on the mantelpiece and sheets of manuscript on my knees, there rises a slight ache of desire.

Time's Dark Stainings Removed

11.6.1981

After twelve years, and nothing done to it, the walls and ceiling of a house begin to look grotty, a bit. (Happy the man who can slap on distemper and paint, with relish and skill. Not me.)

So the walls had acquired a fine grime. Lift a picture, and a blinding square looked out from the surrounding gloom. But the ceiling, especially above the fireplace, was even more intriguing. It had sombre irregular streaks on it, from a decade of pipe-smoke and the invisible upward tremblings of heat from the electric fire.

I must say, those signs of filth did not trouble me unduly. Living there day after day, a tenant gets used to the slow dark stainings of time. He ceases to notice them.

But occasionally a visitor would say, 'It's time you were doing something about your walls. Just look at that ceiling!'

And I would agree that I had seen brighter interiors in my time—and that possibly something might be done about it some time—and then the matter was allowed to drop; until the next visitor came, and eyed with distaste the ingrained soilings and stains. And sometimes a bold visitor would remark on it, and sometimes he or she would maintain a tactful silence.

I think what principally kept me from doing something about it was the frightful chaos I would have to endure—books and furniture in total disarray—while the work was being done.

Well, I spent a long weekend with my friends Ian and Jean MacInnes. To look out of the window of 'Thistlebank' is a little holiday in itself, apart from the kindness and laughter which are always presences in that house.

And while I sojourned at 'Thistlebank', another friend David Hutchison was busy at Mayburn Court with paintbrushes and various pots of paint.

On the Saturday afternoon he drove me down to see the work that had been done. I couldn't have imagined as mine the cave of sweetness and light I stepped into! The living-room was as clean and fresh as a flower; and every book and every picture and chair were back in their places.

How my summer visitors would smile, in such pleasant surroundings—no need for further frowning and chidings.

In the next two days the kitchen was treated with the magic paint-tins and paint-brushes.

The first bright summer suns began to pour into the answering brightness of my council house.

'Bloomsday'

18.6.1981

The sixteenth of June is always, for me and for many another, a special day in the calendar. It is called by literary folk 'Bloomsday'. On 16 June, 1904, two men in the city of Dublin went about their daily avocations. One was a rather bright young man who lived with two acquaintances in a Martello tower and had a temporary job teaching in a boys' school. His name was Stephen Dedalus, and he bears a marked resemblance to the author of the novel, both in his habits and in his intellectual interests.

The other character is a middle-aged man of Jewish descent, married to an Irish woman called Molly. He is a kind of 'advertising tout', and his name is Leopold Bloom.

Throughout the immensely long book, those two drift here and there about the city of Dublin. It is a quite ordinary kind of day for both of them, a kind of boring day. True, Mr Bloom goes to a funeral and he has a dispute in a public house with an Irish nationalist. He sits awhile on a beach and watches two young ladies and the children they have charge of frolicking on the sand. At all times throughout the day a tumult of rather banal thoughts drifts through his mind.

The mental operations of the other protagonist are of a higher order. In a library he argues about the true meaning of *Hamlet* with some Dublin intellectuals. He has a boring and frustrating morning at school trying to teach a class of boys. He converses with medical students in the maternity department of a hospital, afterwards.

Two mediocre characters, in one boring ordinary day—16 June, 1904.

* * *

No writer up to that time would have touched those two with a barge-pole, far less a pen, because literature before that had been concerned with interesting people and interesting important events.

Think of the sound and fury of the Sagas, and their heroes. Think of the royal magniloquence of Shakespeare's characters; and the mighty presences of Nature that move through Wordsworth and Shelley.

And yet this Irish writer, whose name was James Joyce, showed that every living man and woman was, under the surface, endlessly fascinating—and that every life, however dull on the surface, was a jewel of great price; however low a value we place on it ourselves.

So last Tuesday, I paid a silent tribute to a great and a revolutionary writer.

Whether we read his sometimes difficult prose or not, Joyce has literally enriched all our lives.

Mysterious Island

25.6.1981

It's getting on for midsummer as I write this. And midsummer is the time of year when magic is abroad. Fiddlers disappear into green mounds. The young are in possession of the world, and for them nothing is impossible. The first green shoots of corn have broken the earth, that will be the next winter's food.

Now, if ever, is the time that folk should see an island far in the west, beyond Rousay. The Orcadians called this mysterious island Hether-Blether—a rather ugly clumsy name, as if the trows had thought it up.

This dream of an island in the west is a very ancient one, well-rooted in Celtic lore. The Celtic peoples of Ireland and Scotland called it *Tir-Nan-Og*, 'The land of the young'. That name comes off the tongue like music.

In the island of *Tir-Nan-Og*, far in the west, there was no sickness or withering or suffering or death. Always the fields were heavy and gold with harvest, always the orchards were laden with apples; all the stones were precious. No storms beat about the ships and the doors of the people. The people of *Tir-Nan-Og* were themselves young and beautiful for ever, with no ashes in the beard or in the long lissom golden hair of a girl.

An image of a place like *Tir-Nan-Og* has haunted the imagination of men since time began—a place beyond the erosions and cruel workings of time.

The Greeks, the Hebrews, the Celts, probably the Chinese and the Eskimos, longed for such an immortal place; and they longed for it with a greater yearning the older they became.

King Arthur, after his last battle, was ferried by queens to an island called Avalon, 'where falls not rain or snow ... nor ever wind blows loudly'... It was in search of the Earthly Paradise in the west that the Irish monk Brendan sailed west in his ox-hide boat in the 8th century.

How many Orkney men and women in former centuries, burdened with a lifetime of toil, looked from the shore of Birsay or Westray into the glittering emptiness of the summertime Atlantic with a stirring of hope and joy still?

Ordeal by Filming

23.7.1981

'Oh,' I thought to myself, in something like despair, 'not another reading of verse in front of another cine-camera—and especially not an interview probing to the creative roots!'

But so it was going to happen. Half out of vanity, half out of weak-willed desire to accommodate one and all, I had agreed months ago to let a French film-crew, under Professor Jacques Darras (himself a poet) visit Orkney and me on an itinerary through Scotland, to film Scottish poets in their backgrounds.

Time had passed so quickly since the initial correspondence in March, and now it was to happen the next day, Saturday. So, though I drank my share of that delicious white wine at the Pier Arts Centre reception for *Willock o' Pirliebraes* on the Friday evening, I took care not to drink too much.

When I put my head out of the door on Saturday morning about 10.30am, the sky was grey and there was a cold stir of wind. And there, beside the telephone box at the Museum, lingered a group of young men who looked French. And 'Jacques!' they called from below, and pointed at my door. (Obviously I was late for the rendezvous.) Presently Professor Darras and his beautiful daughter Agnes called, and we made plans for the day's filming... I warned Jacques, not once but many times, that he would get poor faltering empty echoes to any questions he might put.

I took the precaution, before we set out, of filling a flask with whisky and putting it in the pocket of my winter coat.

* * *

It looked as though it might turn out to be a day of torrential rain, and that would have been rather a pity, in this summer of beautiful blue days. But only a drop or two flecked the windscreen.

Along the beautiful west coast of Orkney the film was made, mostly. The poems came from a grey shivering mouth. The questions of Jacques Darras got broken halting answers. The whole session wound up at Mayburn Court, with more poems, more questions, more cripple answers.

Camera and microphone sieged me like creatures from another planet and the five technicians and I acknowledged each other's work from time to time with smiles and gestures: for we had only a few words in common.

At last the director said, 'That's that!' The ordeal was over.

We arranged to relax with a talk and a drink, in the Royal later.

But sleep, powered with hunger and barleycorn and an anxious day out in the cold went over me like a great grey wave.

I saw my French friends though, next morning. They were leaving soon on the *Ola*, delighted that they would be able to film the last of Orkney under beautiful blue skies, in cleavings of blue sea.

Speak Softly, or Not at All

30.7.1981

Speak softly, or not at all. The summer is by no means over, and August may yet turn out to be washed by torrents of rain, and wind-ravelled. But so far the Orkney summer of 1981 has been lovely beyond expectation, fairer by far than her five or six elder sisters—grim grey summers of the late seventies.

Friends from Glasgow phoned in the evening yesterday. The rain had been falling in torrents there all day... In Orkney there had been a gentle smirr or two: and the stones and grass dried quickly in the generous sunlight.

The Shopping Week crowds thronged the street with bright faces.

I had to go and feed the two cats Gypsy and Mittens, whose 'mother' was away in Inverness-shire for a week. I thought they would be immensely hungry, not having eaten for twenty-four hours. Not at all—they curled their tongues round a few pieces of liver, then strolled out to the yard and the pier, one to loll on a sunny stone, the other to gaze in wonderment at seagulls and something or other—a crab? a sillock?—moving in the harbour water.

The night was folded 'like a sleeping flower'. It seemed wrong, somehow, to switch on TV on such a night. My friend Peter Grant suggested a car run, to see the last smoulders of sunset in the north-west. The long bronze Cortina climbed Downie's Lane, the rustic road that lies athwart Brinkie's Brae, till it turns from a road to a rut. The Flotta flare was a needle-point; the Inner Holm wore a necklace of Shopping Week lights. We took the Quholm road: the countryside in the fading light was richly patterned with silage patches and with pasture. The east end of Skaill Loch was an unflawed mirror; and why does water make a summer night sky more beautiful?

A curlew wheeled and cried above.

The Brodgar circle communed together in a silence more ancient than rune or song. Trout fishers lingered on the glimmering glooming loch. We topped the Clouston ridge and all below us was darkling still magnificence—Hoy; Graemsay whose tall light winks now instead of that old steady yellow look; Hoy Sound and the magnificence of the wide Atlantic beyond. Stromness was a cluster of festive lights. It was only eleven o'clock; the hotel car park was crowded with cars still.

* * *

PS How the weather delights to scorn our bits of praise or blame! Half-way through writing the above my friend Gordon Wright from Edinburgh called—his coat dark-streaked from a heavy shower, his brief-case beaded with raindrops!

Orkney's Part in the Royal Wedding

6.8.1981

We got only an inadequate idea of the royal wedding last Wednesday morning on my black-and-white antique TV—and indeed the picture seemed to be a bit greyer than it is most days.

But the tumultuous excitement of London, and the solemn ceremonial inside St Paul's, communicated itself. After the marriage ritual itself, the Archbishop of Canterbury delivered his homily, and what startled us was that out of the blue, he quoted four lines of Edwin Muir (lines which, I must admit, I had read only cursorily in the past: but now, in the cathedral, their full beauty flowered).

> '...Where each ask from each
> What each most wants to give
> And each awakes in each
> What else could never be...'

I don't suppose that Edwin, in his wildest dreams, ever imagined that a worldwide audience of 750 million or so would ever, simultaneously, have listened to a piece of verse composed, presumably, in the quietude of his study in St Andrews or London; and now, last Wednesday, in such magnificent circumstances... But so it was, and it fitted in beautifully, and so Orkney played a small but important part in the day.

* * *

In the afternoon of the same day we drove to Marwick Bay. We walked in a cold westerly brine-laden wind towards that beautiful little group of boat-shelters (now, alas, half-ruined) built into the noust, below Howe.

From here the Old Man of Hoy stands well out, a guardian of Orkney—it seems—from the devouring Atlantic. The grass teemed with ox-eye daisies and red clover. Further back along loch-side and road, there were more masses of meadowsweet than I have seen for many a summer.

Having been indoors all the previous day, that walk in the cold salty wind set the stagnant blood circulating merrily.

The 'meer'[1] waited for the incoming tide. The fields were heavy with grass and barley. Going home in the car, the sun came out and made of all the rest of Orkney a ripe surging texture, like some rich coat-of-state.

* * *

In the evening in a house with a colour TV, we saw highlights of the morning's ceremony; without, however, the poetry of Muir or the glorious voice of Kiri Te Kanawa.

1. lagoon (*see* p133)

Three Giant Strides

27.8.1981

I have taken three giant strides into the late 20th century recently. (People have accused me of being backward-looking and in love with the primitive Orkney of old—they don't need to worry any more.)

Readers will be tired of hearing about my telephone that shrills occasionally from its nook on the wall. None of my 18th-century lairds, smugglers, merchants, crofter-fishermen would ever have dreamed that it would, one day, be possible to speak directly to somebody in Australia, as I did the other day.

* * *

Then, in mid-July, my friends arrived from Aberdeen, bearing gifts (as they always do, out of unbounded kindness). This summer, the main gift was a huge heavy cube; which, being installed neatly under the kitchen table and plugged in, turned out to be a refrigerator.

No more pouring out of sour milk a day old in summer. No more cheese half-overgrown with mould by the time one has taken a notion for omelette or Welsh rarebit. Orange juice and lager come deliciously cold to the palate. When a long hard day's work is over, what more comforting than a glass of gin tinkling with ice, braced with tonic water, astringent with a yellow slice of lemon! The cold glass in the hand becomes misty and mysterious—Greenland is mixing its treasures with Japan or Israel or Crete...

* * *

For a few months the winder of my watch had been giving trouble to such an extent that I was having trouble synchronising it. (A fat lot, it's true, our 18th-century farmers and sailors cared about time—the Rackwick men, fishing, gave the sun an occasional glance—the rhythms of the day and the season were so exquisitely grained into them.)

I went into the jeweller's and bought a cheap digital watch. This thing strapped to my wrist has fascinated me ever since. It is all a dance of dark numbers, without hands or winder; its accuracy is so incredible there is never any need for correction. Prompt to the second, the minute, the hour, the digits change as smartly as soldiers drilling... Further, there's a little indicator to tell you the day of the week. Supposing you have forgotten the date—supposing you are so far sunk in inspiration or dotage that you have lost track of the month and the year; all you have to do is press a little black button and here it is, plain and beyond dispute.

I often look at this new watch with awe and amazement for minutes on end, intrigued by the incessant dance of digits. Especially as the seconds pulse on towards midnight, and suddenly 11.59 becomes 12.00; and the little indicator of days thrusts its arrow into tomorrow.

What next—a microwave oven? an electric toothbrush? a dish-washer?

I have, as it is, intruded far enough into the 20th century of late. Time to rest, and wonder...

Pastoral Emptiness to Growth Area

3.9.1981

We see it every day—the Garson shore—a green thrust of land ending in two abbreviated pieces of land that the flood girdles twice a day: the Holms.

We see it, but I hardly ever go there. Last time was a summer evening, five or six years ago, with Peter Grant.

So when Peter said suddenly, one evening early in August, 'What about a walk along the Garson shore?' I agreed at once; though in some ways my tired unadventurous bones would rather have curled up in a chair with a book.

Perhaps we are seeing that piece of untouched green for well-nigh the last time. Soon Stromness's new school is to be reared there; work on the foundations has begun and it is argued that any future development of Stromness will be in this area. There's already a little village of new post-war houses below the Cairston ridge.

If that is to be the future 'growth-area' of Stromness—as the official jargon has it—then in a sense the wheel has come full cycle, because at its beginning this area was the hub of Stromness or Hamnavoe or Cairston village. William and Mareon Clark built their inn here in the late 16th century; there was the farm Hemmigar; a merchant called William Gow had his house and perhaps his business premises here. All have been erased from the map; there isn't a stone of any of these places to be seen.

* * *

It is a rather polluted shore, tins and plastic and slime everywhere. Best to walk on the grassy bank above. The cows in the field watched us, solemn-eyed.

The first luminous shadows lay on the harbour; shadow was added to shadow every minute. Indeed, to use the commonest Orkney expression at this time of year, 'the days are draain' in'...

The two young boys who were with us thought the aim of the walk—otherwise a piece of nonsense to them—was to get to the Holms. But the Holms were still inviolate because of a thin moat of sea.

In the 21st century, this pastoral emptiness may well be the throbbing heart of Stromness. (Best forbid!—no 'throbbing heart' for Stromness, at best a quiet gentle pulse.)

On the way back, we met young foreigners looking for a place to pitch their tent. It could be that some of their remote ancestors stood on this same shore, and at William Clark's inn asked for plenishment for their stormbound ships.

Don Quixote

24.9.1981

All except about forty Stromnessians missed a delightful event one Friday recently—the staging of *Don Quixote* in the Academy Hall, by ATC company of London.

In contrast, Kirkwallians turned out in force to see the same company in *The Tempest* the next evening.

To turn a huge picaresque 17th-century Spanish novel into 'the two hours' traffic of the stage' calls for great skill from the adaptors. The stage props were minimal too, as they would have been in Cervantes' day; and this economy compels the audience to use their imaginations.

Everyone knows the story of the mild old Spanish gentleman who has steeped his brain so much in tales of knight errantry that he decides to end his days in a blaze of chivalry and glory, by becoming a wandering knight himself, fighting against the powers of evil and dark enchantment. Into his service as a squire he takes a seemingly simple villager called Sancho Panza. And he imagines a fair lady, Dulcinea del Toboso, to whom he will dedicate all his acts of heroism.

Together, Knight and Squire sally out, the one on his spindly horse and the other on his ass.

But Sancho Panza is no fool. Promised the governorship of an island at the end of their wanderings, the peasant brings to every piece of fantasy a massive earthy common sense. The windmills that are giants to Quixote are only windmills to Sancho. And the beauteous Dulcinea is only a country lass going home with her water jar. And the great castle is a sleazy inn.

What could easily have been a ludicrous and cruel tale becomes ever more moving and compassionate as the play unfolds. The deluded old man becomes a lovable and tragic character; the coarse peasant is a never-ending spring of comfort to his master—'of the earth, earthy', and yet he has the strength and healing power of earth grained into him.

In short, Don Quixote and Sancho are necessary to each other. We are, as individuals and nations and cultures, a blend of imagination and practicality. Upset that balance, and the world will end with a bang or a whimper.

The players, one and all, were magnificent. Comedy on a TV set seems thin stuff compared to the droll exquisite knockabout and mime last Friday evening in the Academy Hall. The mime of riding (horse and ass) was pure poetry. The mounting of imaginary stairs was so much more fun than if an actual 'wooden hill' had been there. And the whirling of the windmills, and the tilting, were magnificent and so was the music.

After so many adventures, the old sad man wends home, as he has done before. 'There's one last thing,' says Sancho to him at the play's very end. It is the venture into 'The undiscover'd country from whose bourne / No traveller returns'.

But time—all centuries, all places—has been enriched by the lives and adventures of Knight and Squire. Another immortal web has been woven on the loom of mankind.

The ATC drama company brought much laughter to Orkney at summer's end; and we thank them for it.

Next time Stromnessians will turn out in more strength.

A Truncated Meal

1.10.1981

A new turnip, new potatoes. What better meal than that, with melted butter running through it?

Yet the palate insists on some kind of meat to go with the neep and tatties—why, I don't know.

The only kind of meat in my house that early evening was a tin of Spam. Spam, neep and new tatties—already the digestive juices were burbling in anticipation... In a peedie pot the vegetables ramped away.

Then it was only a question of opening the tin of Spam—the simplest thing in the world. There is a key stuck to the bottom of the tin. You insert this key into a minute tin flap, and keep turning the key till the top of the tin comes away—and there is the meat, all ready to be sliced with a sharp knife.

Something went wrong. Three-quarters of the way round the tin, the key (no doubt through carelessness on my part) came off the 'thread'. I wrenched and nagged; nothing happened.

It was very tantalising. The tin was *almost* open. The Spam was clearly in sight—the delicious smell of the Spam rose into my nostrils. Surely it would be possible to wrench the tin open, somehow.

It was not possible. It was, in fact, clearly dangerous. The exposed edges of the tin were as sharp as lances, and after wrenching at the thing for five sweating, cursing minutes, I realised that one slip would lay the palm of my hand open to the bone, with wellings of blood! Were a few slices of meat worth all that effort and danger?

It must have been as difficult to prise a medieval knight out of his armour.

But the human mind is obstinate. I found a hammer in the cupboard, and struck the tin several resounding blows. Other than acquiring a few dents, the tin remained invulnerable.

I gave up—I was beaten.

Meantime the merry dance of tatties and neep in the pot went on. A prod with a fork showed they were ready.

By inserting a knife I was able to gouge out a few ragged slivers of Spam.

It is very bad for the digestion to eat a meal in a rage. I managed, by a great effort of will, to see that the whole business had been funny; at least, it must have been to an onlooker, if such a one had been present.

With a sauce of wry humour, the truncated meal proved to be most enjoyable.

The Golden Age

15.10.1981

We used to be under the impression, when we were peedie boys in Stromness, that we would be young for ever. And it was a burden to us—we didn't want to trek, sticky-eyed and sticky-mouthed, to school every morning, world without end.

Time didn't enter into it; Stromness was there, as it always had been and as it always would be, in an unchanging present. 'Birth' and 'death' were only the vaguest of abstractions to us. Even if we saw a new baby in a cradle, or a funeral going past the curtained window, it was all part of a masquerade.

We knew, theoretically, that we would grow up and leave school and go to some job or other. We yearned towards such a state, as if it were a golden age. Happy the fisherman with his barrowload of haddocks, trading silver for silver with the housewives at the end of the closes, with cats and gulls in attendance! Happy the shopkeeper in his shop, that sold maybe shirts or maybe sweeties! Happy the bellman, the street sweeper, the teachers, the red-faced farmers on a Wednesday afternoon!

Where is this golden age? The saddest thing in life is, that it may never come, or that it may come and we don't recognise it, or that it passed long ago with the shepherds and shepherdesses of Virgil and Theocritus, or that it is only to be found beyond the western horizon, in *Tir-Nan-Og*, the land of the young.

Certain it is that, round about the age of thirty, men and women begin to yearn back towards their childhood as the happiest state they are ever likely to know: the age of innocence and delight.

The old men used to counsel us: 'Mak' na mistake, thee school days are thee best days'...

We didn't believe a word of it; the moralising old bores!

* * *

These reflections stir in me because of the fact that in a few days' time I will be sixty.

Sixty years old!—to the schoolboys kicking a football at Ness, or splashing in the sea at Warbeth, a man of sixty was an aged paltry thing, an ancient bore telling stories in the chimney corner, a muffled bent creature shuffling in the shadow of the Ice Age.

But such is the mystery of this thing called Time, I can still occasionally feel a half-century-old pang of wonderment or delight. And so, thank goodness, do we all.

A Great Stromnessian

22.10.1981

It is strange, and sad, to know for sure that we will never see him again, sitting at the Pier Head smoking his pipe and telling fascinating stories about the First World War; or how it used to be in the Post Office at the beginning of this century, when the Post Office was in Alfred Street, just below the Library, and Mrs Ross was Postmistress; or how the Golf Course got shifted from Warbeth to Ness.

He had an ever-springing well of anecdotes; his memory was richly stored.

All his working life was spent in the Post Office. The huge increase in mail during the war, when 60,000 troops (or something like it) were stationed in Orkney, necessitated many extra members of staff in Stromness, including (for half a year or so) me. We youngsters soon got to appreciate his scrupulous efficiency, and his fair dealings with his subordinates. Much later, he became Postmaster.

He became at last our first townsman, the Provost.

Being the Provost, he opened the first Shopping Week in 1949. Twenty-five years later, he was still around to open another Shopping Week (which had much grander trappings and ceremony, and swarms of colour and noise, than the first one).

After he retired, he took up painting as a hobby. Rather shyly, he would turn up at a friend's door, and offer a square parcel—a painting he thought his fellow-townsman might like. Some of his paintings were extraordinarily good.

He painted a mural in his pier-garden; regardless of the rain, frost or sun. Most moving of all, he set up a tombstone in the kirkyard for his friend and neighbour, the fisherman John Folster, beautifully painted. What will happen to those letters and colours, now that he is no longer there to touch them up from time to time?

He faced up to the problems and joys of literature too—chiefly in order to record local facts that might slip through the sieve of the generations. My favourite among his slim books is the *History of Stromness Golf Courses*, rich in anecdote and character. Indeed, Sir John Betjeman, Poet Laureate, called that book 'pure poetry'—a description that amazed and delighted the author.

He was a selfless servant of our town. He sought no honours or reward. Sufficient for him that he should leave Stromness a little happier, a little pleasanter and less congested, than he had found it as a boy new from the North Isles, at the turn of the century.

We miss his tall slim figure, active still into his nineties, coming home every afternoon from Rae's with his radical newspaper; even after his days with driver and putter were over.

George S Robertson was a great Stromnessian.

The Old Grey Man of Langskaill

10.12.1981

There was an old grey man and he lived in a long hall ('langskaill') in an island with a hill behind it.

He was old, but he was still active and alert. On a fine winter day he and a few of his men would sail out to catch a few haddocks; and they beached their boat before sunset.

Then up to the hall, where a great fire had been lit, and a girl set a chair for him beside the blaze, and another girl brought him a horn of ale.

From the kitchen fires his sea appetite was whetted by the mingled smells of simmering fish broth and roasting ribs of beef. And the cook stood, ladle in hand, hand on hip, and gave a clamorous piece of her mind to a lazy kitchen-boy who had dropped a wooden platter.

And the winter shadows, by mid-afternoon, gathered about the great house. And the fire blazed higher. And the old drowsy man read pictures in the tossing flames and shadows—great things out of the past, proud dealings with earls and bishops, death in the seaweed, death in a longship far in the western sea, death of dear ones in a burning house in Caithness, death in Orphir between the ale-barrels and the Nativity psalms. Death and glory: the old man had drawn his life's nourishment from such absolutes.

Bronze was beaten—the summons to dinner...

Well and heartily the old man ate, stuffing fish into his mouth with greasy fingers, then rags of meat and crackling—and again and again he held the ale-horn to his head and tilted both, at different angles.

All round him was the bright eager brittle talk of the young men and women. How they laughed!—how they chivvied each other!—how they promised a hoard of English gold for the island, once the spring barley was sown and the ships were caulked...

The old man ate and drank and listened. His face showed nothing; but he was filled with bitterest envy of those young men of his, whose lives lay all before them, unwritten scrolls.

The meal was over. The saga-man stood beside the fire to recite. There was ragged applause, then silence, then the first words of a solemn stark beautiful utterance.

Old Sweyn Asleifson of Gairsay was tired of all that. His head sank on his breast.

There, on the edge of sleep, he decided that he was not too old to make one more viking cruise: into Ireland, maybe, or the cornlands of France.

The voice of the saga-man went up and down: words, words, words.

What was better for an old man: to die in his bed, with candles and a priest? or among foreign swords in a treacherous seaport?

The old man's head fell on the winter table, among the harp strokes and the ale-jars...

The Red-Cheeked Ghost

24.12.1981

Three hundred years ago—is it possible to imagine what Christmas was like for a Stromness boy living ten generations since? (We must stop at 300 years, because further back there's blankness—there was no village at all, or at best a few fishermen's bothies under Brinkie's Brae, and a scatter of crofts and farms at Cairston, Kirbister, Quholm, In-nertoon, Outertoon, the Loons.)

This boy, let's say, lives in a poor hut on the shoulder of Brinkie's Brae, sheltered from the west wind. His father has been lost out of a fishing boat five winters ago; his mother helps at harvests and peat-times in the farms round about. But winter is always a hard bitter hungry time in that little stone house.

But, strangely, it is just at this bitterest time of the year that people are most open-hearted and generous.

It is Christmas morning. His mother has gone to the well for water; it is such a cold day she will probably have to break the ice. There is one last star in the sky. Then, in the south-east, over Scapa Flow and the islands, the first flush of dawn.

He goes out secretly and silently, before his mother comes home.

How beautiful!—From an immense black cloud over Hoy Sound, thousands of snowflakes begin to drift down, like a host of silver moths. The roofs of the Hamnavoe fishing bothies wear bonnets of immaculate white.

He calls, shyly, at a croft. The red-faced wife says, 'A guid Yule to thee, buddo,' and kisses him and gives him a little sweet-tasting round cake, pinched at the edges to simulate rays of the sun. So, in the depths of winter, the boy tastes last year's summer.

At another croft, he is given last year's summer to drink, a cup of ale that a red-hot poker has been plunged in, to warm it.

He drifts about Brinkie's like a ghost with red cheeks in the falling snow.

The fishermen are in. They have had a good day. They give him a little bunch of haddocks to take home.

And when he gets home, at last, the summer is burning red and merry with peats on the hearthstone. His mother is making her own little sun-cakes on the griddle, a dozen, one for each month.

And 'A good Yule!' she cries to him as he comes in; and she takes his blue hands in her flame-warm hands; and her voice is like a happy bell in that bare house.

Punch and Judy

11.2.1982

Now that the Drama Festival season is upon us—and a great brightener of winter's end it always is—I must tell of the most thrilling dramatic experience I ever had. That was about the age of six or seven when a wandering man visited Stromness with his Punch and Judy show.

It might have been twopence to get in, in those days.

At once a more marvellous villain than any Macbeth or Iago possessed the stage, bearing his club slant-wise across his wooden chest. And what a braggart he was; he rejoiced mightily in every evil act he perpetrated. No creature was safe from Mr Punch and his murderous club. First it was his dog Toby that stole a string of sausages; Toby was quickly despatched to the canine paradise.

Then the villain looked so pleased with himself, his painted cheeks flamed with self-congratulation; his hooked nose and crescent chin expressed diabolical joy.

Worse than the murder of Toby was to follow: his own baby, a child-in-arms, was despatched for crying too loud and too long. Then Judy, his wife, was sent to her 'long home'. The villain gloated and boasted.

The Stromness children of the 1920s watched with utter awe and delight.

Next to be bludgeoned to death was the Doctor, and perhaps the policeman next.

But justice at last overtook Mr Punch; who, when his luck was out, could whine and cringe in abject self-pity. He was thrown into jail. Jack Ketch the hangman came to deal out justice. By a superb piece of trickery, it was Jack Ketch who danced at the end of the rope, not Mr Punch.

How we clapped our hands at every piece of villainy!

But at last the Devil came for him. Then how he cringed and whined, our hero-villain. The Devil was peremptory and adamant; but he had never had to reckon with such a consummate 'baddy' as Punch. He still had his club and the strength to wield it. After a fearsome struggle, that went on and on, the Devil lay dead.

The Stromness children shouted with joy. Never had they seen such a marvellous character as Mr Punch. No twopence was ever better spent.

Never again, either, was such thrilling drama, be the dramatist Shakespeare or Ibsen or Chekhov or Molière or Sophocles. And I suppose nobody knows who the Italian strolling puppet-maker was who first imagined Mr Punch. (Perhaps he was thinking of Cesare Borgia.)

Vandalism

18.2.1982

The thought of vandalism in a quiet place like Orkney—I have just been reading about it in *The Orcadian*—is particularly chilling to the mind. The idea that good and useful things can be destroyed for pure destruction's sake is something alien to my generation; we just don't understand it; property was to be respected at all times. That tenet was in the very air we breathed, no doubt inculcated (in part at least) by Kirk and School.

'Things fall apart, the centre cannot hold / Mere anarchy is loosed upon the world,' the poet Yeats wrote half a century ago. Certainly he was foretelling the imminent ruin of a great civilization; but the random smashing of walls and windows and aerials is perhaps a symptom of a serious sickness in the heart of society.

Having preached that little sermon, I have a sudden vivid picture of two small boys in the 1920s. They are standing in the Kirk Road; they bend and pick up stones from the road; in a frenzy of joy they send the stones crashing into the windows of a little stone house where nobody lives. 'It's fine, it's all right,' they assured each other, 'nobody owns it'... Then another fusillade of stones smashed the last pane.

It had been a most delightful morning for them both. They went home after a time, to their separate houses for dinner.

Grave stern faces met one boy on the threshold. 'A window's been broken—every pane! Who did it?'... Pale and trembling, he denied all knowledge of it, it wasn't him, it might have been the other boy but it certainly wasn't him.

He was confronted with proof positive. Abjectly, in the end, he confessed. Whether he was smacked or not, I can't remember.

All I know is, I was one of the five-years-old culprits; so what right have I to point the finger at those latter-day vandals?

The Kirkyard

25.2.1982

It was interesting to read in the last *Orcadian* the discussion about the designations 'kirkyard', 'cemetery', 'graveyard'. And it was heartening to read that 'kirkyard' was the word preferred; because it undoubtedly is the oldest and richest and most euphonious of the three.

There is a starkness and coldness about the word 'cemetery' that repels, and 'graveyard' is (to me anyway) only slightly more acceptable.

But the word 'kirkyard' carries overtones and undertones. There is an aura of community and togetherness about it. It is an awesome thought, to know that so many generations of Stromnessians are lying in those few fields beside Warbeth beach. There are still the ruined walls of a 17th-century kirk among the tombstones of the oldest kirkyard. There was a place called 'Monkerhoose' nearby—doubtless a small monastery, whose stones have long since been taken by erosion back among the anonymous stones of the beach.

How we would like to know more about the folk whose names are carved on the stones: the skippers, merchants, ministers, who, long ago, lingered beside Login's Well and saw sailing ships anchoring in the harbour and beyond: whose masters were Bligh, Gow, Franklin.

And when we were younger, how a certain gravestone in the old kirkyard moved us—it commemorated a girl called Ellen Dunne, who died in the mid-19th century, aged sixteen.

And we ought not to forget that there are hundreds—maybe thousands—lying there who have no headstones at all; being too poor, being humble enough to let their names and years be lost for ever.

'Death' is the great taboo word nowadays, as 'sex' was to the Victorians. Earlier centuries acknowledged the inevitable end with carvings of skeletons, hour-glasses, scythes: symbols of mortality.

Nowadays we prefer carved flowers and doves.

The subject ought not to be mournful, for it is as natural as birth and love. And today the sun is shining after two cold gloomy days, and in sheltered gardens there are snowdrops, and soon it will be crocus-time and daffodil-time and lark-time.

Without the certainty of the kirkyard, the lovely things would lose their relish and their sweetness.

Month of the Equinox

18.3.1982

March it is, the month of great gales.

March—the best month for making ale, the old folk used to say; though why March should be a better malt month than August or November, I can't say. Maybe it has something to do with 'the nipping and the eager air'; the fires and frost of winter behind us, the sun of summer to come.

It is, too, the month of the equinox, when light and darkness hang in perfect balance, and there is a stir of excitement through all of creation, a stirring deep underground of the roots, a quickening of the buried seeds. One afternoon you see with delight a single daisy in a ditch, precursor of millions. Daisy: 'eye of day'. And the multitudinous eyes of night, the stars and galaxies, lose a little of their splendour as they wheel down the lessening darkness.

* * *

In March, perhaps, there came a great unrest upon the farmer of the Bu in Cairston, the greatest landowner in the parish, who could like the other great men of Orkney rise and speak in the 'Thing', the parliament, before earl and bishop.

Now that the ploughing was over, now that the seed was locked in the furrows, he wanted to be a farmer no more; the viking-rage came on him. On the beach his longship was being caulked by his plough-men and shepherds and fishermen, who would also be vikings for a month or two under the predatory suns of summer.

There came a morning when the awkward contrary winds of March swung round to nor'-east or nor'-west. Then there was not a moment to lose. They stored honey and ale-kegs and bread and dry fish aboard, and the sail was set, and the oars dripped bright water drops.

Women watched from Ness and Black Craig the hull dwindling under the horizon. Then their men were in the hand of Fate. None knew whether that ship would return freighted with silver and silk and brave stories (saga-stuff), or whether a cripple ship might come in August limping into the Cairston Roads, a patched thing full of woe and wounds.

The hillside heaved bright with winds of harvest, whether it was a treasure-ship or a tramp that returned.

The Mill of Eyreland

25.3.1982

The restoration of old buildings has become a minor industry in Orkney of recent years—and a wholesome and positive industry too, if the original building has been beautiful and useful and a landmark in the parish.

To the Mill of Eyreland a hundred years ago came many of the farmers of Stenness and Stromness with their oats and bere to be made into meal. The rushing burn alongside turned the great wheel, that in its turn activated the ponderous millstones inside. And so the folk of Stenness and round about knew that there would be bread and ale for them in plenty, once winter came.

Then, one by one, the mills of Orkney fell silent; dust settled on the millstones; the burn ran fruitlessly out to sea, and the stonework began to wither and decay.

Ten years ago Ian Heddle of Colchester (but an Orcadian by descent, with a name like that) turned a speculative eye on the Mill of Eyreland, and he decided with the sure eye of a builder that a fine house could be made out of it.

He worked on it in his spare time, in summer and at mid-winter—a real sequence of busman's holidays. And the years passed.

Once or twice he would invite a group of friends to come to the Mill and see for themselves how the work was progressing. (I myself get a kind of sinking feeling, my spirit plummets, standing in an old empty forlorn house—I lack the builder's imagination, who can see in his craftsman's brain what the finished house will be like.)

Then, last Sunday, Ian and Margot Heddle invited us to see the almost finished Mill. An utter transformation had taken place. It was no more like the desolation we had viewed five or seven years ago, than a butterfly is like its chrysalis; than a good statue is like the rough stone from which it has been hewn. All was brightness, cheerfulness, and in perfect order and taste. I have no space to describe the beauty that we saw. (It would take a technical journalist to do that, and I hope somebody from *House and Garden* will come to Stenness some day soon, to do it full justice.)

We ate our bread and cheese, and drank home-brewed ale and talked, while the Burn of Eyreland went past with its clear bubble and undersong.

PS And it turned out that Ian Heddle's grandfather from Westfield, Stromness, had been the first farmer to bring his grain to the Mill.

A New Folk Tale

1.4.1982

Listen for five minutes to an Orkney folk tale.

There were two great kings in the North, Winter and Summer, and they were brothers, and they had small liking for each other. In fact, they went often to war. Then Winter with his icicles and black storms harried the frontiers of King Summer, and spread a greyness and coldness well into June and July even, till the roses were stripped of their petals and the old men sitting outside in their chairs called for scarfs and mittens and bonnets, lest the thin thread of life be snapped in them.

And Summer, in revenge, devastated the frontier regions of Winter, luring out snowdrops while the snow still lay in the ditches, and putting premature songs into the birds' throats. At which outrage, King Winter stamped and roared with rage in his Ice Palace near the North Pole, and vowed vengeance.

Those two powerful Kings had a nephew and a niece, whom they loved dearly; and the name of the girl was Voar and the name of the boy was Hairst (or Spring and Autumn, as they are called in these degenerate times).

And sometimes the little Princess Voar stayed with King Winter, but always her eyes yearned southwards towards the sun. At last it was time for her to go to her Summer Uncle; and south she went, with ferns and daffodils and a basket of warm eggs. But when at last she arrived at the Palace of Summer, there was snow in her bright hair and her hands were blue with cold.

And the boy Hairst was mostly to be found in the bright palace, but at last shadows came upon him and filled the hollows of his cheek and neck; and he longed to travel north to his powerful uncle the Winter King, bearing loaves and ale-kegs and peats in his cart, as a gift.

That was the only pledge and sign of peace between Winter and Summer, the girl with the daffodils and the boy with the cornstalks, whom they honoured and loved equally; and so the year is always one and whole, instead of tearing itself apart.

* * *

I must hasten to say that this is no piece of ancient lore that I have unearthed; I made it up five minutes ago.

A few days ago, the car I was in could hardly get up the Hatston Brae and the Dykes of Binscarth for an incessant fall of grey soft snow. (Spring that day sat demurely in King Winter's power, happy to be there beside leaping flames.)

Today, I am writing this out of doors, on an afternoon of cloudless sun, and my writing hand is warm. (The little princess has left the Ice Palace, she is stooping to pick the first folded daffodil. Soon the Sun Palace will lower its drawbridge, it will throw open its April gate to a beloved guest.)

The Work Ethic

6.5.1982

Suddenly, last week, it became very urgent to write a new play. But nobody has ideas for new plays sticking out of every writing-pad and paper folder.

Suddenly, I remembered a lovely summer afternoon at the West Shore two years ago.

Perfectly balanced people would be quite content to sit on the sun-warmed rock and watch the behaviour of the waves and the seabirds; and to see from time to time a fishing boat borne on the flood-tide, into the green arms of the harbour; and to contemplate pastoral Graemsay with its two lighthouses, and the purple-scarred Ward of Hoy and the Coolags beyond. How sweet, to sit perfectly still, and do nothing, and let the hundred sea sounds brim your ears...

But I am one of those people in whom what's now called 'the Calvinist work ethic' has been deeply grained. That is to say, an idle afternoon is an indulgence, a waste of the small part of time we are allowed on this planet. A quiet half-hour now and then—there's nothing wrong with that—but only in so far as is necessary to renew one's strength for toils and tasks to come.

I always have a notebook and a ballpoint pen handy; the stern voice of Duty is bound, after a half-hour's idleness, to call me back to the smithy of the mind.

I thought, vaguely, about old Bessie Millie, the witch of Brinkie's Brae who two hundred years ago sold winds to skippers who called in at Hamnavoe, to patch their sails or take in water or wait for an easterly to give them a fair passage across the Atlantic to America: there might be a little play woven about her.

At that time, the Age of Enlightenment, not every skipper would bother to climb up the 'series of dirty and precipitous lanes' (Sir Walter Scott's words) to Bessie's hut, and pay the stipulated sum, sixpence, for a good wind. Most sailors being superstitious, the skippers did pay their sixpences, just to be on the safe side. But—let's say—there is one obstinate opinionated ship-master who declares roundly in Login's Inn at the South End that he is a man of reason, he will have no part in the lingering superstitions of the Middle Ages—the other skippers can visit the old rag-bag if they like—he most definitely has no intention of doing any such thing...

And so, that late summer afternoon, I sketched out the play very roughly, and put the scribbled-over notebook back in my pocket.

I felt, rather smugly, that I had worked for my tea. And then, last weekend, when the play was needed urgently, the groundwork had already been done.

Summer Flowers

27.5.1982

The dandelions are suddenly everywhere, in their thousands. Ditches and fields are teeming with them; they are sprouting from the crevices of the flagstones, little bright clusters. They are like companies of lions fed with sun and rain, and rooted in one place for their brief season on earth; and glad for it to be so.

'Tooth of the lion', the French called them away back in the Middle Ages; though how the 'tooth' part comes to be, I cannot for the life of me make out.

Children, we slaughtered them by the hundred, ripping them off by the stem and examining curiously the milky fluid oozing from the hollow stems. And if we smeared our hands with this white dandelion blood, it dried soon and left a dark smear.

It was mostly the girls that occupied themselves with the daisies that too were suddenly there in immense clusters, like stars to a winter sky. There in the fields they sat for hours, weaving daisy chains; and then the girls would wander home along the dusty summer roads wearing those daisy garlands round their necks or in their hair.

It was the wild plants called 'soldiers' that we boys collected, and then matched against each other, striking and striking herb against herb until one or the other was decapitated: a wild sport, that was made pure in a sense by the laughter and the innocence and the pastoral setting.

And the first bees droned from flower to flower, like hot embers of the sun, and the gorgeous butterflies dandled airily among the grasses and stones.

'Do you like butter?' you would suddenly ask your friend. Then a buttercup was plucked and held under his chin and if the buttercup shadow glowed there, between underlip and throat, then for sure he liked butter. (I have never known any young chin that did not take the buttercup glow.)

There were fuchsia bushes everywhere in Stromness; the boys despoiled them of their blossoms, and nipped them off with their fingers below the bloom and sucked a single delicious drop of nectar... So it went on, maybe for an hour, till the close was strewn with slaughtered fuchsia; and our breath had a new sweetness.

And the mayflowers grew in clumps beside ditches and streams, and we brought them home and put them in water-filled jam jars.

The Bay of Skaill

10.6.1982

The sweets of May have spilled over into June. Sun after sun, the days go by. Yesterday the sun was a windless flame. Today there is a faint diffusion of haar, and a mild wind is blowing from the east.

Skaill Bay, and the tide far out, and the horizon indistinct. Thank goodness Skaill Bay is not close to a big city; for on a day like this you wouldn't be able to see the sand for picnickers and sun-worshippers. There are only a few folk on the sea verge. A bus has gone by, north-wards, full of tourists from Skara Brae.

The Hole o' Rowe has half-closed its eye.

From a field inland, a cow is lowing. The small songs of the sea birds flit here and there along the exposed rocks and seaweed. Rustle of wind in the tough links grass. The ebb is quiet; the offshore wind is blowing any sea music back towards the Atlantic. No: occasionally there is a surge, a long-drawn susurration—and again—and once more. Perhaps the tide has turned. Perhaps the hidden moon has given the sea a summons, and soon the rocks and the sand will echo and resound with Atlantic thunders.

On the far curving shore of the bay lies Skara Brae, hazy in sea-haar. One wonders, what would the earliest settlers have made of weather like this? They would not have thought of it as beautiful, for it is only when people have leisure that they think of such abstractions as 'beauty'. I'm inclined to think that to the Skara Brae dwellers, only what conduced to the fertility of crops and animals and fish was meaningful. Beauty and utility were the same thing.

Six such beautiful weeks as we have had in Orkney would have been a delight to them no doubt; for the new lambs would be in the fields, and the crabs would be seeking a way into creels (supposing they had invented such things), and the old men would feel young again while the sun shone. They knew, none better, the exquisite balance of the seasons: and how the earth was turning towards the solstice, when all is saturated in light, a brimming honeycomb.

But the little town is silent and nothing is left of that ancient summer but a few bones and stones.

High over a Sandwick field a lark sifted and spilled out and scattered pure stammering sequences.

Johnsmas

24.6.1982

It was so silent in the house, the boy woke up.

It was—let's say—the year 1832, and the season mid summer. Where had everyone in the croft-house gone? Even the cat wasn't there, hunched up and singing beside the hearthglow.

But the boy could hear the excited barking of Wolf the dog, from far far away, across the grimlings[1].

He got out of bed, his feet cold on the stone floor, and put on his shoes and trousers.

It was eerie, here in the deserted house. What if the trows, or fairies, were to come for him? If they took him away he would spend a long time under the green hill before they let him go.

1. twilight

The boy, Tom, his heart going in an uncertain rhythm, went to the door and opened it a little, and peeped out.

It was very late at night, he knew that. But the whole district seemed to be astir. Tom could see the dark silhouettes moving up the hill against the red glow on the north-west horizon. Some of them carried burdens. He could not distinguish faces. He could tell that the limping shadow was the old man from the mill.

Dare he go out? Certain things were happening on the hill—a cairn that hadn't been there in the morning was on the summit now, and the distant silhouettes were piling their burdens to make the cairn even higher.

And there, beside the well, he saw the girl Peg from the next farm; and she too was peering through the grey air at the queer goings-on on the hill. Well, he must show before a girl that he wasn't afraid of anything. He set off, but slowly, to the hill. And the girl followed him, twenty paces behind.

Surely every soul in the parish was on the side of that hill; he heard a fiddle scratching and scraping, by way of practice: and then it sang like a bird! And like a red-and-yellow earth-rooted bird, the fire woke on top of the hill, and its wings flapped and beat in the wind of midnight...

The faces round the fire were lurid. Tom held back. Another ten paces uphill and he would be recognised for sure. He watched from behind a rock. And Peg, crouched beside him, watched.

A tall young man leaned over the flames, shouting. A hundred hands applauded. The fire sent out a thousand crackles and dying stars. The fiddle sang a new song. Eight dancers hurtled in circles round the fire.

It was Johnsmas, the eve of midsummer, a festival the children had not been bidden to.

And then, beside the fire, amid much laughter, a keg was broached. Twelve young men hurled themselves at the fire, up and over!

Tom saw that his father had lit a heather torch at the great hill flame, and was carrying it very solemnly to his own house and steading and rig.

The boy went home like a shadow. Light and warmth, come winter, would not be lacking. (Or so the old ones thought.)

The girl Peg followed, twenty shadowy steps behind, till she reached the end of her father's field.

Under Moorfea

22.7.1982

A warm bright beautiful day unfolded over Rackwick.

It was not a day to be wasted indoors. I wrote in my pad with a black Staedtler pen, slippered feet up on a rough stone dyke.

Among the huge glittering curling combers on the beach, bathers hid themselves—quick splashes, then out again onto the warm singing sand!

Then down to visit a kind house above the shore, in the evening. We climbed home, late, up a steep grassy road, thick beset with ferns. A little toad jumped in the grass. The sky over the hills was a red rose.

Such a delight, that kind of day in Rackwick!

* * *

Then to wake up, at six or seven o'clock in the morning, to hear the howl of wind in the eaves, and 'blatters' of rain on the seaward window. It was as if a beautiful princess had become a loathsome old hag overnight.

All day the grey haar hung over the valley. Sometimes it would thin out, and there would be a scrap of wan sun. Sometimes it intensified into rain. The plastic barrel at the end of the house was overflowing. We sent the fire roaring up the lum, a mixture of coal, driftwood, and broken peat.

We heard that the gale had all but uprooted two tents in the night.

Fields and sea and sky were half-dissolved in the grey seeping misery.

But we kept ourselves cheerful indoors with writing letters and small impromptu poems, with the old Victorian card game 'Happy Families' and word games.

There was a heaped table and sideboard to dine and drink from.

In the evening we drove to Melsetter and were shown through what must be the most beautiful house in Orkney—a treasury of gracious stonework, fabrics, gardens, woodland, orchard, magnificently sited between Longhope Bay and the Pentland Firth. (There is no space to pay adequate tribute to Melsetter House and to Elsie Seatter, our kind hostess—some day I'd like to have a go at it...)

The car drove back in growing intensities of rain—on the narrow Rackwick road it splashed more like a boat than a car.

An immense dark cloud would loom ahead—and would turn out, at a nearer approach, to be one of Hoy's multitude of hills, rain-hung. We circled the North-house fire, dripping.

Next morning, the sun was in the window again.

Lure of the Tall Ships

26.8.1982

How quickly the golden sands of summer are running out!

There's an autumn freshness in the air these days, heavy August rain-spates, and shadows gather about 9pm, with moths and bluebottles.

Sunday morning began with grey drapings. But as we drove to Kirkwall towards 11am, there were patches of blue in the sky, and the water under the Brig-o-Waithe was brimming full and bright from the sea.

In Kirkwall a large congregation was converging on St Magnus, where the Moderator was to preach.

The little church where we heard Mass was brimming over too with people, many of them strangers.

As we drove north to Birsay about noon, the sun had the sky almost to itself—except to the north, where the high-piled rain clouds had fled.

It was so warm, we had a kind of picnic lunch in the courtyard of the cottage, with Birsay tomatoes and Birsay farm cheese (to name only two items), and we rinsed our palates every now and then with a sweet white wine (but I know nothing about wines; I can tell a good ale or beer when I taste it). And the talk flowed, and photos were taken from many angles, even from the chimney of the outhouse next door.

It gloomed over suddenly, and in the gloom a random midge tickled and bit.

As the car drew near to Stromness, we saw the two tall ships *Marques* and *Inca* berthed side by side at the pier. And what masses of parked cars! And what throngs of people!—It reminded me a bit of the old Lammas Market of the 1930s, with preachers and candy stalls.

Nostalgia for a vanished age had brought half of Orkney into Stromness. Stromness might have known ships of that grace and style two centuries ago. (And of course it gives people a thrill to know that they are actually seeing a ship that had appeared on the TV *Onedin Line* and *The Voyage of the Beagle*, though why this should be is a question best left to sociologists.)

In the yard above the harbour Dominique and Katia were sitting with their baggage. The ferry had left at 3pm that they intended to catch at 6pm; they would have to wait till tomorrow. They were quite cheerful about it.

In a little surge of frenzy the midges began to bite. And heavy raindrops fell. We moved inside.

The *Fortune*

16.9.1982

A curious document from 1770, photocopied, was sent to me a few years ago.

In that year eighteen Stromness men chartered a brigantine, the *Fortune*, to take them to Suleskerry (or Sulisker) for the purpose of killing seals and taking their skins. The men were: Donald Bruce, carpenter; John Groundwater, shoemaker; James Allan, shoemaker; Alexander Sinclair, mason; John Foubister, sailor; David Foubister, boatman; James Gunn, pensioner; Alexander Bruce, weaver; Nicol Taylor, boatman; John Brown, farmer at Innertown; William Cromarty of Citadel; John Simpson, piper; Ian James Mowat, tailor; Magnus Garroch, boatman; Magnus Loutit, boatman; David Linay, sailor; Edward Gray, boatman from Walls; Gilbert Aiken, boatman.

The master of the *Fortune* was Capt. William Malone. On the day of the expedition Malone's wife took ill, and the 'junior ship-master' James Irvine took his place.

(Unfortunately the writing on the document—a petition of complaint to Sir Lawrence Dundas, on behalf of the Stromness men against Capt. Irvine—is so faded in parts, or else the Xerox machine has made it so, that some words and phrases are difficult to make out; besides which the 18th-century scrivener, while striving after a copperplate script, often blundered and scrawled and scratched.)

The *Fortune* set down the seal men on Suleskerry or Sulisker, landing them in a small boat, and anchored close by. The hunters set about their bloody business, and were a bit disconcerted, as they clubbed and skinned, to see the *Fortune* sail off south-east. They completed their work, confident that the ship would return in good time to take them home. But the *Fortune* did not return that night. The weather was not inclement, but they were not clad for a night in the open on a mid-Atlantic rock.

That was only the start of a long vigil. Day after day passed; there was no sign of their ship. They had brought no provisions; they staved off hunger with shellfish and dulse.

At last they reached the point of desperation. Nine of the seal-hunters set out in the ship's boat—probably she would hold no more—for Stromness and succour. They had no sooner got home than the weather broke, so that it was impossible for any ship to get near the rock. The nine remaining seal-hunters were left, unsheltered and half-starved and thinly clad, to the full Atlantic fury.

The document becomes difficult to follow here, but it seems that the *Fortune*, which had sailed to Stornoway, returned some time during the grim little drama, approached the rock and the castaways, and sailed away again.

Eventually the weather moderated; a ship sailed from Stromness, and the nine were taken off. By this time some of them were very ill from exposure—so ill indeed that there was little prospect of them, in the near future, being able to provide for their families.

Therefore, a Stromness lawyer drew up on their behalf a petition against the skipper James Irvine, seeking adequate redress.

There in mid-flow, the story breaks off. We don't know what motivated Irivine to abandon the eighteen men; nor how things went with the men made sick by their ordeal; or whether, at the urging of Dundas, Admiral of Orkney and Zetland, they or their dependants received any compensation.

Equinoctial Gales

23.9.1982

By the time you read this, the autumnal equinox will have come and gone. We will be heading full-tilt into winter. Now the great tides of darkness will begin to swirl about our piers and thresholds.

The equinoxes—so said the old folklorists—brought great gales with them.

How they staggered, with torn sheets and splintered masts, into the shelter of Hamnavoe, the old sailing-ships!... And then, from Login's Inn down to the sleaziest ale-house up some dark close, there was a mighty ringing of flagons on shelf and table, and a broaching of ale-barrels; for sailors new out of a storm were always thirsty men. Silver rattled and rang in tavern tills.

And in her cottage on Brinkie's Brae, Bessie Millie with her cat and hen waited patiently for the skippers to arrive.

How beautifully Stromness was situated in the days of the sailing ships—lying there at the south-west corner of the Mainland, but tucked into a nook facing east with a secluded haven between the piers and the two little green islets. In Stromness, in a westerly storm, you can still hear the immense song and outcry of the wind; but along the street, sheltered by the granite hill and the tall range of houses, only a few airs stir and move.

An enchanted calm it must have seemed to the Atlantic-battered seamen: 'Where the green swell is in the haven dumb / And out of the swing of the sea'.

But let a farmer ride in from Outertown on a horse, or from Stenness, and his hair and beard would be all a blown tangle about his face, and hooves and mane would still be prancing with the exultation of storm! And high up, over the chimneys of Hamnavoe, the rooks would be 'blown about the skies', and the clouds would stream in driven huddled masses out beyond Orphir and Kirkwall and Copinsay.

The west was always a kind airt to Stromnessians. The morning after an equinoctial gale, the beaches from Nethertoon to Black Craig were strewn with driftwood and wrack; and for many days the great Atlantic organ-peal went on and on.

Mr Bluebottle

30.9.1982

Bluebottles are one of the banes of early autumn. Late at night, I sit in the rocking chair looking forward to reading a few pages, when he is suddenly there, Mr Bluebottle—hurling himself at the glowing bulb of the Anglepoise lamp, again and again! At last he gets tired of it, or he is drunk with light, or his wings are singed. Good—Mr Bluebottle takes his departure: where I know not, and care less, if only I can finish the chapter and get to bed.

Vain longing: he comes circling back, Mr Bluebottle, he renews the attack. How he's longing to break the glass of the bulb and incinerate himself on the burning filament. No drug addict was ever more avid for morphine or cocaine than that insect for electric light. Again and again he hurtles himself at the blaze. Sometimes, in his recoils, he lands buzzing and spinning on the very page I'm reading! Sometimes (abomination), he brushes my cheek or my hand, that high-powered ink-blob...

I can stand no more of it. Cover the fire; put out the light, take your book upstairs, read in bed.

But there's no certainty of peace, even in bed. Where has the bedroom bluebottle been hiding all day? He is suddenly there, before I can get pyjamas on, lurching and singing like a mad thing round the bedside lamp.

It is time to match cunning against insane persistence. I switch off the bedlight. I switch on the two lights on the staircase. Mr Bluebottle is dejected, he falls silent; but soon realizes that there's light to be had outside, on the stairs—not one but two bulbs overflowing with heat and radiance, like Caribbean suns. Out of the bedroom he stumbles. I switch off the outside lights and leave him darkling, the poor addict.

It will be possible to read a few pages in comfort, after all—before the poppy drops its petals.

Conversation of the Seasons

7.10.1982

The conversation of the seasons; for each month seems to have a personality of its own.

'In my house,' says October, 'there are witches. There are apples and nuts.'

'I keep the bones of the dead,' says November. 'But a bright one, a saint, looks out through the window, and a candle is burning.'

'I have hundreds of candles,' says December. 'Was ever such intricate jewellery as the first snowflake? There's an inn, a crib, an ox and an ass.'

'The Aurora dances in the north like a princess or a tinker lass,' says January. 'A bird starves here and there.'

'I wear grey patches of snow on my drab coat,' says February. 'But I have a few snowdrops in my hand.'

'I weigh day and night,' says March the shopkeeper. 'There you are, sir—a shillingworth of sun.'

Who brings lambs and first daffodils? April. And she lights a score of hill fires.

May herds the cuithes[1] in legions through the Sound. Old folk begin to think they mightn't die this year yet.

June hardly sleeps. Hardly has she covered the fire in the north-west than it's time to kindle the fire in the north-east. She spreads beautiful cloths everywhere, stitched with flowers.

July is a riot of schoolchildren. And a doucer riot of tourists, saying, 'How quaint!' Fields are scored with green and yellow geometry.

'Well,' says August, 'time to gather all the riches together in a field full of folk.' The Dounby Show.

'I measure night and day,' says September the joiner. 'Not long now, at the longest, the dark.'

Then October again, offering a child an apple in the door. And if you go in, she'll tell you a story of witchcraft at her fire.

* * *

So, indeed, each month seems to have a 'persona' of its own, a flavour and an aura.

I am writing this on the penultimate day of September. The equinoctial gales have done plenty of shouting—rain was dashed in bucketfuls on the east window, to such an extent that it penetrated glass and window-frame, and made incessant drippings on the floor near midnight.

But today is sweet and brimming over with brightness. So September has still a few pleasant words to say: 'Oh, I keep a few jars of honey on my shelf, a few late roses'...

Childhood Reading

21.10.1982

Following the little excursion into Sir Walter Scott territory last week[2], I ought to say a few words about the literature that my contemporaries and I did actually read with joy, in our childhood.

---

1. older coalfish
2. not included in this selection

These were the weekly magazines at twopence each, published by D. C. Thomson of Dundee, full of the most entrancing serial stories— *Adventure* on Monday, *Wizard* on Tuesday, *Rover* on Thursday, *Hotspur* on Friday, *Skipper* on Saturday.

Of course we couldn't afford to buy them all; there was a complicated barter system by which a boy managed to lay hands on most of them.

Gem and *Magnet* (one of them containing the immortal fat greedy schoolboy Billy Bunter) were not so available for some reason, but, whenever they did appear, I liked them best of all.

In general, those weekly banquets of literature were looked on with displeasure by our elders—they were 'trash', not calculated in any way to strengthen and uplift our minds and spirits in the true Samuel Smiles tradition. Yet read them we did, with devotion and gratitude.

(Ah, if only the new novels that stream from our presses nowadays gave me half as much pleasure.)

But most of us, with the approval of our elders, joined the local Library, presided over by Peter Esson when he wasn't in his tailor shop at the foot of the Kirk Road. Some of my contemporaries praised highly the works of Percy F. Westerman, adventure tales; but I never cared for them. Instead, I latched onto stories about English public schools, and the author I liked best in this genre was called Harold Avery. There was a very pious sickly Victorian school story called *St Winifred's, or The World of School* by a Dean Farrar, that moved me to tears. Dean Farrar is one of the few authors who ever melted this stony heart to such an extent... There was another public school masterpiece called *The Fifth Form at St Dominic's*, that left me in a swoon of admiration—but I forget the author's name[1].

But oh, the unparalleled joy of first looking into *The Pilots of Pomona* by Robert Leighton! Was it conceivable that a story could be written about Stromness and printed in a book? Yet here it was, and we read with joy the opening scene of the barefoot Stromness boy being late for the peedie school in Hellihole, because he has been too intent on fishing sillocks at, possibly, Gray's Pier. (After that vivid opening image, the rest of the story I forget, alas!)

Such is one way of entering the enchanted castle of Literature.

A Few Bright Snapshots

11.11.1982

The darkness took an hour's leap forward the Sunday morning before last, and left my digital watch stranded on the shores of summertime.

1. Talbot Baines Reed

That's to say, whenever I consult that silently-pulsing second-devouring thing on my left wrist, I have to remember to subtract an hour. Ah, well: next April my digital and the time on other watches and clocks will be in perfect synchronisation again. (Besides, we didn't go to school not to be able to subtract or add a unit to an accepted number.)

But mention of summertime reminds me—even if the ever-encroaching darkness didn't—that we have put another summer well and truly behind us; and we will soon have to be thinking of Christmas cards and letters to Santa.

Of the summertime of 1982, all that remains are a few bright snapshots in the mind. Particularly I think of Rackwick in fine sun-smitten July days (there was one dark wet day, but it was enjoyable too, driving back from the handsome house at Melsetter among clouds that seemed to be hills, and hills that seemed to be deeper darker immensities of rain). Splashing faces in cold water outside in the mornings, drinking cans of beer at noon, writing poems (2-liners) almost as small as midges outside the open door.

And there were in August the tall ships smelling inside of tar and salt and resin at the North Pier—*Marques* and *Inca*.

And there was Shopping Week, with its masquers and bands and candy-floss and people by the hundred...

And there was the St Magnus Festival, with the exciting new music, and children singing and acting, and the grave rich voice of a great Irish poet...

But there are a hundred other things from the good summer just past that I will not mention, for they would interest nobody but myself. There was that bee, and that gull, that cloud, that dandelion, that wave, that shell, that gust of wind—nothing about them to be said, really; they are indeed all forgotten; but each was unique, and each is gathered now into the unchangeable fabric of time, and is a part of us whether we know it or not.

The Story of Burnt Njal

2.12.1982

The work is in two volumes, superbly bound, with Icelandic motifs stamped in gold on the front covers, and two Icelandic sayings on unfurled pennants: 'But a Short While is Hand Fain of Blow'—and 'Bare is Back Without Brother Behind It'...

The work was published in Edinburgh in 1861. This is a first edition. Not only that, on the front page of Volume I is inscribed, in faded ink, 'To Lady Ashburton, with the translator's compliments, April 18th, 1861.'

The author was Sir George Dasent, and the work in question is his translation of the famous Icelandic *The Story of Burnt Njal*.

I first read *Njal* in the Everyman edition in the nineteen-forties, and was impressed at once by the purity of the narrative. That's to say, each episode flows on, untrammelled by description or digression, in a simple line from beginning to end. If there is description, it is purely functional—the storyteller doesn't obtrude himself in any way. Events unfold in all their starkness and inevitability.

'Inevitability'—the marks of Fate are everywhere in the work; none of the characters can escape what is decreed for him, probably before he was born. Old Njal knows, long before it happens, the time and the manner of his death (but Njal was a 'seer'). The wicked wandering mischief-maker and murderer Hrapp knows that he is evil; in his death-hour—by violence of course—he confesses stoically that his severed arm has worked much devilry; and he seems glad to see it lying there on the ice.

I do not think somehow that *Burnt Njal* will be a classic on the shelves of any Women's Lib library. At the back of every intricate family feud there is a crafty strong-minded woman working the strings. One has the vivid feeling that the Iceland men, left to themselves, would have resolved all their troubles amicably.

So, it must be nearly forty years since I read this great work. I bought the original edition a decade ago in Charlie Senior's bookshop; and it reposed undisturbed in my hill of books till one night last week.

Many of the pages are uncut. The musk of more than a century comes off them. In mid-Victorian times, the paper-makers' and printers' and binders' were noble trades.

Christmas in the Heroic Age

23.12.1982

Christmas, thank goodness, is a lot quieter for Orkney folk now than it was in the so-called heroic age.

No true Orcadian, I'm sure, needs to be reminded of that terrible Christmas in Earl Paul's Hall in Orphir, when the two Sweyns confronted each other, and blood ran while Matins were being sung in the Round Church of St Nicholas, in the next field.

There was another Christmas a few years later, that didn't take place in Orkney though Orkneymen were actively involved.

Earl Rognvald the Second was on his pilgrimage to Jerusalem. In Spain, after sea storms had perhaps ruined their food hoard, they bargained at a certain seaport for provisions. It was coming on for Yule, the darkest coldest hungriest time of the year.

Earl Rognvald and his fourteen skippers were told that he could have the provisions he wanted, on condition that he destroyed the castle of a robber baron who tyrannised the district—Godfrey by name.

It was just the sort of action those Vikings relished, and hunger had put an edge to their war-craft. Earl Rognvald drew up plans for the attack.

And Godfrey's castle was just about to be assaulted with stones, arrows, fire and battering-rams when Bishop William of Orkney arrived on the scene, sternly.

What did they think they were doing? Were they madmen? Didn't they realise it was the holy time of Christmas, when for twelve days the dove takes over from the raven? Let them go back at once to their ships. On 6 January they might do what had to be done... So thundered Bishop William the Old, 'the clerk of Paris'.

Back on the ships they must have endured a miserable Christmas of crusts and sour ale; while in the castle on the hill Godfrey and his bully-boys and his ladies held high revelry.

It was the last feasting that castle would ever do, they had made their last extortions from the little seaport.

On 6 January the Vikings went over and through the castle like a flaming wave.

They had their Christmas feast, the Orkneymen and the Norwegians, very late that year.

St Lucy's Day

30.12.1982

Recovering from a cold, you lie long in the morning.

There's a thud in the lobby downstairs—what can it be?—the postman, of course, has delivered another load of Christmas cards. Well, let them lie awhile, till the mind is full awake.

Reading the Christmas cards and letters lasts a whole pot-of-tea long, while the boiled egg and the toast slowly grow cold. Small leaps of heart-joy!—a distant almost-forgotten friend has remembered you... little pinpricks of guilt—here are kind cards from people you have not sent to!... At last one can settle to the egg and toast.

Then, on the cleared kitchen table, there are things to be done—a few urgent letters written, a few belated cards scribbled in.

Outside, it is a grey day threatening more snow. As the shadows gather, I suddenly remember that it is 21 December, the winter solstice—and past 3 o'clock, when the sun setting over Hoy puts a bright finger on the death wall of Maeshowe. (But not on an overcast day like this.)

But one can have a little private feast of light.

The fire was roaring joyously up the lum.

Here and there about the living-room I lit candles (stuck in bottles some of them), to the number of seven. No electric light, of course. How magical a thing it is, a candle-flame—tranquil, but with a little tremor of life in it: and a kind of radiance that has never been matched by paraffin or gas or electricity. But a configuration of seven flames—it was pure enchantment to sit among them while the windows slowly darkened.

"'Tis the year's midnight, and it is the day's,' said the poet John Donne three and a half centuries ago. Outside was beginning the longest darkest night of the year, the full ebb. Yet already, little eddies of light were beginning to turn round, precursors of the flood-tide of radiance that will brighten hands and stones and flowers next June.

Five thousand years ago Orkneymen built a great chamber beside the lochs to enshrine the last and the first light.

So, among the candle-flames of the winter solstice, I scratched on a scrap of paper a little St Lucy lyric to celebrate the season.

New Year Wishes

6.1.1983

What should we wish for most, in a new year?

Private prosperity and health and well-being—we wish each other that, with a hundred handshakings, in the early days of January—with varying degrees of sincerity.

What else ought we to wish for?—another oil strike in the North Sea? (But such things seem almost as removed from us now as gold-strikes in the Yukon.)

Perhaps we ought to wish most of all for universal peace—what we are supposed ardently to desire Christmas after Christmas. This is perhaps what the Spanish poet Lorca—himself a victim of war—meant when he wrote those marvellous lines: 'I want a black boy to announce to the gold-minded whites / The arrival of the reign of the year of corn'...

May the announcement come soon, because now the whole human race has come almost full cycle; and we are standing on the brink of that chaos from which we emerged with so much courage and imagination, aeons ago.

Another full-scale war, and we are over the brink and into the pit: only it will be much worse, for we are likely to bring down all the rest of the lovely creation with us; and the atmosphere—the air which we 'gather and release' for strength and refreshment, deliciously, ten thousand times a day—that invisible harbinger of life will be so polluted that no plant or tree or fish or horse or man could survive the poison.

So, when we wish each other a peaceful New Year, we ought perhaps to think of peace in its earth-girdling sense.

* * *

Meantime, Twelfth Night is here. The last whisky bottle is empty; the last hangover has been cast aside like a grey rag. All over Orkney, two or three hundred Christmas trees have been dismantled; and Santa's bounty has been hidden away in cupboards.

We turn to face the snows of January and February—never forgetting how beautiful snow and winter stars are. In a cold poisoned cinder of a world, there would be nobody to see those things.

The Ferocious Month

20.1.1983

We are half-way through January as I write this, and already, by mid-afternoon there is a perceptible difference in the light. The old folk used to say (if I remember right), 'By the twelfth of January there's an hour's difference.'... And then, right on the back of it they would say, 'As the day lengthens, the cowld strengthens'.

January indeed is probably the most ferocious month of the year, a growling polar bear.

This morning I was startled by a fusillade of hailstones at the kitchen window—and the garden outside was half-hidden in a grey drift. Then, ten minutes later, a burst of glorious sun out of a chasm of blue—and so the pattern had continued all day, alternate snow-showers and sun-bursts.

And still no one can say for sure how January 1983 is to behave—whether with an immense blizzard that, like three or four winters ago, makes the islands white blanks between the two oceans, or with the blue flashing mirrors of frost that were so breathtakingly beautiful a twelvemonth ago—whenever the swans were penned in their crystal loch prisons.

* * *

For two days, to forget about winter, I tried to imagine that summer day from the childhood of our race when suddenly Eynhallow rose out of the waters between Evie and Rousay, like a great green whale. It had appeared like that before, but even while the folk on the shore marvelled, and thought to themselves what a good place it would be to build a few crofts on, it vanished like a rainbow or like snowflakes.

Iron it was that fixed the island forever in geography and history; for in those days iron was a magical substance, that let the questing hands of men do things they had never been able to do before. Since then iron has become a symbol of cruelty, war, and tyranny.

I imagined it was a boy in a small boat that set out for the impossible shore, and instead of iron he carried silver, a sixpenny piece to send ringing among the new shore-stones.

Anyway, it was a summer day, and the sun shone, and Eynhallow was purchased for the children of men.

Breakfast TV

27.1.1983

Breakfast television—the world is full of more wonders than ever I thought! Who, conceivably, would want to watch TV between 6.30am and 9am in the morning? Mightn't the London businessman having his cornflakes, egg and toast and marmalade, and coffee, be wanting to plan (between hurried chews and gulps) the day ahead, undistracted by coloured shadows in the corner? And his wife: won't she, as always, have her work cut out seeing to that same toast and coffee, and combing the children's hair for school, and fixing scarves round their necks against the winter, without all that chatter going on, and the flickerings, from the box in the corner?

But maybe the urban social pattern has changed lately out of all recognition and families in the early morning behave quite otherwise than they used to do. In fact, it must be so; otherwise there would be no demand for breakfast TV.

All I know is, I will not be viewing (except by some rare accident) because between 6.30 and 9am, I am well into my second sleep.

* * *

Half a century ago, for schoolboys, breakfast was the urgent time of the day. We got out of warm beds about 8.30 or later. (I rather think we had washed our faces the night before, to save time.) Never was a meal consumed with such speed—which was a pity, in a way, because breakfast consisted of one of those long rolls with dimples in the middle, warm from Porteous's Bakehouse, and thick-spread with most delicious butter from the farm of Citadel. One cup of quick sweet tea.

The American clock on the mantelpiece ticked on remorselessly from 8.50 to 8.55am.

Then we seized our bag of books and jotters, and jogged along Ness Road and up the Khyber Pass and on up the fearful slope to Stromness Academy ('shades of the prison house') with, somewhere about the top of the Kirk Road, the tolling of the bell in our ears.

Plenty of excitement for us in the 1930s, without breakfast TV.

A Strangely-Patterned Winter

17.2.1983

A strangely-patterned winter, this, for weather. The snow has behaved most strangely of all. It comes, and goes away, shyly, like a white child. One wakens and draws back the curtains—another snowfall in the gardens and on the roofs—a very small one, that barely covers the earth. By afternoon it has mostly gone, it has dissolved into blue wind and puddles. (But, even so, we have to watch where we put our feet—who wants to end up in a hospital bed getting a leg mended by 'traction'?)

And so the snows of January and early February came like small shy girls, looking round the corner and disappearing again, as if it was all a game. Only high in Orphir and Hoy were cloths of snow spread for a winter picnic.

'Ah well,' said I, when yesterday was a universal grey, 'we won't need to worry more about snow this winter'... Of course there are little blizzards in March and April, that heap up quilts and pillows in the fields. They vanish soon, like white dreams.

Another morning—it is time, reluctantly, to get out of the warm nest of the bed. The drawing back of my red curtains—another snowfall in the night, and this one cheekier and more prodigal than her sisters. She intends to dwell with us a while, this forward one, I think. The sun tries to smite her, to drive her away—she only gleams the more—and every half-hour or so a new blue-black cloud from the north delivers more items for her immaculate wardrobe. This latest snowfall might be a pert obdurate one that lasts to the end of the month—then slinks away like an old ragged woman, leaving hideous thaws behind. There will be maybe a few late snowdrops, to remind us how thrilling the colour white is.

No: this one stayed only a day or two, like all the others. Now she is part of the North Sea or the Atlantic; and may make landfall in some burning part of Africa, where women come with tall jars to that treasury, the well.

Grumbling and Gratitude

17.3.1983

It's amazing, the amount of grumbling we do. A shower of rain comes; people hunch their shoulders, pluck their caps down over their brows, and 'What miserable weather!' they complain to each other.

Miserable weather, indeed! Without rain we would have no blood in our veins, nor milk in our tea, nor beer, nor lemonade, nor roses, nor oranges, nor oaks.

We should turn up our faces thankfully to a shower. (I must admit though, that today's rain is a bit much; it has come down diagonally ever since breakfast-time.)

Still, that's what roofs are over our heads for. So, we ought to be thankful for house and fireside too.

I think it is only when a society is in no serious want—when one knows that there will be abundance of bread and meat and tea for as far forward as we can envisage—it is only in such prosperous times that we indulge the luxury of grumbling about our lot.

In hard times, people are too busy looking for scraps and old boots in middens to grumble. 'Ah, how good, to eat a husk in the swineherd's door!... How delicious this water that I lap from a pool, like a dog...'

Gratitude is not in fashion these days.

I throw the ends of loaves to the gulls and the sparrows and to the proud dreaming drifting swans. Many a person in Cambodia would eat them with relish and wonderment.

You see, stuck on railings, a woollen glove or bonnet that someone has lost. There it hangs, for days sometimes. In El Salvador, or Tierra del Fuego, it wouldn't be on the spike five minutes.

When we were young and turned up our noses at porridge or broth, my father used to say, 'The bairns in Germany would be glad of that.' (It was probably the time of the great recession.)

Gratitude is not in fashion these days. But it puts a relish in living: when we know that an atom splitting could reduce us in a day to want undreamed of.

Orkney Ministers

14.4.1983

The 18th- and 19th-century ministers in their great echoing Manses — life in Orkney must have been lonely for them. Their 'social equals' were only the lairds, and many of them were Episcopalian. But still, laird and minister were the twin bulwarks of society, and one must conclude that the huge Manse was a status symbol. The stipend of £150 a year was generous too, according to the monetary values of the time.

What, then, did they find to do in their big houses, apart from preparing the Sunday sermon?

Many of them were deeply learned men. Rev Dr Charles Clouston of Sandwick was an outstanding naturalist, and one of the founders of the Orkney Natural History Society (Stromness Museum). He it was, tradition says, who finally destroyed the frightful *Book of Black Arts*, burning it in the Manse garden.

A relative of his, Rev William Clouston, was minister in Stromness, He is buried in the Kirkyard at Hoy Sound, under a tombstone of twinned Latin and English. The Latin poets he delighted in; his fascinating account of the parish in the *Old Statistical Account* is made fragrant and sonorous with quotations from Virgil and Horace. I think, judging from the tone of his prose, that he must have been a pleasant man to know.

Another delightful companion would have been Rev James Wallace who ministered in Kirkwall (St Magnus). How gently and sweetly he writes of the islanders, of their innate courtesy, of the comeliness of the women; of the wonders of nature strewn all around.

Somewhat more disconcerting would have been Rev John Gerard of South Ronaldsay. Nothing mealy-mouthed about him; his direct earthy utterances showed him to be sprung from good Buchan country stock. The gentry may well have raised eyebrows at his manifold eccentricities—they delighted the farming folk of South Ronaldsay, and passed almost as soon as they were perpetrated into island legend.

Rev George Low of Birsay is said to have been the best Orkney naturalist of his time.

But the minister with the most encyclopaedic mind of all was surely Rev George Barry of Shapinsay. His enormous book, fruit of a lifetime's labour and observation, was first published in 1805; quite recently a facsimile editon came out, complete with the illustrative prints which in their romantic exaggeration (amounting almost to caricature) seem more astounding than the later more celebrated Daniell prints.

Barry is full of fascinating asides. Readers of modern verse know, of course, that Gerard Manley Hopkins' great sonnet on the kestrel is called 'The Windhover'... In Barry's catalogue of Orkney birds, I was amazed and delighted to find that the contemporary Orkney name for that bird is 'The Windcuffer'—obviously the identical name with a slightly different pronunciation.

So, in a dry list, one comes on a sudden gleam of poetry.

'A Little of What You Fancy'

5.5.1983

It seems—if you are to believe some of the things you read in magazines or watch on TV—that a lot of the food we eat is actually bad for us. Or so they claim. Sugar, for example. But what would the morning cup of tea be without a spoon of sugar? It sets the whole day flowing free and sweet and hopeful.

Salt, too. 'Don't put too much salt on your food!' Not even a fool would deluge his broth or porridge with an overplus of salt. But what (again) would the breakfast egg be without its sprinkling of white savoury grains? (The old wives used to say, when I was a small boy and thought love and kisses nonsense—'An egg without salt is like a kiss without love'.) ... Now I see what they meant, and I thoroughly agree with them.

Eggs, too, one of the great joys and mainstays of life—it seems (the nutritional experts say) too many eggs won't do you any good at all. (Three eggs a week might do—no more.) What, eggs, that have been a joy since infancy! No nobler meal than ham and egg, or sausage and egg, or egg and chips, we could imagine in childhood, youth or maturity... I intend to have my morning egg every breakfast till I can eat no more.

Surely nobody in their senses could be found to say a thing against butter! When we were young we were encouraged to eat plenty of butter, so we could grow up healthy and strong. What's butter but the rich essence of meadow and pasture-land—it is summer's golden unction... Not, it seems, any more. Butter is liable to clog up your insides—hinder the flow of blood in and out of the heart...

Life being so brief, and beset with so many difficult and distasteful things, I intend while the breath is in me to eat and drink the things I enjoy. If you wasted time listening to experts, you'd soon wear yourself down to a grey worried wraith.

Wasn't it Marie Lloyd who sang, 'A little of what you fancy does you good'? It is a good and wise song.

Aberdeen's European Triumph

19.5.1983

In Gothenburg, Sweden, the rain was lashing down last night. Waterproofs and umbrellas were everywhere in the crowd. In Orkney, all day, the sun and the rain had been flying.

It was so pleasant, sitting in a comfortable easy-chair beside a warm fire, seeing the same thing happening as well as—or even better than—

the sodden soaking crowd in the stadium, that had (we knew) a sprinkling of Orcadians in it.

A football match—what should an ageing wheezy rheumaticky person like me want with such a thing, when he could be spending the time more profitably with a book? I should say that in childhood I was passionately devoted to football, though my favourite team was not Aberdeen, but Celtic. (I still feel in the dumps, very slightly, if Celtic get beaten on a Saturday.)

I arrived at my friend's mid-way through the first half, when the play was scrappy and uninspired; after (I was told) a blazing beginning, the score stood at one-all. The red-shirted Dons splashed through puddles near the touchline. The Spaniards' white was splotched with mud. Both teams were tired, obviously, of chasing that heavy ball through the relentless mud and rain.

It seemed like petering out into the poorest of games.

Where the Aberdonians got the fire from—that matched the red of their shirts—in the second half, I do not know. They played so magnificently it was a joy to watch them—the normally dazzling Madrid team looked awkward and commonplace. But never a goal they got, for all their brave brilliant work. The final whistle went.

Surely they had played themselves into the ground! Such disappointment would break the strongest will.

Then, in extra time it came, the flame, the consummation, the crown—a beautifully-taken goal, Aberdeen 2, Real Madrid 1.

There was a breath-stopping moment near the end when a Madrid free-kick seared through the red defensive wall and went, thankfully, inches past the post.

What joy, what triumph! I felt, for two hours or so, fifty years younger.

'Whales!'

2.6.1983

It isn't all that long—a century and a bit, maybe—that Orkney was part of 'the third world' (though nobody had ever heard the expression then—it wouldn't have made any sense).

But no sweeter cry could have been heard along the poor sea-front of Stromness than 'Whales!'

Then everything was dropped—blacksmith his hammer, tailor his needle, shipwright his adze, farmer his plough, housewife her broom—and all the Stromnessians armed themselves for the great whale battle.

I suppose that sometimes as in Westray recently, the whales obligingly beached themselves. But mostly they had to be encouraged shoreward. A fleet of small boats came between them and the horizon. Then the din began—metal was clashed on metal, throats were stretched, the welkin rang hideously with human discord. The school of whales, panic-stricken, made for the shore. One after another, they piled themselves on the rocks.

Then the great festival of butchery began. There were enough whale steaks cut to last an island through the winter (smoked or salted). There was oil enough to keep lamps burning in every window from September to March.

That's to say, if whale oil was suitable for lamps...

Then, burdened, every family set off homeward with its sea-sent bounty.

(The Church officer of the UP Kirk in Stromness, a John Loutitt, got into severe trouble for deserting his duties to go after whales 150 years ago—and on the Sabbath too.)

Nowadays, four or five generations later, we live in an age of affluence. Whales ashore are no longer a treasure—they are an embarrassment and a nuisance.

* * *

There were other sea-given things, like wrecked ships. Barrels of apples, casks of rum, oaken spars and timbers.

If the ocean cast such exotic gifts on our coasts, who shall blame the half-starved Orkneymen for plucking them into their barns and hidey-holes?

As for the foreign sailors, we may hope it was kind hands that drew them to shore.

The First Turf Fire

9.6.1983

It's still cold in the late afternoons, when work and errands have been done. Time then, before the main meal, to put a match to the crumpled paper. The sticks spit, snarl, ignite. Shy little flames appear among the black coal. The flames grow—they leap higher, with glad noises. The fire sends waves of warmth into the coldest corners.

I don't for one moment believe it was Earl Einar (nicknamed 'Torf') who first gave the gift of peat to the Orcadians. They were burning peats long before the day of that violent and lucky man.

The way I see it is this. Three thousand years ago, fuel was scarce in the islands. Miserable cold winters they had, crouched over the warmth given by dried cow-pats. Occasionally a friendly tribe—cousins, perhaps—sent logs of wood to the villages in Rousay and Sandwick.

But the children beachcombed anxiously along the tide-mark, seizing on anything that might burn—a dead tree, a broken rudder, a stranded whale.

This man in Skara Brae, he had three young sons that he sent out to beachcomb for combustibles. The two bright boys wandered about the shore, probing, all morning. The third one, the dim-wit, he left his brothers and he wandered up among the hills.

The two clever brothers were home by sunset, with wet feathers, whales' vertebrae, halibut bones, that might feed a fire in a kind of way.

It was almost dark when the third son returned, the one who was always looked on as 'a bit dim'. And, the poor creature, his caisie[1] was loaded with bits of the hill he had cut earlier in the summer, and left to dry in the wind and sun.

What did the creature do then but throw one of those hard squares of earth onto the struggling fire—so that the fire was almost certain to choke and go out.

The father, having got to his feet, was about to chastise the fool unmercifully when the mother cried, 'Look, the flames are eating the turf! How warm and good it is now, in the house.'

That boy, he never lacked for food or drink along that coast, till he died.

A Mysterious Stranger

16.6.1983

A man came to Orkney in the late '40s. It seemed that he was completely dumb, for he was never known to utter a word. When he got off the *Ola* in Stromness, he showed a card with the name of a croft in a certain island to the men at the pierhead, who almost fell over themselves in their eagerness to tell him where the place was. He must take the ferryboat that left at four o'clock. They pointed. He nodded. He gave them a somewhat sinister smile.

The ferryman tried to engage him in conversation. Where did he come from? What was his business in that lonely place? The stranger mimed the actions of fishing and ploughing... Oh, so that was what the old ruined croft on the island had been restored for, all last spring! Well, well—he wished the stranger all the luck in the world. And if he, the ferryman, could bring him his provisions from the town, he'd be only too glad to oblige.

He paid the ferryman with a fifty-mark note, which, when he changed it at the Bank the next day, caused the ferryman to wreathe his face in smiles. For it was thrice the normal fee.

1. basket

107

Time passed. Twice a week the ferryman brought provisions to the dumb generous stranger. His message list was rather peculiar—apples, oranges, oat-meal, bananas, nuts, potatoes, boxes of sweet cakes (the creamier the better). Never meat of any kind, nor a single bottle of whisky, nor tobacco.

The stranger made a poor job of the fishing, and he wasn't much better at the field-work. But he never lacked for money; he could produce hundred-mark notes like a conjurer. He never read books; he never got a single letter; but the ferryman delivering another box of sweet cakes observed that he kept a copious diary.

Time passed. The stranger visited nobody and nobody visited him. He would scowl ferociously at anybody who approached the house.

He gradually shrivelled into age. One day the ferryman, delivering a box of vegetables and a box of cream buns, found the man lying on the floor. He had fallen and broken a leg. He had lain five days on the floor; he counted the time on his fingers.

Four island men carried him down to the ferryboat. An ambulance was waiting for him at Stromness pier—it bore him off to the Balfour.

By this time he was in a delirium of pain. 'Dumb?' said the staff nurse. 'He's got plenty to say for himself, only I don't know what it is...' The doctor came, and listened, and announced that he was speaking (or, rather, shrieking) German. The doctor leaned down and listened more carefully. Then he turned an awed face to the circle of nurses. 'This is what he's saying:

'"I demand Orkney, Shetland, the Faroes, and Iceland. My patience is exhausted. That is the last territorial claim I have to make in the North Atlantic!"'

A week later, after severe pneumonia had set in, part of his demand at least was granted—six feet of Orkney soil. Also a simple stone with the initials 'A.H.' and the years of his beginning and end.

If the famous Diaries are true, then so is the above.

A Dead Gull

21.7.1983

A lovely late afternoon in July, at the Birsay shore—the same that was so loved and celebrated by the poet Robert Rendall.

The sea has ebbed far out, leaving rockpools for the children to play in. Sea-birds call, far and near, and the voices of children touched to enchantment by the vastness of sea and sky. A tractor stutters in a field nearby—a cow is making a big moan about something or other. The shore flies try to get into your eyes and mouth.

The third day of full unclouded sunshine it is. The faint peach-bloom of haar on the horizon gives promise of another fine day tomorrow. A gentle warm breeze comes off the sea—so that it is not intolerably hot for an old person like me sitting on a rock and writing letters in a notebook.

But there, right at my feet, lies a dead gull, the head buried in the sand, the wing feathers all awry.

* * *

What happened to you, bird of the sea, that you came to this untimely end?

Was it a broken wing, so that you could no longer feed yourself, flying so immaculately from rock-niche to wave?

Or maybe a pellet from a gun ruffled your feathers and dulled your eye.

Or maybe it was your time to die, according to the rhythms of all living things.

Whatever your end was, there you lie now, half-buried, your wings a cluster of crooked pens. Not even the shore insects are interested in you.

No more the silver arcs after fishermen and ploughmen, the little blizzard you make with a hundred of your kind.

And the barbaric songs you gave out only a week ago, those gaunt shrieks for no reason apparent to humans! If it was joy—as lark and blackbird pour forth and round out their exquisite vowels—your gull-anthologies come from a pain or exultation not in our experience, very ancient, from near the beginning of things.

The old folk explained the thing. Lost fishermen and sailors, it was their sea lament.

The heap of feathers at my feet will never stir again, as the tides flow and ebb, 'As though it had never been', to quote an exquisite line from Birsay's poet of the shore.

Black Bags

28.7.1983

Monday is the day of the black bags, when half or more of the Stromness households carry their refuse to this or that corner of the street, for the patient dustmen to carry it to its last fiery resting-place.

At Mayburn Court, there the black bags are piled up like a hoard of Gow's treasure. The cats circle it warily. Gulls in their high circlings look speculatively down.

Yesterday (Monday) I had two enormous black bags to carry down before breakfast. Already, the Mayburn hoard was piling up. In the sunny street below, people passed in their holiday array.

109

Well then—I heaved the first black bag out of the cupboard under-stairs. All went well. It was when I was attempting to heave out the second amazingly fat bag, that it gave a creak of protest. Half-way between cupboard and lobby, a little split showed in the black plastic. The fissure widened—it gaped—the side collapsed—and then my clean lobby was inundated with empty cans, tins, teabags, packets, pokes, bottles, papers; all the effluvium that a household gathers in the space of a week. What a sight to behold, first thing in the morning!

There was only one thing to do—make the mind a blank, and then set swiftly to work with hands, shovel, brush, and thrust the black sickly-smelling treasure into a new bag; tie the neck with string; and carry it down (fearful every moment that another rupture will develop, not in privacy but in the public courtyard, with tourists coming and going, and holding their offended noses).

But the bag held, and I set it gingerly on the growing treasury of black bags—a small triumph.

How delightful, after that holocaust, the pot of tea, the egg and toast, while Gypsy the cat got stuck into cat-food, purring with joy all the time.

The sun poured its temperate gold over the town and the hundreds of revellers. It was the second morning of Shopping Week.

I felt the urge to do some work, but repressed it: for what is the use of pulling against the tide?—and in the course of the day made several new delightful acquaintances.

Filipino Feast

18.8.1983

When my friend Ian MacArthur (from Forres) and I drove through a thick drizzle last Wednesday evening to the Arts Theatre in Kirkwall, we were about the last in the remnants of a queue. 'There are two empty seats left in the gallery,' we were told. I had never seen the theatre so thronged. They were bringing in extra chairs below. (Later, Jack Ridgway who prefaced the show told us that fifty people had had to be turned away.)

What was generating this extraordinary enthusiasm in Orkney? It was, of course, the forty-five singers and dancers from the Philippines.

The show began with a modern Mass by a young Filipino composer; and the ancient but ever-fresh liturgical choruses proceeded to the foldings and unfoldings of the dance—which is (alas) the one art that has fallen out of favour in the western tradition of religion. Painting, music, drama, oratory—but never the dance. Here it was abundantly shown that the dance gives glory as excellently as the others. Gestures of joy, of sorrow, of wonderment, of beseechment, of exaltation—all beautifully choreographed to the changing rhythms of the great sacred song.

After that feast, what might the enthralled hundreds in the Arts Theatre expect? We were given an overflowing cornucopia of spirituals, hymns, songs of freedom, gay rondels of so-called 'nonsense', and a lovely cycle of Filipino love songs, tender and witty and heart-rooted.

Rain—over the hills and waters of Orkney that night the rain was drifting in thin grey saturating clouds. 'That's nothing,' said the delightful conductor—'in the Philippines it rains for six months long!'... There followed an exquisite rain-dance, with umbrellas of many colours suddenly unfurled and whirling and interweaving, and at last presenting a solid phalanx of rain-preventers.

So the night of music and dancing drove on, broken with rapturous applause. And at the end the audience would hardly let the young Pacific enchanters go.

Back they came, and sang as beautifully as I have ever heard it, 'The Bonnie Lass o' Fyvie' (and with the authentic Buchan accent). And yet once more, with a comparatively muted 'Hallelujah'... And then the red curtains closed finally.

Would we be in time for a pint in the Pomona or the Ferry Inn? The hidden moon showed fissures of gold in the north. Perhaps tomorrow would be a better day. We had a dram around midnight.

A Literary Coincidence

22.9.1983

I know that Arthur Koestler, and our own ex-Provost Robertson, have devoted time and study to coincidences, those strange correspondences in the seemingly wayward patterns of time.

I can't honestly say I'd noticed anything of the kind in my own existence—until last Friday at Garth cottage, Outertown, Stromness, where Grenville and Elizabeth Gore-Langton have their hospitable Orkney home.

The previous night, it had struck me that I really ought to read the R. L. Stevenson story 'Thrawn Janet'—it having been recommended by Tom Cotter in the Ferry Inn on Wednesday.

There, right on top of a pile of books, was the Penguin *Scottish Short Stories*, recently published. I was convinced that 'Thrawn Janet' was in this book. But I soon discovered that Stevenson was represented by a story not known to me, called 'The Beach at Falesa'.

I began to read it, soon fascinated by the skill of the story-teller and his masterly limning of character. 'The Beach at Falesa' is a long story, a kind of novella, and I continued reading it in bed till (as Tennyson says) 'my eyelids dropped their shades'.

On Friday afternoon, Elizabeth invited me to Garth to help eat a chicken pie. While we were talking round the fire, Elizabeth happened to mention that, quite by chance, on Thursday evening she picked up a book of R. L. Stevenson stories of the South Seas, and read quite a bit of one story.

That in itself was quite a coincidence. But when she went on to say the story was called 'The Beach at Falesa', and that she was reading it for the first time we were both thunderstruck!

What are the chances of two people in Stromness, on the same evening, picking up a story by R. L. Stevenson, on an impulse? I should think, a thousand to one at least.

Yes, but exactly the same story, out of the considerable mass of RLS's fiction? The odds must lengthen enormously. Might a million to one be stretching it too far?

It may be sheer accident. But it may be that time and chance have intricate patterns beyond our ken.

Braal in Strathy

29.9.1983

Jeremy Godwin of Cumbria, who is known to nearly everybody in Orkney, journeyed this past summer through the district of Strathy in Sutherlandshire, on his way to Orkney.

While he was there he had a close look at a district in Strathy called Braal. He took a photograph of a certain ruined croft-house and he drew a plan of the vicinity. Very kindly, he sent both to me the other day.

He knew I would be interested, because my mother and eight brothers and sisters were brought up in that croft-house towards the end of last century. Their father was a crofter-fisherman called Hugh Mackay and his wife was Georgina Mackay (after whom I was named). Much of the clan Mackay is scattered round those lonely straths and shores on the north coast of Sutherland.

It is not an easy terrain to wring a living from. It seems likely that many of those folk had suffered in the great 'clearances', and had been forced from more fertile places inland to wrest some kind of a living near the sea's edge. (Many of the younger ones, and more adventurous ones, had been urged across the Atlantic to Canada.)

Well, anyway, Jeremy Godwin's photograph sent a pang of memory through me. Once, aged about five or six, my mother took my brother and me for a holiday to Braal one summer. My impression is of great bleakness and barrenness, compared to the green hills of Orkney. I remember falling into a burn. I remember being warned not to go near the sea-cliffs, where a monster called the 'rone' lived. I remember my grandfather reading aloud out of his big Bible, and saying long Gaelic prayers every day about dinner-time. I remember my sweet gentle grannie, and how she gave us milk warm from her cow...

There was a long weary track to a peat bank... Such brief glimpses I remember.

And there wasn't a sweetie shop in sight. Such utter loneliness! How I missed the throbbing metropolis of Stromness!

Braal half a century on is still more desolate, is still strewing the stones of what had been for centuries a good and a gracious way of life.

Kirsty Watt

13.10.1983

Only once a year or so—if you're lucky—a first-rate autobiography or book of memoirs comes into your hands. (I am not all that interested in the lives of film or TV stars, generals, footballers, politicians, best-selling authors, owners of yachts and islands in the sun.)

This book that was lent me a couple of weeks ago is the memoir of a fisher-lass from the village of Broadsea near Fraserburgh. She died in 1923, aged ninety. Her name was Christian (or Kirsty) Watt.

She was crushed by poverty and hard work and tragedy all her life long—so much that it would have broken most women in their twenties or thirties—and yet she had enormous strength and resilience. She had more—high intelligence and a questing, penetrating mind. One who knew her said, 'If she had lived in this present generation, she would have been an MP'... To which someone who knew her even better replied, 'She would have been Prime Minister.' And doubtless, had Kirsty Watt wished it so, there was no height she couldn't have scaled.

She had another gift still—an utterly devastating honesty. The fact is that she came by illegitimate descent from some of the nobility of the north-east (Buchan). She felt herself no whit inferior to them. More than one of those lords and ladies felt the lash of her tongue: for she could express herself with point and pungency. And what is equally amazing, the gentry accepted meekly the scorn and derision she frequently levelled at them. (Most girls would have been bundled out at the servants' door, and the dogs set on them.)

Kirsty had more going for her still—she was comely and beautiful beyond the ordinary. So much so, that at least two young wealthy 'well-born' scions of the same noble family would have taken her to wife. She married, instead, a fisherman from a neighbouring village, and bore him nine children. Many of them—as well as brothers and cousins—died prematurely. Her husband was swept to his death beyond Kinnaird Head. Rather than accept charity, this astonishing woman gathered sea-food from the ebb: until even her strong mind gave way, and she spent the last half of her life in a mental hospital in Aberdeen.

In Cornhill, she became a kind of queen of the place. She wrote her memoirs in pencil on sheets of foolscap. To the end she lashed the warmongers, money-grubbers, and hypocrites in high places.

This is one of the most amazing autobiographies I have ever read. Here is the essential Scotland of the 19th century, with all the grinding poverty and inherent riches of character of its fisher folk and peasants.

The Christian Watt Papers is edited by David Fraser.

Praise and Prizes for Writers

20.10.1983

Booker prize—Nobel prize—what a song and dance about such baubles! What does it matter, the opinion of a few contemporary judges, compared to the near-infallible verdict that time sends down its long corridors?

Think what a few smart-alec contemporaries wrote about Keats and his first book, for example. (Some folk at the time thought their sneers wounded him, fatally—but I very much doubt that.) If Shakespeare had been in line for some Elizabethan 'Booker' or 'Nobel', and had his fellow dramatist Greene been on the panel, he would have been given the thumbs down pretty smartly. Even Ben Jonson might have hummed and hawed a little.

Contrariwise, writers like Alfred Austin and Nahum Tate and Colley Cibber were heaped with honour and praise—and who, except to sneer, reads a line of them now?

Certainly, to be a writer and to get a cheque for something like £100,000 through the letter-box one morning must be not at all unpleasant; provided that one realises as one dances one's way to the bank, the next few generations of readers might give a grave shake of the head.

And anyway, who said all the best writers in the world write in English or German or Italian or French?

It could well be that the world's greatest novelist at this present moment is sitting inside the Arctic Circle, under the Aurora Borealis, writing in some Eskimo tongue. Or he might be in some African jungle, writing his masterpieces in Hottentot or Swahili.

There is simply no way of knowing.

So when it is said, 'Here is your prize for writing the best limerick or epic this year,' let it not be said with great solemnity, so that even the TV announcers catch their breath with awe repeating it. Let it be said with some hesitation, and qualification, and pursing of the lips, and even a touch of indulgent scepticism—lest the long corridors of Time return an empty echo.

Who reads the Orkney authors John Malcolm and David Vedder nowadays? They were very well-known in the 19th century. It is enough to put a shiver on us contemporary scribblers.

Gypsy
10.11.1983

Gypsy the cat has been staying with me for six days, and has just gone back to her own house, with the pier and slipway outside, and the gulls, and sillocks in summer.

She arrived last Friday in a wicker basket, meowing piteously, as if she was to be incarcerated for ever.

Once out of her prison, she went here and there, softly, getting to know the geography of the house. What goes on in a cat's mind? I'm sure Gypsy knew fairly soon that she had been in this house before, in summer, when the light was different.

Soon enough, she was blinking in the firelight and singing cat-songs.

Very daintily Gypsy glides here and there about the house. Very often her black head turns to the kitchen where the cat-food is.

When it comes to food and sleep, she's a tyrant. Six times a day there she stood at the kitchen door, mutely beseeching food. She would, if she'd had her way, have polished off a whole big tin before bedtime. She would never have dared be such a glutton in her own house.

Cats are said to love milk. Not Gypsy—she gives the milk in the saucer a few indifferent sweeps of her tongue and turns away.

Mayburn is not at all like the sea front of Dundas Street. She doesn't want to go out here. She did venture out yesterday, while I was getting messages in the peedie shop below and she got into a snarling scratching tangle with another cat, a resident of Mayburn. The Mayburn cat was of course exerting its territorial rights.

She stole my rocking-chair, where I sit reading most evenings or watching TV. When I came to sit on it, there, stretched out in utmost luxuriance, or curled in a glossy black ball, was Gypsy. Sunk in sleep, she was so beautiful I hadn't the heart to turf her out. The master of the house had lost another privilege.

But oh, what songs she greeted me with in the morning!

Such a golden-eyed welcome to begin a new day with!

Daily Newspapers

17.11.1983

Daily newspapers: I find that I can get by without them. All the news anyone can stomach is on TV, anyway. I'd rather be reading a good book than stuffing myself with wads of newsprint, night after night.

But a pile of newspapers comes in handy, right enough. When you're setting the fire, for example. I've just been crumpling up old newspapers on the hearth, and setting a layer of wood, and topping all with cinders from yesterday's fire and small coals.

To return to newspapers. The first daily that came to our house was the *Daily Express*. Aged seven or eight, it meant nothing to me—except one item, and that was the Rupert cartoon. Rupert was a nice bear and I couldn't have enough of him, day after day.

Then we changed to the *Daily Herald*; in those days a great 'circulation war' was in progress. The *Daily Herald* offered prizes—I remember a complete set of Dickens—to readers who cut out little tokens day after day.

Finally we changed to the *News Chronicle*. A bit older now, I relished the occasional column by a man Ian Mackay who hailed from Wick. It was quite an intelligent paper, the *News Chronicle*.

Daily Herald and *News Chronicle* are dust now. That groves and woods and forests had to be cut down in the first place to give them life!

The boys of Stromness could well do without the *Daily* this or that so long as *The Wizard* arrived at Rae's shop on a Tuesday, and *The Hotspur* on a Friday. Ah, what joy to open their pristine pages and smell the ink new from the press! D. C. Thomson's put enchantment on generations of boys in the 30s and 40s. I don't know whether they're printed now or not.

Our elders tended not to look too kindly on *Wizard* and *Hotspur*. Once I was given a year's subscription to Arthur Mee's *Children's Newspaper*. I hated it—it had designs on children, to make us good smug bourgeois citizens. I was glad when after a year the *Children's Newspaper* stopped coming.

There were still Tuesdays and Fridays in the week, like oases in a barren desert.

The Witch of Leafea

24.11.1983

On 1st November, 1755, the great earthquake took place in the capital city of Portugal, Lisbon. It was such a world-shaking disaster that the whole North Atlantic reeled with the shock, and the reverberations were felt as far north as Orkney.

That day the Outertown folk observed that the sea was very calm and the air sultry. A few fishing boats were out; the crews observed an agitation in the deep waters and a curious white tinge in the blue and green. The agitation and the whiteness increased, until the ocean, in the words of one observer 'gaed like a kirn o' milk'.

Then the sea gathered itself and great waves began to beat on the shores and cliffs of the west; and grew in violence; and began to break its bounds and invade the land.

That day, the laird Mr Grahame was in residence at Breckness. His 'rancelman', George Marwick, happened to be at Breckness on business, 'The sea,' we are told by George Marwick's great-grandson, 'came over at Billia-Croo and ran down in the noust of Breckness'... The big house and the adjacent fields and farms being threatened with inundation, Mr Grahame ordered Marwick to saddle his best horse, and the laird mounted.

There dwelt at that time in the croft of Leafea in Outertown a woman called Annie Caird who was widely believed to be a witch. In all the welter of sea and land that day, Annie Caird was seen running past the house of Brockan, no doubt as terrified as the other folk in the district. But laird and rancelman were convinced that Annie was responsible for the confusion of the elements.

The tidal wave was now breaking on the fields. One wave, larger than the rest, almost took the feet of Mr Grahame's horse from under it. Another higher wave might drown them all. Annie Caird was skirling and screeching in the vicinity; but to Marwick she seemed to be yelling in triumph at the hideous commotion and danger she had created. He was carrying some kind of stick or club, a 'mool-eech'... Marwick shouted above the din, 'I'll either end this or mend this,' and he dealt Annie Caird a violent blow on the head.

The legend is that thereupon Annie Caird the witch disappeared 'in a blue lowe'.

That, as far as the record goes, is the end of the story. It must have been a terrifying day all along the west coast of Orkney. One would like to know how the town of Stromness fared that day—the street must have been awash, the pier houses under feet of water.

For Mr Grahame of Breckness it was such a terrifying experience that, it's said, he never resided at Breckness again.

Crusaders

1.12.1983

Most of the books one picks up are hardly worth writing about. Preserve a decent silence: and hope for better things when you turn new pages.

I got from our delectable Stromness bookshop last weekend Volume One of *The Crusades*. You hear about the Crusades half a dozen times a year, or so; and have to admit to only the haziest knowledge of those world-shaking medieval movements of armies and peoples.

The first fifty pages or so are rather boring and extremely confusing, as Stephen Runciman the author tries his best to put us in the picture; for, in western Asia beyond Constantinople and in Syria and Palestine, there was such a turmoil of tribes and people, as the new religion of militant Islam rose to its full flood.

Then quite suddenly, the Crusades were preached all over western Europe—and men rose in their thousands and tens of thousands to rid the holy places of the infidels.

It is a heroic and a tragic and at times a terrifying tale. First to reach Byzantium, the great centre of Orthodox Christianity, was a hermit called Peter the Preacher and his ragged host. They were cut to pieces by the Turks, an efficient and disciplined army.

The Emperor Alexius of Constantinople had his work cut out, coping with the successive armies of knights from France and Germany and Italy, led by their feudal lords. By magnificent statesmanship he kept his rare jewel of a city from flaw or destruction.

On the Crusaders went, fired by a curious mixture of true faith and a desire to carve out Kingdoms for themselves (the leaders, that is) in Armenia and Palestine...

So, I've been sitting in the rocking-chair, night after night, turning the pages of this fascinating story.

We all know, of course, that Orkney had its own crusading knight, Earl Rognvald II, whose later pilgrimage eastward is told with such verve in *The Orkneyinga Saga*. Earl Rognvald's men in their fifteen ships were hardly spotless pilgrims either on their marvellous voyage through the Mediterranean in 1154.

I know the account of Earl Rognvald's voyage very well. But reading *The Crusades* has helped me to set it in a true context.

We should be glad, at least, that the Orkney leader was called, after his death, St Rognvald.

Christmas, Ahoy!

8.12.1983

What a gay social whirl recently!—especially for a greying chap like me who is becoming more and more addicted to his rocking-chair and fire and book, and pot of tea before bedtime.

Last Friday, quite unexpectedly, the captain of HMS *Orkney* called in the afternoon and invited me for cocktails aboard in the evening at 6.30. At 6.20 the rain was coming down vertically, like broken stair-rods. So Mrs Brass in her reliable taxi came and set me down at the foot of the gangway. After the drinks and pleasant words here and there, at 8pm the flag was lowered and the bugle thrilled out!

Next morning it was the launching of the new edition of *The Men of Ness* in Kirkwall Library, at 11am. The book, the latest beautiful Orkney Press publication, was launched with witty speeches from the Norwegian Consul-General and Howie Firth, of Radio Orkney and the Orkney Press; and the book floated gently in lappings of white and red wine.

Immediately afterwards, I was driven to Ian and Margot Heddle's Mill of Eyreland, Stenness—one of the most beautiful restorations I have ever seen. Over the years we have watched this house emerging from its dusty chrysalis to become a lovely butterfly. And at the Mill, as always, there was generous entertainment.

On Sunday evening, the St Magnus Festival Committee met at Hopedale—and if committee meetings are not my favourite way of passing the time, the good food and ale of our hosts leavened the lump delectably.

(It so happened that all these social engagements came right in the midst of a very busy time for me, when this idle abode of mine was humming like a factory with utter necessities of writing and proof-reading.)

Lunch on Monday, noon, on HMS *Orkney*. I dug my one and only lounge suit out of its place of webs and mildew, and found that rare garment, a tie. And the meal was magnificent. I went home among the shops, humming songs, carrying a reproduction of the ship and a fishing-boat, waves and gulls: a present to all the guests from Lieut.-Commander Childs.

That's not the end by any means. Tomorrow night it's mince pies and punch for the Christmas exhibition at the Pier Arts Centre—and then a meal at another kind house tumultuous with children—and the day after that, a birthday!

Christmas, you have begun very early this year...

Short Story Writing

15.12.1983

I'm looking forward eagerly to the *Orkney Short Stories* book that Orkney Press will be putting out quite soon. And the other morning, listening to Radio Orkney, I heard Howie Firth announce the short story competition for this winter.

It looks to me as if there might well be a flowering in the writing of short stories in the islands. I very much hope so. The talent is there, and the material, waiting to be tapped.

The short story is an extraordinary form to work in. It will rarely be dictated to; it has a will of its own and takes off in totally unexpected directions, to the astonishment and sometimes the delight of the author.

A few weeks ago I put down a rather sketchy little story about the death of a crofter—and there were flashbacks to things out of his past life. And it went well enough—it was quite readable—but there was nothing in it to shake the roots of the imagination.

The 'flashbacks', for a start, were too bare and sketchy. 'Let's try to fill up the first of the dying man's memories a bit,' said I to the pen and paper... And with that the pen got going—it fairly ran and leapt and scampered across the paper, page after page after page—and I was quite breathless by the time I had caught up with it, after three hours or so. And this went on, a full surge and flood, for about five days. (I assure you, there are few jobs in life like the leafing and blossoming of the imagination.)

Yesterday, another 'flashback' got fuller treatment.

The only danger is that the neat original pattern of the story might get disrupted and thrown off balance by those sprees of the imagination.

I am sorry for inflicting such technicalities on non-literary readers. But every craft has its own hazards and delights, and we mightn't bother with them if all was plain-sailing.

So, story-writers of Orkney, yield yourselves and your sails to the winds of the imagination this winter.

Christmas Cards

22.12.1983

Christmas cards—there comes a day in the first half of December that the Christmas cards have to be signed and addresses put on envelopes.

Fortunately, a good writer of script and then a good printer got my box of cards (with a winter poem on them) to me in good time.

Well, nothing could be simpler or happier surely, than to sit down and write the cards. First get out the book of addresses—begin at 'A' and write steadily all the way through to 'Z'—and there, the bulk of your Christmas labour is done!

(Over the past week or two, you have seen to it that there's a plentiful supply of 12½p stamps, plus a few 16p.)

Over the pile of virgin cards, one by one, the pen speeds. Slowly the pile diminishes, and at its side grows the pile of signed and addressed and enveloped cards. And you think to yourself, 'I'm doing fine!'... After about an hour you become aware of a kind of numbness in the hand, accompanied by blunders and misspellings in the writing (a slow numbness is invading the brain too).

Finish the job in one afternoon? Not likely. It has become like labouring in a chain-gang, breaking stone in a quarry!... You struggle on to the letter 'M'.

'That,' you mutter through zombie lips, 'is enough for one day'...

Besides, there have been all kinds of vexations. Friends who should have been in the address book aren't there; others have moved to new unrecorded addresses. Occasionally, my handwriting in the address book is so slovenly that I daren't risk sending a card to such a misty address.

Another mighty day of labour in the quarry—'N' to 'Z'.

Meantime the first incoming cards have begun to filter in through the letter-box. You discover, to your shame, that you're getting cards from folk you haven't sent cards to. (Back to the diminishing blank pile.)

Another task looms: the licking and affixing of stamps. Three-quarters through, the stamps give out ... there will require to be another £5 worth of 12½ps bought.

And the cards for overseas, they must be taken separately to the Post Office to be weighed.

At last all, or nearly all, is accomplished. You must lick the gum on 200 or so envelopes and stick them with a thump of the fist!... I have not the strength left for such a task. I manage, feebly, to tuck the flaps in, as used to happen in the ancient days of halfpenny mail.

* * *

But now with every post the cards come homing in like doves, from old friends and new friends and friends half-forgotten. And the dove-fall is so delightful that the labour in the Christmas-card quarry is quite forgotten.

George Orwell

5.1.1984

1984—mention of that date calls to mind immediately, of course, the novel *1984* by George Orwell.

Bad enough though the times are, with car-bombs in London and Ulster, and the horrors of Lebanon and Central America and other places, Orwell's bleak prophecy has turned out to be not quite so bad, after all.

I read that distressful novel again last week, and could not fail to be impressed by its dark power.

A lot is going to be heard about Orwell in the next twelvemonth. Indeed, there was a very fine programme on TV about his stay in Jura in the late 40s, where he wrote that last sombre masterpiece. (And we were shown him ruining his already delicate lungs with chain-smoking.) There he lived in his isolated farm-house, shunning as many modern conveniences as he could, and tapping out his vision of the future by the light of a paraffin lamp. It was a very different picture from the rosy visions of his boyhood mentors, who saw everything getting better and better as the great goddess Progress strewed ever more lavishly her gifts.

And he skinned the rabbits he caught and he kippered the herring he caught. Enjoyment might come, but only after arduous work.

He had a cold dislike and distrust of people in authority. The 'proles', the despised and downtrodden working people: if hope lay anywhere, it lay with them. If there was an ember of love in his puritanical heart, it was for the poor of the earth.

After reading *1984*, I read an earlier Orwell novel, *A Clergyman's Daughter*, and was deeply impressed. Now I am a quarter-way through *Coming Up For Air*. These are altogether more benign books; though he had begun to cast a cold eye at 'the establishment' long before *1984*.

Let us honour a great and a brave man—and let us hope, at the same time, that his crystal-gazing will never be as bad as all that.

* * *

A happy 1984 to all my readers!

A Pair of Kippers

12.1.1984

An old friend, George Maskell, from the west coast, arrived two evenings ago with a present of a pair of kippers.

Nothing very remarkable about that, you may say; except that those kippers came from the place on earth most renowned for kippers, it's said.

It is a strange thing to say, but I haven't tasted a kipper for years. And why should that be, when kippers are among the tastiest food the sea produces—a rival to trout and smoked salmon?

The simple explanation is that in winter the kitchen window seizes up—the wood swells with rain—and so the smells of cooking must linger for a while. Of all the world's smells of cooking, fried kippers produce the richest oiliest longest-lasting smell (it reminds me of nothing so much as one of those Islay malts, that roll heavy and rich as peat-smoke about the tongue).

So, after kippers, one can go about with the kipper-incense clinging for days, maybe, to the clothes. And right over the cooker is the pulley where the washing hangs—imagine putting kipper-penetrated newly-washed clothes back in the clothes cupboard!

Anyway, it was still the season of Christmas, when rich foods abound, and I didn't see any reason for denying myself one of those famous western kippers. But first, bundle all the washing from the pulley onto the couch next door...

The kipper was so immense it spanned my little frying pan as I laid it with the tarnished side down. Presently the most delectable aroma assaulted the nostrils (the 'Bisto Kids' never smelt anything so good).

But the taste—the rich melting smoky salt taste, it made all the taste-buds in the palate break open and blossom! That kipper was so huge and rich, two people could have breakfasted off it. And the tea and the toast were perfect accompaniments. I have never enjoyed such a breakfast for years. I felt like a whale that had barged through a shoal.

True enough, the kipper-smell lingered for a while. It had crept into the living-room, and there may even have been a whiff or two of it in the bedrooms upstairs... There was the ghost of kipper-incense next morning in the kitchen.

But it was worth it—it was well worth it.

Football Heroes

23.2.1984

Over a period of years, a great local hero for boys from ten to twelve years old, in the thirties, was a footballer. (We had other football heroes, such as John Thomson and Jimmy McGrory, but they were a universe away, in Glasgow, and there was no hope of ever seeing them exercising their magic on a Saturday afternoon. We could get a faint whiff of that magic over the earphones, a hard-to-hear commentary. What excitement, the England / Scotland match each April, either at Wembley or at Hampden! Legendary places those football stadiums were, like Bannockburn or Flodden. And when the news came, in the *Daily Express*, that the 'nonpareil' of goalkeepers, John Thomson, had died on the field of action, saving a certain goal, awe and grief and wonderment came upon us boys, perhaps for the first time.)

Now for our heroic encounters we had to content ourselves with the Market Green, Stromness; where, once a week, Stromness Athletic in their white shirts and dark shorts took on one or other of the Kirkwall teams, Hotspurs or Thorfinn or Rovers.

In those days, half a century ago, Stromness had possibly its best team ever. There were players like 'Yokko' Johnston, Bill Groundwater, Attie and Lammie Campbell, George Clouston: and the great thing about it was that we could see those heroes walking about on the street like ordinary folk. If one or other of them so much as spoke to us, for the rest of that day we trod on air.

I am leaving the greatest name of that invincible band of brothers to the end; for he it was, I think, who—besides being a marvellous footballer himself—welded those young Stromness men into an efficient smooth-working machine. His name was Hugo Munro; he came from round about Inverness; but for a few years he worked in a local bank—the Commercial.

Hugo's few years in Stromness coincided with our first surge of enthusiasm for football. We would have walked many miles to see Hugo's marvellous ball-manipulation, his thrilling goals!

Alas, he was buried this afternoon at Warbeth, not without the laurel of good memories.

Vanished from the Street

1.3.1984

Soon, it seems, there will be no Postmaster in Stromness, when Mr Ian Smith retires.

We cannot remember a time when there was no Postmaster in Stromness: Mr MacLean, Mr Corse, Mr G. S. Robertson, Mr Donald Morrison; and others.

It isn't that long ago that our provost was taken from us, and not only him but the two bailies and the six councillors—all the town fathers at one fell swoop, together with Town Clerk and Burgh Chamberlain. Provost Clouston, Provost J. G. Marwick, Provost G. S. Robertson (who was Postmaster also), and others.

Once there was a bell-man in Stromness. He went the length of the street, stopping here and there to announce a concert, auction sale, or the arrival of a cargo of 'best English coal'. Before and after every announcement he rang his bell. Women appeared at the doors and the ends of closes to hear the cry of the bell-man. The last bell-man was a man called James Leask ('The Puffer'). For the official announcement, James Leask would drop his voice and address a few satirical remarks to the listening ladies. He had one eye. He was a terror to small boys.

There was also a lamplighter. Nightly he passed through the street with (I seem to remember) two long poles, one flame-tipped. Gas-light by gaslight glowed in his wake. He made Stromness a little island of light in the dark sea of winter. But for a few nights on either side of the full moon the lamplighter stayed at home; for the Town Council considered that the moon gave light enough, and kept the rates down too. No one but children of half a century ago remembers what an enchanted place Stromness was under the full moon. Electric lights have cheapened that glory.

Besides, there were the fishermen who sold their haddocks and skate from barrows along the street, for a few pence per pound.

Three or four times a year, the tinkers went from door to door, with knick-knacks and bits of drapery, and possibly clothes pegs.

The Salvation Army made a glad brazen noise every Saturday night at the Pier Head and the foot of the Church Road. All the shops along the street did business till 8 or 9 pm at night. I used to go shopping with my mother.

Only the pubs were barricaded and silent.

'All changed, changed utterly,' as the poet said.

'Comparative' Safety

8.3.1984

I was talking yesterday to a lady photographer-journalist called Ros Drinkwater who was well-known years ago as the leading actress in a TV series called *Paul Temple*. She spent a day and a night in Rackwick, taking pictures of Max Davies for the *Sunday Times*, in connection with Max's new music-theatre work *Number Eleven Bus*.

There were one or two bright serene hours while she was here, but mostly she saw Orkney in a cloud that fell, softly and saturatingly and would rise briefly to let through a little diffused light.

One hates to receive visitors in such bleak weather, when all the land and sea and sky are drained of colour.

Ros Drinkwater thought that soon the lonely places of the world would be taken up by people fleeing from the nuclear threat, into comparative safety.

'Comparative', surely, is the operative word. For while a place like Orkney or the west of Wales might not be within radius of the terrible beast and its aftermath, what kind of life would it be for survivors on the peripheries? I don't mean only that the centres of commerce, administration and industry would be shattered. Then Orcadians, for example, would perforce have to return to a kind of subsistence living that obtained three or four centuries ago: without however, the inherited skills that Orcadians living then acquired almost by instinct. Life might be possible, but it would be very harsh, very cruel, very bitter.

But air and sea would be polluted as well as the earth round about the great cities; and air and sea are never still—they move about every remotest corner of the globe. And so the hideous poisons would be carried to the Eskimos in their igloos and the Polynesians in their Pacific islands.

It may be that, faced with such an immense challenge, the human race will transcend itself and achieve a new vision and greatness. It may be that, following too slavishly the goddess of material knowledge and progress, we have boxed ourselves into a corner from which there is no escape.

Meantime, as the wholesome rain-cloud rose and fell over Orkney on Leap Year day (February 29) the only thing to do was to hope.

Solzhenitsyn

5.4.1984

As one gets older, fewer and fewer writers have power to cast a spell.

Not for years have I experienced the thrill of first opening a book by E. M. Forster, or Thomas Mann, or T. S. Eliot. Those are moments of a person's life which alter his whole outlook on human affairs.

The great moments in literature only happen, I had thought, when a person is young and impressionable. After about the age of thirty, one has grown a hard carapace; it gets ever harder to touch him to the quick with delight and gratitude.

The name Solzhenitsyn has been around for a few years now. I don't know why I had built up a kind of resistance to him. Perhaps I'd associated him with long rambling Slav novels, in an age when novels ought to convey their message with brevity and economy. Perhaps one tends to be sceptical of a name that is bandied about so much. So often, the literary heroes of one generation are seen by succeeding generations to have feet of clay.

Anyway, a book of short stories by this famous Russian exiled writer came to my hand a fortnight or so ago. After a few pages, I knew myself to be in the hands of a great imaginative artist, whose range and passion put him in the same bracket as Tolstoy. It may be that the very vastness of their country becomes a driving-force in their art, giving their books that amplitude. Perhaps our country is too small to throw up writers of this vast power. (There was Shakespeare, of course, but one feels that in its entire history a nation is lucky to throw up one Shakespeare...)

It is a humbling as well as an exhilarating experience to be in touch with a mind like Solzhenitsyn's. One is driven, willy-nilly, to compare one's own writings against such a master. They are seen to be only tales told round the village pump.

My favourite bookshop in Graham Place had only one Solzhenitsyn novel left, *The First Circle*. For days I have been sampling it, a few chapters at a time. In all literature I can't think of a more masterly portrait of a historical character than his few pages on Stalin. (It was for criticising Stalin that the novelist suffered years of exile and imprisonment.)

And now—this writer being prolific—I know there are many months of enjoyment to come.

A Seat at the Pierhead

3.5.1984

Another sign of spring—the public seats are out at Mayburn and in various handy places along the street, until you come to the permanent seats at the pierhead.

How delightful those benches are on a hot summer day when you are weary, and loaded with errands.

For you never know who might come and sit beside you. Permanent bench-loungers like me have known the whole spectrum of humanity, from crashing bores to tellers of enchanting tales, and everything in between.

Easter brought a throng of tourists to Stromness. Then it is diverting—at tourist-time—just to sit and watch the eddies of strangers mingling with the 'well-kent' faces... At high summer, the tourists greatly outnumber the locals.

They used to call the pierhead seats 'the local Parliament'. Certainly, many a thing has been discussed there. But reminiscence always outweighs argument. The Stromnessians are the great ones for looking back to the golden age of childhood. Then, if you are to believe them, the sun of sixty years ago shone hotter and brighter than the stingy sun of our latter years. And everything was so cheap! Twelve and six for a bottle of whisky; eight shillings for twenty Players; bread fourpence a loaf...

This is the way that legend takes over from things as they actually were. A few centuries more, and the doings of our ancestors begin to partake of myth—the world was full of giants, enchanters, and heroes.

A man with a golden tongue, the poet Edwin Muir, saw his childhood in Wyre steeped in the stuff of immortality. From his childhood as a farmer's son emerged all that great wealth of poetry.

Sometimes you will see a man sleeping on a public bench. One February of halcyon weather the 'pierheaders' played dominoes there day after day. Children climb over the benches. An insect like a bee came buzzing there last week. Folk and dogs wait for the ferry-boat to Hoy. Many just sit, content to let the world spin slowly round them.

Latin Disappears

10.5.1984

Twelve years old, away back in 1933 or '34, about thirty of us crossed the gap from primary school to secondary. New children, from the parishes and islands, sat among us at the desks. The elementary steps of new subjects—algebra, science, Latin—were set before us.

It was all a bit strange and frightening. Instead of one teacher for all subjects, now there was a new specialist teacher for every subject, and we shifted class-room to classroom.

Of all the new subjects, Latin was the chief stumbling-block. However did the people in ancient Rome manage such contortions on their tongues? The first word we learned was *regina*, a queen. Very good, so far. But immediately the trouble began. *Regina*—O, queen; *reginam*—queen (accusative); *reginae*—of a queen; *reginae*—to or for a queen, *regina*—by, with, or from a queen... What kind of incomprehensible rigmarole was that?

But *regina*, *mensa* (a table), *insula* (an island)—these were only the lowest blocks in the Great Wall of Latin that we were expected to scale in the course of the next five years. Besides the feminine nouns like *regina*, there were masculine nouns and neuter nouns. These could be mastered by dint of brutish application at the lamp-lit table at home. *Britannia est insula...* The verbs were, if anything, more frightful and contorted. *Amo, amas, amat*—I love, thou lovest, he or she loves.

Oh, why couldn't those Romans have spoken simply and naturally like us? Why was their yoke inflicted on sweating schoolboys nineteen centuries later? (We were told that we had to be masters of Latin if we were going to be a doctor or a chemist or a minister. Nor could we think of getting to a university without acquaintance with Latin...)

Now, it seems, the classrooms of Stromness Academy will no longer ring with the majestic surge of Latin. There will be Computer Studies instead. At one leap we have passed into a new time.

Laureate Memories

31.5.1984

Sir John Betjeman the Poet Laureate has died, and a star has fallen out of the sky.

Many Orcadians will remember Betjeman at a St Magnus Fair a few summers back, when he opened it officially. I had the privilege to be introduced to him by Colonel Macrae, and we exchanged a few words. He had read the poetry of Robert Rendall and was greatly taken by it. George Robertson's *History of the Stromness Golf Courses* intrigued him too—he wrote to the author and told him his little book was 'pure poetry': a remark that greatly intrigued our former Provost and Postmaster, who never dreamed he was writing 'poetry'. But there his work was authenticated from the highest source.

He wrote me later, saying that he had enjoyed a book of mine called *Magnus*.

The list of Poets Laureate is a long one, and not every holder of the august title has lingered long in the ever-changing stream of English poetry.

One wonders if John Masefield, one 20th-century Laureate, was ever in Orkney when he was a sailor. Certainly he mentioned Orkney at least once in his verse. The beautiful girl Morgause—like other Orkney girls no doubt—was taken by seafarers. She became a queen in the Arthurian Cycle: 'King Lot of Orkney took her for his bride...'

A few illustrious names have graced the office—in the 19th century Wordsworth and his successor Tennyson. Alfred Lord Tennyson came to Orkney once in a yacht, and the Prime Minister W. E. Gladstone was on board too. They both received the Freedom of Kirkwall. Tennyson seems to have impressed the Orcadians of a century ago by his dark gloomy presence. He declined to speak at the Freedom ceremony, but Gladstone more than made up for his silence. Tennyson, he said, would be remembered long after his own name was in the dust...

Betjeman was not a great poet but his verse is extremely well-crafted, and in lyric after lyric he celebrated English churches, English railways, English rusticity—so perfectly and so mellifluously that the generations to come need only turn his pages to catch the fleeting fragrance of a vanished age.

Housman and the End of May

7.6.1984

It is the last day of May as I write this—and I do not remember such a May for sunshine and wild flowers.

No weather pleases everybody; today there's a strong breeze from south-east. The earth is so dry that every morning the farmers must be putting longing looks on the western horizon, in the hope that there might be a rain cloud there.

The peat-cutters, though, have had good weather for their work.

And tomorrow summer begins.

Old men towards the close of the twentieth century will be saying to each other over the fires and the ale-mugs, 'Ah, but do you mind on May in the year 1984? That was a month to remember!'... And turning to the young ones they'll say, 'You don't get May-months nowadays like what we got in 1984, oh no, the weather's completely different...'

One of the great lyric poets of our century wrote a marvellous poem— I've just remembered—about the last day of May. Not any particular 31st of May: but rather the ending of springtime in every life, and in the lives of all the young people who have ever lived. Like the stoical poets of Greece and Rome, Housman took a rather poor view of life as a whole. Oh, yes, it is delightful and happy and full of juice when one is young— but alas, it is soon over, age and white hairs come increasingly, and all manner of ache and frustration and bafflement and regret:

> 'Life, to be sure, is nothing much to lose
> But young men think it is, and we were young.'

(But that is from another Housman poem.)

The stark truth is, says Housman, that even youth and springtime— even these—can be sour and flawed. We only think of them as eternally lovely, looked back on from the winter of our days.

Young men, says this poet, are like the shepherds who take refuge in an ale-house on the last day of May from the tempests of wind and rain outside. The chestnut trees and the hawthorn are beautiful, but the storm has ruined everything.

'Pass me the can, lad—There's an end of May...'

The words are heart-piercingly beautiful: but the sentiments run counter to the whole experience of men. 'Hope springs eternal'; even we greybeards are glad to have tasted once more the chalice of this glad young month.

The Masked Fisherman
14.6.1984

One of the loveliest and most moving passages in *The Orkneyinga Saga* is that which tells of the meeting on a beach at Sumburgh, Shetland, between a fisherman and a stranger whose face is muffled up in a hood.

The elderly fisherman is in difficulties—his boat-mate who always fishes with him has not shown up on this particular morning; and he can't fish and work the boat by himself.

The stranger offers to help. He will row, and the fisherman can haul in the fish.

They push the boat out. Very soon, the fisherman wishes he had stayed ashore, for the stranger pulls the boat into the dangerous waters of Sumburgh 'Roost'; the fisherman's panic rises—he rebukes the oarsman—but further and further towards the black heart of the roost the boat swirls and tumbles. Well, but the Shetlander cannot complain about a dearth of fish—hook after hook burgeons with sea-fruit, cod and haddock and skate. He pulls the flashing treasure inboard—hardly a hook is empty. 'Well,' thought the Shetland fisherman, 'if I'm to die today, at least I didn't die destitute' (or so I imagine him saying).

Soon the boat is full of fish; and it is in quiet water, and the stranger is rowing shoreward. The poor fisherman's heart sings for joy!

As usual, there's a crowd of women on the shore holding out hands for fish. The stranger takes his share of the haul and begins to divide it among the shore-folk.

As he turns to walk up the beach, he slips on seaweed and goes sprawling. And one of the old women points at him and screeches with mirth!

Later that day the folk of Sumburgh learn with wonderment that the sea-defying stranger was the Lord Rognvald Kolson, Earl of Orkney and Shetland.

* * *

I was trying to adapt this piece of saga for narrative ends the other day, when I thought it would be interesting to compare the Taylor edition and the Pálsson edition with the 19th-century Anderson edition. But when I turned up Anderson, this episode had been omitted.

There they go again, those Victorians, with their pompous notions of what is true and beautiful! Oh no, they couldn't include such a common story—it might detract from the nobility of the whole work—best leave it out...

And so, at one stroke, the most endearing traits of Earl Rognvald are docked—his love of anonymity, his thoughtless daring, his generosity, his humour, his endless care for his people.

Loss of the *Marques*

21.6.1984

How sad to know that a beautiful ship, and a sailing ship at that, has gone under the waves near Bermuda.

And when you realize that the ship was the *Marques*, that sailed into and out of Stromness two summers recently, the news comes with a special pang.

The *Marques* visited Orkney with a mostly young crew. In this age of easy living, those young folk had not been press-ganged—no, they were paying for the privilege of climbing the rigging and scrubbing the decks and living rough. It was all part of a circumnavigation of Britain, one of those big cultural enterprises undertaken by that bold imaginative artist, Richard Demarco.

Once in Stromness, Richard invited a few of us to sail from Stromness to Kirkwall, via Eynhallow Sound.

7am or so on a cold misty morning in late August, and there we stood shivering on the deck, among a company of blithe bare-footed young sailors, who came and went.

There was little wind, and so the *Marques* made her way out through Hoy Sound with her engine throbbing.

Off the Old Man of Hoy the ship turned north. There were freshets of wind now. The engine throb ceased. The sails fluttered out and filled with wind. And then, in a most beautiful sea rhythm I had not experienced before, the *Marques* leaned north, throwing the grey Atlantic waves from her.

It was one of those dreich summer days, with the west coast of Orkney half-scarfed in haar. And yet the dance of wave and ship and wind was good and invigorating...

How eagerly and courteously those young sailors of both sexes invited us to eat with them down below!—Plain fare, but delicious.

Here and there a scribbler or an artist stood, wielding pencils.

In those adverse conditions it would not be possible to make Kirkwall.

After much intricate manoeuvring, we were put ashore in Rousay. A senior Rousayman said he never dreamed he would see a sailing barque in Eynhallow Sound again...

Next summer, or maybe two summers after, the *Marques* tied up at Stromness again. And, again, crowds flocked down to see her.

Now nobody in this sublunar world will ever see that tall brave barque again.

The Noust at Sandy Geo

5.7.1984

One of the nicest coast walks in Orkney is along the Marwick shore in Birsay to the little geo that holds in its steep slopes the remnants of old boat-houses, built half into the solid rock.

It is said the boat-houses were originally built there because a more favoured noust, a quarter of a mile further north, was blocked by the wreck of a ship. And so the Birsay fishermen had to seek out a somewhat more hazardous boat-shelter.

The walk to the boat-houses begins at the lagoon, or meer, that gives the district of Marwick its name. Down below, the rock pools rich with whelks and limpets, and the organ-tones of the Atlantic. All around, the wheeling seabirds. And underfoot, the tough resilient sward.

Round a few sea-enchanted corners, and there the walker used suddenly to find himself looking down at the steep geo and the cluster of ruined boat-houses...

* * *

I say, 'used to find', because a recent imaginative plan of restoration brought a group of young folk from the south together, under the guidance of a craftsman-builder; and there, in the spring, they set about putting some order back upon this beautiful melancholy place. They built up the walls, put on rafters and roof, recreated little stone-clad hollows for the fishing-boats to nest in.

Last Sunday afternoon, in an air threatening rain, a few of us drove along the grassy track to the place.

It was good to see the work that has been done, so caringly and so well.

But will the boat-houses ever be used again, stored with creels and stacked with oars and sails? Will a new generation of fishermen come and go, as their great-grandfathers did?

It may well come to pass.

As we left Sandy Geo, the haar began to thicken to a dense saturating rain.

An Enchanted Week

26.7.1984

Thankfully, there had not been many changes in Rackwick when we spent an enchanted week there, at Mucklehouse above the shore. (One glimpse of modernity, David Hutchison had installed hot and cold water on tap, and a flushing WC, and electric light—and in his own beautifully restored part there were two TV sets, one colour and one monochrome, and a CB radio.)

Also, on the summit of Greenhill a tall metal mast has recently been erected. What for? I climbed up there one evening, with laboured breath.

Some of the cottages are very derelict now. When I visited Ian and Jean MacInnes in summer 1952, there was an old man living at Shore, between Noust and Greenhill, who sat outside all one day in the sun. The interior of Shore now is a wilderness of nettles and fallen stones.

One curious thing we were told, 'Dandelions never grow in Rackwick'. Well, but the yellow irises were out, and daisies and eyebright and fields rushing with wild flowers.

We were just a few days too early for the clegs. True, a few stole silently upon us, like bandits with knives under their coats; but the dust-grey villains for some reason don't like the taste of my blood, and so they leave me alone. Clegs come about Rackwick in July thick as tourists to Majorca.

But the power of the cleg is as nothing to the annihilating power of the midgies in August. No use putting midgie-repellent cream on your face and arms in mid-August. The midgies in their millions devour the cream and take new strength from it, and they have teeth like sharks!... Then a little wind comes in from the sea, and that mighty host is squandered.

There seemed to be plenty of people in the sea valley, coming and going—but it's a strange thing, the visitors seem to get lost in the vastness—and there you are, alone but for a few drifting sheep and the ducks, hens, dogs and geese.

Sometimes you see two or three, trudging up Moorfea, past Bunertoon, towards the Old Man of Hoy.

We ate great platters of food, and had a few sun-downers, and turned an idle page of a book now and then. I wrote a few verses in my notebook, and the start of a story.

Dunnet Head lighthouse gave out four silent pulses, again and again. And the full moon laid a silver causey on the Pentland Firth.

Summers at the West Shore

2.8.1984

There has been this sequence of sunless days, with light veils of haar lying over the hills and waters, and occasionally drifting so low it leaves a light moisture on the face and hands.

We drove to Warbeth beach two afternoons ago, the silver-grey clouds everywhere. The beach was heaped with sand, and the tide was fairly high. And there was not one person to be seen at Warbeth, on an afternoon in late July!

Looking back fifty years, we seemed to spend a large part of our summer holiday at Warbeth, bathing and picnicking, and searching among the pools for shells, crabs, and seaweed. The Atlantic songs were always in our ears. (But in those days, as always, children were unaware of beauty. They didn't stop every ten minutes or so to exclaim, 'Oh, isn't the sea beautiful today!' or, 'Just look at the seapinks!'... No, we accepted everything thanklessly, like little princes, or little vagrants, as though the swarming beauties and delights everywhere were ours as of right. But deep down, unconsciously, we were being nourished by all those sights and sounds.)

Warbeth was the place to go, in summer, when we were teenagers. Earlier, our feet didn't stretch so far. The West Shore was the place to go, just opposite Graemsay, where the little stretches of sand were broken up by seaward-thrusting reefs. That was our summer paradise, when we were very young. Here the old ones took the picnic things, in a basket, and we were burdened with pails and spades only. How many thousands of sand castles have been built under the 'Tender Tables' in the last century? How many children have trooped in and out of Hoy Sound, bright and shrilling and shivering? And then the sandwiches on some sloping rock above—well they were called sandwiches, with all that sand on them! And the bottles of lemonade that had to be pushed open by wire levers. And the 'rich tea' and the 'Abernethy' biscuits. And the mugs of tea where a shore fly had drowned itself, often enough.

We probed among the little triangular rockpools left in interstices of the reef by the ebb, and found the kind of seaweed that went 'pop' when

135

you pressed it, and tiny semi-transparent crabs, and shells that when you held one to the ear brimmed with the songs of all the seven seas.

So the summers passed, in a long dream of delight and innocence.

Believe it if You Like

9.8.1984

I remember being told a story in Kirkwall nearly forty years ago, that I have never heard since. And now I wonder if perhaps I dreamed the whole thing.

It concerns one of the north isles of Orkney some time at the beginning of the First World War, and a company of sailors who suddenly appeared at the door of the island shop and asked for goods (probably butter, eggs, cheese, bread, etc). The sailors were served with the usual country courtesy. And they tendered coin of the realm for their purchases. And off they went to the shore, where presumably they had a small boat of some kind.

How long it was after that, that irate officials descended on the island, I don't know. But they let it be known, in thunderous tones, that the islanders had had dealings with the King's enemies! The sailors had come from a German U-boat.

How would islanders at that time, who had never seen naval officers or ratings, have known a German uniform from a British uniform? But one imagines the sailors would have been wearing some kind of oilskins. And no doubt the spokesman—the one who ordered and paid for the messages—spoke good English.

If this story had a shred of truth in it, I'm sure it would in the course of seventy years have passed into local legend, and been repeated times without number, and embroidered and shaped in accordance with the laws of folklore.

But I've never heard the tale again. So I conclude it must have been a dream, or else that the teller had spun a piece of pure fiction to amuse us both...

It probably bears some resemblance to the story of a countryman in a remote district of the West Mainland who came to Stromness one day about 1925 in his horse and cart—a rare occurrence for him, who hardly ever left his croft.

Anyway, he got talking to some of the men about the pierhead, and after some preliminary banter about the demerits of Stromnessians and the folk of the district he came from—which satire was almost always, then, a kind of compliment in reverse—he asked in all seriousness, 'Tell me this, hoo's the waar gettan on?'...

You can believe it if you like.

Park where Three Parishes Meet

16.8.1984

It is the morning of the Dounby Show as I write, and this year I don't know whether I'll manage to get there or not.

But through the window the sun is shining, and the sky is blue all over, with just a white summery cloud here and there.

I imagine the animals being judged, under the critical appraising eyes of hundreds of farmers and their wives. And what magnificent animals they are, always—the very finest creatures from the rich fields and hillsides of the West Mainland.

How patient they are too, at their temporary stations—the massive bulls and the butter-breathing cows and the tremulous tinted sheep. Except for a cockerel here and there that rages to the sun against his prison-house.

Yes, but if the Dounby Show was for farmers and farming folk only, Dounby on this day of all the year would not be the tumultuous place it is.

In Kirkwall and Stromness nearly all the shops will have put up their shutters, and cars by the hundred will be converging on Dounby from every corner of Orkney.

In that small park near where three parishes meet—Sandwick, Harray, Birsay—there will be such events as tug-o'-war and Highland dancing and show jumping on intelligent quiveringly-sensitive ponies.

And there will be stalls for books and candy-floss and lemonade. And in an adjacent field there used to be the fairground folk with their 'housey-housey' and fortune-telling and goldfish-bowl booths; but that part of the show seems to have been diminishing in recent years.

What joy, to meet people you haven't seen maybe since last Dounby Show! Oh, it might take a solid hour to make a full circuit of the park, speaking to this one and that.

Then, towards mid-afternoon, to arrive at last at the beer tent. What a struggle to win through that dense throng to the bar with its bottles, cans and plastic tumblers ... then to wash down, deliciously, the dust of the long summer.

Tastes Vanished and Acquired

20.9.1984

When I got home last night, somebody had left a paper poke of mushrooms on the doorstep.

So, this evening I'll have the mushrooms fried with bacon and sausages. With Orkney tatties, where could there be a better meal?

Now that I think about it, the eating of mushrooms is a comparatively new thing in Orkney. I think the soldiers must have taken this taste north with them during the war.

Certainly, in my childhood, nobody in our vicinity ate mushrooms. In fact, mushrooms had a kind of sinister aura. The undersides were 'the devil's pages'...

And nettles—who ever dreamed that some day Orcadians would be making nettle soup? I know, from reading, that the English ate turnip-tops and sorrel.

Never here. In Orkney the edible was confined within a very narrow range.

There were taboo foods, such as mackerel. Mackerel were never eaten; fishermen used them for bait. There were, probably, primitive beliefs about scaleless fish. I have heard it said that mackerel feed on drowned sailors (but then, what fish doesn't?). Nowadays mackerel, fried or smoked, is eaten with great relish in the islands.

Whelks were always sought for by boys—we rifled the rockpools. After they were boiled, we teased them out of the shells with a pin. But mussels, for some reason nobody fancied them... I have tasted them, and they are quite palatable.

But limpets, we draw the line at them. They are for the fishermen only, to bait their line. And yet, two or three summers ago, my American friend Larry Millman sought those delicacies along the shore. I may be mistaken, thinking that he ate them raw. But eat them he did, and called them good.

One popular dish of a half-century ago has vanished completely: stewed rabbit. It is not only myxomatosis that makes our gorge rise—but, before the war, on the Holms, rumour went that hybrid rabbit-rats were running around.

Bygone Brands
11.10.1984

I wrote a few weeks ago about 'fly-catchers', and how every house in Britain used to have those little sticky hammocks slung at the ceiling.

It strikes me that, besides flycatchers, there are many items of domestic use that are no longer sold in the shops (and I assure you there were three times as many shops along the street in the 1930s).

On washing day—Monday—my mother might send me for a packet of 'Robin' starch or Reckitt's Blue, the latter to make the linen whiter.

Also there was a kind of coarse soap called 'Fels Naphtha', used exclusively for washing clothes.

My father smoked a kind of tobacco called 'Black Twist'. The tobacconist—Miss Isa Sutherland—cut a rope of dark tobacco from a huge coil on the counter. I think 'Black Twist' was a very strong tobacco.

The brands of tea were quite different then—'Mazawattee', 'Lipton's', 'Good-as-Gold'. (If you saved enough 'Good-as-Gold' labels, you got a tea-set from Messrs Esslemont of Aberdeen. There are still three cups—one cracked—from the 'Crown Derby' tea-set my mother got. A great ocean of tea must have been drunk to throw those delicate trophies ashore.)

Coffee: we hardly knew the taste of coffee. Very occasionally there would be a bottle of 'Camp Coffee' in the cupboard. On the label—if memory serves me right—there was a picture of a soldier and a tent and possibly a palm tree in the desert...

There was no washing-up liquid; to wash the dishes you dissolved 'Soap Flakes' in the hot water.

Cornflakes came like bursts of sunlight on the breakfast table in the mid-1930s, but they had a forerunner, 'Force', with (I seem to remember) a monocled dandy on the packet; and the slogan, 'Up in the air went Sunny Jim—"Force" was the stuff they used for him.'...

Look for 'the Peedie Summer'

25.10.1984

After gentle pacific yesterday, what a wild storm is raging outside as I write this! In the garden beyond Farafield Lane, the trees are surging, and but for their roots would be up and off, helter-skelter! Waves are breaking grey and white against the piers. The windows are awash with continuous rain.

Is there a lingering tent on the Ness camp-site? I hope not, on a wild raging slut of a day like this.

The children, on holiday, will all be indoors with their computer games and word-processors.

A good day to be sitting at the end of a long bar, drinking Guinness, working up a slow hunger for haddock and chips.

Many a Stromnessian, going for errands before the shops shut on Thursday afternoon, will be saying, 'Here's winter!'

But in fact winter is a long way off, still. Between now and the snow-men (and the 'merry dancers' and lamp-lighting at three o'clock) there always comes a halcyon interlude, known in Orkney as 'the peedie summer'. We can expect it towards the end of October or the beginning of November—a sequence of mild sun-filled days, when we can walk about without coats or scarves; there may be even a few gentle complaints about the unseasonable mildness.

Make the most of that lovely interlude when it comes.

For one day we will wake to a wilder yelling of winds, and the driving rain will have in every drop a little stinging core of ice, and there will be a moan and a snarl in the wrecking harbour waves.

Then it will be time to dig in the clothes cupboard for winter woollies, and fish the hot water bottle from under summer debris (wondering, 'Has the rubber perished? Will it last till February?').

And coal—we can't help worrying about our fires. Nothing has been so depressing on radio and TV than news of that never-ending strike. Will we be lighting fires on the days of the last snow, in February or March? Or will we be sitting like Scrooge, muffled, warming cold hands over a candle-flame?

One of the chief joys of this stormy autumn day will be to set the fire in a merry blaze in late afternoon.

TV Finds its Level

15.11.1984

Sometimes, talking to children, we say, 'Oh yes, in Skara Brae they had stone cups, and stone spoons, and stone telephones and stone television sets.'...

Almost as primitive now as stone TV sets are the black-and-white sets that first reached Orkney in the early fifties (though all that could be seen, to begin with, were drifts of snowflakes across the screen).

But TV quickly caught on. People began to speak about such things as *That Was the Week That Was* and the serialisation of *The Forsyte Saga*. Names like Gilbert Harding and Robin Day were as familiar as neighbours'.

It exerted such compulsion that families stayed indoors, night after night, clustered about the grey shadows on the screen. If neighbours called, they no longer got the kind traditional Orkney welcome. (In plenty of houses, I'm sure they did, still—but the social climate had changed a great deal.)

The twice-a-week Stromness cinema closed down—and that was a real breach in the social fabric of the town. There was something delightful about the coming together, every Thursday and Saturday evening, of so many townsfolk. The tree of drama that had flourished so well in Orkney for a generation all but withered and perished. And no doubt other social get-togethers were drastically thinned out. Were we on the brink of a social revolution?

No, we were not, as things turned out. Folk discovered that they could take so much television, and no more. They began to miss the fruitful relationships, the comings and goings, the visits, that had been so much a pattern of our lives; and having lasted maybe for thousands of years, was deeply ingrained.

So TV found its level, and has stayed there, though in the meantime black-and-white sets have been relegated to the junk heap, and the corner of every living-room in the western world brims with moving colours.

In all of them that is, except this house, where a Stone Age TV hung on doggedly till last weekend.

Sleeping Habits

6.12.1984

Snoozing in the afternoon—that must be a sign that one is getting old. 'Old and grey and full of sleep', as the poet Yeats said, echoing the French poet Ronsard who lived centuries before. Old men and women have been nodding beside the fire since time began.

Hitherto it has always been a slightly shameful thing to drop off to sleep in the middle of the day. It would happen, occasionally, of course, on the days after New Year; or maybe in a garden full of flowers and bees in summer. Then one always woke up surly and ill-tempered, as if time had played a nasty trick. If anybody so much as spoke, he got for an answer a growl or a snarl.

Sleep was for the night only, pillow under the head wrapped in a quilt.

Either one mellows or decays with the years—it depends, I suppose, on how you look at it.

But now, 'sleep comes dropping slow' at any time, especially in the late afternoon or early evening. The difference is that now it comes deliciously, like dewfall, like a drift of puppies. 'Forty winks', the old folk used to call this fireside sleep, or a 'cat nap', or a 'dropping-off'. And one wakes up out of the brief oblivion, not with ill-natured scowls and grunts, but with nods of approval and satisfaction, as much as to say, 'That was good—that was delightful—very acceptable indeed...'

It is nature's kind way of letting one know that life is coming full cycle, time is rounding back upon itself. Stray bits of sleep are for the old and young: young children too are forever dropping off.

'Our little life,' said the greatest bard of all, 'is rounded with a sleep'...
It is a merciful gift of nature, so kindly to close our eyes.

Santa in 1934

20.12.1984

If a modern child were to judge by TV advertisements, Santa has been on his way by about the beginning of November.

Santa must be well clear of the ice-cap now. Santa must be toiling through mountain passes in Norway. Santa must be beginning to be rather fed up.

Fifty years ago, Santa spanned the entire world in one wonderful night! We did not stop to wonder how Santa and the reindeer managed that gift-loaded sledge on Christmas Eve without snow. There was word, indeed, that Santa had given up his sledge and reindeer in favour of an aeroplane. I don't know about the other children, but I much preferred the sledge.

Santa coming down the chimney presented no difficulties to us. Do modern children wonder: 'Won't he get burned? Won't his fine red coat get filthy with soot? Why can't he come in through the door, like other people?'

Santa came down the lum—that was all there was to it—no argument.

Also, in some mysterious way he received the letters that you had sent up the lum a week or so beforehand. No matter if the letter fell back scorched and soot-stained, Santa had got the message. (I suppose, on some very windy nights, the scrap of paper did get sucked up and whirled among the stars.)

Half a century ago and more, there was economic distress over the land—and the poverty was far bleaker than it is today. So, a child could not write to Santa for expensive gifts. All he could hope for was a book, or a toy, or a game. There was always at the foot of the stocking an orange (or a tangerine) and an apple, and a sixpence bright as a star!

With those few gifts, one spent Christmas morning in a state of pure enchantment!

And the decorations rustled at the ceiling; and we drank an occasional glass of spicy home-made ginger wine. And soon it was time for one of the family to go to the bakehouse for the roast goose.

The End of 1984

27.12.1984

The *annus mirabilis* is wearing to a close, and none of the really dreadful things that George Orwell predicted has come to pass. True, there's the prolonged miners' strike, and the fifteen-year-old trouble in Northern Ireland continues, and there is hijacking, distress in Ethiopia, India, Afghanistan, Nicaragua—plus an endless ocean of private anguish and pain that will never be recorded.

1984 is, of course, the most celebrated of Orwell's five novels. More than a year ago, all five were published together in paperback by Penguin Books, and I read them one after the other.

It was a curious experience; it struck me that the very celebrated *1984* was the worst of the five, and three that had been accorded a very small welcome are very fine novels indeed—especially one called *Coming Up For Air*, about a rather unpleasant character who has made a kind of seedy questionable success in business and yet (in the hurly-burly of London preparing for war) keeps a well-spring of poetry inside himself, secure and precious. This is the memory of the little English market town where he passed his boyhood; and especially he remembers a pool where he spent enchanted hours with a fishing rod. He wins a little money on the horses; he pleads urgent business to his paralysingly ordinary wife, and goes off to rediscover the pure source of his first happiness...

It is a marvellous novel; the bits of lyricism in *1984* are tawdry by comparison.

But that has always been one of the ironies of literature—many writers are praised for second-rate work, while their masterpieces are ignored.

* * *

As one gets older, the books that one really enjoys get fewer and fewer. This year only one memorable new book has come my way—the novel *Lincoln* by Gore Vidal, published by Heinemann... Yes, it is about the greatest of all the American presidents: one of the few great leaders that power did not corrupt.

Twelfth Night

3.1.1985

As you read this, after 1985 has begun, we are still in the season of Christmas, though nowadays not many people seem to realize it. There lingers only the shadowy custom that decorations and cards have to be put away, and trees dismantled, before the Twelfth Night (6 January) is over.

The very name Twelfth Night indicates that Christmas is a feast lasting twelve days. It was on that last night that the Magi arrived in Bethlehem with their gifts.

But nowadays Christmas is contracted to the one day, 25 December. What a rush to get cards, calendars and parcels away so that they'll arrive before that date! And inevitably, when you are writing out your Christmas cards, a few names get forgotten. Before the war, to cover up those mistakes, New Year cards were sent—but one always felt slightly insulted, as if to get a New Year card meant that you were somehow a second-class person.

It's said that Oliver Cromwell, three centuries ago, tried to knock austerity into the frivolous giddy tribes of Britain by abolishing Christmas. He had about as much chance as King Canute had with the waves. The dour subtle Scots got over the temporary difficulty by postponing the great feast for a week. They resurrected some obscure Pictish feast called Hogmanay: but then the celebration went on with all the light and peace and joy left out of it—only the dark, berserk midwinter reel was left.

But even so, Hogmanay is one of The Twelve Days of Christmas— the seventh.

Our island ancestors, whom we are inclined to think of as ignorant and bovine compared to our enlightened selves, who can watch TV and read *The Sun*, observed, in a very special way, the entire twelve-day season of Christmas, with little domestic ceremonies of great beauty which have been utterly forgotten—though fortunately they are preserved in the Old Lore books.

So it is still Christmas as you read this—and if you have any forgotten friends to call on, or any little peace-offering to make, you have until Sunday to see to it.

The Faithful Power Supply

31.1.1985

The snow, that has seized up all Europe but Orkney and the north, has broken into our mild oasis at last.

The first indication I had was on Tuesday morning when I was listening, still half-asleep in bed, to women discussing vegetarian cooking. Suddenly their voices ceased. Had the transistor given up the ghost? No—the bedside light, switched on, gave no response.

No point in getting up to a cold house for a cold breakfast. I turned over for another sleep, until the radio voices returned.

There it was, when I drew back the bedroom curtains, snow on the roofs and in the gardens. And a dark lowering sky spitting more cold grey stuff.

I had to get to 'downtown' Stromness—there were urgent letters to post before 12.30pm.

Would the power stay on long enough for toast to be made, tea brewed, an egg boiled? The power—though all day long it gave little flickers and hesitancies—remained faithful.

What a filthy mess the street was in! I had some trouble digging my rubber boots from under an accumulation of boxes, etc, in the cupboard.

The wind howled and moaned from the north-east, and flung cold wet sleet at all the hurrying shivering folk of Stromness. It was the kind of day when the spirit plummets to a very low ebb—and 'joy' is a word excised from the vocabulary.

The human psyche, however, is a strange unpredictable thing. Having posted my letters, and bought stamps, bread, mince and sausages, and turned my face homewards, I actually began to feel at home in the outrageous weather, though my trouser-knees were saturated, and once in Alfred Street, I almost went sprawling in the slush.

The power was still on! The spirits rose. Never have I enjoyed two plates of tomato soup, with chunks of pork sausage in it, so much. At my writing desk a few felicities came.

The fire raged merrily in the grate like an African lion. Only one TV channel, Grampian, was working. I read a new book and was quite happy.

The Blank Screen

7.2.1985

This is the last afternoon of January—and the fearsome month is passing with blown sun and rain, and a strong wind from the west from which we Stromnessians are mostly sheltered.

And we think, thankfully, 'There's the back of winter broken!'— though, to be sure, there will be a few gales and dirty days between now and the vernal equinox.

On the whole, January 1985 has been a kindly month, as Januaries go. It began with a sequence of days like a string of diamonds. We listened on radio and TV, complacently, to stories out of snow-bound England and southern Scotland—but most of all to the sub-zero temperatures from France and Spain. (And we laughed, a little cruelly, about those who had gone south in winter for the sunshine. What were they doing on the Riviera, building snowmen?) And one day the radio said Iceland was the warmest place in Europe.

The idyll ended, of course, with that sudden outbreak of sleety snow one Tuesday morning; and then cobwebs had to be dusted from the rubber boots that are only worn about six days in the year, and the drawer of woollens searched for gloves and the thickest socks.

It is a vivid reminder of how hooked we are on TV when all of a sudden it fails to function in its usual way. Channel 4, which provides the most wholesome fare of all, was a blank, or rather a scramble of black-and-white dots. At best, the other three channels were 'grainy', to say the least...

Into what a wretched state of dependence we have fallen—almost as bad as heroin addicts—when we go grumpily about the house, because we can't view a film we were looking forward to! As if there were no good books to read, as if there were no good friends to talk to. So much are our minds in thrall to moving shadows in a box in the corner.

The snow—probably only the first snow—went as soon as it had come. January is ending with mighty trumpets of wind from the west. In Stromness, one is hardly aware of that airt; but at the kirkyard it bit keenly, where a large company of his fellow-townsmen gathered to pay a tribute of farewell to Willie Marwick.

Sillocks

14.2.1985

Where have all the sillocks gone? I mean the tribes and the flocks of sillocks that used to swarm about the twenty piers of Stromness.

February is not the month for them, of course. But in July and August you will not see them either, of recent years, drifting in silver-grey troops at the end of a pier, at high tide.

There, on summer days fifty years ago, boys and sillocks had their rendezvous.

If you were very hard up, a bent pin and a piece of string might do. But most boys could afford to buy a length of fishing-line (called 'snud') from the little grocer shop of Mr George Linklater, opposite the foot of Manse Lane. And if you bought a penny-worth of snud, Mr Linklater (who was a small rather dapper man and wore silver spectacles) gave you a hook for nothing.

Then the boys went to their chosen piers, Gray's or Clouston's or Copland's or Mowat's, and the contest of boy against sillock commenced.

Of course you baited the barb of the hook with a piece of mussel or limpet previously.

Sometimes—like all fishing for sport—it was a long tedious barren occupation; for either the sillocks were congregating elsewhere or else they declined to bite. (But even a fruitless afternoon of fishing must

146

have been pleasant enough, with the sea-music along the piers and the gulls wheeling above and the spangle of sun on the harbour.)

On other days the sillocks couldn't do enough for you, in the way of giving themselves up, latching onto the hooks time after time, allowing themselves to be drawn out of the water curling and flashing—and then deposited, gulping among a pile of their tarnished companions.

No humans ate the pier sillocks. They were said to be unclean—I suppose because they might be tainted with the sewage. But the cats ate them, and took no harm. The boys sold the sillocks, four for a penny, to the old wives who kept cats.

But the sillocks from beyond the harbour mouth, they were all right to eat; for they had been nourished by the strong pure Atlantic waters, and they sizzled well in the Stromness frying pans.

Rent Increase!

14.3.1985

The whole multitude of Council House tenants in Orkney must have got a shock one morning last week when they got notice of the new rent they will have to pay from April on. The rent for the house I live in is to go up from £12.77 a week to £16.44!

In the year 1934 or 1935 my family went to live in a 'new hoose' at Well Park (now called Guardhouse Park), and the rent was seven and six a week—about 37p in modern money. That was considered to be a pretty stiff rent for a three-bedroom house. Still, there was a bathroom and a kitchen and living-room, and a little flower garden in front and a vegetable patch at the back, and there was gas-light. It felt like moving suddenly into affluence, though it had to be paid for at 37p a week.

Then, for some reason I can't fathom, instead of going up the rent began to get less, first to 31p a week and then to 27p a week, and still the Well Park ladies would say, 'We've paid so much rent for so long that the houses should belong to us!'

After the war, the rents began to climb, but slowly, till in the autumn of 1968, it was still under £1 a week, and that was the rent I paid on moving to Mayburn Court. It was ridiculously cheap.

Then the graph began to climb, each April, steeply. It seems to me, much more steeply than the rate of inflation—in seventeen years the rent has increased sixteen-fold and more.

'Ah well,' as the old folk used to say, 'we should be thankful we have a roof over our heads.'...

I sometimes wonder, would it be wise to buy the house I live in, at the very reasonable price asked? But then, why should a person like me, on the verge of the old-age pension, want to burden himself with ownership of a house? There would be a hundred things to worry about—insurance, for example, and supposing the slates began to come off the roof in a winter gale? One day last summer the outflow pipe began to hurl down water onto the street below—but a council workman quickly came and fixed it. Little things like that are always happening...

On the whole, it seems easier to go on paying this dear rent.

A New Art Gallery

21.3.1985

Enter the coal office in Victoria Street, pass through, and you find yourself in a little enchanted room. This is the new art gallery of Ian MacInnes.

A year ago it was an old junk place, full of coal sacks and cobwebs. Now the walls are whitewashed, there is fluorescent lighting, there are chairs for old folk like me to sit down on (and even a table if you want to make notes), and a movable gas heater.

The four walls glow with oil-paintings by Ian MacInnes: sea-scapes and town-scapes and crag- and rock-scapes, celebrations of the scenes everywhere around us that familiarity has dulled; but here, as Edwin Muir wrote, 'the source of all our seeing rinsed and cleansed'... If it does nothing else, this new little gallery will make us aware of the multitudinous delights all around us. But of course it does more—it enriches our own vision, so that the Orkney we see has a new deeper intensity.

So, Stromness is now more than ever the islands' art centre.

For the tourists, it will be another place that they cannot leave Orkney without visiting.

I am particularly interested because I sat in the same classrooms with Ian MacInnes between the ages of five and seventeen. When he was a boy he had this gift of sketching people fluently, economically, and with a startling lifelikeness. Many Stromnessians saw caricatures of themselves in *The Orkney Herald* in the 1930s, and some were delighted and others were not so delighted; but whatever the subjects thought, no one could deny the brilliance of the sketches.

Since those early days, of course, Ian MacInnes has been an art student, art teacher in Stromness Academy, rector of the same, a student of The Open University (BA with Honours); and now the

148

wheel has come full cycle and, having recently retired, he can devote himself entirely to the service of his great talent.

And we Stromnessians ought to be grateful that we are being celebrated in this way.

Psychology in Numbers

28.3.1985

I read an advertisement the other day—for what, I forget—but the price was £9.99.

There's something extraordinarily bizarre about a price like that. Why not simply £10? It would make it easier for everyone concerned. Even to write £9.99 on a cheque is hardly worth the penny one saves, in time and effort.

So many books nowadays fall just short of a price in exact pounds— £7.95, £19.95 are common on the front inside flap of books.

This has been going on for a long time, since before the days of decimalisation. Even as children we used to wonder at prices in shop windows: 2/11½d for a shirt or a pair of stockings. Why, oh why, for the sake of neatness, couldn't they have made it three shillings exactly?

It seems to be a matter of human psychology. £10, even in these days of mounting prices, is a barrier beyond which tens of thousands of people will not pass. But £9.99—we might just manage that. We'll even get a penny change!

It argues a certain gullibility in human nature: a tendency to be mesmerised by figures, on a mass scale. We like to think of ourselves as rational creatures but we can be influenced by the merest sand-grain or blown cobweb.

* * *

While we're on the subject of numbers, why is there such an aversion to the number 13? Some householders carry the taboo so far that they put 12½ on their doors, or simply overleap the number and are 14. But I have just been reading the autobiography of Maud Gonne, the Irish Nationalist at the turn of the century—and a woman so beautiful that the poet Yeats was stirred by her again and again into marvellous poetry. And 13 was her lucky number.

I have found the number 7 of great help to me, for so many reasons that it would take another article to explain.

April Foolery

11.4.1985

No April jokes this year—at least, none was played on me, but then— it being a public holiday—I was hardly over the door.

I have a feeling that All Fools' Day is not observed so jokingly as it used to be. We schoolboys would say to somebody, 'There's a spider in your hair', or, 'Your boot-lace is untied'—and then, when our victim did something to mend things, we would laugh mockingly and shout 'Hint-A-Gook!' (the meaning of which must be buried deep in seasonal lore). In the course of the same day, we might be 'caught' twice or thrice ourselves, unless we kept our wits about us.

Why, I wonder, is this All Fools' Day observed on 1st April? It might be a feeling of release and exhilaration that Winter is over and done, and Spring is here. The hardships we endured at the time of ice and gales—the things that oppressed us—let's shrug them off in an out- burst of tomfoolery. 'Hey-ho, be jolly. All life is mere folly.'... In other words, there's nothing under the sun to worry about—let all imaginary ills be drowned under the floods of wildflowers and larksong and new lambs.

* * *

But there were other observances, now (I'm sure) almost forgotten, on 2nd and 3rd of April. One of those days was 'borrowing day'. A schoolboy would ask his mate for the loan of his pencil, or a penny. But on the borrowing day, all loans were forfeit—if you were fool enough to loan something to someone, it was his for keeps.

And the other day in early April was 'taily day'. What happened was that you made a tail, out of paper or rope, and surreptitiously pinned the tail onto the back of somebody's coat or jacket. What laughter there was then, when the victim went on his way with his 'tail' dangling behind! How we hooted and jeered and pointed! How the victim blushed with embarrassment, or stamped with rage!

Those folk customs probably go back to the beginning of human society, a score of millennia ago, or thereby. They may have been attempts to contain, within a circle of social acceptability, such fearful things as banditry and piracy—'let's make a game of it'... The 'tails' may have been a way of pricking human pride and arrogance and pomposity. Put a tail on the high-and-mighty one—let him see that, after all, he is a fellow-mortal with the lions and the mice.

A pity, that some things are being forgotten in Orkney...

Cosmic Drama

25.4.1985

Some science programmes on TV intrigue me; though, not having a scientific bent of mind, much of what is said I find baffling. Still, through the drifts of scientific or mathematical argument, from time to time one senses a cosmic drama so immense as to be breathtaking.

A long while ago, some geologist on the radio was explaining how the continents are slowly drifting apart, a centimetre a year or so. So immense is the timescale that once South America fitted neatly into Africa. Indeed if you look at a globe, there those two continents lie, like pieces in a jigsaw, with the immense stretch of the South Atlantic between them now.

Last week, a TV programme was called *Maia*, after a Greek goddess. How do such creatures as dinosaurs exist and flourish on earth for millions of years, and then disappear in a comparatively short space of time; though their fossils remain in the rocks together with fossils of creatures who preceded them? The lifetime of any species covers a large tract of time. It is only yesterday, comparatively speaking, that Man appeared on the earth.

According to the scientist who was speaking, every seventy-four million years or so—I may have the exact figure wrong—our earth is overtaken by a catastrophe. The sun, it seems, has a ghostly twin who visits it, or at least leans over the garden fence, every seventy-four million years. Its approach disturbs a dense wheel of meteors that lie beyond the solar system. It is as if the sun's twin, approaching, kicked over a beehive. The meteors come swarming in upon Venus, Mercury, Earth, Mars, and batter them with such stings and woundings that the cords of the earth can no longer withstand the ecological and temperature changes. So the dinosaurs perished in the new alien atmosphere. But some clever little species, here and there, learned to adapt—among them our primitive lemur ancestors. And they inherited the earth. Now it looks like being a race between nuclear weapons and the next visit of the sun's unruly twin.

The End of World War II

9.5.1985

TV these last few evenings has been brimming over with programmes about the end of the Second World War forty years ago. (It seems, nowadays, that any anniversary—25th, 40th, 70th—is good for a few programmes: they stir up the old nostalgia of reminiscence.)

Who, that lived through those world-shaking days, even as a quiet civilian in Orkney, can ever forget them? The Russians, irresistible since the terrible Battle of Stalingrad, driving on now towards Berlin—the British and Americans crossing the Rhine—the appalling discovery of the human sewers of Belsen and Dachau—the suicide of the mad monster in his Berlin bunker—the shameful end of Mussolini and his mistress—Montgomery curtly dictating terms to a handful of German generals on Lüneburg Heath—then the victory bells and the sky above Stromness fluttering with flags (including, I'm sure, one or two Imperial German Eagles from World War I) ...

In Orkney, we had known for quite a long time that the tide was flowing our way. Early in the war we had gotten used to German air raids over Scapa; our ears had grown familiar with the distant undulating drone of the German engines, heard faintly between the earth-shaking anti-aircraft barrage, and the 'banshee wail' of the air-raid warning and the ululations of 'All Clear'. I think the German squadrons never came back after the summer of 1941—all their bombers were needed for the Russian front...

I think it was the sudden freedom from 'the Black-out' that brought home to us the fact of victory. For years, at night, we had had to grope our way through the abyss of the street, with the merest glim of light from torches. And every window of every room in every house was criss-crossed with sticky tape, to save us from flying glass. We had long discarded our gas-masks.

About 1944, if I remember rightly, the troop-gorged islands were slowly drained of soldiers. *The Orkney Blast* closed down. The Stromness beer-drinkers began to worry about what would happen when the many camp messes closed down; for these oases were everywhere in the otherwise 'dry' town of Stromness. 'The lights are going out all over Stromness,' one mournful beer-man lamented.

But the lovely half-forgotten pattern of lights from a hundred windows and street corners more than made up for it.

A dreadful time was over. But, looking at Belsen films and the ruins of Stalingrad, Berlin, London, Orcadians (in spite of many a private sorrow) had an easy time of it.

A New Ice Age Begins

23.5.1985

There comes a time when the 'fridge' must be de-iced. Actually it ought to have been done months ago; opening the little deep-freeze compartment at the top, there was a great chunk of ice in it that might have sunk the *Titanic*—such a massive wedge of ice that it was impossible to put anything into the deep-freeze. 'You'd better do something about that,' a friend said, weeks and weeks ago.

But time passes, and one does nothing.

Two afternoons ago, in an idle hour, I pulled out the plug and opened the fridge door; and bestowed the milk, cheese, bacon, orange juice into the kitchen cupboard where the mild air is liable to corrupt, sour and rot.

By bedtime, I reckoned, the operation ought to be completed. That immense glacier would be transformed to water. And then I could plug in again and leave the fridge to its own affairs.

(In passing, it ought to be remarked what an ugly word 'fridge' is. A wash of ugliness is going over our language. 'Privatisation' is another ugly word, and so is 'tenderise'. But this is a deep and fascinating theme—no time to pursue it now—except to say that, such is the transmuting power of language, those ugly words, which have already become acceptable, might after a century or two acquire a certain dignity and beauty. But, for the moment, I dislike them.)

By midnight the great glistering bar of ice was still there, seemingly welded forever to the ice-box. But no—there's a little plastic tray below, and it had water in it. Something was happening, but very slowly.

'Ah well,' thought I, 'it will all be gone by morning.'

At breakfast-time the ice was still there—a bit diminished, but hanging on grimly, a white ragged saw-blade. But the little plastic tray was brimming.

I suppose the fan-heater, and my blood and the breath of Gypsy the black cat (who is in temporary residence again) finally put paid to the ice. It was now a slim glistening dripping poker, hanging crookedly by one end. It was possible to dislodge it and put it in the sink.

Then the contents of the fridge went back into their compartments—the plug was inserted—and in that white cube under the kitchen table another little ice age began.

Penguins Are 50

20.6.1985

I think that this year they are celebrating the 50th anniversary of Penguin Books. It was a marvellous time, for young people whose eyes were just opening to the riches of literature. It is strange to think that there had been no real paperbacks in Britain before that, though they were common enough in France and other countries.

Sixpence for a book!—It even brought books within a schoolboy's price range—though there was something of a dilemma, for 'Woodbine' cigarettes were twopence for five, and it was a choice between culture and the pleasures of what J. M. Barrie called 'My lady Nicotine'. (Little did J. M. Barrie know what a killer and a vampire that languorous lady was.)

The first three Penguin titles were *Ariel* by André Maurois, *A Farewell to Arms* by Hemingway, and *Poet's Pub* by Eric Linklater. I have *Ariel* and *Poet's Pub* on my shelves still.

There followed, every month, a galaxy of new titles. I can never forget the thrill of opening such Penguins as *Gone to Earth* by Mary Webb, *Tarka the Otter* by Henry Williamson, *Morning Tide* by Neil Gunn—and scores of others.

Presently, Penguin Books put out branches. There were serious studies in history, economics, psychology, called Pelican Books. Here the going was rougher. I think I had never tried to traverse such a desert of boredom as Bernard Shaw's *Intelligent Woman's Guide to Socialism and Capitalism*, but there were compelling titles too, a spacetime fantasy *Last and First Men* by Olaf Stapledon and an enchanting *The Century's Poetry* in two volumes chosen by Denys Kilham Roberts. There I first came on the poetry of Edwin Muir.

Suppose, in 1936 or 1937, you had a shilling to spend. Look in first at Rae's to see if the new Penguins were in. There was sixpence left over to buy fifteen Woodbines. Between the book and the fags, life seemed to promise perfect felicity for a couple of days.

Poetry of Western Mountains

27.6.1985

This should not be called 'Under Brinkie's Brae' this week, because we have been lately under so many mountains ten times higher than the little hill that guards Stromness.

Once, more than twenty years ago, I must have covered the same route through the west and north of Scotland, but in the other direction, coming home. The memories have long since faded.

Our car journey last weekend was pure enchantment.

The crossing on the *Ola*, though smooth, had been cold with swaps[1] of rain. And Scrabster was drab.

But as the car drove west, past Dounreay and Strathy and Bettyhill, patches of blue appeared. Loch Eriboll lay in full sunlight. It was more than the two photographers in the car, John and Gunnie, could stand. They had to get out and down to the beach with their cameras—

1. swirls

delighted, but despairing in a way that the great magnificent sweep of sea-loch and sky could never be entirely recorded in small rectangles of film, however beautiful; for the scents and sounds and delicate pulsating of nature must be left out.

As we drove south along the broken coastline, the wild enchantment multiplied. A writer as well as a photographer despairs of ever conveying the essence of what passes through the car windows. A genius like Hopkins comes near it in his lyric of 'wildness and wet' called 'Inversnaid'... I found a scrap of paper in my wallet and made a few hasty jottings as on we went, such as: 'bracken and boulders' ... 'long sea lochs with wooded islets' ... 'marvellously sculpted mountains (Stac Polly)' ... 'sign posts with Gaelic names that spell strangely but must be music in the mouth' ... 'the unimagined loveliness of the Summer Isles' ... 'low along the horizon, the Outer Hebrides as far south as Barra' ... 'the roadside ewes and their lambs quite unperturbed by the traffic' ... 'huge scattered boulders left by the Ice Age'.

Some day it may be possible to work those incoherent fragments into an essay of some kind. But the writer no less than the photographer must forever despair of bodying forth those 'mighty presences' and that prodigal squandering of purest lyricism.

I seem to remember that Eric Linklater, comparing (I think it might have been) Barra to Orkney, said our islands were good prose compared to the poetry of the west.

Summer Insects

25.7.1985

Such days of sweltering windless heat there have been—unusual in Orkney. Last Sunday the sun was so hot in the yard I was forced to go indoors and lie down.

Only for four months or so in summer do my windows open properly; winter solders them solid. Full advantage is taken when the weather is mild and bright. Most windows in the house are thrown open, and the sweet airs of summer flow everywhere.

So do the summer insects. A few days ago there was a spider in the bath. I don't know why spiders like porcelain, but there they visit often, sometimes remaining for days in one place. Questions arise: Do they like it there? What do they live on, for days on end?... We used to think they came up the waste pipe—but no, said a 'nature man' on the radio one day, they come through the window.

I have to confess, having a phobia about spiders, I used to wash them away, once they had outstayed their welcome. But nowadays, moved by the arguments of conservationists and other people who rightly see all creatures as having their place in the scheme of creation, I make a long paper spill and gingerly ease the spider onto it and hurriedly—in case it runs back up my sleeve—put it out by the bathroom window whence it came ... But last week's spider went away secretly, by itself.

At least spiders are quiet, but what is one to do with the flies that have invaded the bedroom during the day? In the old days—a decade ago or so—one went to bed to sleep soundly without fail for eight hours or so. Of late years there have had to be aids, including the reading of a book. It is a delightful occupation reading in bed, round about midnight. Two midnights ago I had hardly switched on the bedside lamp, when there was a loud buzzing and a thumping; and there was a summer fly, as mad for electric light as any alcoholic would be beside a pub gantry. It is when the drunken fly bounces off the page, and hurls itself into your face, that it's time to shut up shop. Off goes the light, the book is put aside, the fly retires with its hangover... And if you're lucky, sleep comes fairly soon.

Rain and wind again this morning—windows closed—and presumably all spiders and flies folded under sheltering grass.

No News

15.8.1985

No news on BBC television or radio today, or on ITV...

In many ways, what a relief! How saving on the nerves, not to hear about bombs in Ulster or hijackings in the Middle East, or how nuclear waste is to be got rid of, or the spreading of the desert into Sudan, or of old ladies being beaten up in their houses for the few pounds they are keeping against a rainy eventide.

Yet, writing the above, I realise it is pure selfishness that one wants to cocoon oneself against the terrors that walk the earth, and the ugliness that proliferates everywhere. Let those things happen to other folk, in other places, but not to us—leave us alone in our sty of security and selfishness...

It was therefore all the more heartening that many young people really do care about the cruel things that happen. All praise to the young pop musician Bob Geldof who organised that mammoth day-long pop festival that raised far more relief money than most governments were willing to disburse. From now on, I will treat pop music and pop musicians with far more respect.

It is a sad fact, that it hardly ever becomes apparent in the news until someone like Geldof does such a spectacular thing, that there are such things as goodness, generosity, and goodwill in the world. In fact, there are deep brimming reservoirs of it that will never become exhausted— small acts of decency and courage and self-sacrifice that have never been recorded, and never will be, because they are not 'newsworthy'.

'The devil,' said William Booth of the Salvation Army, 'has all the best tunes', which isn't exactly true, but one can see what he meant... In the same way the devil makes all the headlines.

One can console oneself, that when *The Sun* and *Daily Mail* are no more, there will still abide the Beatitudes, *The Magic Flute* and the odes of Keats. They are much more wholesome experiences than the storms of news that assault our ears hourly.

I was glad to note this morning that we still had Radio Orkney.

Visitors from Abroad

29.8.1985

There must be visitors from almost every nation under the sun in Orkney, in summer.

We had our good Norwegian Orkney-loving friends in July. And before that Katia from France and her girl pupils. And after that Marie Antoinette and Hervé and their three young children, from France also. About the same time, briefly, a grey-bearded jolly Norwegian poet, Finn Strømsted.

At the moment, I have Michael Krauskopf from Germany, who lived in Egilsay for a year—'the best year of his life'—with his goat Rose and his chickens. Michael went to Egilsay to translate a book of mine in peace, but, as it turned out, there was too much happening in the Egilsay sea and shore, fields and sky to bother with transient things like book-translation.

But I have never had Japanese visitors before. Osamu Yamada came to see me, on literary business also, and brought his sixteen-year-old son Hiro with him. He brought gifts, the most beautiful one being a little iron bell that is hung outside houses in Japan. Depending from the bell is the script of a poem. On still evenings, if there is a little movement of air, the bell gives out a small pure sound; and in this conspiracy of wind and iron, the loveliness of the lyric is enhanced. I asked Osamu to translate the poem, but he was afraid he might ruin its delicacy. He will send a good translation when he gets home to Ichikawa City. (I have a feeling that those Japanese lyrics are so pure and fragile that any translation would scatter the rose petals.)

'Oh,' said Osamu, 'the poet was very poor. He died young.'... I said they had the same occupational hazards as many of their Western fellow bards.

Twice, on County Show Day, Osamu and Hiro saw the Queen Mother! They were amazed! They were delighted!

Gale Warnings

5.9.1985

The wind was blowing in great wild gusts from the west. You could tell by the dark 'fans' of wind spreading across the harbour, through the morning window.

Brinkie's Brae stands, a guardian, over Stromness, in such weather. But once you're out of its shelter, in Stenness or Innertoon, the gale can blow you about like a leaf. And anyone in search of sensation ought to go to Yesnaby on such a day, to view the Atlantic rampant against the crags (whose battlements, walls, bastions, towers are crumbling year by year in that perpetual battle).

'Gale warning, force 9,' said the weather forecaster at 5pm, 'imminent, Fair Isle'... But the gale had been with us for some time.

Along with the gale, the sun shone in all its late summer magnificence. Why does the sun seem to shine brighter in a high wind? The wind puts a burnish on it—the wind evokes splendours unseen on a calm day. All around the sky, too, roamed packs of dark grey cloud—rain-bringers. Some places not too far away were getting deluges and downpours. The sun, in the afternoon, took an even brighter lustre from those rainclouds.

It was possible to sit on a bench at the Pier Arts Centre and enjoy the sky drama.

In the evening, my visitor told me that the moon, nearing the full, had risen large and harvest-red over Orphir.

Orcadians in former centuries used to think that work always went better when the tide was flowing and the moon was rounding out. That might have been the reason why my pen all morning had flown with such fluency across page after page (and I had thought, beforehand, that it was going to be a difficult piece of work). The moon was shedding her silver increase.

Late at night, making a pot of tea, I saw through the kitchen window the brimming orb in the south... Two days to go till full moon—better pack as much work as you can into that time.

One of the rainclouds had trespassed into the Stromness sky. My visitor had come with an umbrella.

Stromness Street Names

26.9.1985

A friend from Glasgow enquired, 'Why Alfred Street?'

Alfred Street begins right under my house and goes as far as the foot of Hellihole Rd, when it becomes Dundas St.

As everyone knows, there is only one street in Stromness, but at one time or another in the past it was deemed advisable to split up our one and only, unique and remarkable street, into separate streets—possibly to make it easier for the postmen.

If memory serves me well, Alfred St was named after a son of Queen Victoria, who was Duke of Edinburgh in his day, and did his stint in the Navy—and that brought him to Orkney.

I think it was of Alfred, Duke of Edinburgh, that the then custodian of Maes Howe enquired after his mother's health—and remarked that Queen Victoria was 'a fine aald body'—and bade him be sure to tell Her Majesty that he was asking after her...

The other sections of our street present no problems, with the exception of John St. I think I may have written about this before and received no satisfactory answer. Who and what was this John, so to dignify the north part of our street?

There is of course no doubt about Victoria St. But still I think it a great shame that the original name for that part of Victoria St between Graham Place and the Coal Office should lose its fine original name, Plainstones.

Why, one wonders, was it called that? Couldn't it have been there that the first flagstones were laid, that changed our street from a winter quagmire to a river of stone?

(Concerning flagstones, I hope it is being noticed how our flagstones are being progressively eroded and broken, month after month, year after year. Where is the stone-mason who will instruct the young unemployed in the quarrying and dressing of flagstones, so that our street may be preserved and renewed?)

There is a joker in every pack—and Khyber Pass never fails to evoke exclamations of wonder and delight from the tourists—and hundreds of camera-clicks...

Mealtimes

3.10.1985

Up to the 1939–45 war, the vast majority of Orcadians recognised four mealtimes in every day: breakfast, dinner, tea, supper.

Breakfast might be porridge on winter mornings, but cornflakes were beginning to creep in, in the 30s. There was rarely an egg for breakfast, except on a Sunday morning. But I remember doing a milk round as a boy, and sniffing with pure enchantment bacon frying in the kitchen of 'a posh house' at 8.30am.

The main meal was dinner, at 1pm. No great imagination went into any dinner-time menu in the working-class homes of Orkney (or, for that matter, I'm sure, anywhere in Britain).

The food was wholesome, but boring, especially for children—variations on broths, mince, stew, fish, liver and bacon, and great quantities of tatties. Nearly always there was a pudding—rice or Creamola or (rarest of treats) an apple pie.

I am a bit confused in my memory of 'tea' at 5pm. There were floury bannocks and bere bannocks and oatcakes and bakehouse bread, together with cheese and various jams, home-made rhubarb being the commonest. But I think 'cooked tea' only came in with the war, and continued after it. But 'tea-time' on Sunday was special, for then there were all kinds of home-baked cakes and sweet biscuits. (Oh, those marvellous sponges with the raspberry jam, and the ecstasy of date-cakes!)

And supper—you held out slices of bread on a fork to the glowing ribs of the range, and had toast and cocoa. And maybe, if there were tatties left over from dinner-time, fried tatties.

* * *

We knew, from reading, that 'the gentry' in England and suchlike places had dinner in the evening; they had had 'lunch' or 'luncheon' round about midday.

Were the gentry right after all, in their eating rhythms? For now, more and more, the working classes eat their main meal in the evening. And I must say that I only begin to feel really hungry about 5 or 6pm.

The names change, too. 'Come for supper,' someone will say. And it turns out that 'supper' and 'dinner' are almost interchangeable. It is very confusing to those of us whose earliest suppers were toast and cocoa.

The Open Window

31.10.1985

There comes a depressing day, usually one morning in September, after heavy rain, when neither the bedroom nor the bathroom nor the kitchen windows will open: and then you know for sure that the summer is over, and the windows won't open again till about May.

A depressing thought. For there's a stale air in the bedroom whenever you have occasion to go into it; and in the kitchen what are you to do about the clinging smells of soup, fish, bacon, etc?... Kippers are the most delightful of meals, but I don't want everything to smell of kippers for days on end.

There came a wild wet storm on the night of 10th October; thunderous winds, crested seas, lashings of rain. And so everyone on the street went about, buffeted. 'Winter's here!'...

And the *Ola* didn't sail till the afternoon on the 11th.

You would think, from long experience, we would have known about the 'peedie summer'. The cycle of the seasons is bred in the bone, over centuries, over many generations. Like some strict musical form, it should tell us that there is a mild sweet gentle interlude before the mighty orchestrations of winter.

So it has happened, in 1985, as nearly always. About a week ago it came, sun and sweet airs, and even in the evening such mellowness you could have had an hour's conversation over a garden wall, or at the foot of a close, or over an upturned boat on a pier.

Fogs drifted over, light as gossamer, and like gossamer drifted away on a stir of air.

'Surely the windows will open this morning!' I thought after several serene days and nights. Not a chance. I heaved at it—it was obdurate. Well, even a breath of air isn't worth rupture or a heart attack.

Still another bright morning, like a diamond, to add to the precious string! The 'peedie summer' is being particularly good to us this October.

Gypsy meowed outside the bedroom door, wanting her breakfast.

I gave a forlorn tug this morning to the bottom half of the window. Up it went, and a current of sweet air poured in! Same with the bathroom window.

The world was almost as happy as Spring.

The Price of 'Civilisation'

14.11.1985

A fascinating series of programmes on TV, every Monday evening, *The Triumph of Western Civilisation*, displayed with a good commentary and fascinating photography and artwork how the western mode of living, with all its paraphernalia of progress, has permeated every corner of the globe, and modified other cultures and civilisations, like the Japanese, Chinese, Aztec, African.

Nothing has been left untouched by the questing probing European mind.

So, a working-class family today probably lives in greater comfort in its council house than a medieval baron in his damp cold draughty castle. The baron didn't have TV, an electric toaster, and a car. Nor did he know when he might be murderously assaulted in the night, either from within or without. For 'law and order' were pretty crude instruments in medieval times.

I have been dipping into the *Vinland Saga* which shows pretty conclusively that Norsemen touched the continent of North America 500 years before Columbus. From the point of view of bodily comfort, how dreadful those long sea voyages must have been a thousand years ago: soaked to the bone with storm and spindrift, rancid food, stale water, and the ever-present menace of being washed over the world's edge... In Vinland (North America) they got a foothold for a year or two, before the 'Skraelings' (Red Indians) drove them out.

In part, it was to obviate such discomforts and dangers that western civilisation took the turn it did, some time in the 17th century. The human intelligence must be freed, in some measure, from the brutish burden of flesh-and-blood.

It is nevertheless the title of the series, *The Triumph of Western Civilisation*, that one takes exception to. It is so smug and self-congratulatory.

For, how many other civilisations of great beauty and delicacy have been ruthlessly trampled on so that European ideas could dominate the world? A door has been opened to immense material ameliorations. But one door leads inevitably to another; and there is a price to be paid; and the same science that has given us the electric toaster could conceivably make of the globe a smoking cinder. And where would 'the triumph' be then?

Better Leif Ericson seeking west with his crew of grey-faced famished seamen.

Christmas in Hamnavoe, 1085

19.12.1985

In the harbour called Hamnavoe it was cold and dark and silent.

A small hamlet of wooden huts: that was Hamnavoe nine hundred winters ago. It was sheltered from the west, it had good fishing nousts but it was often a hungry place.

This Yule night it was dark and cold in the fishing hamlet. Not a glimmer of hearth-flames in any hut, not the shout or the song of a child.

If there was hunger, the Hamnavoe folk had taken their hunger to where it would be cured—across the north end of the voe and over the ridge to the little castle at Cairston where Thorkel the laird kept Yule.

Not that the poor folk of Hamnavoe would have dared show their faces at Thorkel's feast. Only the important people sat down at Thorkel's table, to cut slivers from the pig's head on the platter and have ale-horns replenished by the serving-men and girls.

The Hamnavoe fishermen and their families would have to feast in a humbler way, from the great pot of broth with chunks of ox-flesh in it, and the thin ale of the second brewing. But they were happy in the barn, especially after the piper began to get scarlet in the face with the booze and the blowing.

In a lull of the merriment, they could hear from the big hall the harp-strokes and the measured chant of the poet reciting the old poems of Thor and Balder.

And the farm children and the fishermen's children squalled and skirled and laughed by themselves, outside under the stars. The farm children broke and tasted dried sillocks, those bits of sea-silver out of summer seas, that the fisher-folk had brought.

Round the hall fire the laird and the skippers—the harp silent now—began to complain about the royal taxes and the earldom taxes—a ruination, if such burdens were to be inflicted again next year.

In the barn, the piper was drained of wind and bloated with ale. The Cairston farmfolk and the Hamnavoe fishermen spoke in anxious whispers about the rents they were charged by Thorkel the laird. No wonder he and his kind could eat venison and drink out of silver cups!

A boy entered from the night outside and let in stars and silence.

Then they heard it, a thin thread of plain chant on the midnight: the monks at Warbeth three miles away, on the shore of Hoy Sound, singing a Christmas psalm.

Bygone Hogmanay

26.12.1985

Hogmanay and New Year—it used to be a strange time for children, especially after the pure enchantment of Christmas.

We realised that New Year had little to do with children. It was a time for old folk—and everybody over thirty was old—to lose themselves in fantasy.

Stromness was 'dry' between the two wars. We boys would watch, with some puzzlement, a group of men waiting at the bus stop in the evening for Wishart's bus to come from Kirkwall with a cargo of mysterious parcels—it was the New Year whisky, wine and beer.

Round about 10pm we began to yawn—it was long past our bedtime. On this one night of the year we were permitted to stay up till midnight.

(I seem to remember that, on Hogmanay, a horde of 'guisers' in fancy dress went through the town—a few dropping in at friends' houses: Chinamen, Red Indians, Bullfighters, etc. It was a custom that seems to have died out some time in the early 30s. It was probably a remnant of the New Year song—that marvellous winter chant—that every Orkney home must have experienced for centuries.)

Suddenly, drama burst upon us! The *Pole Star*, on the stroke of midnight, sent up a whole fusillade of rockets. Every boat in the harbour blew her siren. We ran to the door to see that garden of rockets flowering in the sky. Everybody shook hands—'A Happy New Year!'

Soon after that, I suppose, we were glad enough to get to bed. In those days, most of the first-footing was done on New Year's Day. We young ones were amazed at the way the townsfolk behaved. Taciturn men were suddenly talkative, or sentimental, or amorous, or aggressive, or reminiscent, or even lachrymose. And it all had something to do with the little tots of yellow liquid in the little glasses.

In the afternoon, after the one and only roast beef dinner of the year, we went in our Sunday suits in solemn procession to the Museum kept by Mrs Lyon. The most astonishing exhibit was a lifesize wooden 'idol' brought home from the South Seas by some sailor or other.

Why Come to Orkney in Winter?

16.1.1986

What boreal magic can take Europeans to Orkney, in the depths of winter?—unless it is, perhaps, to see the sunset glow in the heart of Maes Howe round about the solstice, or that world-famous anarchic game, the Ba' in Kirkwall?

My two German visitors have gone on this morning's *Ola*, having arrived on the wretchedest day of the year, Hogmanay, in bitter cold wind and rain. Someone in the Highlands, on their way north, had told them there would be no shops open for days in Orkney, so they had taken a supply of cold food with them. And eventually Kevin and Cordula got settled in a cottage in Orphir, and got on with their work, which is writing; and they managed between times to visit Brodgar, Maes Howe, the Cathedral, the Round Church of Orphir. The Cathedral organ was playing Buxtehude, which delighted them...

'Why do you choose to come at this time of year?' I asked them wonderingly—for the wind howled and the rain lashed much of the time, and the great darkness was over the land ... 'To avoid the summer tourists,' they said.

I think it was two Christmases ago that young French friends came, Dominique and Katia. Since I had last seen them, they were married, and they had a baby with them, two months old. They had earlier mentioned a midwinter visit, but I had thought it was 'only a way of speaking'...

But here indubitably they were, all three, with not a room booked, and Orkney clad in armour of black frost. Shelter was found for them at last.

But with all the comings and goings, invitations and festivities of the season, I lost sight of them for days. Storms howled, rain lashed unmercifully. The only tranquil person I saw that midwinter was the baby, Benoît.

They all got bad colds to go home with; on the *Ola*, driving the length of Britain, a Channel crossing, another long drive to the High Alps in the south of France.

Other people have in the past mentioned the possibility of them visiting Orkney round about the solstice and after. I plead with them, for all our sakes, to bide at home till the daffodils are out and larks begin to sing.

A Fall of Snow

30.1.1986

Another blanching of snow through the bedroom window this morning—the fourth or the fifth of the winter.

It will not last. As I write this, passing noon, the rain is coming down in torrents—the fleeting whiteness will soon be gone.

Last Thursday—16 January—Stromness had no snow. Stromnessians were amazed to see cars entering the town bonneted with snow.

Cars going the other way, into Kirkwall, suddenly found themselves, between Stenness and Finstown, entering drifts of snow—it seems there was a hard demarcation line; on one side plain road, on the other side a snowtrack.

As one gets older, the snow becomes ever more of a nuisance. I think one will never lose the pure enchantment of the first-fallen snow, the transfiguration of the ordinary world, the hushed spell of frost, the islands lying out there like white whales. That first fairy-tale few days is never lost—time is finished with us, if it ever is lost—but then old folk begin to worry. 'What if a pipe bursts? What will become of me if I fall and break a leg? The electricity might fail—what about my fan-heater and TV programmes? I can feel already, in my bones, the miseries of the thaw to come! Why, this might even be the start of the next Ice Age!'...

So we old ones grumble, frayed and fretted between aftersight and foresight.

Gone are the days when we hurled snowballs at each other in the school playground, in the merry snow wars of half a century ago. We were little sculptors, building snowmen with bits of coal for eyes and buttons down the thick quilted coats. We had far more joy than any competitors in the Winter Olympics, hurtling on home-made sledges all the way from Oglaby to the foot of Hellihole, under the ringing stars!

And our breath smoked, and our eyes glittered, and our cheeks glowed like apples. And we ate great hunks of bread and jam, to quell the snow hunger. And we slept eight or nine hours out, with stone hot-water bottles at our feet. And we hoped against hope that more snow had fallen in the night, millions of tons of snow, a great white trackless oblivion—so that school next day would be cancelled.

Demanding Gypsy

13.2.1986

That otherwise delightful cat Gypsy, who has been staying with me for a week, has been driving me crazy with demands for food.

As soon as she hears me stirring in the morning, there she is waiting outside the bedroom door, faintly meowing. Then, as soon as I open the door, what a rush of affection, such deep sonorous purring out of her black throat! Then a wild tumble downstairs, and before I've drawn the curtains she is at the kitchen door, importunate and pleading. Breakfast-time!

I had been instructed in how much food to ladle out of the tin onto her plate. No gourmet on this earth goes at her food with such relish and delicacy. At last, the plate licked clean, she seems to sigh, 'Ah, delicious!...'

Then for a while she sits in the window, alertly watching the life of Stromness below; the shoppers coming and going at the little shop, but I think she's especially interested in the neighbourhood cats and the poor hungry birds of winter.

All this time, I'm writing away at the kitchen table.

But if I go next door, to consult a book maybe, Gypsy loses all interest in the world outside. With a soft thud she is down on the floor, and flowing rapidly into the kitchen—she needs more food!

I ought to know better. I ought to send her about her business till her proper mealtime. But even a heart of stone might pity that yearning pleading look. Another dollop of catfood—rabbit, beef and heart, chicken, liver—is emptied onto her plate. Having devoured the second breakfast, Gypsy might retire to the rocking-chair for a snooze, dreaming maybe of goldfish and birds-of-paradise.

But she's aware of the least movement round the kitchen door. That means: more food.

Yesterday she overdid it. Weary of her clamour in the late afternoon, I opened a tin of lamb. She ate it, rather slowly, I thought. Then, ten minutes later, I went through to see to the fire, and Gypsy had been sick on the rug! A disgusting performance. She seemed ashamed of herself.

Half an hour later I was having my own supper. She appeared, coyly, at my elbow. 'Have you a trifle to spare?' She devoured, with exquisite delicacy, bits of cold meat from my fingers, and later, at supper time, a trifle disdainfully, fragments of cheese.

Then she curled into sleep in the rocker for the night.

Origins: Nothing for our Comfort

27.3.1986

We used to think of scientists and mathematicians as, apart from their one speciality, being desiccated unimaginative creatures.

Of late years we are having to revise our ideas quite a bit.

Paradoxically, it is 'the priests of the imagination', the artists, who seem to be dry and cold.

My friend from Oxford (Hugo Brunner) and myself were a bit late in switching on Jonathan Miller's long TV programme called *Origins* last night; having had a nice meal (with Guinness) in the Ferry Inn.

At once we were plunged into a far more fantastical realm than *Alice in Wonderland* or Hieronymus Bosch. Jonathan Miller was trying to explain to us where it all came from, the galaxies, the elements we move through with all other living things, the atoms that are inconceivably small and yet as complex in their way as the galaxies.

But this programme was only an interim report, what science has found out, to date. Perhaps it is only a scratching of the surface. But, even so, it is sufficiently extraordinary and weird and wonderful. We are asked to swallow incredible things, compared to which the miracles of some medieval saints are straightforward bits of common sense.

The screen was filled, from time to time, with mathematical equations of bewildering complexity. One or other of these might be a clue that leads a step closer to the heart of the mystery.

Mystery it must remain, especially to a layman. But some mysteries are comforting; these latter-day ones have nothing for our comfort at all.

The universe began, we are told, with 'a big bang', and the explosion is still going on, the galaxies are flying apart from each other at speeds that the mind cannot take in.

But the layman is still entitled to ask, 'But what was there before the "big bang"?' The mind is so constituted as to demand, perhaps stupidly, what in the 18th century was called 'a First Cause'...

Perhaps best not to torment ourselves with overmuch speculation. The mind was made for the homespun of story and myth, not over-complex aridities.

We had a late dram beside the fire—matters which the human frame can understand and enjoy.

Assiepattle and the Stoor-Worm

10.4.1986

There's more to fairy-tales than just a little whimsy and fancifulness, a bit of narrative to send a bairn to sleep at bedtime.

I'm quite sure that many of them must have been attempts, on the part of a whole tribe or people, to come to terms with some difficult perplexing situation.

This struck me the other day when I was trying to tell over again one of the very old Orkney myths, the one about 'Assiepattle and the Stoor-worm'. (It is to be one of a series that will form the text of a book of drawings, etchings, prints, etc, to be called *A Scottish Bestiary*.)

A certain Kingdom in the north was threatened by the Stoor-worm, an unimaginably huge and ferocious monster. Unless seven maidens were delivered to it daily, as food, the Stoor-worm would destroy the kingdom. At last Stoor-worm tired of this diet. The King's daughter must be delivered by a certain date. East and west, north and south, the King's couriers rode, looking for a hero to vanquish Stoor-worm. If such a one appeared, he would have the princess for his wife.

There was a lazy dreamy creature of a farmer's boy called Assiepattle (because he was always beside the fire).

Assiepattle rode to the shore off which Stoor-worm lay. He lit a torch and set out in a small boat. When the beast yawned, in rowed Assiepattle at his open jaw, and down his gullet, and he thrust the torch into the oily liver. Stoor-worm burned internally, in a great blazing magnificence of pain. In his death agony, the heat of his forked tongue created the sea channel between Norway and Sweden. He cast his teeth thrice—Orkney and Shetland and Faroe. What's left of his liver smoulders on in the volcanoes of Iceland.

And so the layabout, the dreamer, became King in due course...

This myth must have come out of some terrible peril that threatened a North European tribe in an age before recorded history.

These dangers are a constant—and perhaps were never so real as today, when nuclear extinction hangs over the whole human race.

It is never the men of force and power who solve those problems. Ulysses the cunning one found the way into Troy. Assiepattle, 'the no-good', killed the Stoor-worm.

Might it not be that only a pure exercise of the imagination can reconcile us to the terrible equation $E=mc^2$?

The Child, the Eagle and the Mother

8.5.1986

I remember, a long time ago, reading in our Primary textbooks at school the story of the child, the eagle and the mother.

It is one of those stories that live on in the memory, a bit faded maybe, when all the other stories in that textbook are completely forgotten.

This story must have taken place at harvest-time, maybe two centuries ago. The men were cutting the corn, the women following, gathering and binding the sheaves. One of the women had an infant, and she had laid it in the shelter of a stook while she worked.

Suddenly there was a great commotion in the air, a stoop and threshing of wings, and the harvesters looked up to see an eagle flying off to its eyrie with something white in its talons. At first they thought it must be a lamb. But when the woman looked behind the stook for her child, it had vanished.

The people must have known where the eagle's nest was.

I seem to remember that it was the young mother herself who climbed the hill to the eyrie, fought off the fierce bird, and took her child out of the nest—and so, perilously, down and home.

(I have read somewhere, since, that it was the men who got the child back—but somehow I like better the version of the woman doing it by herself—it is somehow more humanly and artistically satisfying.)

It was so long ago that we read the story in the classroom that I remember being very impressed when somebody of the older generation said that the events of the story actually happened in Hoy. Imagine that—a story in a book actually happening next door, so to speak! For we lived in the light of common day—stories only happened in magical places under the horizon.

Last summer I mentioned this story to a young man who is a poet and ornithologist. He was very sceptical at the idea of a golden eagle—for I had somehow convinced myself that the thief was a golden eagle—being able to carry off a child.

I was turning over the pages of Barry's *History* the other evening, and there—in his fascinating Nature section—Barry mentions the story as happening in Orkney, right enough.

Caged Dragons

15.5.1986

The recent nuclear 'incident' in Russia, horrifying as it is, and full of menace for the future, might yet be of some use if it gives us pause to sit and consider our part in the whole web of creation.

For three centuries now 'science' and 'progress' have been the abstractions to which most people give their allegiance.

Most of human ingenuity, imagination and endeavour has in the past three centuries been devoted to what we complacently call 'the conquest of nature'—a pathetic and arrogant phrase, if ever there was one.

And the great majority of mankind have willingly gone along with the scientists, 'the priests of progress'. Haven't the scientists proved over and over again, during the past five or six generations, that they can deliver the goods? They have made life easier for all of us. A modern working-man is probably surrounded with more comforts of a physical kind than a medieval king.

We can span the globe in search of holidays in the sun or the snow. Many of the diseases that scourged mankind in the past have been eliminated. (True, there are always new woes of the flesh slipping in here and there, like AIDS.) But the horizons before us seemed boundless. There seemed no end to the benefits that 'conquered nature' would bestow on us. Until, a few days ago, something broke down in a nuclear plant in the Ukraine, and the wind began to blow clouds of poisonous dust here and there over the whole globe.

'Nothing to be really worried about,' we are assured, over and over. But on the radio, this morning (8 May), it seems they are having more trouble in quenching the nuclear fires than was at first thought. The dragon is still astir and roaring.

Hundreds of caged dragons (nuclear power stations) lie here and there about the continents. How strong are the cages?

One begins—I hope not too late—to feel more and more sympathy with 'the green parties' that are trying to ease their way into political power, and with Friends of the Earth.

It is time, maybe, to think that we have gone far enough in 'the conquest of nature', and to think of nature rather as our faithful and kindly and much-abused mother. There are still the sun, the waters, and the wind, that have never failed us. Is it beyond the wit and daring of the scientists to co-operate with nature, for the benefit of all created things—animals and plants as well as human beings?

Perhaps the cost will have to be a considerable drop in the standard of living, for a long, long time. And even that, when you think about it, may be no bad thing either.

Never Cast a Clout

5.6.1986

'Never cast a cloot / Till May be oot'... is that rhyme or spell still said on the streets and roads of Orkney?

There comes a day in May when one begins to feel the burden of the winter clothes: the thermal underwear and thick jerseys. There is a longing for the freedom of lighter things. The rhyme must be centuries old; and must have been begotten of experience. For those who 'cast a cloot' early in May may have a few shivering days before the month is out.

I've heard it said that the May in the rhyme doesn't refer to the month at all, but to the mayflower, the primrose. When the mayflower comes out in ditch and bank, then summer is round the corner; it's time to shed the heavy coat of winter.

Always it surprises us, the sudden rise in temperature, which sets in well before May. I can always tell by the butter at breakfast time. That yellow stone on the dish, that you have to carve hard chunks out of to spread on the toast—quite suddenly the knife glides through it, it yields gently, it spreads its brightness evenly over the toast.

Quite suddenly, too, the grate doesn't devour coal like a ravenous dragon. A couple of shovels will do, of an evening. The coal bunker is full to overflowing.

You and the coal man agree—there'll be no need of a bag of coal next week...

But always the most dramatic change is in the light. Suddenly the long darkness is up and away: or rather, it confines itself to the few hours round about midnight. For a week or two, the late spring light can be disconcerting and upsetting. What has happened to the delightful darkling hour or two with a book, or listening to Mahler on a tape? The sun is shining at 8pm—one ought to be outside. The TV set in the corner loses much of its compulsion.

One of the glories of winter is the visiting moon. From October to March we northerners see her in all her unfolding and fading glory: the sickle, the axe-blade, the full sphere, the wilting blossom, the cinder. The summer sun banishes, almost, the moon. But not quite. The other night, going to bed, there through the window was 'the queen and huntress' with her full silver orb.

And suddenly too, the heavy winter quilt on the bed is too much. Last night the weight of it kept me off sleep for an hour and more. It's time to search the cupboard for the lighter summer 'downie'.

World Cup Football

12.6.1986

People watch snooker on TV—old ladies and children—who have never been inside a billiard hall in their lives. And the names of the snooker stars are more familiar than the folk who live at the end of the street.

The season of snooker is only recently past. There is something fascinating about the game: the absolute precision required. The slight subtle touch of ball on ball; the wild foray that sets them in a scatter, helter-skelter, all over the green baize table. The moving colours themselves fascinate the eye. There is the inexorable escalation of a big 'break', and the miss by a whisker that can bring a 'frame' down in ruins about a player's head.

It is exciting and soothing at the same time...

Some time—I forget when, because I don't like watching it—falls the season of darts.

But these days it is all football—the World Cup—from Mexico. Football enthusiasts are in the midst of an enormous banquet; which would be even more sumptuous if Mexican TV was holding up well under the strain. But there have been severe technical troubles, in the early stages at least.

What chauvinism it causes, that World Cup! How the expectations of the multitudinous fans of (I suppose) every competing nation, are built up, often on slender bases, by the media... One image throbs in the memory from eight years ago, in Argentina—Ally MacLeod the Scottish manager with his head drooped in his hands, in silent anguish...

And tonight (4 June) the Scots play again, against Denmark. Thank goodness, we are taking things more modestly and soberly this time. Any defeat will not be equivalent to the Battle of Flodden.

But, compared to fifty years ago, what an incredibly rich banquet for football-mad boys! Then we kicked a ball about in some park or other, with coats for goalposts, most summer evenings and every Saturday. But Saturday afternoon was a special time, for then there was a football commentary from Ibrox or Pittodrie. In the early 1930s, we listened, headphones clamped to ears, to the merest whisper of a voice, and far off, rising and falling, the roar of the crowd... It was a great miracle, though we could only follow the course of the game with great difficulty.

In the mid-30s came the loudspeakers, and that was an immense improvement. Scotland v England, at Hampden or Wembley, was the greatest drama that could be imagined!

(We had been born just too early for the 'Wembley Wizards' of 1928.)

To have witnessed that, on colour TV, would have been (for us boys) to live an immortal hour.

Festival-Time

3.7.1986

Yesterday (Johnsmas Day, 24 June) was one of those brilliant days that we automatically think of whenever 'midsummer' is mentioned—but we only get the overbrimming blue and gold once in five years, maybe, at Johnsmas.

And why is 24 June midsummer, when, as everyone knows, the longest day is 21 June? I suppose, for the same reason that we celebrate Christmas on 25 December rather than three or four days earlier, at the solstice.

Having lunched at the 'Hamnavoe', Peter Grant and I drove leisurely round parts of the West Mainland. Larks above, and the newly shorn fields that make such vivid yellow patches on the hillside. There was a faint bloom of sea-haar on the horizon, harbinger of good weather. But soon the haar thickened into a thick bank over Hoy—it stirred, heaved silently, and came pouring and swirling into Stromness, driven by a rising east wind. When finally I got home, the half-gale had come howling so fiercely through the open bedroom window, it had lifted the lino and I could only get the door open with difficulty.

We have had a few late nights this week, at Festival-time.

There's something specially delicious about a drowse in the late afternoon. One is not in a deep sleep: time drifts through the brain like muted music.

After a pie out of a tin and peas and new tatties (Egyptian), it was time to be in the car and on the road again, bound for the Phoenix and *The Lighthouse*. It is a powerful piece of opera, sure enough, marvellously sung against the stark textures of the orchestra, with the Flannan light flashing from time to time and the foghorn blorting. The tragedy happened in the midwinter of 1900.

So many old and new friends to speak to, lingering afterwards outside the door of the theatre. That is half the joy of Festival-time.

It was still light. The horizon was still hazy with haar, but the wind had blown the dome of the sky clear.

It was Johnsmas night, midsummer. A century and a half ago, in Orkney, the country folk would still be recovering from the all-night fire festival. A hundred fiddles would be hanging silent on the walls. The farmer who had cleansed his field by walking round it with a blazing torch would be looking at his green corn with more confidence. On fifty hilltops all over the islands there were only the black ashes of another Johnsmas celebration.

Rackwick Holiday (1)

24.7.1986

We are getting near the end of a week-long holiday in Rackwick, Hoy.

There is an almost infinite variety in this sea valley. Every day is different from what went before and the following day. Rackwick, beyond any other place in Orkney, keeps its own astonishing weather. Or rather, every day is a little book of weathers, and the pages keep turning.

Yesterday morning, from the Mucklehouse above the shore, we agreed that it looked like rain. So, we thought of rubber boots, or maybe a day indoors with books and writing-paper.

By lunch-time—and this place sharpens the appetite marvellously—there were patches of blue showing through the grey over the Pentland Firth. Then the sun was out, the valley was all joyous dancing colour and freshness.

The two collies, Glen and Snoopy, ran here and there and barked with sheer delight. (In general, I have no great liking for dogs, but I've never known such delightful dogs as dapple-fawn-coloured Glen and black-and-white Snoopy.)

The nine geese go here and there in a tight little company, and Sid the gander stretches his neck and hisses if you come too close.

A starling chirrs all day long, in the eaves, and brings worms to her hidden brood. And one morning, very early, she found a fissure in the ceiling and fluttered about in Alan Grant's room; but then, fortunately, she went out by the way she had entered.

The wet floor of the valley is covered with bog cotton, and the yellow iris are out, and the wild roses. Some day soon Betty Grant will pick some wild flowers to lay on Betty Corrigall's lonely grave between the two parishes of North Hoy and Walls. A few weeks ago, she met by chance at a railway station in Glasgow a woman, a stranger, who had been reading the sad story of Betty Corrigall in a book. This woman's own young daughter had died very recently. She asked Betty Grant to lay flowers on Betty Corrigall's grave.

It would be possible to write a hundred pages about this marvellous place. Our next-door neighbour, David Hutchison, would need twenty pages all to himself. Perhaps we can say a few more things about Rackwick next week.

Rackwick Holiday (2)

31.7.1986

I never remember being on the road to Braebuster, Hoy, before. We went by car from Rackwick one fine afternoon. We are familiar with the look of Ward Hill and the Coolags from Stromness. Weird it is, and a bit frightening, to see them twisted out of shape from this new angle: the Ward a looming cone with a deep cleft in it, Coolags and Kame flung out wildly to the West.

And there suddenly, below us in Hoy Sound, was the *Ola*, outward bound. On this fine day, her bows were plunging deep in, as she rode the blue surge (where Hoy Sound, Pentland Firth and Atlantic mingle).

Returning, we visited the Hoy Kirkyard. If you have a taste for such places—and I do—it is one of the most lyrical God's-acres in Orkney. How many generations of the nameless dead, reaching far back beyond the tombstones, lie here? How old is the roofless kirk, flourishing inside with all the sweet wild tangled growth of midsummer?

Such acres of bog cotton this summer—such profusion of wild red roses! And curlews calling. And peat-cutters in the moss, with heaps of coloured plastic bags near the cuttings.

Two days later, and all was changed. The wind from the South had got up in the night. Grey clouds, half rain, half haar, muffled the hill tops. The hills of Rackwick seemed to conspire together, like old women keening for a death.

The bay below Mucklehouse was a smother of white. No boat, a century ago, could have fished out of Rackwick on such a day. The waves came in in wide curving crests, and flung themselves high up the beach. I watched the wild scene for a while, from David Hutchison's sea-facing window.

In the evening, the storm moderated a little. When at last I stood outside to take the air, while Peter and Betty and Alan walked up to the phone box, there over Moorfea was a little gleam of blue, precious as an opal, but more transient.

Inside, I lit the paraffin lamp and managed to draft the chorus of a St Magnus play, one of several choruses I sketched in Rackwick. There seems to be no place like it for setting the images free, in a lucent ordered flow. That work done, I felt I had earned some sleep.

But, before bed, we had a drink and told a few stories till away beyond midnight.

Next day we packed and sailed home on the *Geira*.

Giant Hogweed

14.8.1986

No wonder the neighbours must have been tired of my drying-green, stuck in an odd corner of the Mayburn scheme. It has never been used these eighteen years. Every summer a forest of hogweed grows there, dense and luxuriant. In the shade of those poisonous plants, slugs and snails breed and proliferate, and venture out on piratical raids on the well-kept gardens round about. And cats hide there, when they want to meditate for a while, unseen.

This summer, for some reason, the hogweed jungle has flourished tall and strong and sinister as never before. I would look at it from time to time in passing, and shake my head in utter bafflement. A scythe, sprayings of weed-killer—these were called for; but I did little about it.

Then one day this week my friend from Ayr, Brian Murray, who spends all his summers in Orkney, arrived at my house with a large garden fork and a parcel of black plastic bags, and said he would like to tackle the dense hogweed jungle. He sounded like one of those medieval knights-at-arms who calmly volunteers to enter a forest of dark enchantment. Once Brian makes up his mind to do a job, there's no use raising objections... I retired to bed for a couple of hours in the late afternoon, thinking guiltily of how I was spoiling a good man's holiday.

When I looked in later, half the forest was felled. Hundreds of black snails, bewildered by the light, had taken themselves off. We refreshed ourselves with a pint or two of lager.

Next day was crystal calm and clear, except for one magnificent thunderhead over Hoy that was emptying curtains of rain over Scapa Flow and the South Isles.

In two or three hours in the early evening the last of the hogweed jungle was uprooted. A dozen black bags held the once-mighty weeds. The black-and-white tailless cat from next door didn't know what to make of the sudden clearance. The black snails were a defeated and dispersed army. How many roses and lettuces would now be left in peace!

There on the low wall sat Brian, triumphant, eating the last of a cheese sandwich and drinking the dregs of his tea from a flask.

I'm sure all the neighbours were relieved. I was able to report next morning to the Housing Department in Kirkwall that the dark enchanted forest had vanished from Mayburn—for the time being, at least.

To Yesnaby as Evenings Draw in

28.8.86

Now summer is hastening to an end. The evenings 'draw in', as the old folk used to say. There is, sometimes, an eager nip in the air.

And yet, as if to compensate us that the height of summer is past, we have been rewarded with a week of magnificent skies: great shifting segments of deepest blue, enormous silver-grey clouds that drop, here and there, bounties of rain.

My friend from Germany who used to live in Egilsay, Michael Krauskopf, arrived two evenings ago. 'Would you like to walk to Yesnaby?' said he. I never much like walking anywhere, so I said 'No' at once. However, we would drive to Yesnaby in his borrowed car.

I asked, would he not like to view Stromness from the top of Downie's Lane—that road that peters out in a track not far below the summit of Brinkie's Brae? So there we drove. The growing skirt of Stromness, clustered about the inner voe, was spread beneath us. Through the Finstown Gap, eastward, a glimmer of sea...

Then on, in the direction of Yesnaby. Would MK not like to see Mousland, on the far side of the Black Craig, which he'd never seen? The car turned up the road marked 'Cauldhame'—and then there must have been some confusion, I must have directed MK along the wrong road; for we found ourselves in the Loons, near the Waterworks. Surely MK would like to see Stromness reservoir for the first time? It is a beautiful desolate place, the little artificial loch that supplies Stromness with its water. A raincloud hid the sun—the surface was a pewter sheen.

This time, nothing must keep us from Yesnaby. 'I like this road very much,' said MK, as we drove towards the ugly remnants of that wartime naval gunnery range. It would have been a magnificent sunset, except that two querns of solid black cloud crushed the sun. Far out over the Atlantic we could see a slow-moving curtain of rain, and a thicker wedge of rain.

There was still an hour's light in the sky. It might be pleasant to sit with a lager and sandwich at The Braes, and watch night coming down. Alas, there were no sandwiches, but we had lager and crisps.

Flotta flourished its flare, and the lights came on in the little oil island.

There, over Orphir, stood the full moon. The moon, that is one of the glories of our winter, tends to be ignored in the late bright skies of summer. The great cloud continents hid, too, most of the stars.

The Gairsay Viking

11.9.1986

When you pass the little island of Gairsay, driving along the straight Rendall road, you wonder how Sweyn Asleifson could have kept all those retainers all winter long, in 'the long hall'.

But it happened, year after year. As soon as the fields were ploughed and sowed, the longship was out of its shed, new-caulked, with maybe a new patch or two on the one big square sail. There might have been a farewell supper. Then, one morning when wind and tide agreed well, Sweyn's ship was out and away—through Eynhallow Sound, maybe, or The String.

Then, while the corn rooted, when showed the first green braird, Gairsay was an island of women. There were a few old men, too feeble for plunder and piracy now, and children making bird-cries down at the shore among the sea-birds. The boys and girls caught a few sillocks off the rocks. The old men set creels here and there, off Rousay. So it was, all summer long.

But women dominated the island: often arguing (it might even come to hair-tearing, now and again), singing seal songs and corn songs; tending to cows and swine and sheep; making butter and cheese; brewing a special strong ale for Sweyn's homecoming. Sweyn always came home. A few oarsmen might come home wanting an eye, or some fingers, or hirpling on a crutch, but Sweyn always came home whole and laughing. He was growing old, and feebler than he used to be, but he always came home with silver and bolts of fine broadcloth... Nearly always, one place on a thwart was empty—a young shepherd or ploughman had been drowned, or killed by an Irish arrow.

The corn rose green into wind and sun.

The long summer weeks passed. The corn began to take a first burnish.

It was then that, increasingly, the women began to turn their eyes from the embroidery frames and the cheese-making, to the sea.

178

Still there was no sign of the sail.

Sweyn had promised not to go on another spring cruise. The autumn cruise, after harvest—he promised the Earl that that would be his last voyage out of Gairsay. After that old age, the winter fires, a quiet 'straw-death'.

Ah, there was the ship, bearing home, keeping well clear of the Eynhallow roost! And there, at the helm, sat the old skipper.

That August, there was a great home-coming feast in Gairsay, and a sharing of the spoils.

Then the sickles were in the ripe corn, dawn to sunset.

When the harvest was gathered in, Sweyn set out on his last harrying. But this time Sweyn did not come home to preside over the Yule board.

The citizens of Dublin, tired of Vikings, had lured Sweyn into a trap. And there they put swords into him. Perhaps—such was the mentality of those medieval Orcadians—Sweyn was glad enough of that.

Starting Secondary School

18.9.1986

It was not an entirely doleful day, going back to the school at the age of twelve.

After the lightness and freedom of bare feet all summer, to put on stockings and boots and clump about in them, gave you a certain dignity and importance.

Besides, we were moving from the Primary to the Secondary. New mysteries were about to be unfolded to us: geometry, Latin, science.

Instead of one teacher, we were to have several teachers, and between periods we shifted from one classroom to another. Imagine that!

Our primary class was shorn in two—an 'A' section and a 'B' section. The 'A' section contained potential academics, but more likely clerks and shop assistants. The 'B' section turned to learning handicrafts and gardening. Looking back, the 'B' section seems to have been the better bet.

So we ran quite eagerly in answer to the bell that first morning.

There was an initiation ceremony to be undergone by the boys, called 'dumping'. Two louts some years older than yourself seized you by wrists and ankles and dumped you on the ground several times. It could be quite a painful experience. Then you were beyond doubt a member of 'the Higher Grade'.

I think we must have had new school-bags, to hold all the textbooks. Sternly we were told that all textbooks had to be covered with brown paper, at home, without delay. The textbooks had been passed down through several years. The names of the scholars who had had them before you were written on the fly-leaves.

I opened a Latin grammar and was struck into dumb dismay by the 'cases' and 'declensions'. What kind of a language was this? How had the ancient Romans ever got their tongues round the words? *Mensa*, a table. Fancy calling a table by such a weird name!

We had lost half our class, but there was an intake of twelve-year-old boys and girls from all over the West Mainland and South Isles. We could not help but notice how well-behaved they were, compared to us Stromnessians.

Mapmakers' Mess
9.10.86

What a mess the old mapmakers, and others, have made of our fine place-names!

Last week I got a welcome letter from North Ronaldsay—and it struck me, just when and how did that island lose its original name, Rinansay? For it was a beautiful name.

Tourists have visited me this summer from 'Papa Westray'—an extraordinary name to give a unique island, still called by the inhabitants Papay ('Island of the Celtic fathers'). I think it may not be too late for the islanders to get up a petition to have the rightful name restored. The island isn't, after all, a little offshoot of Westray.

Some of the names that soldiers and airmen applied during the war are still used—e.g. Skeabrae, of which the old venerable pronunciation was something like 'Skay-braa', I've been told. There was, I think in Flotta, a war-time battery that the soldiers called Stanger, correctly enough; but they used the hard 'g'. They may, in fact, inadvertently, have stumbled on the truth; since the original was, presumably, 'Stanigar'... somehow or other in the lost centuries the Orcadians had consented to the soft 'g'.

The power of the printed word carried immense authority a few centuries ago, when printing was new, and the names of places were being taken out of the mouths of the people and set down, apparently authoritatively, on maps and in documents. 'Waas', for example, in Hoy. Some Scottish cartographer quickly came to the conclusion that that was the vulgar pronunciation of the true name Walls. Down it went on the map. And the people of South Hoy woke up one morning to find themselves living in a parish with a new name ... it was the same with the folk of Kirkwall.

This erosion has been going on constantly. The biggest island in Orkney was, in Norse times 'the island of the horse'... Some wretched bureaucrat, probably a Scotsman at the time of the impignoration[1], thought it might be best to call it Mainland: he couldn't get his tongue round 'Hrossey', in any case.

We Stromnessians ought to be glad we're not living in 'Shoreside', a name we were once threatened with.

The Eventide Club

16.10.1986

On the very verge of being an old-age pensioner, I took shelter from a driving smirr of rain on Monday forenoon in the Eventide Club at the Pierhead. Really I had no right to be there, for there were still eleven days to go. But seeing I was so close to the admittance age, I thought nobody would take umbrage. I didn't want to get soaked through, and maybe die of pneumonia before the time.

Really, it's a nice place, the Eventide Club. Comfortable chairs to sit in, at a fine fire to keep the peedie room warm on a cold afternoon. Piles of magazines to read: *National Geographic, Newsweek, Reader's Digest*, etc.

There's a darts board, but I don't suppose we of the rheumy eyes and shaky hands would be much good at darts. But old men can still enjoy a game of draughts or dominoes. We oldsters have much more childish glee in winning games than younger folk; not altogether a good sign.

I'm glad to say there's no TV or radio as yet. Let not any kind-hearted benefactor think of bequeathing such disturbers of the peace. Old men are glad of silence, after so many years of noise—either that, or to hear themselves talking, preferably about the great exploits of their youth, when beer was sixpence a pint and a 2lb loaf cost fourpence.

If it so chances that a member gets drowsy in the club, he can boil the kettle and make himself a cup of coffee. Or he can wash his face at the wash-basin, if he has forgotten to do it before breakfast.

A toilet? There is one almost as old as Hamnavoe, certainly a lot older than himself, just round the corner.

Over the mantelpiece hangs a panoramic view of Stromness, Scapa Flow, Orphir, Hoy, Graemsay, and the Sound, by the late George S. Robertson, who showed what was possible for old men to achieve when he took up painting after his retirement.

I tell you, when we old chaps have done our shopping, we might be glad to lay our bag down and have a cup of coffee in that delightful room that looks out onto the very hub of the town.

1. Norway's impignoration, or pawning, of Orkney to Scotland was in 1468.

Flying to Turnhouse

13.11.1986

If one has not flown in a plane for a time, it is natural I suppose to be a bit apprehensive. Especially if there has been a wild tempest from the west the day before; and this present day of flying is not that much better.

My friend Ian MacInnes drove me to the airport. Drinking tea, we saw a plane from Shetland coming in to land. A squall of rain met the travellers as they disembarked; they struggled, coat collars up, into the shelter.

A little plane took off for Stronsay and possibly Eday—another for Westray.

And then, at 2 o'clock, it was time to go. Once boarded, I had trouble with the safety-belt—which was only to be expected as I always have trouble with contraptions.

The plane was full and was bound for Aberdeen, Edinburgh, and Birmingham. The filthy weather flaunted itself over Orkney, with bits of flung sunshine here and there, and the fragment of a rainbow.

The engines roared into life and grew to a steady intense pitch of sound. And, after the preliminary canter along the runway, suddenly we were up and off. The plane eased itself higher and higher, and surged singing through the cloud-mass into blue sky and dazzling sun. Below, through rents in the cloud, we could see 'the wrinkled sea'.

Soon, the pilot's voice announcing that we were crossing the Buchan coast. The untidy cloud carpet below shredded thin. The rich checkered straths of Aberdeenshire lay below now, in full sun. Soon we were bouncing gently onto a runway at Dyce.

What a vast transformation there, since I last flew! It is like a huge bazaar of shops and bars and cafés—and so many people in transit! I all but lost myself in that vast labyrinth, and had to ask my way back to the starting-place.

As it happened, there was a delay of twenty minutes or so—'a technical fault'. Forty minutes later, in the growing darkness of Hallow-E'en, we touched down at Turnhouse.

(I almost forgot to say, we were 'frisked' at Dyce by a security man. The only dangerous thing I was carrying was a little pewter spirit-flask—and they let that go...)

Return to Rose Street

20.11.1986

One remembers always, having lived there for six years, what a beautiful city Edinburgh is. But each time one goes back, the full vividness and grandeur of the city flow over again, like a half-forgotten tide returning.

There was a succession of cold clear days when I was there, and it was a delight just to walk around here and there (but never *too* far, for walking isn't my hobby).

Many things have changed in twenty-five years, but mainly small ephemeral things, like the buses and the shop-fronts—that noble skyline in the afternoon winter light can never be changed (at least we may hope not).

The traffic is frightening, to someone coming suddenly from Orkney. I would huddle among a flock of waiting people on the pavement, and then when I saw them beginning to surge across the street, I went with them like a sheep. Alone, I would have stood there till I was a statue...

Then I discovered that when you board a bus, you must have the exact fare. There are no longer conductors to give you change, and advise you and chide you if they think you're going over-far for threepence. So one spends a great deal of time in small shops handing over pound notes in the hope of getting plenty of change for the driver-conductor.

The trees were in their autumn colours—very lovely to a treeless islander. Every little gust of wind sent a swirl of red or yellow sere leaves about the pavements, rustling.

I was curious to see Rose Street and the pubs where many of us spent happy evenings in the late 1950s. The Abbotsford was one of the 'poets' pubs' then—a very handsome Victorian bar, quite unchanged except that the bar-persons are women, nearly all of them. My friend Paddy Hughes and I had lunch there one day, and glasses of 'real ale'. Another delectable tavern was Milne's Bar, two hundred yards along Rose Street. It now calls itself 'the poets' pub', and is hung with pictures of all the Scottish bards of a generation ago; but inside it is changed utterly, all modernised and facelifted; but fragrant still with the ghosts of dead poets—MacDiarmid, Goodsir Smith, Campbell Hay, Garioch.

Midwinter Festival Revived

18.12.1986

'Christmas is abolished!' said the Cromwellian colonel to the lairds and ministers assembled. 'There is to be no more of those foolish fiddlings and feastings in the middle of winter. Life is real, life is earnest. You'd think those poor people of Orkney would know that, without having to be told. Tell them, from now on it's work as usual on that day!'

So the lairds of every parish told the grieves and the grieves told the crofters and the fisher-folk. Also the ministers announced it on the following Sunday from every pulpit.

The women were even more angry than the men. The Yuletide ale had been, for a week, briskly fermenting, and they were just about to bake the little sun-cakes that were eaten by the whole family, with joy and solemnity, every Christmas morning.

As for the men, Christmas was the very happiest day of the year for them, when all their year-long comings and goings and drudgery were caught up into the joyous reel of the fiddlers.

As for the children, Christmas was an experience so mysterious and beautiful that their lips trembled to think of it even...

There was no question of any work being done that day, let Cromwell's colonel say what he liked.

(Across the hills in midwinter moved the trows in dark hordes under the stars, thousands of them. To do a single stroke of work, at that season, would be to invite the trows into the houses, secretly, to steal away their beautiful children.)

There was an old man who lived by himself in the hills. I think he must have been a sailor at one time. Anyway, he could read his few books by lamplight. He turned the pages, and discovered an ancient manuscript that described a very old Celtic midwinter festival called 'Hogmanay'.

The old sailor went from croft to croft telling the women that their ale hadn't been brewed in vain. He told the fiddlers to get their music ready. He told the children they could laugh and get presents after all (though, to be sure, it wouldn't be as beautiful and blessed a time as Christmas).

So the islands rejoiced, a week late, for a century or two to come.

Disaster at Hogmanay

1.1.1987

When we were boys in the 1930s, Stromness was a 'dry' town—there were no pubs or clubs or licensed grocers.

We were curious, on the last day of the year, to observe a group of citizens waiting anxiously near Wishart's shop on the evening of 31 December. What on earth could they be expecting there, at that time of night?

They could only be waiting for the last bus from Kirkwall. Presently it drew up, and then a stir of excitement went through the waiting townsmen.

I can't remember whether buses had 'boots' in those times, but anyway the bus seemed to be carrying a most precious cargo. One by one the Stromness men bore their parcels away.

The parcels contained, of course, bottles of whisky, or maybe crates of beer or stout. So, Stromness was sure of this little rivulet of merriment at least, after the New Year came in. (Some difference to today's torrents, cataracts, and waterfalls.)

Never did Stromness men tread the stone streets and closes so carefully, going between bus and doorstep. You might think they were carrying silks of Cathay or doubloons from the Spanish Main. No wonder: for each bottle of 'Johnny Walker' or 'Crawford's Three Star' cost twelve shillings and sixpence—a very large sum of money in those days—a quarter of a working man's weekly wage—maybe £25, translated into modern currency.

There were heart-rending stories of men stumbling in the dark, and the Hogmanay parcel falling out of their arms, and after the tiny crash of breaking glass, a stream flowing down 'the Syre[1]'; and a most rich and powerful scent of the quintessence of corn lingered in the air for a second or two, before a darkling breeze of the dying year bore it away.

And that was all the man got for his quarter-week's wage! And maybe his bairns at home were crying for a crust, and gathering their thin coats around them as the wind of the New Year bit with a sharp tooth...

Sledging

15.1.1987

Maybe Orkney will be snow-covered by the time this appears, but this early Thursday afternoon the air is silver-grey and still, and hushed, as if waiting for something. I think it was usually on a day like this, in my childhood, that the old folk used to say, 'It's a bed for snow.'

Then, as a most delightful gift to us youngsters, the magical white flakes began to drift down from the grey skies, fast and silent. And an old one would say, 'Old Mother Carey's plucking her chickens.' Then the old folk retreated, grumbling, to their firesides. To them the snow was a nuisance and a danger and a blood-thinner. (Maybe it reminded them of their latter end.)

To the children of Stromness the first snow ushered in a week or so of pure enchantment.

---

1. open drain

First of all, sledges had to be dug out from under the stairs and from garden sheds, and the cobwebs dusted off. The steel runners were all rusty; but not for long.

The favourite sledge-run was from Oglaby down past St Peter's Manse and the Braes and Kirkness' blacksmith yard and the Library to the street. This went on all day, beyond early sunset and the first star, till the sky above was ringing with stars in the ink-blue night, and even the toughest sledger was exhausted with all that silver excitement, followed by the long trudge back to Oglaby gate—time after time.

Meantime the old folk heaped the coal on their fires, and lit their paraffin lamps, and tried to forget about the silent drifting millions of snowflakes outside. 'Time for bedtime cup of cocoa,' an old wife would say to her silver-haired man. 'Oh,' says he, 'I think I have a cold coming on. See if there's a drop of New Year whisky left in the cupboard. I would be the better of a good strong toddy...'

The Poets on Winter

22.1.1987

'As the day lengthens the caald strengthens', the old folk used to say, drawing on a great hoard of folk-memory. It's true enough. Looking back over many years, January seems always to be the month to be feared, with claws and teeth of ice. It is the month when Robert Burns was born—'"Twas then a blast o' Janwar' win' / Blew hansel in on Robin'...

There is a dark rich magic in this time of year that Burns loved and exploited to the full. It's impossible to imagine his greatest poem, 'Tam o' Shanter', in a summer setting: a storm, with darkness, was essential.

His cantata, 'The Jolly Beggars', is a winter-time extravaganza. He weaves his magic about a winter-evicted mouse. 'The Cotter's Saturday Night'—that pious pastoral—falls in wintertime, when hearts and hearthstone burn more brightly. Many of his lyrics too, are stoked to winter ardour—'Oh, wert thou in the cold blast...' Does not the whole world sing 'Auld Lang Syne' at New Year?—though nearly always they get the words wrong.

It may be that high summer is too obviously 'practical'—with abundance of flowers, birdsong, fleeces, honey, sunshine—and poets like a thin soil to work in, so that the beauties of art can vie with the overflowing riches of nature.

The coldness and cruelty of winter is in one of Keats's greatest poems, 'The Eve of Saint Agnes'. He makes a marvellous distillation from the bitter wind, the shivering sheep, the frozen breath of the bedesman that was 'like pious incense from a censer old'.

Possibly the joy of winter for artists is the knowledge that the seed is lying under the snow, with all of summer's abundance locked in it. The waiting and the longing are more wonderful than the consummation.

Twelfth Night—that is, January the sixth—Shakespeare called one of the happiest of his plays. Another he titled *The Winter's Tale*: a title to enchant any audience, because it is at the time of darkness and snow that people draw in to the fireside to listen to the old men's stories. Even nowadays, I suppose, TV has more viewers than on lingering rose-scented evenings.

Firelighting

19.2.1987

The lighting of the fire in the hearth can be a very chancy thing. Every day the fire has a kind of personality of its own. It is a benign and cheerful being, most days, especially in winter.

Apply a single match to the crumpled paper, and away it goes on its merry dance all through the evening till midnight. It asks nothing in return but the random shovel of coal.

Just occasionally it lets me down. I came home rather late one evening to find that the fire had kept a red glow at the heart of it. 'Oh, true and faithful fire!'... It being Burns Night, I was anxious to see a Burns programme on TV. Whether the fire was sullen that I had deserted it for so many hours, I do not know; but it responded to no kind of coaxing or delicate feeding. It was offered in desperation, fat, sugar, new sticks, a white cubic 'fire-lighter', a sheet of newspaper was spread to create an updraught... Nothing doing: it died there, in front of me, on the midnight. And I had missed most of the Burns programme. And in my exasperation I had sat down on my spectacles and wrenched the frame and dislodged one of the lenses... I went to bed that night, very bad-tempered.

But after that the fire was as well-behaved as ever; until one day last week. I applied the match, up went the paper in a blaze; but the cinders and coal responded so sullenly that I couldn't account for it—until I realized that, in a fit of absent-mindedness, I had forgotten to lay the structure of sticks! (I get a bag of lovely firewood once a month or so from a kind friend.) But on this particular day the fire took pity on me, and though it was only the feeblest glow to begin with, an hour later the flames were like a meeting of all the most cheerful folk you ever thought of—Tam o' Shanter and Mr Pickwick and Falstaff and Sir Toby Belch and Godfrey Ritch of Stenwick—all that nodding and gossip and laughter of flames—all those benign circles of warmth.

An Orkney winter evening can be a joy, if you have a fire and a book and a few sheets of paper.

From Orkney to New Zealand

26.2.1987

A friend wrote from the North Island of New Zealand yesterday, away on the opposite end of the globe. It is summer there still, and the kind of summer we Orcadians have never experienced—temperatures in the eighties, and orange and lemon trees in the garden where you can pick your breakfast on those golden mornings.

She went on a walking tour, away to the northernmost tip of New Zealand. The nights were so warm she could sleep under the stars, without a tent for cover. And the long Pacific breakers rolling in, to bathe among. And there suddenly was a beach, sixty miles of uninterrupted sand—a long tawny ribbon stretching as far as the eyes could see. And on the sand, a Maori exercising his horses, who offered her one to ride on; and away they went, plunging joyously—girl on horse—skirting the breakers.

Away in the distance, snow-draped mountains three times as high as Ben Nevis. To this land of mountains and seas, Scottish emigrants—many of them Orcadians—sailed by the boatload last century; and no wonder.

And yet the cities of New Zealand seemed too new to her, creations of today—and the sense of history that is everywhere in Scotland seems lacking. (Except for the Maoris and their mysterious beautiful culture.)

How lovely, to be on the sunny side of the globe from October to April!

Here, in Orkney, the latest snow is slowly shrinking from the gardens. Yesterday, near the end of winter, was colder than any day this season; even under the thick quilt, with a hot-water bottle at my feet, it was cold.

Yet there are signs of cheer. Spring is putting forth first delicate impulses and tremors. 'There are snowdrops in the garden,' a passer-by says... 'Not long now to crocus-time'... 'The daffodil sheaths are picking up'...

What could be lovelier than an Orkney springtime; even today, with those summer images from New Zealand in my mind; even now, when small birds sit shivering and starved on the roof-spouts, waiting for a handful of crusts to be thrown among the grey lacings of ice?

'Spike'

5.3.1987

There have been so many deaths this past winter. I hadn't seen Bob Johnston for years, since he went to Aberdeen to work on the *Press and Journal*.

But I used to meet him every Monday morning, when I went to read proofs for the *Orkney Herald*, published on the Tuesday. (Gerry Meyer, then editor of *The Orcadian*, always drove me from Stromness—which shows that there was never at any time bad feeling between the two Orkney papers; not even at Election times, when *The Orcadian* supported the Conservative candidate and the *Orkney Herald* was staunchly Liberal.)

There we sat together in a little boxed-in office in a corner of the printing works, Bob Johnston and I; and every now and then Jack Twatt the editor would bring in another sheaf of proofs, new from the 'hot-lead' linotype machines.

And there, all morning and some of the afternoon, we went over District News and WRI reports and the doings of the three Councils—Orkney County, Kirkwall, Stromness, occasionally pouncing with our pencils to make a sign in the margins. What we had a certain distaste for were the long boring advertisements in small type from wholesale firms in the south. Bob Johnston was very careful to see that there were no mistakes in his weekly 'Stenwick' instalment, because he was the only begetter of those masterpieces. And I had an eagle eye on the proof of 'Island Diary', a column of which I was author.

Occasionally Ernest Marwick showed up from the *Orkney Herald* shop, to read the proof of his weekly reflections on Orkney life and lore, 'Sooan Sids'.

There were slack periods between proof-reading; and then Bob and I would lean back in our chairs and talk. He had a dry laconic marvellous sense of humour. The only thing that awoke in him something like passion was cricket. The Test Matches he followed ball by ball, stroke by stroke, as if they were parts of some breath-taking ritual... We talked sometimes about books, though our tastes differed widely. Agatha Christie was for him the great modern master of narrative. And I held out for E. M. Forster. We agreed, amicably, to differ.

And sometimes, unknown to me, Bob was studying some quirk of my physiognomy, so that he could put me in his amazingly witty 'Spike' cartoon... Later, we would laugh together about that, too.

Wedded to the Sea

12.3.1987

Imagine, if the *Pole Star* no longer sailed in and out of Stromness...

It's not so long ago that it seemed possible the *Ola* might no longer make its daily crossing out of Stromness, when the 'short ferry' crossing was being hotly debated.

The successor of the little *Hoy Head* is no longer based in Stromness.

Where is the flock of trawlers that used to seek sanctuary in Stromness from the North Sea storm?

Stromness has been wedded to the sea almost from its beginning.

And the host of little fishing boats moored off the piers, that went out with lines and creels, and came back with haddocks and lobsters... You would meet a few local fishermen, most days, climbing up to the Lookout between Guardhouse and Citadel, where an ancient cannon stood, to look through their 'glass' at the west, in case there were trawlers poaching within the three-mile limit...

We would listen to the old men telling of the great days of the herring fishing, when you could walk from Ness to the big Pier, stepping from deck to deck, so thick were the herring boats in the harbour.

And always the rasp of saws and the thud of hammers in Stangers' boat-building yard at Ness.

* * *

What will Stromness be, in the 23rd century (supposing there are any towns and cities and villages left at all, under the clouds of nuclear poison)?

There might be a guide showing troops of tourists round the deserted streets and the ruined piers. 'This,' says the guide, 'must once have been a fairly prosperous little place. Its business had obviously to do with the sea, and fish... Over there, at the edge of Hoy Sound, tens of thousands of scallop shells were found, and crab shells... There were found, in many of the ruins, primitive harpoons, and exotic objects from all over the globe that had obviously been brought home by local sailors...' Even today, it's said, the seagulls make the most melancholy outcries of all over this place. *Hamnavoe!* they cry. *What's become of you? We're the long-dead mariners and fishermen that you reared and nurtured and sent out, centuries ago... Where are our crusts and our pieces of fish?*

Water Supply

26.3.1987

How many good things in life we take for granted—for example, our water supply. Turn the tap, fill the kettle, flick the switch, and in ten minutes the breakfast tea and egg are ready. Meantime you can wash and shave comfortably.

We should think sometimes of the Stromnessians of a century ago. There were six public wells between the Market Green and Ness: Market Green Pump, Church Road Pump, Brewery Lane Pump, Hellihole Pump, Distillery Well, Spence's Well—and to one or other of them our great-grandparents had to trudge once a day at least with their yoke of buckets, in all weathers. The North End was scantily served; the South-Enders were more lucky. A few houses had private wells, in their backyard or even inside their houses.

In the year 1896, Professor Matthew Hay of Aberdeen University inspected the many wells of Stromness. He took samples from each, and had them analysed. His report makes horrific reading to us hygiene-minded moderns, for nearly all those wells were polluted to some extent.

The wonder is that our ancestors didn't die like flies of cholera or typhus. For the sewage drains—such as they were—leaked into the wells, to a greater or less extent, by secret underground courses. It was not pure sparkling water that was brought every morning through the three hundred doors of Stromness.

We pride ourselves on our waterfront, unique perhaps in Europe: a pleasant scape to look at on a fine summer morning. Professor Hay didn't think so. For the raw sewage was thrown over the piers into the sea, and the whole line of the waterfront was a reeking cess-wash, especially in hot weather.

The situation was very much aggravated in the herring season, when the population of Stromness quadrupled. The herring-boats were willing to pay for the foulest water.

Professor Hay's report led to the construction of the Waterworks at the Loons and tapwater and water closets that flushed.

After that, Stromness water was celebrated. A farmer from Stenness used to visit our house when I was very young. He always asked for a glass of 'Stromness water'. There was thought to be no water like it, for flavour and wholesomeness, after Professor Hay had come and gone.

Persons from St Andrews

9.4.1987

An old grumpy man of books and papers like me looks on every unexpected visitor with suspicion and a touch of resentment.

What do they mean, knocking on my door without warning? I might be very busy, deep in some work or other. (Every writer carries in the back of his mind the archetypal image of Coleridge, the early 19th-century poet, in a cloud of laudanum writing part one of that magnificent word-tapestry, 'Kubla Khan'. Part Two is clear and vivid and pulsing in his mind, waiting for the pen to set down the words on the sheet of paper. There comes a knock at the door; Coleridge's servant comes into the study to say that 'a person from Porlock' has called to see him, on urgent business, and won't go away. So Coleridge goes to the door to speak to this tradesman, who very likely is pressing for a debt to be paid; and after their business palaver is over, and the poet returns to his desk, the vision of 'Kubla Khan' Part Two has vanished forever! It is one of the strangest incidents in literature.)

Well, this Orkney writer is no Coleridge, and no vision so rich and strange will ever visit him... But imagine my consternation, last Thursday, when nine students from St Andrews University stood at my door in the bleak cold weather. I was in a great hurry; we made vague promises to meet each other, somewhere very soon. (They were leaving on Saturday's *Ola*.)

We did have our get-together, the very next afternoon, in a farm cottage a mile from Stromness. Outside, the March weather couldn't have been more sluttish and spiteful. There were talented musicians among the students—a fiddle came out, a clarinet, a guitar. For an hour the district of Cairston was enriched with glees, choruses, folk songs, rounds. It was as good a tonic as an old recluse like myself could wish for. In between times, we ate scrambled egg sandwiches, bere bannocks and cheese, and drank tea, and talked.

The storm outside might not have existed. It was the same tempest that drove the *St Sunniva* back to Aberdeen, and kept some of the party from going to Sanday (for the *Orcadia* didn't sail), and kept others from walking through the rainy hills of Hoy.

What would have been a gloomy afternoon at Mayburn Court turned out to be happy.

Frayings and Wearings-Out

23.4.87

In a house, of course, there are always little frayings and wearings-out. For a year or more one lives without accident or nuisance—and one lives in the house thanklessly, thinking that nothing will ever go wrong any more. A spider in its finished web, a bird in its completed nest, must feel the same.

The wild wet month of March caused the coal-shed door to stick: not entirely, but there was enough friction between door and jamb to cause worry. I remembered with something like horror the last trouble with the coal-shed door, six or seven years ago. The door refused to close, it was suddenly too rain-swollen for its frame. The wind got up in the night and kept slamming the door against the iron railing. All night long it went on, like the clanging of a mad black bell! I tried, in the early hours of the morning, to muffle the hideous clangour with rugs and blankets. It was no good... Was this hideous thing going to happen again now—whereby much of the South End of Stromness would be kept awake; and very likely blaming me? Ah, no, for my friend Russell Smith arrived soon, from the Town House, and re-hung the door. How relieved I was!

A few days later, I switched on the immersion heater; for it was cleaning day in the house. There was no answering light. Fortunately my little coal fire heats the water to some extent. Once more the Town House sent Stephen, the electrician, and that ailment was sorted.

Returning from the town this morning, I started putting some messages[1] in the fridge. It didn't have the Arctic cold it ought to have. I put my finger in the ice-cube rack; it was melted water. And the white plastic catchment tray brimmed with water. More trouble! the 'household gods' were angry about something ... then, greatly relieved, I saw that in an absent-minded moment I had switched off the fridge myself; it must have been yesterday evening. And so now the cheese and the milk and orange juice are cold to the touch once more—as if they had come out of an igloo in Baffin Bay.

An Iron Discipline

7.5.1987

I had a letter yesterday from a young friend in Edinburgh who is studying hard for her final degree exams, while outside the sun blazes down and that beautiful city is awash with life and colour.

I remember the situation only too well, from thirty years ago.

1. shopping

No city on earth could be so lovely as Edinburgh when students return to it after the Easter holiday. During one's absence, everything is changed. The dour grey wintry city has suddenly opened like a flower; the trees are clothed in fresh young foliage; the gardens everywhere, but especially in Princes Street, are lyrical with flowers; even the citizens look free and happy as they go about their business. The girls' dresses are like butterflies' wings...

For the students, especially those preparing for the finals in June, it is altogether different. We had to shut ourselves like monks in our narrow cells, and dedicate ourselves to books. We had to rule our days with an iron discipline. It could be fatal, for one minute, to peer through the curtains of the Marchmont 'digs', or out of the Library window, at the magical world of springtime beyond: the sun-splashed gardens with the new flowers and birds, the young happy sun-tranced people everywhere (for it was all right to be a student if all you had to sit were the end-of-session exams).

Back then, sternly, to the pile of textbooks and notebooks on the desk: the *Anglo-Saxon Reader*, Chaucer, Elizabethan Comedies, Metaphysical Poets, Pope and Swift and Dr Johnson, the Romantics, the great blocks of the Victorian quarrymen-novelists.

Sometimes, in a weak moment, you might think with delight of the Brough of Birsay, or the marvellous valley of Rackwick, or the water lapping high about the Stromness piers, or St Magnus on a market day. But they weren't 'weak moments' at all—they gave you strength to attack once more the mountain ranges of English Literature as yet unconquered.

But at evening, we refreshed ourselves with beer at 'the poets' pubs' in Rose Street—the Abbotsford and Milne's Bar; for there has always been a kind of mystical bond between ale and poetry. 'I often wonder what the Vintners buy / One half so precious as the Goods they sell'...

Edwin Muir Centenary

14.5.1987

Tomorrow—15 May—Edwin Muir would have been a hundred years old. It's hard to imagine him a very old man—there was such a spring of timelessness in him always, even when he was unwell or depressed. But he, being curious about time and the mysterious workings of time always could imagine himself as a kind of Old Testament wanderer —just as he drew from his childhood in Wyre the pure waters that sustained him all his life long.

I first met him and Willa in the lounge of the Stromness Hotel one summer afternoon in 1951. They had invited me for afternoon tea, as I had applied to be a student at Newbattle Abbey College when the new session began in October. I was very nervous, and had had some beer in the bar below to fortify myself for the interview. As things turned out, I needn't have worried, because the Muirs were both most kind, and did all they could to put me at my ease... To tell the truth, Willa made a more immediate impression than Edwin; probably because she spoke much more and told anecdote after anecdote, each one ending with a gust of full-throated laughter. All I can remember about Edwin that day was that his eyes had 'the blue flash' of mirth in them that Willa describes in her book of memoirs, *Belonging*—and that he smoked many cigarettes—and that he told me he had read a short story of mine in *The New Shetlander*; on the strength of which he accepted me for Newbattle... They had driven that afternoon from Kirkwall, and on the way had picked up two young men who (it turned out) were fairground pugilists... When Edwin dropped them off, they thanked him courteously—and then one of them said, 'And thanks to your mother too.' Willa laughed very much at that. But the incident gives some idea of how young he looked then, with his wide blue eyes and full sensuous lips and tranquil expression... Whereas most of us are chained inexorably to time, Edwin could move about at ease in that mysterious dimension—'I see myself sometimes, an old old man... With old man's staff and legendary cloak.'

In January 1959 he died, and was outside time at last. As Prospero said to the exquisite singer Ariel, 'Then to the elements/ Be free'...

The End of a Toaster

28.5.1987

'How,' you sometimes think in an idle moment, 'will I ever begin the day properly without the toaster?' For the toaster had stood on its little side table for so long, and so faithfully, that nothing could ever go wrong with it. It must have been a faithful friend for a dozen years, at least.

One morning recently the toaster went on fire! I switched it off. The fire went on. Then I saw that a bit of crust had fallen off the slice of bread and was leading this independent fiery life of its own.

At last it burned itself out, and I thought, 'A sensitive machine like my toaster can't take such punishment, and survive'... And at the same time it occurred to me that you are supposed to unscrew the bottom of the toaster from time to time and clean out the toast-grains that have accumulated. For three years or so I had neglected to do that. Once unscrewed, a great torrent of toast-grains fell on to the table, and made a little hill that I could only stare at with awe...

Once that refuse had been cleared away, I tentatively switched on, to see if the toaster had survived the conflagration. Faithful friend—it responded at once, its little parallel coils of wire gave out a reassuring glow.

Alas, it was a last gesture of bravery and friendship. The flames had been too much for it, after all. Next time I slid the slices in, and switched on, the response was coldness and darkness. It might be the fuse! But it was not the fuse. The toaster had been mortally wounded.

Well, of course, either it will have to go to the electrician or a new toaster will have to be bought. Laziness and procrastination have prevented anything being done about it, as yet. Meantime I survive on 'Ryvita' and oatcakes with the morning tea; and they are good enough, in their way, but they do not have the marvellous taste of toast—the second encounter of earth and sun (the first having been the ripening cornstalks).

Some people swear there has never been toast like the toast of their childhood, when they held a slice of bread on a fork in front of the glowing ribs of a stove. They may be right—but in those days we had the hunger of childhood to enhance every joy.

Colditz on the Heights

4.6.1987

So, that great building at the back of the town lies empty and forlorn, since last week.

To tell the truth, I have such mixed feelings about the old Stromness Academy that I neither mourn nor rejoice. 'Aa,' the old folk used to say to us, whenever we showed reluctance to shoulder our school-bags in the morning, 'thee school-days are the happiest days o' thee life'... That kind of talk only confirmed for us the stupidity and staidness of our elders. For most of us, it was a huge prison-house. We would count on our fingers how long it would be till we were fourteen, and our sentence expired, and we were free forever.

I suppose there must have been happy hours up there, on the side of Brinkie's Brae; but I have to dig deep to find such moments of felicity. We boys enjoyed playing football in the park at 'playtime'. I enjoyed hearing about the kings and heroes of Scottish history—Wallace and Bruce, Mary Queen of Scots, Bonnie Prince Charlie—and as 'religious instruction' consisted mostly of stories out of the Old Testament—the patriarchs, and Joseph and his brothers, and David and Goliath (all beautifully read to us by Miss Smith, our primary teacher for three years)—I first got a taste for the art of narrative, told by ancient anonymous masters. Certain poems, too, like 'The Burial of Sir John Moore' and 'Fidelity' and 'To a Mouse', brought awe and delight.

I will not mention such things as parsing, analysis, mental arithmetic, or 'drill', for even to think of them at this remove is painful.

If I say that late Friday afternoon was the most glorious time of the week—better even than Saturday's full freedom—and that there came a day in early July each year that glowed with the full light of summer and freedom and boundless joy, because on that day the seven-weeks-long summer holidays began, I think perhaps that sums up what school meant to me and thousands of other boys and girls from Stromness and the South Isles and West Mainland... In justice, I should add that a later generation of pupils took a much kindlier view of that Colditz on the heights.

Pilgrimage to Wyre

11.6.1987

What a disgrace, never having been to Wyre, source of some of Orkney's greatest literature. I'm thinking not only of Edwin Muir, but of Bjarni Kolbeinson, a poet from seven centuries back, whose father was Kolbein Hruga, laird (or the medieval equivalent) of Wyre and by all accounts a rough, ill-tempered man. At any rate, mothers in Orkney until fairly recent times used to threaten ill-behaved children, 'Cubbie Roo'll get thee!'...

Cubbie Roo's son became a famous poet in the north, and was Bishop of Orkney at the time when Earl Rognvald Kolson was canonised.

It is passing strange to think that those two poets, so far separated in time, might have sat at the same hearthstone (or, at least, over the same foundation stone).

* * *

Saturday morning, May 16, broke bright and fair. (If it had been stormy, I'd have left Wyre till another day.)

There were so many 'pilgrims', two boats had to ferry them from Tingwall. The Sound was calm all the way.

Wyre has a fine long pier, which it certainly didn't have in the time of the two poets.

There's a long gentle incline from the pier to the Community Centre. Some of the Wyre ladies had prepared food—delicious sandwiches and cakes, and tea—which we had outside; though now there were masses of cloud mingled with patches of blue.

At the wall of the ruined chapel of St Mary, some of Muir's Wyre poems and prose extracts were read. Cameras clicked like insects all around. The music of the words hung gently in the early summer air.

Most of us managed the gentle climb to the summit of Cubbie Roo's castle, and then we saw vividly what the small boy Edwin Muir saw— 'the islands lying thick around' ... 'unseen straits between them lay'... It is a very beautiful outlook, all around, and the environing isles give a sense of security and peace.

Very moving it was, too, to see the Bu farm and the garden and fields.

The afternoon ended with music and dancing in the Community Centre.

The Solan visited Rousay pier before returning to Wyre for the other passengers. About twenty scattered drops of rain fell.

The car was waiting for us at Tingwall jetty.

Macbeth Country

18.6.1987

So here we are, in the middle of Macbeth country, with a village called Cawdor nearby and the town of Forres, which is mentioned very early in the play, five miles to the east. We drove through it yesterday, on our way to visit the Abbey of Pluscarden, so beautifully situated in a green fertile fold of the hills.

There Father Giles, one of the Benedictine monks, showed us round. Very lovely indeed are the new stained glass windows. The abbey, ruined at the Reformation, is slowly being restored to its original grace and beauty. Here is tranquillity that obliterates the sinister doings of King Macbeth.

But was he such a monster as tradition depicts him? History is always written by the winning side in any dynastic dispute, and the sons of King Duncan emerged victorious in the end. So Macbeth was fitted with the coat of an evil reputation, and so Shakespeare depicts him as a great villain in a tragedy—a royal scoundrel who, however, manages to utter some of the greatest dramatic poetry ever written.

It was an age when men in high places used violence and blood-letting as an everyday acceptable procedure. We have to look no further than the Norse earls of Orkney—e.g. Hakon in Egilsay.

Macbeth seems to have ruled in Scotland for quite a while and after his death was buried in Iona among the other medieval Scottish kings. The logical outcome of Shakespeare's play is that such a monster would have been thrown on the dunghill, in horror and revulsion. Instead, they folded him in hallowed ground.

Returning from Pluscarden, the road runs through 'the blasted heath' where Macbeth met the three witches. The medieval moorland is now rich agricultural land. There is a mound for each of the three witches. Might they not have been three 'gangrel bodies' who cried out to a victorious well-loved thane in passing, 'Oh, Macbeth of Glamis, it's you that ought to be Thane of Cawdor'... 'No, King of Scotland is more like it...'

But indeed the past is a mystery that can never be fully unravelled.

Midsummer Myths

2.7.1987

Midsummer in Orkney—and a few very daring people (or foolhardy people) went to Brodgar on the Solstice midnight and drank some Highland Park in the centre of the stone ring. I told one of them the next day how very lucky she was to be there talking to me; for they had all been flirting with a supernatural danger. The trows: the trows are abroad in their thousands on midsummer nights. People have been dragged or lured or cajoled to the trows' abodes inside the hills, and been lost to human ken. But not, of course, for ever. Sooner or later— after half a century, maybe—the trows get tired of their guests and invite them to leave. The midsummer revellers, in the past, thought they had been gone for half an hour or so—or maybe it had all been a dream, a piece of midsummer madness—but when they emerge into the midsummer light again, they find that they are strangers in a familiar land. All their generation has vanished or grown so old as to be unrecognisable. Only they, the enchanted ones, are not a day older than when they entered the trows' castle.

I suppose you are fairly safe if you aren't children (especially very beautiful children) or musicians. For some reason, the trows are specially delighted with innocence and beauty, and music and dancing ... so, when we drove home with a certain world-famous composer the other evening, after the Consort of Musick in St Magnus, I told him he ought to go right indoors when we got to Stromness and not come out again that night...

I'm pleased to say, he is still with us.

* * *

A little boy in New York nearly two centuries ago heard his father telling him this story—at bedtime no doubt. Being a glutton for narrative, the boy made it a part of himself. And when he grew up, he wrote a very famous story called *Rip Van Winkle*. The theme is immediately recognisable. The child's name was Washington Irving, and his father was a Shapinsay man.

Rackwick Rain

23.7.1987

The rain began in the late afternoon, yesterday, and it thrummed and threshed all night, and was even fiercer at breakfast time this morning. Little pools had formed in every crevice and hollow. To stand outside for two minutes was to be soaked. The Rackwick rain has an intensity unknown elsewhere in Orkney, I'm sure.

But yesterday afternoon, earlier, I had done a thing I had never managed before—to climb up to Bunertoon, the highest croft-house in the valley, by the shortest steepest way, close to the sea cliffs. Fortunately for nervous folk like me, the cliff edge has recently been stoutly fenced, so that one has a definite sense of security. But it is still hard on the lungs of an ageing bronchitic like me, and I was very safely herded, with frequent pauses to get the breath back, by David Hutchison and Betty Grant. And there it suddenly was, Bunertoon, in its patch of green.

Soon Archie Bevan was putting glasses of his delicious ale into our hands. We sat outside, in the mild grey air, talking, seven of us.

There is a new addition to Bunertoon, created from a wall of what may be the old byre—a sun-room, made by the talented David Hutchison out of fish boxes, and discarded windows, looks out over the Pentland Firth. On a clear day one can see the *St Ola* leaving Scrabster, and chart her passage almost to the Old Man of Hoy.

Bunertoon, in case you don't know, is the Orkney home of Sir Peter Maxwell Davies, composer.

The Rackwick air had whetted our appetite for a plentiful and delicious lunch of curry. There were wines to go with it, but I stuck with the local brew.

We went home, singly or in small groups. By then the rain had set in, intense drenching stuff. I was glad I had brought another pair of trousers to Mucklehoose.

By a driftwood fire, and candlelight, the three Grants and I played whist—at which Peter and I were defeated rather heavily by Betty and Alan.

The tattoos of rain beat steadily on the roof till beyond midnight. We cheered each other—not that we were despondent, but we had experienced more sunshine during Rackwick weeks in past summers—by saying it would be a warm bright day tomorrow.

But we didn't really believe it, quenching the candles.

And the rain throbbed and threshed all night, and the wind moaned.

The Stromness Correspondent

20.8.1987

For some years I was Stromness Correspondent for a newspaper only the older folk remember, *The Orkney Herald*.

It was wartime—1944—and though a great deal was happening in Stromness, with thousands and thousands of soldiers milling around, for the townsfolk themselves it was quiet days. All the young men, for one thing, were in the forces. The 'black-out' at night kept folk at home.

So, what was a Stromness correspondent going to write about?...

There were always WRI meetings, and monthly debates that brought soldiers and townsfolk together, and church services. Also cinema and variety in the Garrison Theatre (now the Swimming Pool). Occasionally 'stars' like Sybil Thorndike and Gracie Fields and Nat Gonella flew in to entertain the troops. I will never forget a magnificent performance by Sybil Thorndike one Sunday afternoon, in which she mingled dramatic and lyric poetry. The like will never be heard in Stromness again.

It was forbidden to write anything about weather conditions or the movement of troops or the coming and going of ships, like the *Earl of Zetland*, the troop-carrier.

But by 1944 all the excitement had ebbed from Orkney. The great German air raids of 1940 and 1941 were never to be repeated. No longer were the night skies of Orkney raked with searchlight beams. The fleet was securely locked inside Scapa Flow. Our gas-masks, that we were supposed to carry around everywhere, gathered dust on the shelves.

None of that could be written about. What could a correspondent do then? A famous journalist, C. P. Scott, had said, 'Facts are sacred, comment is free'. I tended increasingly to hold the exactly opposite tenet, and allowed my imagination to drift at random here and there about the town and the townsfolk. A few people were amused, some were outraged. Many severe rebukes were administered to me, by direct confrontation on the street or 'Letters to the Editor'.

It began to dawn on me that imaginative writing, and not journalism, might be my true calling.

Convalescence in Kirbister

27.8.1987

I have been for nine days now living in the country, in the pleasant district of Kirbister, recuperating after the nasty 'bug' that sent me to hospital for a brief stay.

It is quiet here, with wholesome country airs, and with good food and good company one quickly recovers one's well-being.

For a fortnight the thought of reading and writing nauseated me, but this morning I wrote with eager relish for two hours before lunch... And while I was writing indoors, the sun lay warm across the pastures and the ripening barley.

What a joy, this summer, to eat lunch outside in the garden! It has been one of those cold grey summers when indoors was more attractive than garden or beach.

We look for great things from late August and all of September and half of October at least.

And while we were having lunch in the garden, Radio Orkney was telling us all about the arrival in Kirkwall of the Queen Mother and King Olav.

The weather forecast had mentioned, rather ominously, a 'front' moving towards us—another of that ruffian gang of 'fronts' that has been harassing us ever since July came in. We hoped devoutly that the 'front' would leave Orkney alone till after the *son-et-lumière* this evening. Just then a gust of wind blew the paper napkins from the table over the garden. 'Here,' said I, 'comes the "front".'

All afternoon the blue sky has dwindled and drifted westward over Birsay, and a wash of grey has sought to dissolve the sun...

Outside are the lovely hills of Miffia and Kringlafiold, and through my bedroom window I can see a thin sliver of Stenness Loch. There are big farms near and far, for this is a fertile region of Orkney.

My lost appetite is back, healthier than ever. And I sleep on a lovely bed like a sailor after a twelve-hour watch.

No throngs of tourists in this green corner of Orkney. A few old friends from the south find their way: Brian Murray from Ayr, and Michael Krauskopf from West Germany, and Dave Brock from Stockport with a lovely Loch Swannay trout.

Three Empty Spaces

3.9.1987

An old radiogram under the window, vintage 1948, useless for eighteen years or so (but regarded as a handsome piece of furniture when it was new). A washing-machine bought in 1965 or so, useless for seven years. An electric fire with three bars that has been gathering dust and rust for seventeen years, and might explode if it were to be plugged in... You get used to these useless clutters after a time; they seem to be a piece of the house like the rocking-chair or a well-loved picture on the wall.

But one day in summer, Betty Grant pointed out to me that the once-handsome radiogram was being systematically eaten by an army of woodworms. 'It should be got rid of at once,' she said.

What happy evenings we had, in the 1950s and 1960s, listening to the old 78rpm discs: 'On Wenlock Edge', T. S. Eliot reading his Quartets, Beethoven's Violin Concerto, and 'Life is just a Bowl of Cherries'... Well, it has been silent too long, and now the worms are devouring it and might soon devour other things made of wood.

I even had happy hours working the washing-machine and the spin-dryer, manipulating heavy coils of rubber and cupfuls of 'Daz'.

That ancient electric fire, a gift from Charlie Senior, poet and bookseller, warmed my early days in Mayburn.

All were now about to be sent packing into oblivion.

To get rid of such heavy articles, you must first arrange with Orkney Islands Council, and fix a suitable date for the collection.

The day before radiogram, washing machine, electric fire were to be removed, I had to go to hospital. In the midst of my fevers and mighty coughings and grey distaste for life, I remembered about that date with the OIC removal men.

Kind friends were there, early in the morning, to let the three removers in.

When I came home at last, how strange it was to see empty space where those three useless things had been. Never a pang for the happy industrious useful artefacts they had once been. Such is the ingratitude of men (or of 'persons', one should say, in deference to Women's Lib...).

The Free Kirk

8.10.1987

Whatever name you give it, Stromness can't do without the Academy Hall, or the North Church, or 'the Free Kirk' as everybody called it when I was young.

Since it became the Academy Hall a decade or more ago, over and over again it has proved its worth not only to Stromness but to all Orkney, and the great world beyond. A list of the great musicians and poets who have performed here makes impressive reading.

The acoustics are excellent. The building is beautifully sited, right at the heart of Stromness and slightly elevated so that the belfry dominates the street, looking south from the pierhead. Sailing into the harbour, the silhouette of the town would be much diminished without it.

It was built, too, at a time when working in stone was still an important and proud craft. Outside, the building would stand for centuries. Unused, I imagine that the interior would quickly disintegrate, and quite soon only an empty shell would stand there.

Surely it would not cost an excessive amount to put in fire-doors ... if our main theatre is to be some area of the new school at Garson, expect very meagre attendances on a winter night, from the old and the frail and those who don't have cars...

* * *

One man knew the whole history of that building from its beginning, and of the Kirk before it that stood on the same site: Peter Esson, tailor and librarian. Peter Esson's knowledge of the immensely complex history of religion in Scotland since the Reformation was vast.

For him, the crowning glory of that history was the Disruption of 1843, when a great flock of ministers walked out of the General Assembly in Edinburgh and formed the Free Church of Scotland.

Among those ministers was Rev Peter Learmonth, who became the first Free Kirk minister in Stromness. Those ministers of the Disruption sacrificed a great deal, their kirks and manses and secure stipends... As a young woman, Peter Esson's mother had been a servant at the new Free Kirk manse. When one of her sons was born, she called him Peter Learmonth Esson... His tailor shop, where men congregated to tell stories and comment on the passing scene, was right in the shadow of the Free Kirk.

I'm sure it gave Peter a feeling of immense satisfaction and security.

Orkneymen in the Nor'-Wast
15.10.1987

I saw a strange, gruesome, and moving programme on TV last night, about the fate of Franklin and his sailors and his two ships *Erebus* and *Terror* that, in 1845, were crushed by ice, seeking the 'north-west passage'.

As we Orcadians know, Stromness was the last port that the expedition visited before they disappeared forever. They watered at Login's Well at the South End. And it was an Orkneyman, born at Clestrain House on the Orphir shore, who at last discovered how the ships had been crushed like matchwood in the ice, and of how the sailors had drifted greyly into death by starvation and exposure.

The man who put the clues together, with the help of Eskimos and certain relics they showed him—medals, ribbons, cutlery—was John Rae, a physician in the service of the Hudson Bay Company.

Dr Rae employed mainly Orkneymen to go with him among those white wastes. He was given a huge reward for his solution to the great enigma. A century and a half ago, exploration of the uncharted parts of the globe—Africa, northern Canada, the interior of Australia—held as much fascination as star travel nowadays.

What emerged from last night's TV programme was that the sailors of *Erebus* and *Terror* had been fatally weakened by lead poisoning. The ships were provisioned for three years, and a great deal of their food was what we nowadays call 'tinned', but those early 'tins' contained a high proportion of lead. To keep food for so long in this novel way must have seemed, in mid 19th century, another triumph of science ... but the sailors were eating slow death with every mouthful.

There, as proof, we saw the exhumed bodies of two of Franklin's men who were among the first to die. The Canadian pathologists found great quantities of lead in the bodies (which lay there, coffined and under headstones, as if they had died two days ago: time and corruption held in check by the ice). We even saw a pile of the battered 'tins' that had killed them.

As for the 'north-west passage', one might think that geographers, mariners, explorers should have seen the impossibility of finding a way through that vast desert of ice.

Windmills on Burgar Hill

19.11.1987

Good luck to the windmills on Burgar Hill. Given that wind technology is only in its infancy, might we not expect windmills in the future to gather ever more power from the clean element of air—so that in a century or so there will be hardly a hilltop on earth that isn't crowned with its windmills and the villages and cities round about living without dread of the terrible nuclear dragon we have invoked? If it turns out that way, what companies of pilgrims will flock to Burgar Hill to view the first of the many...

All the elements are our friends—air, earth, water, fire—if they are used with proper reverence. There is enough water in motion everywhere to light half the globe. As long ago as the early 1920s, the playwright Bernard Shaw crossed over from Scrabster to Stromness on the *St Ola*, and that mighty outpouring of waters—the Pentland Firth—impressed him as being able to provide half of Europe with power. (I have no record of his exact words.)

Deep under the peatbanks, down under the black seams of coal, smoulder the central fires at earth's core. People who live near volcanoes know all about that awesome power. It may be possible, some time soon, to harness that red slumbering force.

Anything, I should think, is better than placing all our hopes on the dragons of uranium and plutonium. We are looking into ciphers and secrets that ought never to have been disrupted in the first place. Its first gift to us was horrible enough—Hiroshima and Nagasaki. Chernobyl was but a dark whisper in passing.

I have a great deal of sympathy with Friends of the Earth.

The Burgar windmill isn't the first time that air has been our friend. Think of some oarsman at the dawn of time who, weary of rowing, hung up his coat at the prow. And the wind filled it and the prow sent the spindrift flying and the little ox-hide boat surged through the sea with this new thing—a sail.

Eye Trouble

10.12.1987

What a curious thing—not being able to read any more, or only with strain and difficulty—I, who used to devour books by the barrowload! (That, however, is only a way of speaking. Actually I am a rather slow reader, one of those who get bogged down in long sentences, and have to start at the beginning, sometimes more than once. But I did read for two or three hours every day.)

About thirty years ago, in Edinburgh, a specialist in the Infirmary told me I had eye cataracts. And he said they might develop slowly, or quickly. As for wearing glasses, it didn't matter much, one way or the other.

For thirty years I noticed hardly any difference. True, there was short-sightedness. How embarrassing, to pass old acquaintances on the street and not greet them. Almost as embarrassing, to wave a hand to someone who, as he comes closer, turns out to be a total stranger! Of late years I've begun to nod to everyone I meet.

In the spring of this year, I began to notice a quite rapid deterioration in the left eye, which was always the weaker. There came a perpetual blur or mist—it was what Milton called 'dim diffusion veiled'.

There is no question, now, of beginning to read long books like a novel or a biography. I hoard my vision for poems and brief essays (and that may be no bad thing, in these days of literary long-windedness). Or I listen more than I ever did to music. There's an Austrian called Mahler who pleases me mightily, and hardly a day passes that I don't hear some of his mighty harmonies.

In Kirkwall, in September, the visiting eye specialist said it would be best if I had an operation some time early in 1988, in Aberdeen.

Strangely, I can write as fluently as ever. 'Alas!' I can hear some readers groaning. But I'm sure they wouldn't want to deprive me of one of my remaining pleasures.

Christmas Decorations

24.12.1987

We geriatrics can only faintly recapture the marvellous magic of an Orkney Christmas in the 1920s.

I assure you, it was no wild materialistic splurge that passes for Christmas nowadays. Most Stromnessians were poor by modern standards. We children didn't know that we were poor—riches and poverty as they are computed on, say, the Stock Exchange, meant nothing to us.

To be rich, then, was to be struck with wonderment and delight at something very simple.

The hanging of the decorations, for example.

Last year's decorations had been bundled into a cardboard box and hidden in the attic or under the bed. Ah, they were found at last, with all a summer's dust and ruins of spiders' webs among them! And maybe mice had chewed them.

To buy a new decoration cost one penny from Rae's shop. Well, two or three pennies could be rustled up from somewhere, to repair the ravages.

And then the decorations old and new were nailed to the rafters, radiating from a centre, in a kind of star: red and blue and yellow and white—never had our kitchen known such richness. From the centre of the star depended a silent paper bell. 'Heard chimes are sweet, but those unheard...'

Then a very ancient ceremony was performed, though to us children it was new every Christmas and a matter for secret laughter—the hiding of the mistletoe twig somewhere among the decorations. Some day soon a visitor was bound to stand directly under the mistletoe, and would be mightily surprised by a kiss.

A mistletoe kiss meant the giving of a box of hankies or a pair of socks... And such laughter.

Oh, it was so rich a time it would take several columns of *The Orcadian* to do justice to one tenth of it. I must confine myself to decorations only.

There was no tree. I believe there was not one single Christmas tree in Stromness until the late 1940s. But we had enough to be going on with. The multicoloured paper star whispered above our heads, and the paper bell rustled whenever the door opened.

There came the melancholy day when the enchantment had to be dismantled and put into a cardboard box and hidden away in cupboard or attic.

Then we were aware of the grey of winter.

Soup

14.1.1988

One of the delights of winter is soup—good thick nourishing broth that will outbrave snow and gales.

A few weeks ago a friend was here and she made two or three pots of broth the like of which I have never tasted for richness and nourishment. It all started with the simmering of a piece of lamb... After that, the vegetable additions were made.

I made vague enquiries as to how this culinary masterpiece was achieved: and noted, vaguely, ingredients and method.

Yesterday, being cold but pleasant outside, seemed a good day for the mutton broth.

So, after the morning's work was done—a piece of writing concerning the voyage of the seven-year-old Queen of Scotland, Margaret, from Norway to Orkney—I set to work on the vegetables and the cereals. All seemed to go well, all seemed to promise fair. I couldn't find the little jar of mixed herbs, but I threw in some rosemary at the last minute. And I chopped up the boiled piece of lamb and added the pieces. And I toasted brown bread.

Certainly the broth, when I ladled it into the plate hadn't the rich dark colour of Kenna's. That didn't seem to matter so much.

It was the taste that let me down with a thud: especially as I was very hungry. There wasn't enough salt, for one thing. There was too much rosemary. (In my childhood the housewives of Stromness knew nothing about mixed herbs or thyme or rosemary or bay.) The onions were harsh and seemed to scour the delicate mucous inside my mouth.

It was not a masterpiece.

Still, I was so hungry I supped two platefuls.

I used to make quite good soup, years ago. The skill seems to have deserted me.

I'm sure one or two kind ladies will oblige with recipes.

(PS The broth on the second and third days had improved enormously! I think, maybe, a thread of time has to enter the subtle weave...)

Short-Lived Daughter of Winter

25.2.1988

February, someone said the other day, is the awkwardest month, plastered with mud and shivering with sleet. But I think of it as a shy young month, poor it may be and in rags, but carrying first snowdrops and crocuses in her cold hands.

No one has even dared to divide the year into its four seasons, so confused and perverse our weather is. For example, we call 24 June midsummer: though summer has hardly begun. The sun may be highest in the sky then, but the full warmth and flowering come weeks later (if they come at all).

The same applies to midwinter. Merely to mention the word 'January' is to evoke images of blizzard and storm.

Something has been happening to our seasons lately. Winter the tyrant has been mild and inoffensive for three years past. 'Oh, how lucky we are!' we say to each other on the street... But the following summers have been so disappointing, the blue and the gold all tattered and tarnished.

Looking at TV programmes, weather patterns seem to be changing the world over. The life-giving rain doesn't fall on great tracts of Africa. In Bangladesh the flood waters drown crops and cattle.

'A green Yule makes a full Kirkyard', the old Orcadians used to say. Indeed, they seemed to welcome snow in its due season as a life-giver and preserver, warming the buried seeds.

As for the four seasons, I have always thought (it is a rough-and-ready measurement, to be sure) of February as marking the end of winter, and May the end of spring, and August the end of summer, and November the end of autumn.

So, hail and farewell, February, shy and cold and short-lived daughter of winter. It is you who lets us have our first teatime by daylight. It is you who whispers to us, 'One morning soon, you'll open your eyes to spring...'

Spring-Cleaning

3.3.1988

A kind of frenzy used to fall on the folk of the northern hemisphere—especially the women—about this time of year, when I was young. This springtime madness was very distasteful to us youngsters.

Spring-cleaning time! cried the women, with the light of battle in their eyes.

You would come home from school one dinner-time to find the familiar kitchen-cum-sitting-room looking as though a hurricane had passed through it. The wallpaper with nice red roses on it lay, a heap of ruins, on the floor. There, on the table, new wallpaper with violets and bluebells on it was being cut and pasted with a mixture of flour-and-water, and hung, strip by strip, on the stark bereaved walls... Ham and eggs for dinner that day...

And the cat crying among the debris, more lost than we children were.

All the women in the close went around in the mad March days, the light of battle in their eyes. The mats and rugs, that had lain so cheerfully at the hearth or the bedside all winter, did not know what was coming to them. (Only the very grand houses in Hamnavoe had carpets, in those days.) The mats were hung over clothes-lines and were unmercifully beaten, with carpet beaters, till the stoor rose in clouds about them.

The linoleum was scoured till it gleamed with wax polish and smelt good. Up went the feather duster among the dead flies and the cobwebs in every darkest corner.

The 'bed-sacks' (for only the wealthy had mattresses) were manhandled like truants or malefactors till the chaff lay smooth and even from end to end.

The brass ornaments shone like beacons.

'Maybe the door should be green this year'... So green paint was slapped on the kitchen door—and, if any was left in the pot, on the mantelpiece too.

What an upset! What wilful disorder and obstruction!... What on earth had come over the Hamnavoe women?

Yet, when all the chairs and newly ironed curtains were in their places again, we had to admit that there was a delicious clean smell in the house—as if a flower had opened.

Next, it was the turn of the men. They began to look speculatively at the garden shed where the garden tools had lain all winter, gathering dust and rust.

Equinoctial Blues

31.3.1988

I think there must be a condition called 'the equinoctial blues'—i.e., a kind of depression and melancholy that falls at this time of year, just when one ought to be most joyful that the dark days are over and we are moving into the boundless light of spring and summer.

But there it is. One can hardly put a thought together without a leaden lump coming into it somewhere... There are jobs to do. One thinks, 'What's the *use* of doing this or that?—It all amounts to a nothing in the end'...

Of course it doesn't amount to a nothing at all. We humans are so conditioned that we must always be doing or making something. Otherwise, we are obscurely convinced, chaos will come again. And so, in some way too subtle to be comprehended, every thought and every action sends delicate ripples through the whole web of creation, and influences not only the future but the past also...

I see I am now in danger of being carried off on some metaphysical tide. So I will stop here, on the brink.

What were we talking about? The *morbus equinoctis*. It is not merely that we are sipping the last dregs and eating the last crusts of winter. It was true, in a literal and physical sense, for our great-great-grandfathers. This time of year was the period called 'the lang reed' —the very barest and hungriest time on the crofts and small farms. The cupboards were all but empty, all over Orkney; the first-fruits of spring were still biding their time. Many of the old and the weak died, not in the depths of winter so much as in the cruel first light of March.

We modern Orcadians don't have to contend with such deprivations and hardship. Still, we carry about inside us vivid ancestral memory. In the midst of a modern sufficiency and amplitude of material requirements, the old worries, despairs, and anguishes touch us.

We don't shake off the past as easily as all that.

And yet every day now brings its delights—crocuses in a garden, the longer slants of light, the urge—in spite of all—to do something new.

Interfering with 'God's Time'

7.4.1988

Deep down, one feels that there is something not quite right about it, interfering with time—with 'God's time', as the old folk used to say— stealing an extra hour of light in spring, adding an hour of darkness in autumn.

The pulse of a whole nation pauses, then moves into a new rhythm. All but the animals and plants and birds; they remain true to 'God's time'.

But when you think about it, I don't suppose it does people any harm to get up an hour earlier, and to go to bed likewise... The gastric juices seem to adapt, quickly enough.

We are told, too, that it's all a part of being welded into the United States of Europe; for the 'Common Market' nations all keep to Summer Time all the year round—and so might we, soon.

Still the faint unease persists. Nature ought not to be interfered with in this way.

The wrench in time struck me forcibly, yesterday evening.

It had been a marvellous afternoon, bounteous with sun. At Warbeth the first daisies were out. The gentle wind from the north-east, though, still remembered the recent snow. Children and dogs ran along the sand, beside the pulsing gleaming ocean.

For months I had got used to lighting the fire in late afternoon, drawing the curtains, and listening to music on tapes (since the world of books has been closed, though only temporarily). And then the TV news, which is hardly cheerful stuff at any time. It occurred to me the other day that only dark events, violence and swindling and the other deadly sins, are considered newsworthy. There are tides of goodness flowing everywhere in the world: but it seems we don't want to know about them.

Well, then, here I was yesterday afternoon late, and the fire beginning to smoke and crackle and flame, and piles of tapes ready to select from; but something was wrong. What was wrong? The lovely lingering light of early spring, that was upsetting everything, wrenching the room and the whole landscape through the window from their winter frames.

It is strange to be upset by light and beauty. We will all get used to it, in a day or two.

Novels on Film

14.4.1988

A film, *A Passage to India*, was announced in the *Radio Times* for showing on TV—and I didn't know whether to be glad or sorry.

Make no mistake, the novel *A Passage to India* by E. M. Forster is one of the great novels of this century.

But how often the film-makers fail to do justice to a great work of literary imagination! I think I have not seen one Shakespeare play excellently done on TV, or on 'the silver screen'. Nor any other great work of imagination, if it comes to that.

The trouble is, the film-makers have to leave so much out. For example, the style of the story, the overtones and suggestions, the subtle interweavings, the surge and pulse of the prose. In other words, a whole dimension has to be left out in the transposition from book to screen.

So, of course, it happened with *A Passage to India*. The magic garment of the original story-teller was missing. The film-maker, though, had done a masterpiece of patching and stitching, so that the film could be enjoyed in, and for itself. But to one who has read the great novel a dozen times, maybe, the film was perhaps not so enjoyable as to one who had never turned the marvellous pages.

There is one great novelist who, time and again, crosses the great chasm from book to screen in triumph—Dickens. One reason is that Dickens created what the same E. M. Forster called 'flat characters' rather than 'rounded characters', and TV and film rejoice in flat characters rather than in characters that are subtly and delicately delineated, and are even given life by apparent contradictions now and then. Another reason is that the Dickens novels came out originally in regular episodes, rather like the TV 'soap operas', and so they slot neatly into the mass modern art form. *Pickwick Papers, Oliver Twist, David Copperfield*—TV has done them over and over, and they never fail.

It seems, though, that this week I have failed my readers. What, a 'Brinkie's Brae' without once mentioning Hamnavoe or Gypsy the cat or the glory of the new daffodils! Much more of this highfalutin meandering into literary and film criticism, and they'll be giving me my books...

Flowers Spun from Light

21.4.1988

Suddenly the daffodils are everywhere, the indomitable ones, the flowers spun from light.

They sleep all winter along the roadside ditches, underground, hoarding their strength and beauty for spring. Then they turn in their sleep—'Time to be up and about. The first lambs are on the hillside. We thought we heard a lark singing the day before yesterday. I distinctly heard a spade going into the wet loam in the tattie-patch next door. Time to be about our business.'...

That's what one imagines the daffodils saying to one another, in the earth-cells where they have endured all winter the darkness, cold, and tempest.

But they play it canny. No use rushing into the light, like mad dancers. So they wrap themselves in tight green coats, with hoods up, and give a canny look here and there. The first brave venturer, she calls to the others that it's all right, 'There's only one last streak of snow on the Orphir hills—The sun's at the right angle—The crows are flying with twigs—The kids are stuffing themselves with pieces of chocolate egg—Time for our dance to begin'...

Only the bravest daffodils are convinced, to begin with. A few cautiously remove their hoods and look around them at the lovely late March earth and sky. They didn't think such beauty could exist anywhere! Their job is simply to make the awakening world more beautiful still...

Now they come in crowds. They jostle in ditch and field and garden. They wave a valediction to the coloured little splinters lying here and there; the crocuses have held their fair, and packed their silent music and gone.

The world belongs to the daffodils. Never were there such lovely clothes—not even in the courts of Solomon or in Irish palaces where the princesses wore saffron.

But what's this?—A cold blast, a storm from the east, a huge blue-black cloud grinding out snow-flakes. The golden flowers surge and sway in the gale, pellets of hail batter their cups, grey flakes drift onto their petals and melt there.

Some folk think, 'Poor flowers, we'd better take some of them inside, to our vases and bowls'... Indeed, they make every room rich and rare.

But the daffodils are strong as well as beautiful. They endure the batterings of snow and tempest. They are there, lovelier than ever, when the sun comes out again.

They run, rejoicing, in long lines all over the Orkney landscape, a golden web.

New Glasses

28.4.1988

I got my second pair of glasses the other afternoon, brought back from Kirkwall by a friend. This was the 'everyday' pair, which should be worn all the time so that friends can be recognized on the street, and Stromness is no longer a community of grey shadows.

It has been no real comfort for me to watch TV for months. One eye has to be shaded so that the dim figures seen through the other eye can have some kind of life...

So I put on the new glasses and switched on TV. Figures shimmering with vitality, with intent vibrant faces, were striking balls of amazing solidity and vivid colours. It was a snooker match.

Then I went to the sea window and looked out. The Orphir hills, that have been faded and far away for so long, leapt to meet me like a friend. I thought it might be possible to step onto the Outer Holm, as we had done many a summer day in boyhood from a flattie. As for the harbour,

I could relish every little moving corrugation. The houses and street and the people going past had a striking immediacy and solidity.

I realised that I was seeing the world as I must have seen it forty years ago, before what the blind poet Milton called 'dim suffusion' began to veil it gradually. Poor Milton, he was possibly (by that description from *Paradise Lost*) suffering from progressive cataracts too. But three and a half centuries ago nothing could be done about it. You slowly went blind.

There are one or two minuscule hazards with the new glasses. One is liable to bump into pieces of furniture. It takes the eye a while to judge distances exactly... Then the glasses keep slipping down my nose so that I have to keep shoving them back. No doubt the tightening of a little screw will fix that. Then the two pairs of glasses are forever getting lost, so that I have to grope into a dozen corners before finding them. (And as you get older your patience has a shorter and shorter fuse.) So a friend said, 'Always keep them *in one place*'... And that I intend to do.

Yes, there are two pairs: the first pair I got are for reading. 'Now,' I thought, 'for a feast of books'... It hasn't worked out that way. In the long period of non-reading, I got into the habit of listening to music instead. Old age brings laziness as well as ill-temper. It's far too much of an effort to go tunnelling into books—'words, words, words', as Hamlet said. Much easier to listen to the tapes.

And anyway, in the meantime, I have those amazingly vivid moving pictures on TV... But I expect I'll be glad enough to go back to my books quite soon.

The First Morning of May

5.5.1988

Imagine Stromness a hundred years ago, on the first morning of May.

What are all the girls doing up so early? Why have they all gone trooping to the upper slopes of Brinkie's Brae?

They are all there. The servants who work in the big houses, scouring and sweeping—the prim daughters of shopkeepers and skippers—the lasses smelling of fish from the piers—a few farm girls smelling of milk and butter—a troop of Gaelic-speaking girls from the herring booths at Ness.

You would think there was going to be some great fair on Brinkie's Brae.

And now the sun is clear of the Orphir hills, and dew sparkles on the grass-blades.

The girls of Hamnavoe, with much laughter, and a few protests and tauntings, bend down and wet their hands on the dew and spread the dew on their faces. Their faces glisten for a moment before the dew melts.

Then, in little troops and companies, or alone, the girls of May walk or trip or run down a dozen closes to their houses and work-places.

Some ill-natured old man will say, 'Where have you been, you slut? What about my porridge?'

And some herring-merchant will say, 'What nonsense! I pay you to gut and salt herring. You'll work an extra half-hour tonight...'

Some wicked old wife at the end of a close will sneer, 'Make them bonny, will it, the May dew? It'll take more than a few dew-drops to make them bonny, Jemima and Peterina from next door.' (But that same old dame, when she thought no one was looking, she dabbed her cheeks with dew too, at her tattie patch.)

The master at the school says, after the morning prayers, 'I could not help but notice that, this morning early, certain girls from this school went to the slopes of the hill behind and indulged in a piece of ignorant superstition, namely the washing of their faces in the May dew. I hope they think it made them look more comely, because I must tell them here and now that I notice no whit of difference in their appearance, none at all... If those same ignorant girls nod off and drowse in the middle of the geography lesson, I'll have something further to say'... And he brought down his stick on to his desk with a loud *Thwack!*

And a poor cripple lass down a pier weeps because she hasn't been able to get to the hill.

And so the lovely month of May might have come to Orkney a century ago.

The Gab o' May

12.5.1988

Another awkward May morning—the wind still in that bitter quarter, the east, and grey clouds threatening rain.

May hasn't been a kind month to us, so far. Ah, well...

There's always work to be done. I sat at my desk and opened a note-book, on several pages of which were scrawled first drafts of a Brodgar poem, written six weeks ago or so. I tried to imagine the setting up of the stones over what must have been a great stretch of time: generations, maybe centuries. And the kind of early Orcadians who quarried and dressed the stones and dragged them from Vestra Fiold and erected them in the pits prepared for them. And what they thought they were up to. It is impossible to enter into the minds of such people.

I discovered that, to my cost, when I went over the first drafts with a pencil. It was pretty awful. Whole sections had to be cut out. Other sections might be worth working on. There were fleeting felicities here and there. But I did not give myself much hope that the poem could ever be made satisfactory, either to myself or a publisher or to some readers at a future date.

So I retired from the contest bruised and battered, but with a faint hope that some day (the little host of scribes in the subconscious working on it secretly in the meantime; this is a phenomenon of all artistic creation, without doubt) I might turn those scarred pages of the notebook again.

I had to go out in the evening for a prescription to the surgery. A cold grey evening still. Some neighbours were grouped about a lost cat—'a very nice friendly cat'—that had somehow strayed to Mayburn Court. But nobody, including myself, would offer to take the gentle forlorn creature into the household... 'Where has it come from?'... 'Radio Orkney has mentioned a lost black-and-white cat in Kirkwall.'

'Could it have leapt onto some lorry and come all the way to Stromness?'... That seems highly unlikely.

When I came home with my prescription the creature was still there. And it followed me up the steps, so touching and so trusting. And it followed along the balcony to my door. And it would have come in like a shot. And I had plenty of milk.

After I had shut the door against it, I felt a bit like D. H. Lawrence after he had thrown that log of wood at the golden snake in Sicily.

All I hope is, that nice cat gets home safely.

* * *

All is forgiven, beautiful month of May. This morning, there's sun and blue sky and a kindling warmth in the air... The wind has shifted into the south-east.

What the old folk called 'the gab o' May'—a period of dull cold weather—might be over early this year.

Orkney Churches
19.5.1988

St Peter's Kirk at Skaill is such a fine building of its period, and is such a familiar landmark alongside the road to Birsay, that it would be sorely missed if it had to be demolished. I hope it isn't too late to put in a word for it. So many of the Kirks and 'big hooses' that set their stamp on the parish are decaying. Meantime a greyish wash of architectural uniformity is going over Orkney.

It's interesting to note that most Orkney churches were built beside the sea: so many that we must believe it was no mere accident. There is symbolism in it somewhere. Perhaps the sea was the symbol of eternity. And there, above the shore, the parish Church stood, instructing those who were dust in those things that lay beyond the boundless horizons, things marvellous and undreamed of.

Now I must hasten to defend myself from those who will be quick to point out that St Peter's in Stromness, for example, was built well back from the sea, on the side of Brinkie's Brae, in fact. True, but its predecessor stood where the kirkyard is now: some walls are still to be seen. In the 19th century a place called 'Monkerhouse' was still spoken about— but the little medieval monastery, if that is what it was, has gone into the sea—there has been so much erosion round our western seaboard.

It will be quickly pointed out too, that St Magnus—the greatest minster of them all, in Kirkwall—stands well back from the shore. But it seems it wasn't so at the time of its building. The Peerie Sea has shrunk so much in a millennium that it is a mere vestige of what it once was. 850 years ago those going into the Cathedral could hear its waves lapping—the wash mingling with the bell-voice on a holy day.

There are, of course, a number of UP Kirks and Free Kirks that seem to have no kinship with the sea. It is very likely that, in the 19th century, people were ceasing to think in a symbolical way. Utility was everything. They prided themselves on their progressive ways. 'What does it matter where we build our Kirk?'—I can well imagine them saying just that. Thereby, all unconsciously, they were admitting that a great richness had gone out of their lives.

Holiday in Shetland (1)

9.6.1988

The *St Sunniva* left Stromness for Shetland at noon on Sunday, and never surely was there a calmer sea all the way. The big boat never rocked in Hoy Sound, and, further in, the famous Sumburgh Roost might never have been there.

But we sailed blindfold, for the slight sea-haar when we left Stromness thickened the further north we sailed—Yesnaby and Westray were ghost places, and Fair Isle might not have existed.

The big boat went on in this mild thick silver-grey air, with its load of tourists and its hame-faring Shetland folk, and three of us going in quest of a wider 'simmer dim' than even Orkney can show.

And we ate two nice meals on board, and drank a little beer, and watched the silver-grey haar thicken to a dense fleece of fog. It was so thick in Lerwick we didn't even know the *Sunniva* had docked till one of the stewards told us. (We hadn't gone to watch the afternoon film. Fancy that, a cinema on board, as well as a shop and a music group— how the old-timers who used to sail pre-war on the North boats would have been amazed!)

Of Lerwick, there was nothing—it was entirely blotted out. But Gunnie did see our car-hirer on the pier with a new red Ford Sierra waiting with the keys and necessary forms, a very friendly lady, and in a few minutes we were off, headed north, out of the blind town. And sometimes the fog wove thicker, and sometimes shredded out a little. There was a constant stream of cars with mist-diffused headlights coming from the north—from Sullom Voe, thought Gunnie.

Gunnie knows Shetland well, and loves it, having visited it many times recently while co-operating with Liv Schei in the newly-published book, *The Shetland Story*... I've been to Shetland only once, in 1950, helping to 'cover' a Shetland/Orkney football match for *The Orkney Herald*, and as the brief visit was filled with celebrations and socialising, I have only dim far-away memories... It is partly to atone for this shameful ignorance that I am in Shetland now.

In the fleece of fog, Gunnie took the wrong road only once, and then she realized it was the next one further on. We dropped down a rough narrow road, and didn't see the sea far below; and there to greet us at the lonely beautiful cottage Grobsness in the district of Voe were the owners, John and Liz Somerville. They were all kindness, and gave us coffee and schnapps to warm us up, and information as to the basic workings of the house.

The boreal light still seeped through the fog when it was time to go to our comfortable beds—and it was still only 11.30pm.

When I woke up on Monday morning, a night wind had blown the fog away; there was even a flying gleam or two of sun.

Holiday in Shetland (2)

16.6.1988

The place is called Grobsness and the cottage is on a steep peninsula set into one of the many voes that go gleaming here and there from the Atlantic and North Sea into the Mainland of Shetland.

It's a lovely cottage with all modern conveniences and so we don't have to fetch water from a burn a mile away and scour the beach for driftwood.

From Grobsness, up a steep road, we make expeditions here and there. The weather has been marvellously kind, after our arrival ten days ago in dense fog on the *Sunniva*.

Since it is impossible to compress all the richness and beauty and generosity we have experienced in Shetland into a short article, a few impressions will have to do. (Maybe next week a few more impressions will be inflicted on you; but so long as you think maybe of packing your bags for Shetland instead of the Costa Brava or Blackpool, that may be no bad thing.)

Two days ago, the sun came out, unclouded, but there was still a chill in the wind. So we thought of going to some sheltered place for a picnic.

Gunnie drove us up the steep road and we didn't stop till we came to a little farm beside the sea. It is marigold time in Shetland—never in Orkney have I seen such masses of marigolds, in fields and shallows and ditches. The larks were pelting down songs so joyously and continually that after a time there was too much wealth of sound; one involuntarily stops the ears.

Everywhere the voes striking deep into the lane—round every corner a new richness of blue, that the wind stroked to a deeper intensity.

It is the time of lambs too, and brown lambs and black lambs seem to be as plentiful as the white lambs. Their little wavering bleats wake us in the morning.

We carried the picnic baskets across a field of new grass and got shelter behind one of those huge rocks that Shetland is studded with. All around us in a beautiful blue ground-mist grew the wild flowers called squill.

One bird was very indignant at our arrival, an oyster-catcher. It flew round and about high and low, hurling lyrical insults at us; but soon it must have decided that there was no real harm in us, for it fell silent.

Then we spread the rug and made impromptu sandwiches of the rolls, cheese, tomatoes and ham we had bought in the little shop in Voe village, and washed it down with lager out of cans.

I'm sure that the picnic place, that Monday afternoon, is one of the loveliest places this earth has to show. I can never hope to bring it to life. The only poet who could was Gerard Manley Hopkins. He would have been utterly enchanted with the 'wildness and wet' of Shetland.

Holiday in Shetland (3)

23.6.1988

We met, in the first days of June, so many delightful people in Shetland.

George Peterson, teacher of English in Brae, visited us in Grobsness and invited us to see a performance of the Papa Stour Sword-dance by a group of his boy pupils. (They were leaving in a few days to do the Sword-dance in Norway.) An intricate beautiful dance it was, to chant and fiddle: a kind of ritual battle ending in peace and reconciliation. The mystery is, how did all those heroes of Christendom—St Denis of France, St James of Spain, St George of England, etc, come to be rooted in the lonely isle of Papa Stour? The dance was being performed there in Sir Walter Scott's time... We had a delicious lunch in the dining hall of the new luxurious Brae school.

That same afternoon Jonathan Wills, editor of the *Shetland Times*, met us off the Bressay ferry. After giving us another delightful meal—a kind of chowder with monkfish—Jonathan drove us through Bressay to the Noss shore, pointing out all the tumultuous birds and wild-flowers that make Shetland so beautiful at this time of year. He pointed to a croft—'That's where Baby-face Nelson was born, who was Al Capone's driver'... Jonathan lives in a fine house by the shore, facing Lerwick. The ferry, which sails, I think, every half-hour—they have amazingly cheap and frequent ferries connecting all the Shetland islands—brought us back at late evening to Lerwick and the car.

One day we drove to a small jetty. On the way we had lingered at a little hill and bay where half the lambs were black or brown, and Gunnie took a score of pictures at least. There at the jetty was waiting Henry Anderton and his boat. A short crossing brought us to his tiny precipitous island of Vaila, where he lives in a hall restored and embellished by his ancestors: a lofty dining room, one wall of which is totally occupied with oil portraits of his family, with a musician's gallery above. It was a cold day and Henry restored the four of us with generous glasses, and later fed us with one of his own 'farmed' salmon, and rounded off his hospitality by circumnavigating his bleak rugged island, taking us on the way through a black arch of rock, with the cold sea seething all round.

One Saturday evening we were invited to a party in Skeld. Again, there was nothing but boundless generosity, friendship, music and laughter. The hostess Debbie said, 'I thought you mightn't like sea-food, coming from Orkney'... The many kinds of sea-food tasted delicious, and the Foula lamb; and the impromptu music and comedy from Dave and Cluny was a better show than anything I've watched on TV lately... A most lovely breathtaking serene sky in the north-east, driving back to Grobsness at 2.30am, and the voes gave back unwavering, the loveliness.

It was lucky for us three strangers that Gunnie knows so many good people. She stopped the car one evening at a farm at Culswick, and there we had a wonderful reception from Sandy and Mary Fraser and their young daughter Osla. Below the farm was a loch that the sea had breached in a storm, a long while ago, and the cottages still cluster round the wetlands.

Holiday in Shetland (4)

30.6.1988

A prosperous town Lerwick is, with all the bustle round the harbour and foreign ships in, and with a strong heartbeat to it. I thought of little Stromness, sitting so tranquil under its granite hill, only lapped lightly by the late 20th century.

One sunny day we thought of visiting the northern islands, Yell and Unst. There are frequent cheap efficient ferry services linking the islands. Yell, we had been told, was a sprawl of solid peat. We found the people and the places we visited altogether pleasant, from the well-stocked shop near the pier to the Aald Haa, Burravoe, where Mrs Garrioch presides over what is going to be a fascinating local museum, to Mary Ellen Odie and her husband who have a beautiful garden with a stone-age broch at the end of it...

We couldn't linger too long in Yell; there was the ferry to catch for Unst. The weather continued so bright, day after day, we could hardly believe our luck. Unst is a greener island than Yell—and Gunnie knew so many places we could have gone to. We settled for a most beautiful beach with a roofless medieval church, St Olaf, at one end of it. And then the coverlet was unrolled on the sand and the picnic lunch set down on it.

Then, having eaten and drunk, there was nothing to do but let the wave of early summer go over us, in warmth and peace and brightness.

Whenever we got back to Grobsness, late most evenings, there was that precipitous perilous road for Gunnie to negotiate in the car. Half-way down, Kulgin had to get out and open the gate... Then, at the garage door, what a welcome we got from the cats, especially little Tammy with the many-coloured coat; she rolled about on the dusty road in pure welcome; but it may just have been that she knew Kulgin was going to give her supper.

The Atlantic mouth of the voe is guarded by islands, Muckle Roe and Vementry. It is the utter desolation of Vementry that is so impressive—high and dark and uninhabitable—some late romantic painter ought to have chosen Vementry for his 'Island of the Dead'... Back home, I found myself writing a poem about Vementry and Stone Age people in a ship beaching at Vementry, all the sheltered fertile voes being denied them by earlier settlers; and they were full of courage and foreboding and hope.

Holiday in Shetland (5)

7.7.1988

It was something (as they say) to see Mousa Broch, and the four flares of Sullom Voe with the peat cutting near it, 20th-century energy cheek by jowl with immemorial hearth fires; and Scalloway set among the lovely bridge-linked islands in the west.

We would have needed another month to see all the places we wanted so much to visit. Much better that, the yearning for more, than to be pining for home twice or thrice a day.

Some of the places were too wild and rocky for my weary bones to traverse. But it was quite pleasant to sit at Grobsness while my three friends went to the cliffs of Eshaness or Noss. Shetland began to work like yeast in the imagination, and I was able to sketch in my little red notebook seven or eight drafts for poems, in the midsummer solitude of Grobsness.

The day came for us to depart—Friday, 10 June.

There were last messages to do in Lerwick. Kulgin and I drank coffee in Solotti's cafe where the waitresses wear milkmaids' bonnets, very becomingly. How strange, that Colin and Gunnie should have thought we had gone on a pub crawl!...

We delivered the rented car to its garage, and were in good time to climb the steep gangway onto the *Sunniva* before she sailed at noon. The sun shone on Lerwick and Bressay as we left.

Well, we were certainly fortunate with the weather. What my impressions of Shetland might have been after the days of storm, I do not know. What we experienced was a wild and wonderful place, as if some young gypsy had emptied her pack before us, and here and there among all the squanderings of bog and desolation we found places of purest lyricism and enchantment. Whereas Orkney, in comparison, is a neatly apparelled place, sober and slightly complacent. Only along its western seaboard, from Westray to Hoy, Orkney forgets its green hoard of pasture and history, and becomes a poet.

The Sumburgh roost was as gentle as a pond. Off Westray, Captain Duncan invited us to his bridge and soon the familiar landmarks began to fall into place. Scabra Head, Marwick Head, Yesnaby, the Old Man of Hoy, Black Craig. Little green Graemsay seemed to be opening the gate into Hoy Sound for us.

It was 8pm, and we were home. The dog Nuff heard Gunnie whistle from the rail of the docked ship, and he went half-mad with joy.

The seal of summer, the westering sun, lay over Orkney too. Maybe this year, for a change, the season would be fine.

Highland Park Distillery

4.8.1988

You run into tourists from further south, who say what a drab summer it's been down there. Also the weather-men on TV keep up a low lamentation.

Well, here in Orkney we've had our grey days too, but all the same it has been one of the better summers of this decade. For example, I feel I oughtn't to be at this table this morning writing, at all; for outside, July is squandering its rich torrents of gold. It's been that way nearly all week, except for one memorable afternoon earlier this week. I'll enlarge on that presently.

But earlier, in June, we had twelve sun-filled days in Shetland. Then, a few days later, we experienced those mysterious silent battles between sun and sea-haar in Rackwick. No summer would be complete without those cosmic encounters.

Two days ago my friend Hervé from France and I decided to visit the Highland Park distillery. Imagine this—living all my life in Orkney and never seeing the inside of that famous distillery! (But many a time and oft I've tasted the fruits of it.)

So, in we go, Hervé and I, and sit awhile in a waiting room until a sufficient crowd gathers; and then a young lady guide takes us round, describing every station of the whisky-making process from the malting-floor to the full casks, stamped with their dates, waiting for the twelve years of maturing to pass... 'It would cost you £500 to buy a cask,' said our guide, 'but then the Excise would slap on an extra £5,000...'

At the end of it all, we visitors sat in a little theatre and—a glass of the pure malt in our hands—saw a well-made film of Orkney in general and of Highland Park in particular. Then we went into a little shop and signed names in the book, and Hervé bought Highland Park badges—very well-designed logos—to take home to his friends in France.

It was when we emerged into the afternoon again—after those vaults of deep alchemical enchantment—that we ran into melodrama in the shape of rain. I am not speaking of ordinary rain—drizzle or shower or downpour—but into such intensities of rain as you only experience three or four times in a lifetime. Old-time Orcadians used to call such rain 'a hellyifer'. It was as if buckets of water were being flung at us, again and again. Between the door of Highland Park and the car we got drenched. 'Surely,' I thought, 'the least we can expect is a bad cold out of this...' But no fevers or chills have arrived so far. Maybe that dram, earlier, saved us...

Icelandic Sagas

18.8.1988

I had a visit one morning last month from Professor George Johnston and his wife Jeanne and his friend Professor Blisset. Professor Johnston's speciality is the Nordic languages. Besides being a well-known poet himself in North America, he has translated Icelandic sagas and the verse of the famous modern Norwegian poet K. Ødegård, who visited me one Saturday night a few years back, on his way from Iceland to Ireland.

Professor Johnston came with a gift of books—his translation of the latest collection of Ødegård poems, including a group of Orkney poems (and the visit to Mayburn Court is one of them), and two books of his own poems, and his translation of an Icelandic saga I hadn't known, *Gisli's Saga*.

It was only earlier this week that finally I got down to reading this new saga. What a relief, among the clutter and introspection of 20th-century narrative, to find a story as clean and sharp as an axe!

There must be something in the far northern latitude that creates a hunger for stories, and gifted tongues to tell them. It is a remarkable thing, that those comparatively few farming and trading families produced such a rich crop of narrative, in medieval Iceland. It may have been the early darkness of winter, the people grouped about the hearth, the low flames burning in a lamp here and there, the circling ale horns, that unleashed the tongues for story-telling.

There may also have been the need to reassure the family as to its 'title-deeds' and credentials in this new huge island of glaciers and burning mountains—their ancestors who had first fared west out of Norway had been brave and resolute men, who had established themselves by hard work and foresight. And so, in comparative peace and security, this present-day farmer could sit down with his family and bond-men and serfs and pass the winter in 'a feast of story-telling'...

The strange thing is, many of the sagas tell of wild lawless men, breakers of the peace, doom-driven... They, in Iceland as in ancient Greece, are the heroes who meet death with a taunt or a jest or words of wonderment... And so was Gisli the outlaw. And so was many a one in our own *Orkneyinga Saga*, that imperishable scroll.

Early Tourists

There might have been fifty tourists each summer in Stromness when I was young, before the war, in the early 30s. But maybe I'm exaggerating. Or maybe there were far more than memory suggests.

There was no mistaking them. For one thing, they did nothing; and everybody in Stromness worked at something or other. Also, they were forever stopping and looking around, up closes and down piers—and what on earth did they want to look at such common ordinary places for? Also, you could tell them in the far distance even by their language—they spoke a very grand English, and they put the words together in such a way that the Stromnessians said they 'chanted'. (And this, when you think about it, is very strange, because the modern tourists are forever telling us how musical our speech is. I suppose it amounts to this: the way one speaks in one's own community is the norm, and any variant partakes (however slightly) of that quality of formal artificial utterance that we call 'song'.)

A few of the tourists played golf. We lived in those days near the golf course and our services were called upon as caddies. We followed those grand rich chanting folk round the course, humping their golf clubs. At the end of the round we were magnificently paid with a shilling. *A shilling!* A silver shilling was an immense amount of money in those days. You could buy twenty 'Gold Flake' cigarettes, or six bars of Cadbury's milk chocolate... Sometimes a very wealthy or generous golfing tourist would give you one and six. (The modern equivalent, I should explain to younger readers, is seven and a half pence. And that should let you see what progress we have made in half a century.)

Some tourists, like the eccentric professor, came every summer. He had the reputation of being a 'woman-hater' and he wouldn't sleep in a hotel room that had a tree outside the window.

There were grand ladies who set up easels at the foot of Melvin Place, for example, to paint a delicate water-colour. (They didn't need to worry about cars: there might have been ten or twelve cars in the whole of Stromness.)

Concerning cars, there was one piece of melodrama that shocked us children to our very souls. Two ladies drove their car down the Warehouse Pier to get it hoisted onto the deck of the *Ola*—but something went wrong and the car drove onto the *Ola* and into the harbour over the side. The two tourists were dead when they were brought to the surface.

There was also a bearded man with a dog who lived in a tent at the Lookout, but he was more a tramp than a tourist, and he may have sold small things from door to door. The imminence of war was in the air, and so this Scottish itinerant—it was rumoured by idle mischievous tongues—was a German spy. But I'm perfectly sure he was just a young man with a shaggy beard and a dog and a tent who, as the song says, was born under a wandering star.

Isabel Gunn

1.9.1988

Two weeks ago I received through the post a remarkable story, in the form of a poem published in Canada, *The Ballad of Isabel Gunn* by Stewart Scobie, who is descended on his mother's side from Orcadians.

This Stromness girl, Isabel Gunn, must have been born about two hundred years ago. She grew up and fell in love with a Hudson Bay man, an Orcadian too, called John Scarth, who was probably home on leave. Either the girl was persuaded by John Scarth to go with him to 'the nor'-wast' fur-trading posts, or else she was so infatuated that she argued him into the deception. (No women were allowed at the trading posts—I suppose it was reckoned in those days that women were too delicate for North Canadian winters—and also there was the danger of jealousies and feuds breaking out, to the detriment of work.)

At any rate, the Hudson Bay agent in Stromness, David Geddes, signed on a certain John Fubbister, obviously Foubister—in those days people weren't too particular about the spelling of names.

And this John Fubbister—who in fact was Isabel Gunn in man's attire—sailed across the Atlantic on the ship *Prince of Wales* (Captain Hanwell, master), in company with John Scarth. John Scarth explained to anyone who would listen that Fubbister was his cousin.

Once they arrived at Moose Factory, Scarth was sent on to his duties at Eastman River, while Isabel Gunn was allotted to Albany, where she laboured among the other workers, many of them Orkney men; and she must have carried off her deception with great skill, for no one seems to have questioned her true identity.

Whether her long separation from Scarth cooled her ardour for him—it is suggested in this long poem that his work engrossed him too deeply, for he was a good dedicated Company man—or her starved heart and the strain of deception drove her to it, will never be precisely known, but Isabel Gunn bestowed her affections on a Fife man, David Spence, a fellow labourer. Nature, as they say, had its way, and Isabel Gunn became pregnant; but right up to the hour of birth no one, it seemed, knew or suspected. On December 29, 1807, the labourer

Fubbister came in great distress to the house of Alexander Henry, a Hudson's Bay official, and soon after gave birth to a boy child.

Meantime, fate had struck a bitter blow—David Spence was drowned in Red River when the boat he was in overturned. Isabel Gunn and her infant were looked after well by an Indian woman, Ke-che-cho-wich.

John Scarth, summoned to see his 'cousin', hurriedly set down a purse of coins beside her bed, and left, and Isabel never saw him again.

She returned to Orkney with her son, lived in great poverty, begging for food and shelter (as the poem says), 'from Stronsay to Hoy', and wintering in a broken Dounby mill.

She died in Kirkwall, probably in 1861. I am hoping soon to get fuller information about these extraordinary events.

It is strange, I think, that this extraordinary story has not been gathered into Orkney legend... I for one had not heard of it till now.

Discovery of a Poet

15.9.1988

Last time there was a postal strike was in the early 70s, and it seemed to go on for a long time. I remember it chiefly because, that winter, BBC Radio was running its annual students' verse competition, open to students at all the universities and colleges of Scotland, and I had been asked to be one of the assessors. The normal thing would have been to read the verse as it came in, batch after batch. But this was impossible because of the strike. But at last the strike ended, and then the floodgates were opened! An *immense* parcel came thudding into the lobby one morning, and it contained the songs of about a hundred singing birds from the Scottish seats of learning, typed and on sheets scrawled or neatly printed—every variety of script was there, and the full range of lyricism poured forth. Alas, since the human being is not by nature a maker of verse, many of the 'poems' required only a cursory glance to be set on the growing pile of rejections. But here and there, now and again, through the wordstorm, a genuine utterance could be heard—a fragment of larksong—and these gems were put aside for further consideration.

And then, suddenly, there came a group of six or seven poems by a young student who knew more than a little about the art of poetry. It was like coming on an oasis in the middle of the Gobi.

This very good poet turned out to be a student at the Glasgow College of Art and the name on top of each page was Elizabeth Lochhead.

It seemed to me, at the end of that immense labour, that Elizabeth Lochhead was the clear winner. As I boarded the plane for Edinburgh, armed with my notes, I devoutly hoped that my two fellow judges would be of the same opinion.

We met, a day or two later, in a pub near the BBC. After five minutes or so of cautious probing, I think I let go the name Elizabeth Lochhead. One after the other, my fellow judges nodded agreement over their glasses of beer. Elizabeth Lochhead was unanimously the winner.

A telegram was sent to her Glasgow address. Within two hours, she was in the studio in George Street, Edinburgh, being interviewed—and brimming over with joy too, as I remember—and an actress with a beautiful voice, Sandra Clark, was reading the few poems that had emerged with credit from the competition.

That poet is now well-known far beyond Scotland. Nowadays she is called Liz Lochhead. She has delighted Stromness audiences with her superb verbal artistry.

That's really all I remember about the last postal strike. But if the present strike has, concealed somewhere in the mountain of mail, as rare a treasure, I won't complain over-much.

Labyrinth of Books

6.10.1988

Why are there some days when everything seems to go wrong, like this morning?

I was going to have written so many letters this morning. There was that brief holiday from letter-writing while the postal strike was on. I kept perversely, with one part of me, hoping that the strike would go on for a month or so; so that the work I had to do could flow on unimpeded. But the postman's visits twice a day are so pleasant—the rattle at the letter-box about 9.45am and again about 3.45pm. Sometimes it's only a letter saying I should open it *at once* because if I do I might soon become a millionaire: and such communications go to light the fire. But where would we be without the tidings from dear friends near and far?

I got into such a tangle this morning with the letters that had to be written! The birthday present for a friend in Edinburgh wouldn't fit into the padded envelope I had already addressed. Another letter disappeared—what had happened? Maybe I had shoved it into the big birthday envelope by mistake; in which case the so-carefully-sealed envelope would have to be opened again. (Eventually the lost letter was discovered loitering on the couch.)

Then, details had to be copied from a book into an article I had written some time ago—a few factual things; nothing simpler than to fill in the blanks, once the book was located on the shelves. The book refused to be located on the shelf of Orkney books. Blood-pressure rising by the minute, I tore those shelves apart with frantic eyes, looking for *The Ice-Bound Whalers*. Nothing doing. It is there, somewhere, hiding. I could imagine it perversely sniggering from its hidden niche. I could imagine it saying, 'Let this be a lesson to him, once and for all. Let him arrange us books in decent order, not rammed in here and there in utter disregard. Then there's a chance we books might have civilised dealings with him...' I admit the justice of these biting remarks. The times I have wasted searching for books in the huge labyrinth of books that I call my library!

Well, I did get one letter written, but that was merely to sign my name on the Electoral Registrar's form. And there may yet be time, before going out to lunch in the Ferry Inn with three friends, to write to Gypsy the cat (who's always first on the list).

Normally the phone keeps a pious silence while I toil at the writing desk. This morning it rang *thrice*, just as a flow of words was building up.

What with looking for lost and missing books and articles, the living-room table is a wild chaos, mixed up with heels-of-loaf and flower petals.

And still, in the next half-hour there's the fire to clean and set.

Hundreds of books mock silently from the wall. The phone looks ready to leap into another wild outburst of ringing at any moment.

I ought, first thing, to have consulted my horoscope.

The Street-Devouring Dragon

10.11.1988

Now that the street-devouring dragon is nearing the Bank of Scotland, having eaten its way since early summer from furthest North End— with a pause for Shopping Week—pedestrians this past day or two have to make a loop round by the Town Hall (I always like to think of it as the Free Kirk) on to Church Road and so on to Post Office and Pier.

And sometimes the dragon roars and rends, laying bare the old entrails under the street; and whenever it comes on a stubborn granite bedrock, its roars are fearsome to hear; and the narrow chasm of the street flings the echoes near and far.

The workmen who are setting the new pipes, etc, are very cheerful and considerate.

Would this lifting up and laying down of the street have been a golden opportunity to re-pave Stromness with the lovely old flagstones that were once such a unique characteristic of the town? It seems not. Maybe nobody knows how to quarry flagstones any more.

These past few days, the little loop between Manse Lane and Church Road has been quite populous with people. I remember this side close well, having spent early childhood in the near vicinity. I always thought it a pleasant enclosed place, with a garden belonging to Mrs Brown whose husband had been the local registrar, and the tall-steepled kirk itself with Peter Esson in the tailor shop below, who seemed to be the guardian of the kirk and knew its history from the Disruption on. Facing Church Road was a cast-iron lion head that spouted clear water when you turned the knob. It was a wonderful corner. Miss Matheson our teacher lived at the foot of the steps, and next to her, facing the street, her brother Bill Matheson the saddler, whose shop was full of horse collars and bunches of raffia. Across the street from the saddler's was the sweetie-shop of Janetta Sinclair, where I was a faithful customer with my Friday halfpenny. In Janetta's shop window hung an enormous clay pipe.

I tell you, it was a busy corner! Nearby was the Commercial Hotel and Mr Robertson the lawyer's and Mr Brough the jeweller's and the two shops of Mr J. D. Johnston, draper, and Isa Sutherland the tobacconist, and the butcher's (Harcus).

Further up the Church Road—we always called it Kirk Road, and with good reason, because there were three kirks on it, the Old Kirk, the Free Kirk and the Pisky (Episcopal) Kirk—there were gardens with tall trees where rooks built untidy nests in Spring. And below was the fisherman's pier, and the boats and the gulls.

It was a delightful segment of Stromness for a child to grow up in.

When the street-devouring dragon comes, some time within the next year I suppose, to Mayburn Court, I hope to take a holiday far from the fumes and the shattering noise.

No Praise for the Dog

24.11.1988

Letters with next-to-impossible requests come from time to time. The Scottish poet Maurice Lindsay is compiling an anthology of poems about dogs for Aberdeen University Press. And he asked if I'd care to submit one.

I take care to avoid mentioning dogs whenever possible in my writing. If they *have* to appear, a sinister aura clings about them. I would never think of joining a Dog Lovers' Society.

With cats, it's quite another matter. I've been enchanted by cats since infancy. I feel a tingling in my fingers whenever a cat has to come into a story or poem. Every week I write a letter to a cat called Gypsy. I wrote a whole book about a cat once. The wisdom and mystery in those amber eyes, that 'change like the changing moon', as the poet Yeats said...

Tourists forever speak about the multitude of cats in Stromness. I think cats must have been a part of the populace since Hamnavoe began, whenever that was—probably well before the 17th century. Forever there will be cats where there are boats and fishing folk. There are fish-heads to be eaten, rats to be controlled, winter fires to sit at (washing the paws and singing).

I, being then a small boy aged six or seven, in Plainstones, Stromness, saw a tawny-coloured mongrel dog apparently asleep with a bone beside its wolfish skull. But no, it wasn't asleep; it had one savage eye on me. Wishing to be kind to the brute, I pushed the bone with my foot nearer its mangy snout. The next I knew, the monster had seized me by the knee and was savaging me unmercifully! Whereupon the whole of Graham Place and Victoria Street pealed and echoed with my yells of shock, anger, fear; and with a ragged circle of drill-marks from the teeth of the ungrateful hound in my leg I was rushed to the chemist's near the pierhead, where iodine (or something like it) was applied—and the cure was more painful than the wound.

So I wrote regretfully to Maurice Lindsay, saying that my muse had a marked aversion to writing about dogs—and giving the reason. Maurice Lindsay wrote again to say his anthology would not be devoted entirely to the praise of dogs; might there not be a poem in the traumatic childish encounter? Nothing doing.

Then I remembered how two years ago I had written a prose-poem about a wolf for *The Scottish Bestiary*. Maybe 'Wolf' would do? So it seems 'Wolf' will do. So now something will happen that I'd have thought impossible a month ago—I'm to be in a collection of dog poems...

Christmas in Literature

22.12.1988

Perhaps, in the next day or two, you might want to escape from the coloured blizzards and extravaganza on TV, and from over-much cake and wine, jollity and crackers and tinsel, and just be alone for an afternoon with a book.

Literature has been a good handmaiden to Christmas, from the time of the medieval ballads and carols. No lyric so chaste and perfect as: 'He came alle so stille / There his moder lay / As dew in Aprille / That falleth on the spray'...

In school we were presented with Milton's 'Ode on the Morning of Christ's Nativity'. I remember thinking, 'What a crude ugly poem!'... Milton is not for young minds. Only with experience come the full power and tenderness of the 'Ode'.

There was one rather sad Christmas poem at school that a few of us liked very much. You hardly ever see it in anthologies. It is by R. L. Stevenson, and is about a storm-beaten ship trying to make the open sea out of a bay, in vain. There's a young sailor on board who can see his own house on shore; and crusted with salt and weary with hauling sails, can almost see 'my mother's silver spectacles, my father's silver hair', and the blink of fire in the hearth.

Everyone, I'm sure, knows Thomas Hardy's 'The Oxen'. The child in the poem longs to believe that the oxen are kneeling in the byre on Christmas Eve; the mature man who wrote the poem knows that it is unlikely. From this tension of longing and stoicism came a flood of marvellous poetry and story that continued all through Hardy's life.

Dickens ushered in the modern Christmas of plum puddings, turkeys bursting with stuffing, the storm of gifts in coloured wrappings, merry children in the snow. Yet that cold desolate miser Scrooge, at the centre of *A Christmas Carol*, had to have that festive frame, otherwise he would have lost much of his power.

A few winters back, I used to read two Christmas pieces by James Joyce: the magnificent short story 'The Dead', and the Christmas dinner scene from *A Portrait of the Artist*, that ends in tears and rage and bitterness (in Ireland, where the story is set, it is still going on, the anger).

The 20th century has given us, too, T. S. Eliot's 'Journey of the Magi'.

But we needn't go so far afield. In *The Orkneyinga Saga* there are two thrilling Yuletide episodes, the burning of the first Earl Rognvald in Papa Stronsay, and the feast in Earl Paul's Hall in Orphir, that also ended in violence and bloodshed... The human element is never absent from the pure original story. The red threads go here and there, helter-skelter, through the tapestry. (Herod's horsemen rode through the streets of Bethlehem, their swords unsheathed.)

There are the beautiful Christmas rituals, from Thomasmas (the solstice) on, that were observed in Shetland crofts until well into the 19th century. These simple ceremonies must have put a great beauty on the dark cold northern midwinters... In Orkney, probably, the long lovely festival must have been dismantled a few decades earlier.

Game at the Year's End

29.12.1988

Seeing that it's midwinter, it might be fun for once to have a game before the year's end—imagining every month to be a stage in Orkney's history, (especially Stromness).

In January, then, the first-comers arrive, full of hope and fear. They draw up their skin boats at Warbeth, Breckness. How busy they are, gathering and building stones against the tempest! Will the ewe die, or the cow? Their existence hangs by such slender threads.

In February, the great-great-grandchildren of those first-comers have learned to read sea and tides and fishing grounds. The stones were good, the houses stand strong.

March: many deaths among the old folk aged thirty-five or forty. Let their bodies be mingled with the elements. Let the bones be stored in the chambers of death. New children come crying into the world.

April: a marvellous boy has fashioned and fired pots. There are exchanges with other villages along the west coast of Orkney, a bartering of fish and cheese, exchange of stories, unfolding of new mysteries. Such as, if the earth is broken and seed of wild barley planted... A girl puts spring flowers in one of the new pots.

May: hundreds of years have passed, many generations. It is no longer a little tribe in the west, poor and free. No: there is a great chief in Stenness, between the two lochs, a rich powerful presence. To him, richly dressed, splendidly housed, rents must be paid. Let them—the Breckness tribe—send one delegate to the assembly. One by one the stones are being dragged from Vestra Field to Brodgar and set up. It will be a circle of great power and mystery.

June: there is no peace. Nor can the little king in Stenness protect them more. Tribes are surging north in strong ships. They land, they establish their boundary stones and cut tribal marks on them. They must rear a strong tower, a broch, against the new tribes still surging out of Scotland and Ireland.

July: the stone castles, the impregnable brochs, everywhere. The Celtic tribes do not expect a bright-haired enemy from the east, on long ships like wolves. They kneel, one after the other. They yield up their keys. The yoke is put on their necks.

August: how happy it is in Breckness after harvest, after the summer Viking cruise: the ale-feast in the long hall, the vaunting and the epic chanted to the harp. Till word comes, there is more trouble, the two earls are in dispute again, the king in Norway must tax the farmers more.

September: the shadows deepen. Scots officials sit on the high stools. The Scottish earl will have a magnificent new Palace in Birsay. *Send a score of labourers.* The old law book is burned. New writings, in Scots, are made on the parchments.

October: ships from Spain and Norway and England shelter in the bay Hamnavoe. 'What are we doing here, in this storm-beaten place?' In Hamnavoe, that hamlet, the gold is ringing on the ale-barrel in William Clark's new inn... There are fifty houses in Hamnavoe now, and new foundations dug every day...

November: nothing but trouble, generation by generation. That trouble-maker Alexander Graham, beseeching the merchants yet once more for money to outface the Kirkwall magistrates in the law courts. 'No sooner is the pirate Gow out of the story but this Graham upsets us'... 'No, but Graham is for liberty and independence. Support him. He is the spirit of the age.'

December: nothing but trouble, though we sit in comfortable houses outfacing winter, with plenty to eat. The lovely earth is slowly being saturated with poison and pollution. There are enough bombs to blow it to smithereens. There will never be an end to worries and hope and laughter, under Brinkie's Brae and over all the earth.

The Ozone Layer

12.1.1989

It is amazing, how mild the past three winters have been—a visitation of snow for two or three days at most, and sea and sky more tranquil than in many a summer. And now, in the first days of 1989, the pattern looks as if it might be the same for this winter (of course, by the time you read this, eight days on from the time of writing, we might be knee-deep in snow and slush, or battling into tempests from north-east... it never does, to be too confident, prognosticating Orkney weather).

Still, three mild winters in a row—that is a small matter for wonder, at least. The older generation were always suspicious of seasonal mix-ups. They had their direful bits of folk wisdom, such as, 'A green Yule maks the kirkyard full'... They were all in favour of winter being really wintry, and big snowfalls were welcome, because under those quilts of white the earth was warm, and the seed slumbered healthily, waiting for the trumpet-blasts of March. If the winter was wintry, then summer would most likely be full of greenness and blossoming and increase.

These intrusions of quickening and growth into midwinter—they would have shaken their wise old heads about that, and feared greatly for the year to come...

Nowadays we are better informed, by newspapers and TV, or at least we like to think so. Some knowledgeable people tell us that the weather-patterns are changing because our ignorant, arrogant intrusions into the delicate web of nature, for the sake of 'progress', have made a hole in the 'ozone layer', and that in consequence of 'the greenhouse effect' the whole globe is heating up—and something, the 'greenites' insist, ought to be done about it; such as, we should stop using that pressurised foam when we shave in the morning, or when we hunt down with squirts of vapour the bluebottles that disturb our reading on early autumn nights.

I feel instinctively that there is a great deal of truth in those warnings. I feel that the new tyrannies of 'science' and 'progress' and 'profit' are wreaking great havoc in the ordered patterns of nature, and that the raveners will have to be restrained if our earth is to remain a pleasant and habitable place.

Perhaps it is too late. Perhaps the human spirit is too torpid with affluence and comfort, at least in the west, to face the great challenge.

Bernard Shaw thought that it was in such conditions that the great advances in evolution were made. Somewhere, deep down in the human spirit, there is a vigilance, a readiness, a longing to launch out into unknown seas...

We must hope so. In the meantime all we Stromnessians can do is hope that the dangerous rays pouring through 'the ozone layer' don't melt the ice-caps gradually; so that our grandchildren, building their houses higher and higher up Brinkie's Brae, never see on a calm night the old town drowned under the sea. 'That,' they'll say, 'was Graham Place'... 'And those two shimmering sunken hulks were the Town Hall and the Hotel'... 'The two blue islands of Hoy over there, they're the Ward and the Coolag, they used to be part of one land mass'...

The Master of the *George*

19.1.1989

January, 1726—and a fine ship, armed, has dropped anchor behind the Holms, in the 'Clestrain Roads'... That might have struck the townsfolk as strange, in the first place. Why couldn't the ship anchor in the harbour like other ships? (In those days, more and more sailing ships were sheltering in Stromness, and provisioning, and trading. The magistrates and merchants of Kirkwall were none too pleased about that.)

Some old seaman, sitting in the seaward-facing window of the Arctic Whaler or the North Star, might have levelled his glass at the strange ship beyond the Holms, and read the name *George* painted on the bows. However sinister and storm-battered she looked, the name was reassuring; that was the name of the King; she must be a leal and a true ship.

But that line of guns? For sure, the cannon must be to defend her crew and cargo against the French freebooters... All through that century there were wars against France. It seemed that France would be the great enemy from the beginning to the end of history.

Meantime the shopkeepers bought in eggs and cheese and beef and chickens from the crofts of Cairston and Innertoon. They anticipated good business. Sailors were always short of such delicacies.

Along the dingy webbed corridors of the ale-houses, barrels of the oldest ale were trundled. Sailors get tired of rum at last. Their throats are salted. Nothing like good local ale to bring the songs and dances and silver coins out of them.

But no small boat was launched from the *George*. Shadowy figures moved about on her. It seemed the skipper might be unwilling to make contact with the townsfolk... The old seaman with the telescope reported that he had seen in his time more honest-looking sailors. Some of them seemed to be nervous and acting under coercion. There was a captain; but even he seemed not to be in entire control of his ship.

A 12-year-old girl, Bessie Millie, watched from her mother's hut on the side of Brinkie's Brae. Then she began to wander about the piers and closes like a little sybil, crying out that the sooner that bad ship was up and off, the better it would be for Orkney. 'Now, Bessie,' said Mr James Gordon, the magistrate, quite severely, 'you be a good girl and stop disturbing the peace.'...

Now, at last, after a day's uncertainty, a small boat was lowered from the *George* and the captain was in her and two sailors rowed her to the harbour steps.

Half the populace of Hamnavoe were there, of course, keeping well back, for Mr Gordon the magistrate and Mr Graham the merchant stood at the top of the steps to greet the master of the *George*.

He came up the steps, a dark handsome smiling young man—if rather unkempt and poorly clad for a skipper—and he spoke civilly, in a low grave voice, to the two leading townsmen.

The 'chorus of Hamnavoe men' couldn't quite make out what was being said.

But suddenly, first Mr Gordon and then Mr Graham seized the skipper by the hand and wrung it over and over, as if they could hardly believe their ears.

Finally, Mr Gordon turned to the crowd and said, 'This is most extraordinary—most gratifying!... A few of you at least must remember

John Gow, who signed on for a sailor twelve years ago, when he was a boy of fourteen... Well, here he is again, come back home, master of that fine ship out there. I welcome him on behalf of us all.'

Captain John Gow, his face darker and leaner by a dozen years at sea, raised his hand to this one and that in the crowd that he recognised.

A shout of welcome went up from the men of Hamnavoe.

And young Miss Thora Gordon, watching from the window of her father's big house, declared that she had never seen a more handsome sailor; no, never in her life.

Local Traditions

2.2.1989

I was writing at my table yesterday morning when a buzzing came in my ears that lasted for half a minute. In my childhood everyone knew what that meant—either someone was dying at that very moment or someone was going to die... Since people are dying every second of every day, somewhere in the world, that's a safe enough bet.

And if we 'made faces' at someone, as children do from time to time, out of pique or mockery, our elders would say severely, 'If the wind changes, you'll look like that forever.'...

On a spring day, in the fields, we would pick a dandelion 'clock', and blow off the grey globe of seed until the last seed was away on the wind, counting with every blown breath. And that was the way we told the time.

The milk teeth slackened and came out, leaving a growing gap. If you put a lost tooth under the pillow and slept on it, there would be a silver coin there in the morning. Some good fairy rewarded you in this way...

There being no television, or even wireless, on winter nights, we would sit for long solitary spells watching shapes in the fire. If you had a strong subtle imagination, you could see almost anything. The shapes among the coals were probably better for children than plenty of TV programmes.

Sometimes we would go for a very long walk, as far as the Black Craig. We were assured by our elders that, every seven years, somebody 'went afore the face' of the Black Craig. But in my lengthening life-span no one has fallen over the Black Craig. The last recorded accident there must have happened a century ago and more, when a herdie-boy was lost. I think his name might have been Isaac Mowat.

Then there was 'the mineral well' just below the farm of Brownstown. I remember being sent there with a tin can to get water for my mother's asthma. Lots of Stromness families took buckets and cans there. It must, I think, have been a medieval Saint's well, and children of my generation were the last pilgrims (though we only went because we were told to go). Now, I hear, that well is a ruin. After the war a local hotelier sent a sample of the water to be analysed in Aberdeen. Back came the word; the water had no discernible curative properties. Stromness, it was plain, could never become a spa. Yet faith, it may be, is a greater impulse to wholeness and health than any salt or iron... It would be interesting to know more of the history of the well, after which, it seems likely, Hellihole takes its name. 'Mineral Well' it was called in my childhood— that is an indication of the growing power of scepticism and science.

And the gulls wheeling and calling at the end of our piers—what were they but reincarnations of drowned sailors and fishermen? I seem to remember that one old woman, throwing bread to them, had a name for each seabird.

The 'Quiet South End'?

9.2.1989

It's a quiet place, our South End of Stromness. Life has an easy gentle rhythm. You can work without fear of distraction.

It wasn't always so quiet. No—the South End was where the important things happened.

Depending on how you look at it, we South-Enders have come down in the world, we exist in a backwater, we don't count any longer. Or else we are endowed with the most precious thing left in this crazy late 20th-century world: tranquillity.

Where I am sitting writing this, in Mayburn Court, there was once a small distillery, where two kinds of malt whisky were made—Old Orkney and Old Man of Hoy... Imagine the stamping of hooves, the shouting, the heavy thunder of barrels, when a consignment of Stromness whisky was about to be shipped south—the clashing of doors, the trundling and the levering and crack of whips...

Where the Museum is now was once the Town Hall. Once a month, the grave bearded councillors trooped through the door to discuss the affairs of the town, to fix the rates, to discuss whether Stromness really needed a reservoir in the Loons together with piped water and sanitation.

Further south, there was the steady beat of hammers and rasping of saws and whining of planes. At Stanger's yard at Ness, there was a new hull growing on the stocks.

And oh, on a Saturday night the one and only policeman in town led two fighting beer-sodden wretches to the cells up a dark close in Alfred Street. And in Billy Clouston's pub where now our little grocer shop is, the landlord and the moderate drinkers gave sighs of relief, and some-body called for another round of schooners of ale.

A few decades earlier, young men from Stenness or Birsay signed on for whalemen in the ledger of David Geddes, agent, in Alfred Square. And some came home with enough gold sovereigns to buy a little croft and get married, and some never saw Orkney again.

If you wanted to post a letter or a parcel, you dealt with Mrs Ross, Postmistress, where Mrs Black lives now, at the foot of Hellihole. A letter arrived one day for someone who had just died. Mrs Ross, Postmistress, said to the telegram boy, 'Write *Deceased* in red ink on the envelope—it must be returned to sender,' and the telegram boy wrote, *Deceased in red ink* on the envelope; and Mrs Ross was very angry; and the postmen could hardly get the mail sorted for laughing...

Candlemas Day

16.2.1989

I'm not sure what girls in Shetland did, in the way of ancient divination, the Orkney lasses didn't do too.

Of course those touching and lovely ceremonies have been well stamped on by education and the new religion of progress and aff-luence. But girls still scan the pages of magazines for astrologers' fore-tellings, a weary dull exercise.

Well, then, in Candlemas on February 2nd—and I suppose few cand-les are lit anywhere in the northern isles for that—it was thought a good time for the island girls to know about their future husbands. It was the crows in the fields that decided the matter: never who the young man would be, of course, but the general direction of his dwelling.

The dawn was hardly up when a lass would get out of bed and take her shawl about her and look from the open door for a crow in a field.

It was an anxious moment. Her mother, almost as anxious as herself, might be looking from the ben window, and a few white faces of younger brothers and sisters, some mocking, some solemn.

The girl ran helter-skelter at the crow in the field. And the crow rose and flew off. This was the moment of truth. For, to whatever quarter the crow took flight, in that airt dwelt her husband-to-be.

(It is likely that most of the lasses had, overtly or secretly, a boy that they fancied more than any other boy in the island... How glad our croft lass must have been if the crow took wing to the hill, where (say) Robbie the shepherd lived; for her heart for the past month or two had fluttered whenever she passed Robbie and his few ewes on the path.

240

But suppose the crow flew towards the shore where the fishing boats were safely noused? There were none of the young fishermen that, at the moment, she had an eye for. But here was the crow saying, 'Come on—follow—you're to be a fisherman's wife and smoke fish and knit long Atlantic stockings and rock sea cradles for the rest of your life...')

There was one dire possibility. The crow might rise and wing its way in the direction of the Kirkyard. That meant only one thing: that the girl would die an old maid.

So, smiling or downcast, the island lass walked back across the winter field and went inside—looking as though she had just gone out to see how many eggs the ducks had laid—and the mother was ladling out porridge into the bowls, and the young brothers and sisters were sniggering behind their hands at the table, and 'Daddo' with his thick black beard was looking solemn in the high chair.

'Inspiration' and Work

2.3.1989

Sometimes a writer gets asked, 'Why do you write, then? What's your inspiration?'

Because everybody thinks a writer, artist, composer, weaver, potter, *must* be inspired.

Well, maybe. But if there is such a thing as inspiration, it comes some time during the composition of the work, like wind or fire.

But work: the main thing is work, the slow labour over years to perfect a craft, to learn one's limitations and potentialities. To work as a stonemason or a carpenter works, that's the secret, learning at last to be in complete harmony with one's material.

So a writer writes in order to enjoy bread-and-butter and beer. He writes to keep the deadly enemy boredom at bay. He writes because at last it is the only thing he *can* do, and he can no more help doing it than a spider can help spinning a web.

I warn young people who want to write, 'Beware of inspiration. Don't believe anyone who tells you, you must wait for "the spark from heaven to fall". Because if you wait for inspiration, nothing worthwhile may ever visit the blank page.'...

Further: 'Write every day, whether you feel like it or not, otherwise whatever skill you have will leave you. If you have nothing to write, choose a subject quite coldly, and let your imagination work on that.'

There is a wise passage in the Old Testament (maybe Ecclesiastes)— 'Whatsoever thy hand findeth to do, do it with thy might.'

One morning last year, after I'd cleared the breakfast things from the table, I sat there looking at a blank page and found I had absolutely nothing to say—the mind was as blank as the page. It is then a question of waiting, maybe for as long as half an hour, for a subject to announce itself. After a while, for some reason, the Ring of Brodgar came into my mind. There were sixty stones originally: how about making a very brief poem about each stone, as the original builders might have celebrated the dragging of it from Vestra Field, and its setting up on the moor between the two lochs?

At once the images came swarming in like birds to one place. There is something exciting about letting the imagination go free among mysterious rites and customs and attitudes of mind, and yet the solidity of the stones, and their mathematical exactitude, prevented too much extravagance.

So the poem came, over two or three days. Needless to say, many of the small verses were flawed or deficient, and had to be ruthlessly abandoned (even as contemporary Brodgar has great gaps in it). A score or so remained that were passable.

I shoved the notebook away and forgot about it—until one day recently there was a good idea to make a series of Orkney prints and poems. And then the almost forgotten Brodgar 'peedie poems' were brought out and winnowed once more.

But we began with 'inspiration'. So many descriptions of it have been given that I hesitate to say anything more; except that very occasionally, it seems that one's own directing will is hushed and laid asleep, and then words, images, rhythms, appear on the page that the writer knows with joy to be beyond his own capacities.

Sorry for being so boring this week—but the question is asked so often that some sort of answer must be given, some time.

A Drive to Birsay

9.3.1989

A company of us drove last Sunday afternoon to view a house in Birsay that our Edinburgh friend Sigrid has recently bought.

Barnhouse is situated in a pleasant part of that loveliest of the Mainland parishes. Right below is the village, The P'lace, called after the ruined Renaissance palace built there by Robert Stewart, Earl of Orkney, half-brother to Mary Queen of Scots. It is said that part of the evidence brought against him at his trial for treason was a mistake in Latin grammar. In an inscription over the big house he had carved 'Rex

Scotorum' (King of Scots) whereas what he wanted to boast in stone was only that he was a son of the King of Scots.

A lovely and gracious building it must have been when the last mason had packed and gone. The Stewarts had exquisite taste but power seemed subtly to corrupt some of them, so that Robert and his son Patrick had a distorted vision of the community they lorded it over. The people of Orkney were there to carry out their sovereign will, regardless of the rights that had come down to them from their independent Norse ancestors.

The vainglorious dream faded, and the palace began to crumble...

Right below the house is the shore that Robert Rendall came to know so well as a boy, on holiday there from Kirkwall. Later, he wrote marvellous poems about Birsay and its people, and a prose book *The Orkney Shore*. He was, besides being a poet, an authority on shells.

The tidal island of Brough of Birsay stands out in the Atlantic, steep and green. That such a few acres, sundered by the sea twice a day, should be so richly stored with history, is marvellous. For here a greater earl by far than the strutting peacock Robert Stewart had his palace: Earl Thorfinn Sigurdson, who 'ruled over nine earldoms in Scotland', and who was not afraid to meet his irate overlord, the king of Norway, on a ship confrontation... If the Norse earl's palace was here, surely the bishop's church, the cathedral, would be on the Brough too? I like to think so—also that the body of Magnus lay here before it was brought with psalms to St Olaf's in Kirkwall... But some historians think Bishop William's church may have stood near the place where the parish church is now.

Steeped in history and perennial beauty this parish is. It happened to be a fine bright day between two storms when we visited Barnhouse. Already to the north-west, there was an infusion of grey into the blue, and the little white clouds above were teased out and shredding: a sure sign of imminent gale... There, to the north, was the Noup Head of Westray and its lighthouse.

Presently, after tea and cakes and a small dram to wish well to the new house and its owner, we moved off home in four cars.

The Lady Nicotine

16.3.1989

'No-smoking Day' yesterday, all over Britain—and I didn't need to do anything about that because (except for an occasional festive cigar) I threw my collection of pipes into the dustbin eight years ago, and never really missed it, except for a faint pang of desire when I was enjoying a pint of beer.

But cigarettes—that was a different and much more difficult yoke to break out of. Some of us began to smoke 'Wild Woodbines' at the age of twelve, at the beginning purely as a dare and a kind of showing-off, hating every puff and every shred of tobacco that stuck poisonously to the tonsils.

But we persisted, and before we were aware of it the heavy yoke was on us. We were the abject and miserable and furtive slaves of the Lady Nicotine. At the school playtime, we resorted to the boys' toilets with our scraps of 'fags', for each 'Woodbine' was too precious to smoke all at one go—and the lighted match was passed round—and we dragged the blue-grey reek down into our lungs, lingeringly, deep down. And the bell summoned us back to Latin and Maths, and the teachers knew well enough what we had been up to by the smell from our hair and jerseys and fingers.

Twopence for a flimsy packet of five 'Woodbine'. Twopences weren't so easily come by in those pre-war days, and so we resorted to many questionable practices to lure or cajole the odd penny, from parents chiefly. 'Oh yes, I'll go for those messages, no trouble'... And I would bring the bread or sausages back, with a silent twopence added on for porterage.

The twopence of course was laid on the tobacconist's counter.

But even here, sometimes, there were difficulties; because the tobacconist might say, 'You're not sixteen'... Then a lie had to be added to the purloining, and I would hasten to assure the tobacconist that the cigarettes weren't for me—of course not—how could he ever think such a thing?—they were for some neighbour.

A pristine packet of five 'Woodbines'! What a rare jewel to have won, by superlative forethought and deceit! One more day's happiness...

The greatest joy in those early days was football, in any field or open space. We couldn't wait to get our hideous homework done (geography or Latin irregular verbs) to be out playing football, South-End *versus* North-End... I began to notice, after a year or two, that I couldn't run along the touchline so swiftly or blithely as formerly. Fifteen minutes of play, and I was completely exhausted; the lungs laboured and the legs were like lead.

Curiously, I never connected this sudden disability with the joys of smoking (that had an extra thrill in that it was forbidden, and had to be done subtly and secretly). It just so happened, it seemed to me, that my footballing days were prematurely over.

And then, suddenly, 'My Lady Nicotine' turned and hung heavy chains about me, and threatened me with imminent 'early dark'.

But that's another story.

Sailors in the White-House

6.4.1989

Strange, to think of Bligh of the *Bounty* in Stromness. Yet in Stromness he was, in 1780, an officer on *Resolution*, on the way back from Captain Cook's last voyage, when that famous navigator 'left his body on a distant shore'.

In the White-House, Stromness, lived Mr Stewart of Massater in South Ronaldsay. Why would Mr Stewart, a moderately wealthy farmer (and, perhaps, merchant) be staying in a Stromness house? Very likely, because 18th-century Stromness was a thriving port, and Mr Stewart had an opportunity for his young family to become acquainted with sailors of quality. Doors might open for them, to advancement or to matrimony.

So, Lieut William Bligh finds himself invited to dinner at the White-House. Perhaps Mr Stewart and a magistrate or two had rowed out to pay a courtesy call to the naval ship anchored in the harbour and left their cards.

It is hard to know whether Lieut Bligh relished the prospect or not. After such a long voyage, it must have been pleasant to walk on firm ground again, and to taste fresh meat and vegetables and new bread.

Lieut Bligh's character has, over the past two hundred years, been so blackened by legends of sadism, puritanism, and tyranny, that only of late years have attempts been made to clean his image.

Perhaps he will forever be an enigmatic figure. Certainly, as far as his craft went, he was a superb and resolute navigator.

If only we had a record of the conversation that went on that evening over the dinner-table in White-House!... We can only imagine, and conjecture. Mr Stewart a bit ingratiating, perhaps; Lieut Bligh curt and gruff, but gallant to the ladies of the household; the servants coming and going with the dishes and the bottles of claret... And the sea-coal fire leapt high in the grate.

There, right across from Bligh at the dinner table, sat a very young man, hardly more than a boy: the son of the house, George Stewart. The shy melancholy youth hardly opened his mouth; from time to time he stole glances at Bligh, and at the ship he could see through the high window. There was a look then of great longing on him—while the women chatted all round, and the sailor sipped moderately at the wine in his pewter cup, and Mr Stewart kept saying, in a score of different ways, how his boy longed for a sea career, and how good he was already with sail and compass and chart, and what a wasted promise it would be if he had to spend his life over the new kinds of farming (in which he wasn't interested) and a merchant's ledger...

Lieut Bligh appeared not to notice, but all through that tedious meal he was taking stock of the boy, weighing his character against the unknowable mystery and menace of the sea, and—by the time they were at the cheese and port—he liked very much what he saw. This very handsome Orkney boy would make a good sailor.

Far off, beyond Hoy, on that still evening, they could hear the muted music of the Atlantic.

* * *

The rest of the story is well known: how young Stewart was a midshipman on the *Bounty* at the time of the mutiny, and returned to his wife and child in Tahiti. There he was captured and put, a prisoner, on board HMS *Pandora*, and was drowned when that ship foundered on the Barrier Reef.

The poet Byron made him the hero of his poem, 'The Island'.

* * *

Soon, as we all know, the voyage of the *Bounty* is to be re-enacted on this second centenary, with many descendants of the original crew participating. It is not known whether there are any descendants of Midshipman Stewart and his Tahitian wife, Peggy. It is fitting that an Orcadian brought up on the lands adjacent to Massater, the eldest son of William Mowat, should take the part of Stewart.

Academy Library—Old and New

13.4.1989

Stromness Academy library in my time, in the late 1930s, consisted of about a hundred books along one wall of the classroom where Mr Paterson taught us English.

The English classroom was, I think, the most pleasant in the school, looking down over the roofs of Stromness towards Houton, Scapa Flow and Hoy.

It was there that some of us first began to be intoxicated with words, rhythms, and rhymes: the 'Immortality Ode' of Wordsworth, Shelley's 'Skylark', Thompson's 'Hound of Heaven', Rossetti's 'Blessed Damozel', Coleridge's 'Ancient Mariner', and the tragedies of Shakespeare. I don't say that we got anywhere near the heart of those poems and plays—it was rather that their incantatory quality touched the quick of us.

And there too Mr Paterson gave us our first sips of modern poetry—MacDiarmid's lyric about the animals going into the ark ('Auld Noah was at hame wi' them a'...) and a haunting lyric by Kipling ('They closed the way through the woods'...).

There, against one wall, the school library slumbered—all the hundred volumes of it—and was only disturbed briefly now and then, towards the end of the school session maybe when the exams were all finished and we could hardly wait to break out into the seven-week-long freedom of the summer holidays.

The only book I can remember from the hoard is a book of five stories by Joseph Conrad[1], about a couple of seedy characters who ran a trading post on a river bank in West Africa. The atmosphere of heat, claustrophobia and menace lingers. I thought, 'What a marvellous writer this Conrad is!' But I never afterwards read anything of his quite so good...

Last Wednesday afternoon we visited the new Academy library at Garson, four of us, and were pleasantly received and shown around by the librarian, Mrs Joanna Ramsey.

The pupils of the 1980s have spacious and well-stocked apartments. Everything conceivable is there to help them cross the border into the enchanted lands of literature, and any other subject they may feel called to. There are computers—which we of the 1930s could never have imagined, any more than we could have imagined people actually walking on the moon... We ascended an iron spiral to a quiet study room where senior pupils can get down to serious work.

No library could be more conducive to a true love of books and knowledge.

We almost lost ourselves in the labyrinth of the new school. Further on, a swarm of workmen were busy putting finishing touches to the last phase: a theatre and entrance hall.

A school with an actual theatre!—If there are any potential Barries, Bridies, or Byrnes in Stromness and the parishes of the west, this fine high, bright, rich-sounding playhouse will surely evoke whatever talent there is.

Bessie Millie

11.5.1989

I have heard that Bessie Millie's house—or its foundation—has been found, or claimed to be found, on the side of Brinkie's Brae.

Now I'm waiting for somebody to take me to the place. (For Bessie's dwelling ought to be as well-known as Alexander Graham's in Graham Place—or Gow's (vanished, alas!) on the Cairston shore.)

I think Bessie wouldn't have been too happy in, say, the month of May 1789. In May and for the rest of the summer, the harbour wouldn't be

---

1. *Tales of Unrest*. The particular story was 'An Outpost of Progress'

sheltering storm-beaten ships, as it had all winter and spring: and so Bessie would be lacking a scattering of silver sixpences from super-stitious skippers who wanted a good wind to take them to Bergen or Boston or Cadiz... But still... But still, sudden storms had been known to blow up in June and July, and so Bessie kept her water-pot handy; an enchanted pot that, stirred, could conjure wind and weather.

Meantime, in early May two centuries ago, the sun emblazoned the harbour and Scapa was a spread of blue silk.

Bessie fed her few hens and sniffed the first warm air of summer.

Then she went inside her hut and added a peat or two to the fire, and she took the cat on her knee, and she nodded into sleep.

Oh, it was a terrible dream, a nightmare! Bessie dreamed that she was being led out, bound, through a crowd that mocked her and spat at her and (when they could, for men were guarding her) struck her. Where were they taking her? Bessie lifted her poor insulted head and saw she was being taken to a stake, and a man was standing beside the stake with a rope and faggots for burning...

Bessie woke from that dream in a cold sweat.

Then she knew what had set the dream going. Some impudent lasses, going past her door, had shouted that she was a witch, and a hundred years ago they'd have burned her at the Gallowsha in Kirkwall.

Ignorant young hussies! Of course she wasn't a witch. Wasn't it doing a good service, obtaining fair winds for ships and sailors? No one had ever accused her—nor could they—of driving ships onto rocks.

So Bessie had a drink of milk and went out to see that Whitie the ewe and her two new lambs were doing all right.

How tired she was! It must be the warmer airs that followed the lambing snow and the withering of the daffodils.

There was not one sail in the harbour.

Bessie went inside and put her boot among the smouldering peats and went to sleep again in her chair.

It was a most astonishing dream that came—not frightening this time, but amazing, impossible! There in her dream was the harbour of Hamnavoe, enclosed by the Holms and Ness, and the houses and shops on their little piers or on the hillside. In her dream Bessie saw two long piers, and the strangest-looking vessels coming and going, that seemed to have hearts beating inside their iron hulls and long tubes smoking. As she looked, another of the weird dream-ships, throbbing and spilling wisps of smoke, came quickly up through Hoy Sound and turned into the bay. Not one of those ships had a sail; a wind-drinker.

Bessie woke up, and this time she laughed. Dreams were funny things. Would this be the way of it in a hundred years' time...? 'If so,' thought Bessie, 'there won't be much of a livelihood for the likes of me.'

A Golden Summer

8.6.1989

Tomorrow comes June, and that reminds us of childhood summers: even though we were inmates of the prison of school till early July.

Seven weeks in July and August were one long dream of sun-drenched happiness—in boats, fishing sillocks at Gray's pier, bathing at the West Shore and Warbeth, running everywhere on bare feet, having picnics on the rocks with sandwiches, 'rich tea' biscuits, and Gowans' lemonade. And all lapped in the gentle flame of the sun.

Of course we know in fact that it can't have been like that at all. Weren't there rainy days? Days of misery over a broken friendship? A day (maybe) of falling into a nest of nettles?

There were such miseries, of course. Our minds are so constituted that they remember only the precious things. Time is a panner of gold by a stream below a mountain veined with ore: the debris and trash are riddled out.

There seemed to be one summer in particular when we were never out of a boat. The boat belonged to Ian Cadger's father, who was engineer on the *Pole Star*. This rowing-boat was kept at John Folster's pier, I think. John Folster was a fisherman with a small house on a pier hidden away from the street. A quiet inoffensive man he was, only mildly mutinous because he had to travel by bus to the Pomona Inn at Finstown or the Smithfield at Dounby for the beer he missed so much (Stromness having been 'dry' by this time for a decade). John Folster caught lobsters and haddocks in his fishing boat off Yesnaby and the west coast.

That summer—it must have been 1931 or '32—morning to night we were never out of the little dinghy, Ian Cadger and I and maybe another favoured friend or two. We would row to the Holms, and that was quite an adventure, like landing on some Treasure Island. The house on the Inner Holm was then a ruin. There was mystery and strangeness on the rocks on the Clestrain side of the island.

Every afternoon there was a great event that couldn't be missed: the arrival of the *Ola*. The *Ola* in those days was a narrow black ship that carried only a few tourists in summer, and one or two cars occasionally; many Stromnessians called her 'the mail boat' because she carried all the Royal Mail—it was just before aeroplanes began to poach on her rights.

Small and black though she was, the *Ola* made a superb curve, coming out of Hoy Sound into the harbour. Her bow cleaved the quiet water. It was then that boys set out to get 'the *Ola*'s waves', in dinghies and flatties. Five or six dizzying ups-and-downs, our knuckles white on oar or gunwale, and maybe our faces a bit white too, with fear and delight.

Many an afternoon we spent drifting idly along the waterfront, under the piles of the *Pole Star* pier; as far south as Stanger's deserted boatyard; as far north as 'the New Pier' where the *Hoy Head* berthed, and little seemed to happen on the long golden afternoons.

Stromness was quiet that summer. We couldn't imagine it otherwise. On the side of the hill the school-prison waited to receive us again at the end of August.

Tourists you could count on the fingers of your hands. Two tourists came to John Folster's pier one day—they had heard he owned a model ship made of bone, maybe (my memory suggests) made by French prisoners-of-war in Napoleonic times. Wouldn't John Folster sell it to them? They mentioned sums of money, rising as high as five pounds—a fortune! They bargained for a long time. The bone ship passed from hand to hand. We boys watched. The tourists left without the whalebone ship.

Such a marvellous summer it was!

Gerard Manley Hopkins

22.6.1989

There was a century ago an English poet called Gerard Manley Hopkins who got no further north than the southern fringe of the Highlands, just north of Glasgow. There he wrote a magnificent lyric called 'Inversnaid', all in praise of 'wildness and wet'.

So I suppose we oughtn't to be speaking about him in an Orkney newspaper at all.

But I feel that his life and writing was a seeking for the sources of things, from which new life springs perpetually to renew the earth that is forever being soiled and filthied by industrialism and the wounds that men inflict on the environment.

To do this work of cleansing he had to throw away the old worn moulds of language, and mint words and images as if they were being used for the first time.

The week we were in Oxford, we seemed to run into Hopkins everywhere—a crude way of putting it—rather, his sweet fresh eager spirit was everywhere welcoming.

I may have mentioned last week that one of the first things Hugo and Gunnie and I did in Oxford was to visit a Hopkins exhibition in the Bodleian Library, where the whole history of his short life is told in manuscripts, photographs, letters, drawings. Particularly fascinating are the manuscripts of his poems, early and late, which are unlike poems written in English before, or ever will be again, so daring and revolutionary they are in imagery and technique.

The exhibition is still going on because 1989 is the centenary of his death. He died in his early forties in Dublin, where he was Professor of Greek, on 8 June 1889.

On the anniversary, Hugo said there was to be a Requiem Mass in the Church of St Aloysius, Oxford, in the early evening; and would I like to go? Of course I wanted to go. There the great poet had been a curate in his youth.

Alongside St Aloysius, bulldozers and builders were at work behind a stockade, and Hopkins wouldn't have thought too much of that, all the noise and machines, and men transforming themselves into moles to delve into the lovely earth.

Inside the church, all was solemnity and calm and a subdued delight: the still sources of the spirit were being stirred a little, for the consolation and refreshment of the heart.

I had a feeling that the congregation were all lovers of the poetry, though I did not know a single one of all the sixty or seventy people present.

The priest who preached the sermon knew the man and the poet; his homily was jewelled with quotations from that small sheaf of poems that has added such treasure to our literature.

The spirit of such a great and humble man—he never sought fame for himself, but left his friend Robert Bridges to do what he liked with his poems, and they were only published to an astonished world in 1918, thirty years after his death—his spirit is everywhere; but perhaps, that evening, it was especially there in that little church in Oxford at evening Mass.

In his life he was never in Orkney; but one can feel his spirit here too, in the rapture of a skylark singing, in the cold clean thrilling wash of the sea against Yesnaby and Birsay, in the midsummer rush and cluster of the wild flowers with the morning dew about them; and in the fish and the animals and folk, every one distinct and unique, a never-to-be-repeated joy.

Ecclesiastes

13.7.1989

My friend John L. Broom and I don't always see eye to eye on matters of religion and literature, but we never fall out seriously with each other.

I am thinking of his letter on the book of Ecclesiastes in last week's *Orcadian*. JLB, quoting from that magnificent poem the passage beginning, 'Go thy way, eat thy bread with joy, and drink thy wine with a merry heart...' calls it 'one of the most powerful expressions of hedonism in the whole of literature'. The passage is not an invitation to gluttony and drunkenness, surely. It is simply what any good honest person ought to feel, sitting at his own table after the heat and burden of the day.

There is that other famous passage quoted by JLB, 'Whatsoever thy hand findeth to do, do it with thy might; for there is no work, nor device, nor knowledge, nor wisdom, in the grave, whither thou goest.'

The beginning of this marvellous sentence is simple common sense. What is the point of doing any work unless you put into it your whole heart and strength? That, in passing, is what is wrong with so much of the work people have to do nowadays, that it is boring and repetitive and soul-destroying.

As for the second part of the sentence, there can of course be in the grave no work nor device nor knowledge nor wisdom—but so far from being 'a denial of immortality', as JLB claims, what is abundantly implied is that immortality will perhaps confer on us new faculties, insights, delights, and freedom that we can't conceive of at the moment, being (as Shakespeare said) clothed in 'this muddy vesture of decay'.

JLB calls Ecclesiastes 'this most pessimistic of treatises'. What the poet of Ecclesiastes has done is to confront mortality and time and chance in the same way that great poets have always done—for example, Shakespeare in his tragedies, the great choruses of Sophocles and Euripides, Dante in *The Divine Comedy*. Such a confrontation with death has been the common concern of serious poetry right up to the moden age—Yeats, Eliot, MacDiarmid, Muir.

As for the poem Ecclesiastes being the kind of patchwork that JLB claims it to be—one pious author in a fit of rectitude trying to put to rights what an original 'unknown agnostic' wrote—the law of aesthetics is against any such possibility. Certainly, in early literature, there were many collaborative hands. The Border ballads were not written down by one poet working alone; it might be said that a whole community shaped them orally in the course of generations. It seems highly unlikely that Homer was one blind man with a harp. And what of the ancient literatures of Ireland and Scandinavia?

I think many hands may indeed have worked at Ecclesiastes, but one hand produced the version that we have. Whoever he was, he did the work magnificently. The result is not a patchwork, but a seamless garment throughout—a wonderful poem that confronts fearlessly whatever darknesses, time and chance have in store for Everyman; and is yet able to break out in the same kind of irresistible joy that Milton and Beethoven knew: 'Let thy garments be always white; and let thy head lack no ointment.'

Orkney Tatties

20.7.1989

The other day, I had the first Orkney tatties of 1989—and how delicious they tasted!

The story of 'the new tatties'' adventures is intriguing to think about.

There comes a time, in April, when last summer's tatties are virtually played out. Likewise the neeps are tough and fibrous, and clapshot doesn't taste good any more.

And there, suddenly, in the shops are new potatoes—rather expensive—and from a great distance, Egypt or Cyprus.

So everybody rushes to buy the new potatoes, and they taste not bad—'all right'—but nothing really to make a song and dance about.

As the wave of early summer breaks over the northern hemisphere, the potato crop ripens nearer and nearer home. 'There's Cornish tatties in the shop today.'... So we buy Cornish tatties, and they seem to have more sap and relish to them than the earlier exotic tatties.

Meantime the Orkney tatties planted in early April still slumber in the back gardens, waiting their hour. I have heard knowledgeable folk saying that 'Shopping Week' is the best time for lifting the first shaw. And there, pale globes and spheroids along the prongs of the garden fork, lie the new Orkney tatties.

They hardly need cleaning, just a flush from the tap to remove bits of soil; then the boiling, and the kitchen filling slowly with a summer fragrance; and then the marvellous taste of them, in their golden coats of butter. Many a time, since childhood, I've heard the old men saying, 'I could make a meal of new tatties and butter'... And it's true, but of course a piece of good haddock, or a few slices of corned beef, or lamb chops, are an excellent accompaniment.

New tatties go along with lupins and butterflies and larksong to make every Orkney summer memorable.

* * *

It would be intriguing to know when the potato first came to Orkney: some time in the 18th century, perhaps.

We can imagine with what suspicion those round earthfruits were regarded; for the Orcadians have always been conservative by nature, until use and wont have proved the worth of the importation.

Once tasted, it must have seemed a wonderful kind of food, that might even banish hunger forever. (The Irish, alas, thought the same, until the terrible potato famines decimated the rural populations in the mid-19th century. There is, alas, nothing entirely perfect under the sun...)

I think there was potato blight in Scotland and the islands too... But the potato was such a marvellous experience that there could be no question of abandoning it. An aura of magic clung to it. I know, when I was young, Orkney men used to carry a tattie in their jacket pocket; they thought that it kept away such troublous things as rheumatics.

The First Shopping Week

27.7.1989

It seems so long ago, the first Shopping Week of all, in 1949.

It has grown and grown since then, out of all recognition. This year, there were new flags of all colours fluttering outside Mayburn Court, and even stretching the length of Ness Road.

So many events occurred this year that a sizeable booklet has been produced as a programme—quite different from the flimsy yellow sheet of forty years ago, which included daily such island-shaking events as the daily arrival and departure of the SS *Hoy Head* from the South Isles.

Now the *Ola* and the *Sunniva* bring in tourists by the hundred. Do the accents of Glasgow predominate in the jostling streets?—for this is the Glasgow Fair fortnight. (In about an hour I must hasten to the pier to meet an old friend from Blantyre, who knows Stromness and Shopping Week well. Was it late on the Saturday night of that very first Shopping Week?—Whom did I meet round a reeling corner but this old friend of mine, who had never been to Orkney before, and had never said he was coming—and I thought I was experiencing a vinous vision—a not unusual thing in those days, for me. But it was him right enough, and together we watched the midnight rockets spangling the sky over the Holms... How the mind betrays one! That strange meeting wasn't the first Shopping Week at all, but perhaps 1959 or 1960.)

Well, on the very first Shopping Week Stromness was hung with flags of every nation under the sun. Stromness being a town of seafarers, there must have been a hundred kists in attics stuffed with flags. Alas! with the weathering of forty years few of those original flags can be left. The late Provost Robertson counted, if I remember aright, over nine hundred flags.

Furthermore, there was no Shopping Week Queen in 1949, no royal carriage and outriders, no platform and awning in the Town House garden for the opening speeches. If my memory doesn't deceive me yet again, Provost George S. Robertson declared the week of revelry open from the open back of a car.

I must ask younger readers to imagine Stromness with one pub only, not the five that are nowadays as busy as beehives. *One* pub, for all that tumult of folk who came by the busload from all over the West Mainland (there weren't so many cars then either) and who flocked up from the South Isles on the *Hoy Head*—not to speak of the tourists that poured off the *Ola* and the BEA plane. The Glasgow accent predominated.

I have a vivid memory of the beer-drinkers that first Saturday night overflowing the one narrow public bar, all the way down the walled close that is no longer there, across the street, and the outer fringe of them were uptilting their beer mugs around Alexander Graham's fountain. It was a sight to move one to awe. (I speak, of course, as one of the then active participants in that slow yeasty dance.)

I can't remember all that happened in the third week of July 1949. The shop competitions tended to be not quite so imaginative or colourful as the competitions of 1989. But there was obstacle putting on that much-to-be-lamented Putting Green at Ness, and sports and football matches at the Market Green, and a pet show and a baby show, of course.

As for the weather, it was probably the kind of patchwork we always expect.

We enjoyed it very much; but I must have had a very sore head on the Sunday morning, in common with many another.

The May Burn

3.8.1989

A few days ago my friend Brian Murray and I walked up 'the burn' to the Back Road.

If that doesn't seem a spectacular thing to do, imagine what a host of memories is stirred up in a person of my age by that steep brief ascent.

All is changed completely since the days when 'we ran aboot the braes and paidled in the burn'.

Remember, this little hidden thread of music is the May Burn, after which the housing scheme takes its name. Right beside the Back Road there was, until the 50s, a small square reservoir that must have supplied the Distillery with its water.

Where the May Burn has its origin I do not know, possibly some-where in the Loons, 'the wet places', behind Brinkie's Brae. It was flowing before the first fishermen set up a bothy on the shore of Ham-navoe. Lieut Bligh of the *Bounty* may have heard its music, going up to dine with Mr Stewart one evening in 1780, at the White-house.

Sometime in the 19th century a distiller must have dipped his finger into that burn and tasted it. 'This water,' said he, 'would make very good whisky.'

Then for a while the May Burn was a busy place, while stones were brought and dressed and set for the building of a distillery, together with a spacious yard, and offices, and massive storehouses built into the rising slope where now is the housing scheme of Faravel. Then the great stills— that could still be seen, forlorn giants, in the late 40s—were set in place; and the reservoir was built to gather the sweet delicious waters; and the great vats were brought in; and distiller and excise-man sat in their offices, and the labourers were approved and engaged. The barley came in in cartloads, and the vats began to burble. The neighbouring ducks, it's said, got drunk from time to time, after a good feed of 'the draff'. Back they reeled, a disordered army, rising and falling, to the safe barnyard at home.

Soon after that 'Old Orkney' malt whisky began to be famous, and the modish advertisements of the day—collectors' items now—leaned heavily towards the sophisticated and the romantic.

However, I am not speaking of personal experience of the Distillery at work. For when we were boys the 'Old Orkney' distillery was already dead. The shutters were up, the gate closed, a fust of decay had settled on the stone complex. The storehouses on the higher slopes began to look like particularly grim prisons.

It seemed to have no inhabitants but Mr Fred C. Kelly the exciseman and Mr Wylie the caretaker.

It all meant little or nothing to us children. These strange grim forlorn buildings were simply there; they always had been and possibly they always would be. We didn't care, in those long-ago summer afternoons.

Little did I think that I would one day live in a council house there, and look through my seaward window at the May Burn emptying itself into the harbour below.

Origin of the Dounby Show

10.8.1989

How does such an important market come to be in Dounby?

Some folk would say, 'It's obvious—for there's Dounby, at the very centre of the West Mainland... Where else could the fair be?'

But there's little magic in the obvious. I think, somewhere, there must be a story.

For example, the great Earl and his three sons.

Sigurd the eldest son ruled the roost in Birsay, on behalf of his father. And Hjal had the big house and collected rents in Harray. And Einar kept his ships on Skaill beach and ruled over the lands in Sandwick parish.

Sigurd said to his father one day, 'I'm thinking of setting up a market for horses in Birsay, on the lower slopes of Revay Hill. We should do a good trade with people coming in from all the districts.'

The old Earl said he thought that a good idea, if a fair amount of the profit was paid into the Earl's treasury.

Hjal tethered his horse at the banks above the shore and walked across the ebb to the Earl's palace on the Brough.

'I've just had a good idea,' he said—'a horse fair, with dancing and piping in Harray. Beside the loch, maybe at Merkister, seems to me a good place for the new fair.'

'It will be hard getting folk to ride to two August horse fairs,' said the old man. 'I give my permission, on the usual percentage basis, but I do not think that this fair will be a great success.'

'We'll see about that,' said Hjal of Harray.

The very next morning the third son, Einar, rode up the coast to Birsay just as the Earl was setting out for Graemsay with the hooded hawk on his fist.

'I have a small request,' said Einar.

'Don't make it too long,' said his father, 'for this hawk is new and fierce and he is sinking his claws into my fingers.'

'I just ask you out of courtesy,' said Einar, 'knowing you will grant it to your youngest and truest son. I'm thinking of establishing a new horse fair somewhere in Sandwick, maybe at Tenston or Quoyloo. The like of this fair will not be in all of your highness' lands. Besides the horses and the hucksters, there'll be a team of acrobats and also a variety of games such as wrestling and archery. We will have good profit—a new ship for me and a new garden for you at the back of your palace.'

First the Earl laughed till his beard shook in the wind and the falcon had to be taken from his fist by the falconer.

'I see,' said he, 'that the spies of my three sons have been going between the three Bu farms, listening to the talk at the ale benches, then riding home with the gossip.'

The Earl stamped with his foot on the ground. 'There will be a fair in August indeed,' said he, 'but it will be my fair, and it will be set up at the place where the three parishes meet, at Dounby. And my treasurer will stand at the gate leading to the booths, and he will take the silver pieces for admission.'

Later he shouted from the side of Greenay, till his three sons standing under their separate lintels heard his voice clear in the summer wind, 'I hope I will have the pleasure of my three sons' company at my great horse fair!'

The hawk, high against the sun, looked down on the ripening cornfields of Birsay, Harray and Sandwick.

Hamnavoe Market

31.8.1989

An old school friend wrote to me in hospital, hoping we might have an early reunion over an end-of-summer talk and a drink. I had to reply that I wouldn't be out for the Dounby Show, but we might have a dram on the day of Stromness Lammas Market.

The Stromness Lammas Market! Readers under fifty will look at each other and shake their heads. Such a date is not and never has been in their calendars.

Let me assure them, before the war, the second Tuesday of September was one of *the* great holidays in Stromness—more joyous, I think, than Christmas or New Year.

Slowly the excitement built up. A few days before, the little canvas village of booths and shows had arrived suddenly, and been established at the pierhead and round the waterfront. The booths were inhabited by exotic 'market-men and market-women' and their dogs.

Stromnessians were offered a taste of the excitements of the fair: shooting booths, coconut shies, swing boats, 'roll-the-penny' booths, maybe the Wall of Death or a boxing booth, and the King of the Fair was a man with full red cheeks and a bristling moustache called Charlie Rigolo who ran a kind of primitive casino, with wooden cards and a numbered board and a spinning arrow.

Newly back in the prison of school, the arrival in town of 'the market' opened a gateway into fantasy. Gimcrack it may have been, but for us children it was high festival, a harvest dance, a station between the sun of summer and winter stars. We would not have put it that way, of course, but we felt it instinctively. Hardly was school over and our tea down our throats, than we were off to the booths and the market-men. Mainly as light-hearted observers of the scene we moved from booth to booth, because we were saving up our pennies for the big day, the first Tuesday in September.

Then, that wonderful morning, it being a holiday from school, we brought out our hoards of pennies, which might be supplemented by 'fairings', a silver sixpence from a parent or a neighbour. Fabulously rich, with five shillings maybe in our pockets, we set out for the fantasies and enchantments on offer at the pierhead.

And the street was thronged! Up the piers came folk from the South Isles. Buses and gigs and carts deposited revellers from the seven western parishes, the men in dark suits and the girls in flowery dresses (and the more daring of them scented and lipsticked).

The Stromness food-sellers had stalls up that day too, selling fruit and sweeties and ice-cream. Guilio Fuggaccia went here and there with his ice-cream barrow and his hound. 'Cheap today, free tomorrow!' he intoned. And 'Last card!' bellowed Charlie Rigolo from his canvas casino. And a little furtive man with a tripod and cameras dodged among the thickening throngs 'snapping' country boys and lasses. The swing-boats cut arcs against the sky. Children who had had luck at the coconut shies came proudly bearing a goldfish in a bowl. Cheeky town boys blew peas from their pea-shooters at any likely target. There were balloons and whirring birds made of wood shavings. The crowds parted now and then to make room for a drunk—for us kids an unusual frightening sight, Stromness being dry then.

The chatter of the cheap-jack might hold us for an hour, as he tried by blandishment, allurement, and mockery to relieve stubborn farmers of ten-shilling notes.

There might, near the Fountain, be a circle of preachers.

What good was ordinary food to us, on such a day? We crammed in sweeties, fruit, ice-cream, chocolate, chips, from morning to night, inebriated with excitement, variety, colour, music, voices.

At night flares were lit here and there among the booths and the fair was splashed with the leaping lights and shadows.

It was almost too much. We went home with heavy eyelids, empty pockets, and queasy stomachs. But the wonderment of the day would endure all the following winter; and still does, after a fashion.

Robert Rendall

14.9.1989

One of the great lacks in Orkney today is that the poetry of Robert Rendall is not available[1], unless one is lucky enough to pick up a copy of one of those four memorable books at a sale or in a second-hand shop.

It is sad to think that there must be many Orcadians, especially younger ones, who have had no opportunity to read these poems, some of which are among the most remarkable of this century, with a relevance far beyond Orkney and even Scotland. Robert Rendall's lyrics achieve timelessness and universality again and again.

We older Orcadians first realised that another remarkable literary man was among us when a very thin book of poems was published in 1946: *Country Sonnets*. In fact it wouldn't have been such a remarkable book but for one single poem in dialect called 'The Fisherman'.

The other poems in that first book were technically correct, but in a fading Georgian tradition. 'The Fisherman' was a rare and perfect gem.

Well, we all held our breaths when it was known that RR, in 1948, was about to publish a second book. Would 'The Fisherman' prove to have

---

1. Rendall's *Collected Poems* came out in 2012

been nothing but a happy accident, never to be repeated? Would RR be another of those 'one-poem poets' who are fairly common in literature?

We needn't have feared. *Orkney Variants*, the next RR book, was a box of gems: 'Salt i' the bluid', 'The winter lift is glintan down', 'See this is Liza's but and ben', and many more. The mouth of the poet was touched again and again with the Muse's fire.

The vein must peter out, the pure gold must surely come to an end! There was no sign of it in the next volume, *Shore Poems*, though RR took a risk by eschewing the dialect in which all those earlier lyrics of genius had been written and using only English. The third book has at least one sonnet that is as fine as any sonnet of this century: 'Renewal'.

There was, in RR's last years, a fourth volume, in which the graph of achievement is on the wane perhaps, but not to any serious extent; his swan-song is full of memorable pieces.

The rest was silence.

It is extraordinary that a poet of such high endeavour and achievement has never been reprinted. It can't be allowed to continue, surely. We can't deprive young Orcadians of such life-enhancing rare delights.

I can already—and not before time—detect a reviving interest in the work of this modern poet. It is not stuff you blow the dust off; it is 'as vivid as a pulsing star'. It is an inheritance for all Orcadians, especially the young. It tells us islanders what we truly are.

Robert Rendall and Stromness were thirled to one another in many ways. His unique shell collection is in our Museum. In the last years of his life he was a well-known figure in Stromness, when he was a resident in St Peter's House. Many Stromnessians—not least Ian MacInnes, who painted his portrait—were included among his best friends.

RR through his poetry still has friends to make, in the near and in the distant future.

Lyrics

12.10.1989

There came through the post the other day a brief letter from a friend in Australia, enclosing (on some fine material—silk, I think) a 'haiku' in the original Japanese. It is a thing very beautiful to look at, and the Japanese characters give it a deeper mystery, all the more so because one can't read them. The poem is set out on the pink silk in two vertical columns, beautifully proportioned. You might call it 'visual music'.

My correspondent enclosed a translation of the haiku: 'I must write some letters but outside there are spring flowers'...

Does that sound to you like a let-down? Surely poetry ought to have a greater depth and range and subtlety? Surely (you might think) anybody of quite ordinary gifts could turn out a score of poems like that between dawn and sunset?

One answer is that the beauty and profundity lie in the very simplicity.

We shouldn't forget that nearly all the essence of a poem is lost in the translation. The whole history of Japanese culture gives this haiku delicacy and validity. It's true, a Japanese reader will get far more out of the poem than one brought up in our western tradition...

And then the marvellous way they have of presenting the poem, in that exquisite lettering on fine-spun silk! As if, with beautiful courtesy, one was being handed a gift on an ivory dish beside a fountain.

* * *

Our whole way of looking at poetry is conditioned by the way we were taught Wordsworth, Tennyson, Masefield, etc in school.

But every culture has its own mode.

What, in contemporary Orkney, are we to make of the poems of Rognvald Kolson, earl and poet, or of Thorbjorn Black or Little Oddi, famous bards who went on the Jerusalem pilgrimage more than eight hundred years ago? They seem, translated into 20th-century words, to be at best a kind of savage chant. 'I am glad that the Bringer of Wine had words with me, this autumn—a strong attachment I felt for the French lady. Out of love for the aristocratic maiden, I make food for the eagle. Stone and cement will crack and collapse'...

By 'food for the eagle' is meant corpses slain in battle. At the time Rognvald and his pilgrims had set fire to a Spanish castle... In an interlude of the battle Earl Rognvald made the poem.

Those who listened and delighted in it—the fighting Orkneymen, Icelanders, Norwegians—expected that kind of imagery; it was part of their tradition.

What might have surprised them, and outraged the more conservative of them, was that the battle-song began with praise of a young woman. How could the two elements be mixed?

Here we might be hearing one of the first love lyrics, that were to sweep through Provence and eventually all of Europe in the centuries to come: precursor of Ronsard, Donne, and Burns...

Here again, any translation ruins the original.

But there is, I think, an old Chinese lyric that may claim to be one of the great lyrics of the world, in that it preserves its freshness and poignancy even in a foreign tongue, and after many centuries:

'I will sit under the apple-tree and be a soldier no more'.

Largesse

19.10.1989

Last year, only a few kids came round the houses with their carved turnips on November 5. I suppose, nowadays even 2p is hardly worth knocking on a door for. (In my childhood, one halfpenny was the usual dole.)

But there were occasions when money spattered like rain on the street—for example, after a wedding. Then the town boys gathered outside the bride's house, and either the bridegroom or the groomsman appeared on the doorstep and showered the crowd with coppers. Then for five minutes or so there was a hot fierce struggle—like bubbling porridge—to get as many pennies as one could from the stamping feet and foraging hands. And you had to expect to get a bruised knuckle in the mêlée.

This ceremony was known as 'giving the ba' money.'... I have heard that it derives from a time, many generations back, when the bridegroom presented a football to the local boys. Maybe we were expected to buy a ball with the money substitute; but what we bought was toffee or ice-cream.

There was another cloudburst of money once a year, and this happened on the South Pier. Tour ships called at Stromness in the 1920s and 1930s, especially one called the *Duke of Clarence*. Everybody young and old went down to see the *Duke of Clarence* when she docked, especially to see the rich 'toffs', who spoke in very swanky accents and were equally astonished to see such crowds of 'the natives' of the Northern Isles.

As beads and cheap tinsel things were thrown to the Tahitians and the Cherokees, pennies and ha'pennies were showered among the Stromnessians, to the no small delight—tinged, I seem to remember, with a kind of contemptuous paternalism—of the well-heeled tourists.

Again, the pier heaved like boiling porridge—and the wonder is that nobody was nudged inadvertently into the harbour.

I remember one visit of the *Duke of Clarence* because several of us got into trouble at school that afternoon.

The showers of pennies had lasted so long from the deck of the tour-ship that we didn't hear the school bell ringing. What a panic there was!—What a breathless stampede up the Boys' Lane!

But it was no good. We were met by the stern headmaster, Mr McAuley and herded into his room. What punishment was meted out I cannot remember; I think it was only a stern reprimand. I think Mr McAuley dealt rather gently with me, as I was the youngest of the defaulters, aged seven or so.

I can't even remember if I had enough *Duke of Clarence* loot to make the escapade and the reprimand worthwhile.

All Saints' Day

9.11.1989

November the first today—All Saints' Day.

Television and newspapers tend to show us all the sensational unpleasant things that happen, and their perpetrators. No wonder the pessimists among us tend to think of a world awash with evil; and so get gloomier still. And if it isn't evil, vain foolish things seem to happen over and over—'All is vanity'...

We ought to be glad that the calendar is starred with saints' days: 'those who in their lives fought for life... They left the vivid air signed with their honour'...

The Saints are recorded. At least a few of them appear in Dictionaries of Saints, etc. And the chosen among them have their own days in the calendar. And it may be that their sweet subtle powerful influences touch the doings of men and women on earth, and remind us continually that there are things worth living for that have nothing to do with money and holidays in the sun and penthouses in Paris or Miami.

But today is All Saints' Day, when *all* the hallows that have no stars in the calendar come together in a mighty chorus. In that choir are surely set those who would have been most astonished to be called saints. But we all have known a few of them in our time—the patient, hard-working good cheerful women whose lives were dedicated to their families, and whose goodness overspilled upon neighbours' doorsteps and upon the whole community, and who gave a fair welcome to strangers. And their men-folk, some of them, who worked hard at their trades for small reward all their days, and rarely complained, and were a part of the communal harmony, and had room in their lives for the timeless stories (beyond the trashy 'real stories' they read in the newspapers). And the children, 'trailing clouds of glory'. And the old folk with the silver light on them.

One thing may be common to those 'ordinary people'—they seemed to have a natural piety in their conversation and bearing, whether they went to the church or not.

Since we hardly know anything about saintliness, and since nearly everybody is patched here and there with perversities and all kinds of selfishness, it would be foolish to class all the good folk we have known in our time as saints. Yet they all had the potential to be gathered into that freshness and radiance which is forever at work cleansing the earth of its foulness and its fevers.

They are dust in the kirkyard. And they are a part of 'the choir invisible'. Sometimes, in a quiet hour, the music comes down to us.

Perhaps we don't realise what influences for good are working on us on a day like this, All Hallows.

* * *

I feel chastened, as though I had spent the morning writing a sermon; and I have no training or talent for such things... Excuse me this once.

Strange to think that we are almost at the door of winter.

But it is through the open door of winter that the stars shine brightest: 'all the fire-folk sitting in the air'.

The day after All Saints is All Souls.

Return of the Rats

23.11.1989

Suddenly the clock changes, 'at one stride comes the dark'—and we think winter is here.

And we bring in the coal earlier and spark a match to the kindling in mid-afternoon. And we consider it might be time to think of thicker winter clothes. (A friend in Glasgow has sent a long wine-coloured scarf so kind and comfortable to neck and throat that on dry days it is possible to venture along the street without a coat.)

The low sun in the afternoon puts bronze squares rather than gold on the wall.

I bought a quilted hot-water bottle a few weeks ago.

Signs of Christmas get earlier and earlier. By the time Christmas comes, the huge brash commercial wave has spent itself, is drained of meaning; especially the primal meaning—a poor child born into a world of power and money and corruption, the WORD come to give meaning to what seems the chaotic babble and idiocy of history—*that* is all but drowned in the wash of money and profit.

But the true meaning endures, no matter how it is covered up and bundled away.

Enough sermonising for today...

The days get shorter and colder. More than human beings are feeling the cold. Three mornings ago I was sitting in the kitchen writing when I heard a scrunching and a scrabbling behind the skirting-board. Our friends the rats—or one of them at least—are back after a long absence... I admit to a small shiver of fear and distaste. (Such an evil reputation the rat has earned for itself over the centuries.) After that brief heart-stopping spasm, I managed to get caught up in the theme again and continue my writing.

Maybe the rat, or rats, I thought, are just passing through, exploring old runnels and tunnels on the way, and have now quit the premises.

Next morning, getting near the climax of the story I was writing, there they were again, gnawing away at something—mortar or wood—and a beading of sweat came on my forehead.

The imagination feeds unwholesomely on such a small sinister hint. Suppose the rat succeeded in boring a hole into the kitchen!

Every time I went in, for the rest of that day, I paused on the kitchen threshold, looking for rat signs. Suppose bright fierce predatory eyes glinted from beside the cooker! (Seven or eight winters ago, I had had such an experience: in the end, poison and the blocking up of vents and points of entry put paid to them.)

But there was nothing. Yesterday the rats were silent. Perhaps they have moved on; I hope so.

Whether they are on the increase, generally, I do not know; other folk have had experience of them too.

Perhaps we should all keep a saucerful of Eynhallow earth on our window-sills.

The Telephone

14.12.1989

Having a phone in the house is, I'm sure, a great boon; even when some stranger phones at the very time when your work is going well. (We all know the occasions when you answer the startling phone-bell to hear a voice saying, 'Is that you, Willie?' or, 'This is Ina here—I just wanted to say...' and you have to say, as politely as possible, 'Sorry, you've got the wrong number...')

And here's another mystery. Sometimes a friend phones from the south, and the voice is as clear as if he or she were sitting in the room. Another evening, and you can hardly make out what they're saying for all the fuzz on the line...

I suppose it must have been seriously considered, having a phone installed free in every old person's house. Most old folk can't afford it—and they are more liable than anyone to sudden illness. Besides that, they would feel less lonely and cut off.

I see they have phones in cars now—but only 'yuppies', I suppose, and high-pressure executives. I should imagine it must be a great hazard to phone for the latest stock-price figures while driving a powerful car on a busy road.

I can't remember when we Stromness children first became acquainted with phones. I think it must have been even later than knowledge of 'the wireless'. There can't have been more than a dozen motor-cars in Stromness in the 1920s; anyway, it was possible for boys to play football on the street, and to slide down Hellihole on sledges from Oglaby to the Library, without cars being a nuisance... At first sign of the two policemen, of course, the young footballers scattered. Or if a window got broken, there was the wrath of the householder to face.

But phones—they were for the families who owned cars and wireless sets.

I think I must have been well into my twenties before I first used a public phone, and then I must have done it under compulsion, and urgently. All I know is, I had to have a friend in the phone-box with me to instruct me in proper dialling, and when to put the pennies in the box.

Now, I'm told, they have a machine that can relay documents instantly to the furthest ends of the earth.

Time marches on. Will there ever be a time when you can actually see the person who's phoning you? That might be an advantage, or a disadvantage, depending on the caller; and whether one would have the alternative of letting one's own visage be seen.

All in all, though, once a phone is in the house, it would be a loss to be without it. The only time—apart from having the work schedule broken—when it becomes irksome is when I'm sitting fascinated by some TV programme; but this happens rarely; and if you know the caller well, you can always say you'll ring back in half an hour or so, and no hurt feelings on either side.

Preparing for Christmas: 1920s

21.12.1989

It's hard to imagine a Christmas without TV or radio. The only newspaper we saw in the 1920s was the *Daily Express*, and the only thing I followed in that was the adventures of a bear called Rupert.

But, even without these modern aids, there was wonderment in the air.

From a box somewhere, in a cupboard maybe, was unearthed a box of decorations from last winter. The dust was blown off them, they were unfolded with a thousand rustlings of coloured paper, and they were tacked to the living-room ceiling (the living-room and the kitchen were all one). Last was unfolded the paper bell, and it was hung right in the centre. Then sprigs of mistletoe were cunningly concealed among the decorations; so that unexpected and gift-bearing kisses could be given.

There were certainly no Christmas trees in our houses in the 1920s. I seem to remember the red holly berries, though.

But the shop windows were decorated, I think, with frost-silver edgings. With joy we looked into Spence the baker's window, full of round iced cakes with sugary coloured script: 'Lang May Yer Lum Reek', and 'A Merry Christmas'.

I suppose white Christmases were as rare then as they are now, but memory always sets our young Christmases in a scenario of snow and stars that glittered with a purer intensity than usual.

Certainly there were no blizzards of cards such as come fluttering through the letterbox now. There might be a dozen cards on the mantelpiece, and most of them seemed to be faced with celluloid.

And the cakes—a Scotch bun, rich and black and heavy—and a big round fruit-cake, waiting for the marzipan and the icing. But the cakes, I think, must have been baked in November.

And the bottles of home-made ginger wine...

And the letters to Santa that went flaming up the lum, or fell back half-scorched. No matter. Santa had somehow got the message.

On Christmas morning it was all a dream of joy, even though the loaded stocking at the bed-foot might contain only a book or a game of ludo, and always an apple and an orange, and maybe chocolate and a sixpence.

The clouds had opened and bestowed inestimable treasure.

Meantime the adults in most households went about their own business—such as, taking the goose or duck to one of the local bakehouses to be roasted.

And neighbours and friends came and went. And after the paraffin lamp on the dresser was lit, there was ginger wine and slices of marzipan cake; and sometimes, amid cries of delight or consternation, a kiss was given under the mistletoe. (But such nonsense was for the adults only.)

Then in mid-evening, the guisers came.

Impressions of 1989

4.1.1990

Apart from great international events—like the political stirrings and upheavals in eastern Europe—every one of us has his or her own private impressions of the year 1989.

It was another mild winter—and let's hope 'the greenhouse effect' hasn't got anything to do with three mild winters in a row.

Since our council house rents had been climbing more and more steeply each April, I thought it might be a good idea to buy this house I've lived in for twenty-one years. And so I applied, in the springtime.

And, though we know in theory that spring is bound to come, it always breaks over us with the joy of wild flowers, returning birds, and the lengthening light.

It remains a happiness that one can still spend a few hours at the writing desk between breakfast and lunch. For all writers and artists live under the shadow of the possibility that the gift, or whatever it is, may be withdrawn... So three more books got into print, and were liked, disliked, or tolerated, in the usual way. As the years pass, one ceases to care overmuch.

A great adventure in early June, into England, as far as Oxford, on a sleeper on an all-night train! (Not that I did much sleeping for all the bumping, swerving, slowing down and speeding up...) But to awake in London, and see for the first time Buckingham Palace and Hyde Park! And on to Oxford and the dreaming spires, and a kind house and family where new friends were to be met. Perhaps the most memorable event was a centenary Mass for the death of the great Victorian poet, Gerard Manley Hopkins, in a church where he himself had been a priest.

Six weeks, including the whole month of August, were spent in hospital in Aberdeen, undergoing radiotherapy—a very extraordinary experience, lasting five minutes a day, that went on for five weeks. The efficiency and kindness of doctors, radiotherapists, and nurses, are a proof of the success of the National Health Service. (Not to speak of the cheerfulness and quiet bravery of the patients in Ward 6.)

Nothing much has happened after that. I went quickly back to the old routine of writing, reading, and listening to Mahler and Sibelius on tape. (Thanks to Dave Brock for keeping me well supplied with Mahler and Sibelius.)

I got a taste for porridge in Foresterhill and so I've been having porridge for breakfast. Nothing so good on a winter morning.

Oh, I almost forgot the Festival in June. There are so many impressions—the outstanding one, perhaps, Sir Peter Maxwell Davies' talk on three Beethoven sonatas...

I clinched the purchase of the house in early November.

Some early guests were rats between the walls. They disturbed my tranquillity for a few nights and days. Thanks to Oliver Tait, I think they have packed and gone.

Such intensities of frost this winter! Even my cheerful fire has taken a long time to warm the room. The second snow came overnight, last night.

A happy New Year to all readers.

'Chief o' Scotia's Food'

11.1.1990

Porridge on a cold winter morning—I suppose northerners have been comforting themselves with porridge of one kind and another for centuries.

And of course, in the days before cornflakes, porridge was an important part of our childhood diet. And of course we didn't like it much; together with mince, stew, soup and boiled fish it was a thing to be endured rather than enjoyed. The only food we seemed to enjoy was ham-and-eggs, sausages, kippers, and especially cakes, chocolate and sweeties.

As cows munched hay we took our spoonfuls of porridge, mechanically, and 'because it's good for you'... we often wondered, I'm sure, how the things that were good for us were on the whole unpleasant.

But anyway, we grew out of porridge, weaned away in large part by the 1930s craze for cornflakes, which swept our generation like a prairie fire.

For one thing, there were no lumps in cornflakes. For another, there was no sticky smudgy pot to be cleaned.

For decades thereafter, porridge was a food of which we had only theoretical knowledge.

'The halesome parritch, chief o' Scotia's food'; even Burns' mother had told him it was good for him.

Last summer, I had to spend a while in hospital in Aberdeen. Porridge was on the menu, among other items, every morning.

I must say I enjoyed my first plate of Foresterhill porridge so much, that thereafter I had it nearly every morning. I was able to tell the sister-in-charge: 'Foresterhill porridge is really good'...

So when eventually I got home, I thought seriously of making porridge every morning first thing. Three things held me back: the thought of steeping the stuff, the probability of 'lumps', and the certainty of a mucky, sticky pot to clean afterwards.

For my birthday, a friend gave me a small non-stick pot, along with two wooden stirring spoons. I bought a packet of porridge, and found out that no steeping was required. A little five-minute stir and simmer, and there on the table was a plate of most delicious hot nourishment, laced with cold milk.

Now I have it nearly every morning.

How the locusts have eaten all those years of grain-rich cold-defying corn.

Now I see clearly what Burns meant. And I'm sure many an ancient Celtic bard before him had sung the praises of porridge.

Burns' Day

25.1.1990

How quickly it comes round again. January the 25th, one of the great days in every Scots person's calendar, along with Hogmanay and November the 30th.

It is, of course, Burns' Day, the day when 'a blast o' Janwar' win' / Blew hansel in on Robin' in an Ayrshire cottage in 1759.

It is extraordinary how this farmer's son caught the imagination of an entire nation, and has held it for more than two centuries.

In our Orkney childhood the name of Burns must have been one of the first of the great legendary names that people talked about, along with Bonnie Prince Charlie and Robert the Bruce and Mary Queen of Scots. There were Burns songs like 'Mary o' Argyle' and 'A Red Red Rose', and (of course) 'Auld Lang Syne', and bits of verse, generally of the more sentimental kind.

When we were 'scholars', about the age of eight or nine, we were presented with a poem called 'To a Mouse', and given the task of learning it by heart.

It must have been quite difficult for us young Orcadians to grapple with the alien Scots tongue. What were we to make of such phrases as 'a daimen icker in a thrave'? We solved the difficulty of 'Oh, what a panic's in thy breistie' by turning it to playground merriment, by substituting 'pancake' for 'panic'.

And yet the poem, for all the language difficulty, caught our imagination and enlarged our sympathy.

This—I can see now—is a sign of really great poetry, that it appeals to the innocent mind as well as the mature mind.

There remains the mystery of why Burns has a day to himself in the calendar, when poets like Shakespeare, Dante, Pushkin, and Goethe are not honoured in this particular way.

It may be that Scotland had suffered a series of defeats and humiliations in the decades before Burns. There was the failure of the Darien Scheme (which was almost certainly a blessing in disguise). There was the Union of the Parliaments in 1707, when Scotland ceased to be a sovereign nation and was called for a time 'North Britain'. There was the crushing of the Jacobite Rebellion. Not all Scots by any means supported the Rebellion, yet the brutal defeat of it on Scottish soil must have been a deep humiliation to most sensitive Scots. And their language was in grave danger; weren't the upper classes in Scotland doing their best to get rid of 'Scotticisms' from their speech, and to ape the received speech of England?

So, when the Kilmarnock Edition was published, Scotland had suddenly a new hero, who reminded the Scots of their past glories, and put strength and joy back into their threatened language, and at the same time appealed to new stirrings in the human heart: the notion of the dignity of all men and women, even the poorest and the humblest. The vision went deeper, until all of creation was involved: the mouse and the mountain daisy are made of the same dust as men.

Stromness v Kirkwall

1.2.1990

There is somehow a feeling that the local war between Kirkwall and Stromness that began maybe about the year 1700 has never really stopped; though there have been long intermissions and uneasy truces, the seal of peace has never been truly affixed.

Some Stromnessians feel, rightly or wrongly, that the royal burgh has never really forgiven us for that humiliating defeat in 1746, when Alexander Graham took the case of the Stromness Merchants to the final court of appeal, the House of Lords, and won a famous victory (not only for Stromness, either, but for all the small trading ports of Scotland).

The ultimate defeat was doubly humiliating for the Kirkwall merchants, in that the earlier law processes had seemed to promise them victory.

In one respect, Stromness ought to be ashamed too; for in the end Alexander Graham was a lonely hero, seemingly deserted by the fainthearted among his local peers, and a hero financially broken.

Possibly 'the war' had started a full century earlier, when ships from the Baltic and Europe first began to call at the growing village in the west, called then (variously) Cairston, Hamnavoe, Shoreside, Stromness.

What if this upstart village and its shopkeepers and traders were to become a serious threat to Kirkwall? Nothing is settled and secure. There had been a time, admittedly far in the past, when Birsay had been the administrative and ecclesiastical centre of Orkney; and in those Norse days Kirkwall, 'the bay with the church', had been the upstart village.

Could the centre of gravity be shifting again?

Indeed, after Graham and his pyrrhic victory, it seemed that Kirkwall was slowly and increasingly losing ground to Stromness. It was to Stromness that the Hudson Bay ships came, and the Davis Straits whalers. There was a brief time in mid 19th century when the population of Stromness was greater than Kirkwall's. And the momentum seemed to be increasing.

The invention of the internal combustion engine was, possibly, the saving of Kirkwall.

Battered sailing ships no longer needed, with such urgency, the shelter provided by Brinkie's Brae and the Holms.

Slowly the balance reasserted itself. Stromness entered on a long period of decline that lasted right up to 1939.

Such an incident as this acrimonious debate about the short sea crossing is but another skirmish in a war that might go on for a century or two yet.

And at the end of it all there might be a new capital of Orkney entirely: Houton, or Flotta.

'The Cup that Cheers'

1.3.1990

What more delicious taste than the first cup of tea in the morning? It has been going on for so long that it's hard to imagine life without tea.

What did the women do before the mid-morning break; and when did they begin to pour from the steaming teapot again in the afternoon, and again before bed?

For three generations at least in Orkney tea-drinking has been an established ritual. (Coffee came in much later, and is preferred by some people, but it seems, to me at least, a much inferior kind of refreshment.)

But tea-drinking isn't so deeply rooted in our island way of life as all that.

I remember a good lady in Birsay telling me that when she was young tea was drunk only on Sundays, as a special treat.

So, what did they drink before that? Milk probably, and when milk was scarce they supped their porridge with ale. Even the children did that—probably not the strong ale that ploughmen drank in the evening, but thin stuff from a second or third brewing.

It is intriguing to imagine how tea first came to Orkney.

No doubt, in the lairds' houses, then in manses, then in the merchants' houses in Kirkwall, it was sipped and savoured. Tea was very expensive. Lairds' wives and ministers' wives had brought the habit no doubt from London and Edinburgh.

As for the commoners, let them stick to their milk and ale.

But then, some time in the late 18th century, word was brought secretly that that night, in the dark of the moon, a Dutch ship would anchor in 'the Cairston Roads' (that is, behind the Holms). The message was whispered to certain merchants. One by one they were sworn to secrecy. There would be trouble if the excisemen got to hear about it.

So, after dark, a couple of yoles[1] set out from this pier and that, with a few strong reliable men in each.

And presently they were under the big looming shadow of the Dutch ship, behind the Holms.

The Stromness spokesman addressed the shadowy figures above, along the ship's rail. How many casks of rum? Did they have a sack or two of snuff? They would take as much tobacco as the Dutch skipper could spare...

Up above, as their eyes got accustomed to the dark, the Stromnessians could see the Dutchmen shaking their heads. No rum. No snuff. No perfumes. No tobacco. Only boxes of tea. They could have twenty large boxes of best China tea.

Whereupon there ensued a long loud passionate argument between the Stromness merchant and the Dutch skipper.

1. small two-masted fishing boats

'Tea!' shouted the merchant. What could he do with tea? Nobody in Hamnavoe had ever tasted the stuff. He would be ruined! Here he stood, risking his neck for some Chinese swill nobody would buy or drink...

In the end, however, the twenty boxes of tea were eased down into the yoles. Money was exchanged—a tinkling like small bells in the quiet dark night.

They parted, the Dutchmen and the Hamnavoe merchants, with cold farewells.

But the illicit tea was all sold before that winter was out.

Rev William Clouston

8.3.1990

The *Old Statistical Account of Scotland* (the Orkney volume), compiled between 1795 and 1798, continues to be fascinating reading.

It was written by all the parish ministers of Scotland two centuries ago. Of course some of them were good at the job of compilation, others not so good.

Stromness was fortunate because the minister of Stromness and Sandwick at that time was Rev William Clouston.

What he has written about his combined parishes and their people is balanced, lucid, and reasonable.

Two centuries ago, ministers in their big manses had, it seemed, plenty of time to follow their inclinations. Some of them, like Rev George Low of Birsay, were outstanding naturalists. Rev George Barry of Shapinsay wrote an extraordinarily comprehensive *History of Orkney* (1805), that took in every facet of life in the islands as it was known in his day, and ended by being much more than a mere history.

In the long winter nights those ministers pored over old tomes and manuscripts; and studied shells and pieces of rock, and roots and grasses and feathers, through their early microscopes.

We know, from the evidence, what Rev William Clouston was up to in his study in the manse at Stromness. He was reading Latin poetry, especially the works of Virgil—the *Aeneid* and *Pastorals* and *Georgics*. He delighted so much in that ancient and ever-young music—what Tennyson called 'the lordliest measure ever moulded by the lips of man'—that his account of Stromness and Sandwick is interspersed again and again by quotations from the great classical poet. Virgil was no poet of a dead language to Mr Clouston. Over and over he relates the conditions of farmers and merchants of his two parishes to conditions among the fertile hills and valleys of Italy two thousand years ago; and so the present resonates with the past, and a kind of timelessness is achieved.

But this minister was no dry stick of a pedant. He cast a charitable eye on his parishioners. Yes, he says, they use a great deal of their cereal crop to make malt for brewing. But their work is so hard that they deserve to rejoice from time to time; and besides, the winters are raw and cold.

He is all for balance and toleration, in matters of religion as well as in everything else. In that sense he was a true son of the 18th century.

I think this tolerant, charitable man is buried in the old part of Stromness Kirkyard, at Warbeth. And half of his tombstone—if I remember truly—is in English words, and the other half is engraved in his beloved Latin.

May the earth lie kindly on his good dust.

Women in *The Orkneyinga Saga*

12.4.1990

Leafing through a favourite book again, the other day—*The Orkneyinga Saga*—it was soon plain enough that there was no need for 'women's lib' in Orkney's medieval history. In it, women play as prominent a part as men. Not, of course, in actual statecraft and piracy and battle. But it often seems that women in the *Saga* held the strings of action, and the men were puppets miming to their will.

There is Earl Sigurd the Stout's mother, a kind of witch. It was she who wove the raven banner of victory for her son Sigurd. The army that followed the banner was always victorious, but the standard-bearer was always cut down.

It was she who made the magnificent remark to Sigurd, when he doubted whether he should fight a battle in Scotland, the odds against him being seven to one: 'I would have brought you up in my wool basket, if I'd known you'd want to go on living for ever.'

Lady Macbeth had nothing on an earlier *Saga* lady called Ragnhild. The first Earl Thorfinn had five sons—Arnfinn, Havard, Hlodver, Ljot, and Skuli. And Ragnhild was married to the eldest, Arnfinn.

It seems she just got tired of him—'she had her husband done to death at Murkle in Caithness'. Then she married the second brother Havard, who bore the bountiful nickname 'Harvest-happy'. And indeed it seemed that Orkney flourished under him.

But Ragnhild got tired of him too. At a feast given by Havard, Ragnhild spoke privately with a nephew of Havard's called Einar. She urged Einar to murder his uncle, and so become Earl, and then she would marry him. Einar was reluctant to begin with. But in the end he and his men set upon Havard in Stenness and killed him.

All Orkney was shaken with revulsion. Ragnhild rejected Einar, and sent for another nephew of Havard who was also called Einar (Einar 'Hard-chaps'), and she urged Hard-chaps to kill his cousin the murderer.

Hard-chaps knew what kind of a woman he was dealing with—'It is often said that your speech is different from your thought'... But in the end this Einar, to win the earldom and the ferocious bride, killed his cousin Einar.

But Ragnhild didn't marry the second Einar either. Instead she wooed Earl Thorfinn's fourth son, Ljot. 'The Orkneymen,' says the *Saga*, 'preferred to serve a son of Thorfinn Skull-splitter'...

Ragnhild must have been a beautiful and a fascinating woman; because Ljot, knowing full well the risk he was running, married her.

The second Einar was naturally 'very ill-pleased with his lot...'. He raised a rebellion against his uncle Ljot, but it failed, and he was killed.

No more is said about the amazing woman Ragnhild.

We have, in the *Saga*, to set in the scales against her a wonderful woman like Thora, the mother of Earl Magnus, who made the great feast at Paplay in Holm on the day of the peace-making, Easter Monday, April the sixteenth.

The Unfolding Drama of War

3.5.1990

There were some lovely May mornings fifty years ago. We went to school and somewhere along Alfred Street—I seem, vaguely to remember—it dawned on me that Hitler had invaded Holland, Belgium, and at the same time struck at France.

'Well,' we thought, 'now things are happening.'

Then Churchill was Prime Minister.

The Germans would never break into France, we knew well, because of the Maginot Line, which was impregnable. The Jerries were in deep trouble now.

To us senior pupils of Stromness Academy it was all like a game, or a play. We heard the news from France on the wireless and in the *Daily Express*.

Soon a slightly odd note struck. It seemed the German army had somehow gotten into France, after all. They had gotten in round the north corner of the Maginot Line, which didn't extend beyond the place where France joins Belgium.

A place called Sedan seemed to be in the news a lot. Then Mr Churchill the new Prime Minister came on the air and said that a battle he called 'The Battle of the Bulge' was being fought. To our amazement 'the Bulge' was on French soil, and growing alarmingly by the day.

Still, General Gamelin would sort things out soon. How careless of the French, all the same, not to have extended and sealed the Maginot Line!

Thereafter, it was all rout and confusion, as the German army broke through all along the front.

And yet the Stromnessians, as I remember, were never worried or afraid. We were spectators at a darker play than we had anticipated, but the unfolding drama continued to fascinate us.

There was no more talk of the 'Battle of the Bulge'. Mr Churchill spoke of the Battle of France in thrilling resounding defiant words.

I think by May 1940 we had long discarded our gas masks.

We were waiting to leave school for ever. We would soon be in the Army or the Navy or the Air Force. It seemed, on the whole, an exciting prospect for us; even though only news of disasters poured in.

Meantime a civilian army called the LDV was hurriedly formed (Local Defence Volunteers). The name was quickly changed to the Home Guard. A few of us joined, and were given guns and forage caps and arm-bands. Lord Haw-Haw the German propagandist said those part-time soldiers could not expect any of the courtesies of war if they fell into the hands of the invading German army.

We took turns to stand guard all night at the Telephone Exchange behind the Masonic Hall.

It was really, for us youths, a lovely and an exciting summer.

We had not the least doubt of ultimate victory, though it was hard to see just how that could be achieved.

Poet in the Prison-House

24.5.1990

'Now,' said the teacher in Wyre school, 'the multiplication table.'

Nine times one is nine, she chanted, smiting the blackboard with a pointer.

The children of Wyre took up the chant.

Nine times two is eighteen.

Nine times three is twenty-seven...

The mouth of one small fair freckled boy moved but no sound issued to join the chorus.

Nine times seven is sixty-three.

The boy was thinking, 'The buttercups and mayflowers will be bonny round the Castle this morning... The sun will be putting a sheen on the waves... I can almost hear the kye from here, new out of the byre, taking big sweet slurping breaths of wind.'

Nine times nine is eighty-one.

There was a silence in the classroom.

'Edwin,' said the teacher, 'are you with us or not?'

The boy looked confused.

A few of the pupils laughed.

'You'd better pay attention, all of you,' said the teacher. 'It's an hour and a half till the bell. I hope you've all done your homework for history.'

The pupils murmured submission and acquiescence.

They ate their pieces and cups of milk at playtime, sitting at the desks, whispering, smiling, mocking. A boy pulled a girl's hair.

The teacher sat at the high desk, writing in the register.

Swans flew over. Down at the shore a whitemaa[1] cried. The inattentive boy heard the scrunch of a keel on the stones. The men would be back from the haddocks. Suddenly there were thousands of gulls on the shore, screaming. He heard the voice of Willie Sutherland at the far end of the island, shouting to the horse.

The pointer thwacked the blackboard.

Time for history.

It was the Scottish Wars of Independence. Every little tongue flowered with names and dates: Alexander III, the Maid of Norway, Edward I, John Balliol, William Wallace, Stirling Bridge, Monteith.

At last the heroic heart-stirring name, Robert the Bruce, and his immortal field, Bannockburn.

Without much joy, the pupils repeated names and battles and dates.

Battle of Bannockburn, 1314.

The boy thought with horror of the mingled hosts, the rearing horses, the pits, the screams, showering arrows, blood and wounds and death, and the King on the hillock with the gold circle on his head. Long, long ago... Here, in a page of their school history book, was the story of the battle, in a few phrases. Which was the true battle, the event or the story?... It was hard for a boy to know.

'Edwin,' said the teacher, 'you're in a dream again.'

It was four o'clock. The day in the prison-house was over.

The school door was choked briefly with pupils, then they were scattered, laughing and shouting, all over Wyre.

* * *

I remembered early this morning in Foresterhill Hospital that today, 15 May, is Edwin Muir's birthday.

So I've tried to imagine a long-ago day in the school in Wyre.

1. kind of seagull

Home Thoughts from Hospital

31.5.1990

Who would choose to spend the lovely month of May in hospital, far away from Brinkie's Brae and the Hoy hills and Scapa Flow?

Sometimes one has no choice. At any rate there are trees outside the ward window, getting heavy with foliage, and a north-east sky. Blue and silver with promise of summer, or grey with the rain the Aberdeenshire farmers are crying out for.

And I see more folk coming and going in an hour—nurses, doctors, cleaners, patients, porters, newsboys, mobile library ladies, mobile shop ladies—than I might see in a whole month in Stromness. This little single side-ward is like a front room at the side of a busy street.

Furthermore you are not allowed to be bored, for there is always something happening: dressings, blood tests, mealtimes, blood pressure, temperature, pulse-beat, medicines, and cups of tea, hoovering and mopping.

And all done with the greatest kindness and courtesy and despatch.

* * *

But one can't help wondering about Orkney in May and what is going on there. Letters come and they are like draughts of fresh air. Folk from Orkney call from time to time, and I'm kept abreast with the local events and folk. *The Orcadian* comes winging in once a week; I read all about the amazing OIC[1] election. Peter and Betty Grant—naturalised Orcadians—never fail; I'm sure I would be very lonely without them.

* * *

There used to be a local saying when I was a boy, that the cuithes came swarming through Hoy Sound at 'the first drink of the May flood'.

The month was full of proverbs and saws. 'Never cast a cloot till May is oot'—meaning, I suppose, keep your winter garments on till June, for the May airs can carry deadly chills.

May—early May, the first—can bestow beauty on girls, if they wash their faces, with proper ceremony, in the high dews.

Nothing is lovelier in the north than the lengthening light of May. The west brims with promise, and we often waste those magical dawns with over-sleeping.

The ditches are transfigured with wild flowers. There is a field above Warbeth beach that is richer, for a few weeks, than any eastern carpet.

The larks throw their skeins of song on the wind.

On banks here and there—beside the Loch of Skaill, for example—there are endless profusions of primroses (or, as we called them, mayflowers).

1. Orkney Islands Council

Such a precious month it is, that it seems made for young people. For us who are older, to walk abroad in May is to have the memory enriched, and to be permitted yet one more drink at the fountain of youth.

The Sunday School Picnic

14.6.1990

It must have been about this time of year, in the early 1930s, that we went on the Sunday School picnic.

I'm sure they still have Sunday School picnics, but nothing like sixty years ago. Because, in the first place, we didn't go to the seaside in buses, but, much more excitingly, in horse-drawn carts, provided (I'm sure) by the farmers of the congregation of the UP Kirk (Victoria Street).

Every little Sunday scholar was there, at the appointed time, with an aluminium mug tied round his neck with string. Then off the carts set, over the thrilling bumps and ruts of the road.

It must have taken a considerable time to get to Skaill or Swanbister, the only two places I remember. The horses kicked up dust from the road, the wheels creaked and sang, the fields of sheep and cows went slowly past, and the peedie crofts with flocks of hens round the door. At last there was a gleam of sea, and soon after that we were there.

What happened then? We were probably treated to sandwiches and lemonade, cakes and milk. We ate till we could hold no more. Not the best of preparations for the sports to come, on the greensward above the beach.

Oh, they were delightful, the races! No straightforward running—that would have been boring—but sack-races, egg-and-spoon races, three-legged races. Our Sunday School teachers, I think, were the referees.

What laughter, under the blue summer sky, as the sacks went blundering and tumbling towards the finishing tape. 'The secret,' we told our friends, 'is to place your feet in the corners of the sack...'

In the egg-and-spoon race, no decent boy or girl would put a thumb on the egg. But who was to know, in that broad field, if the rules were broken or not? The eggs, made of clay, were always falling among the buttercups.

More waves of hilarity from the touchlines!

Modest prizes to the winners—maybe a sixpenny piece.

By that time we were all as hungry as hawks again, and the egg sandwiches and the beef sandwiches and the cakes and chocolate biscuits and bottles of Gowans' lemonade were devoured among the dunes.

And probably the more energetic kids paddled in the sea. And all too soon the sun hung over the Atlantic, and it was time for the sleepy horses to draw their loads of satiated sun-soaked children slowly home to Stromness.

This happened summer after summer, and only once was there so much rain on the day that we spent the picnic in a barn; and that wasn't so much fun.

Festival Poets

5.7.1990

This is the first year since the St Magnus Festival started that I haven't been able to go to a single performance—not even the poetry recital on Saturday morning in the Pier Arts Centre, always a glittering occasion.

And Gunnie Moberg the photographer always manages to get a picture of me standing with the Festival poet. But not this year, though it would have been a pleasure to be in a picture with Liz Lochhead.

Next year, I hope.

But I met up with Liz after all, when she came to visit me on the day of her departure, and left me a copy of her play *Tartuffe*.

She gets more and more famous as the years pass, as poet and dramatist and performer—and rightly so.

And that other regular poetry feature, the Johnsmas Foy, I had to miss that too, with its nautical flavour this year...

The Festival has been fortunate in its choice of poets, a succession of illustrious bards, beginning with the veteran Norman MacCaig.

And we have had the Poet Laureate, Ted Hughes, and the poet who would certainly be the laureate of the worldwide Irish if there was such an illustrious post, Seamus Heaney. Also Stewart Conn, Richard Murphy, Edwin Morgan, Iain Crichton Smith, Douglas Dunn. (Forgive me, any poet I have inadvertently left out of this galaxy.)

Some of those poets stayed at Garth, the highest cottage on the Mainland, hospitably looked after by Grenville and Elizabeth Gore-Langton (now Earl and Countess Temple of Stowe). Looking out over Hoy Sound and the open Atlantic, those poets must have thought Orkney an unforgettable place indeed.

Seamus Heaney, who may well be Ireland's greatest poet since Yeats, spread good-fellowship wherever he went. Three beautiful Stromness sisters showed him Brodgar and Skaill Bay in the late midsummer 'dim', and he thought of them as 'the three graces' or 'the three muses'.

Ted Hughes fished the lochs, conducted by a man (Dave Brock) who knows the Orkney lochs and all the subtleties of trout, but alas! they were unlucky.

Are we running out of illustrious poets to invite to our Festival? There are verse-makers by the score and by the hundred. It takes time often to sift the grain from the chaff.

It has been suggested that an overseas poet ought to be welcomed. A name that occurs is Knut Ødegård, the Norwegian, who has been inspired by Orkney after a single visit. And another Scots-Gaelic poet, the veteran Sorley MacLean. The problem would always be there, as to whether the poems ought to be read in the original language, or in translation, or in both.

There is still a wide field to choose from.

'Wet' and 'Dry' Times

12.7.1990

I haven't been drinking beer for the last three months or so, not because I've joined the temperance party, but for a temporary private reason.

I got quite a shock, as an old and faithful adherent of beer and ale, when I heard on TV one day last week that the price of a pint might be going up in some places to £1.20, or more.

When my generation first got a taste for beer, after Stromness went 'wet' again in 1948, the price of a pint was one shilling and twopence (or about 6p in modern money).

Temperance had had a quarter-of-a-century reign in Stromness, so when the one and only pub re-opened in 1948, in the Stromness Hotel, there was something slightly furtive and guilt-ridden about going up to the long cold narrow austere bar for a pint. We looked right and left along the street to make sure that no respectable citizens were observing us—and then made a quick dash up the narrow lane to the temple of Barleycorn. And there we tasted the creamy frothy nectar till 4pm (closing time).

After 4pm, we didn't care so much who saw us coming out, for the beer had put a false bravado on us.

Then home, through the legend-haunted town, for our tea, and maybe a snooze.

So it went on, while more and more taverns opened their doors, and successive Chancellors put the price up, but slowly, a penny this Budget and twopence that.

It has to be remembered that that quarter-century when Stromness was 'dry', was not normal at all in the history of the town.

Rev Peter Learmonth in 1840 or so records that there were nearly forty taverns, bars, and ale-houses in Stromness.

The townsfolk waited in dread for the return of the Davis Straits whalers each August, for the whalemen had plenty of money and they had had little to drink but melted ice all summer.

And it seems there were wild scenes on a Saturday night, during the First World War, when English marines and Irish navvies melled with flying fists and bloody noses outside the taverns. Such scenes, it's said, influenced Stromnessians to vote 'dry' in 1921 or 22.

So what happened to those locals who liked their drop of beer? They had perforce to take a bus to the Pomona in Finstown or the Smithfield in Dounby; and it's possible those commuters drank more beer there than they would have at Billy Clouston's at South End or Flett's in Dundas Street.

Some folk claim that Stromness declined commercially in those twenty-five drinkless years. Others say that the tone of family life in general improved.

The Second World War brought thousands of soldiers to Stromness, and 'wet' canteens sprang up like mushrooms, and you had only to be civil to a soldier to be invited into the camp for a pint... So the drinkless generation quickly rediscovered the magic, and they were quick to vote Stromness 'wet' again two years after the war ended.

The Putting Green

2.8.1990

I'm glad that they have a Putting Green back at Ness this summer.

Stromness has lacked that fine pleasure ground for too long.

I haven't managed a round yet, but perhaps I will before the evenings get chillier.

I think—giving it a brief glance through a car window in passing— that it is not so big as before. How could it be, with the bowling green occupying the top half of the field? So I expect the new putting green has only nine holes, whereas in the days of its glory, from the 30s to the 60s of this century, it occupied the entire field and had eighteen holes, each with a character of its own.

What brought me first to the Putting Green as a small boy was that my father went there every afternoon in summer, after he became too incapacitated with arthritis to work.

There, on the bench in front of Mr Tom Craigie the greenkeeper's house, sat a row of the town elders—Mr Wm Thomson, retired sailor and publican—Mr Bill Spence with a silver beard, the baker—Mr Bill Robertson, retired baker (father of George Robertson, later Post-

master and Provost)—a Captain Hutchison from the North End—
Mr Jimmy Bruce, postman and watchmaker... And others whose names
I forget.

There they sat and discussed the great issues of the day, local,
national, and international.

At last, having put the world to rights, they decided it was time to
putt. Then battle was joined, usually in foursomes.

What mingled joy and earnestness those ancients would devote to
their game! What cries of anguish or delight if they succeeded in
'stymying' an opponent—that is, getting their ball between the
opponent's ball and the hole.

They weren't above resorting to questionable tactics, such as giving
a loud cough, or making a snide remark just as the opponent was
squaring up to strike a delicate shot.

I could observe all this, because my job was to lift the wooden
numbered pins out, or retrieve a ball that had wandered into Mrs
Craigie's flower-beds alongside the green, or lift the balls out of the
hole (for several of those old gentlemen were too stiff in the joints to
bend so low). Those menial tasks I performed with pleasure.

Younger Stromnessians will not know that the lower half of the
green was a series of little hills and hollows, and it was among those
tantalising irregularities that a game was won or lost—often by good
luck, occasionally by superb skill and timing and gamesmanship.

If the grass had been newly mown, and one chanced to miss the hole
at the first unlucky stroke, the chances were that growing exasperation
would make a player miss it again and again...

Then victors and vanquished would rest their aged bones on the
bench, and talk, laugh, gossip, and speculate until the urge to play
overtook them once more.

Many a gentle innocent afternoon I spent on the Putting Green at
Ness, in bygone summers.

A Wilderness of Paper

30.8.1990

I have lived for years in a wilderness of paper, that has been getting
wilder and wilder.

Of course this happens when you write for a certain time every
morning, and letters come winging in on almost every post. Also, you
clip bits out of magazines sometimes that you think might be interesting to read some time later.

So, pieces of paper continue to drift about the house like snowflakes and from time to time they get shovelled to one side like snow, but without order or system.

Fortunately, I have a few summertime friends who know how to deal with snowdrifts of paper. Especially I was wanting to find manuscripts of published works, and also working manuscripts, and miscellanea. My friend Brian Murray from Ayr set about that task with apparent relish, and it took him days, and in the end the chaos of papers was there in ordered piles, in envelopes and folders neatly annotated; so when my friend Kulgin Duval came last weekend to collect the finished MSS, I could put my hand on them at once.

(Brian Murray is my good neighbour, each holiday time, but in mid-August he has to set off back to his headmaster's desk in Ayrshire.)

Then remained the letters—and not just a few letters either, but a blizzard of them that has been lying about the house in black bags and old suitcases, a thirty-years epistolary storm... Certain of those letters are of interest to one national establishment; but how were the important letters to be sieved and saved from the monstrous thirty-year letter-fall?

I could never attempt such a task.

How fortunate I am in my friends! Peter and Betty Grant from Aberdeen have been staying with me, and they got stuck into those immense drifts. It took them a whole day, till midnight, and I think at the end of it they must have been exhausted.

Next morning, down went nine black bags of shredded letters to 'the dust-cart' (as we used to call it).

Not only did they remove that intimidating weight of papers from my house, but they covered my bedroom and upper staircase with a fine carpet (but I think I mentioned all that last week).

Slowly, once more, letters come sifting in twice a day; but from now on I will not be such a hoarder of them, there will be no more dense snowdrifts.

Poets of the Sagas

6.9.1990

A very attractive pamphlet on Maes Howe has recently been published by Her Majesty's Stationery Office.

It is well illustrated with good photographs and with prints and drawings from past centuries. And it has an intelligent and lucid text.

Fascinating always are the Norse runes, most of them carved by Earl Rognvald's crusaders when they came back from their crusade (or, more accurately, pilgrimage) in the mid 12th century: CRUSADERS BROKE INTO THIS HOWE.

It is known that Earl Rognvald, a famous poet himself, had other poets in the fifteen ships that left Orkney for the Mediterranean in 1150. *The Orkneyinga Saga* is starred with their lyrics; but most of the poems were made by the earl himself, notably his sequence of love poems to the Countess of Narbonne in France, Ermengarde.

Some poet among the 'Jerusalem-farers' may well have written on the walls of Maes Howe: INGIBIORG THE FAIR WIDOW—MANY A WOMAN HAS WALKED STOOPING IN HERE—A VERY SHOWY PERSON...

A constant theme of poetry, before and since, is how all pride and beauty must come to the dust of death at last.

One poet mentioned in the *Saga* who did not carve in Maes Howe was Thorbjorn the Black. (The Norsemen were not all blond. Thorbjorn must have had a beard black as midnight to get such a name.)

Thorbjorn was among the sailor poets, but only one of his verses is recorded, telling of the crusaders' landing in Acre... It was the last poem Thorbjorn made. Some kind of fever broke out in the crews, and Thorbjorn and some others died.

Thorbjorn must have been honoured among that company of poets, because another poet called Oddi wrote an elegy for him: 'I saw the friend of the King buried in the High Church. Now earth is over him, and a southern sun brightens the stones'...

So Thorbjorn did not live to enter the dark howe in Stenness and carve a rune by the light of torches.

It is a touching story—all the more so because of the laconic manner of its telling.

Nothing is said about Rognvald's sorrow over the death of his friend.

And what would the King of Bergen have thought of the loss of one of his laureates?

Not the cold sun of the north touched his howe, but he lay lapped in bright Mediterranean light, under the stones of Acre.

Remembered Autumns

11.10.1990

We didn't think a great deal in our Stromness childhoods about the changing months and seasons.

All we were sure of was, in late August we had to set out once more to the prison-house of school... A week or so there, and we were let free into the magical Lammas Fair, that (alas!) only lasted one day.

We were aware that the paraffin lamp was lit earlier and earlier on the kitchen table. And we were aware, not unpleasantly, of the increasing flames in the range. (There was one queer time—it must have been the miners' strike of 1926—when there was no coal to burn, and Stromnessians burned pitch in the stove. I remember the ugliness of those dripping flames that seemed to give no heat.)

By the lamplight I suppose we did our homework, reading and spelling and history. I was more interested in games like ludo, snakes-and-ladders, and blow-football.

Delightful it was, on a fine autumn evening, to run outside with a few other boys and play games like 'pikka' and 'hide-and-seek'.

Sometimes there was devilment afoot, and we knocked on doors and ran away, and hid round a corner till the householder opened the door upon vacancy, and shut it again, muttering imprecations about boys and what should be done with them.

Then home, hungry, for supper, that might be fried tatties and bread and butter, and cocoa. (Sometimes there was hot milk, a horrible drink, especially when a skin formed on the surface, and came away disgustingly in your mouth.)

Then, on cold nights we went to bed with a brick heated in the oven and wrapped in an old bit of blanket... How wonderful, to lie in bed and listen to a storm raging outside! (Nowadays storms make me uneasy; so far do we drift away from the innocence that accepts everything and delights in everything...)

The moon came and went, a glory on the harbour water. The stars went in their great wheel across the sky. We accepted it, it was a part of our heritage—we were not in the least thankful. Or rather, the truth is, we lacked the hypocrisy that comes over us in later life, when we stop and exclaim, 'Oh, look at the sunset!'... 'Isn't the moon just a picture! Lovely, wonderful!...'

I am thinking in this brief essay of the month of October mostly. About the middle of the month I had my birthday, and I'm sure there was a plum pudding made by my mother with threepenny bits hidden in it. I got quite angry if other children found the threepenny bits before me. But somehow, mysteriously, one of those small silver coins always got inserted into the last spoonful.

Right at the end of October was Hallow-E'en, when we dooked for apples and nuts in a brimming tub. Very watery occasions—the streaming hair had to be dried with a rough towel—we had to work hard for our fruit and nuts.

We may have been dimly aware of even more magical times to come—the first snow in November, the first whisper, 'Christmas' and 'Santa Claus'.

Strategy for the Fire

1.11.1990

There's an exciting encounter with the hearth every morning, for you never know whether the fire will work or not... It becomes very important, of course, that the fire should work as the days get colder.

The paper takes fire from a match and the sticks from the paper; up the chimney it goes in a fine 'bleeze'.

Everything is going well! You go into the kitchen to write a note or put on the kettle, and when you come back the fire is all cold and black—a few creaks and sparks that will soon be no more.

So, begin again...

Obviously, you have choked that merry beginning with too many coals. But the newspapers for kindling are not what they used to be either. Not so long since, the *Radio Times*, for example, made a good fire-starter, but now the pages are all glossy and they burn sullenly.

I have driftwood from Marwick and Warbeth, and a bag of well-cut sticks from a faithful friend, and they burn well. And the coal is of the very best quality.

It used to be, that sheets of crumpled newspaper, a stratum of sticks, a topping of coal—then the match applied, and the fire was merrily on its way till bedtime.

I seem to have lost my skills.

It all depends on the person who builds the fire. A fire is like a horse or a kite, it obeys some people and other folk it gives a hard time to. Those unfortunates have to bully the kindling, and shout at it—and often that makes matters worse. You get to your feet, your hands black with smoke and cinders and soot, defeated for the second or third time... and with a coldness in the spirit as well as in the flesh.

After that there's no help for it—you have to resort to 'fire-lighters', those white cubes impregnated with paraffin or some other highly flammable ingredient... If *they* (the fire-lighters) don't work, you might as well take a hot-water bottle and get warm in bed.

But it never really comes to that. Always, sooner or later, the fire decides to be your friend—sometimes, if you speak nicely to it, it's up and off at the first application of the match. Such a lovely sight—like a young tiger wakening from sleep in the dark jungle, purring and stretching and unsheathing its claws. At last shaking itself and coming to vivid pulsing life! Then you give it its just reward, a feed of more coal, a shovelful.

What happiness then, to sit in the rocking chair and enjoy the flame-feast; quite forgotten the gloom of early winter outside, or the moan of the wind in the lum.

A fine morning today, but cold. It will soon be November.

Today I've planned a fine strategy for the fire. I will build it, soon, of crumpled paper and sticks and small coal. The frying pan is full of cold sausage fat. How cunning!—I will spread that sausage fat on top of the coal, and we'll see what that will do.

Surely the fire will be pleased with the offering. Surely it will go up the lum, dancing and singing in its yellow dress...

If, however, it's in a bad mood and decides not to co-operate, what a mess will be left for me to reassemble.

Recollections on Radio Orkney

8.11.1990

Yesterday afternoon, at home, I very much enjoyed listening to tapes of Ian MacInnes's and Eric Flett's peregrinations through Stromness, originally broadcast earlier this year on Radio Orkney.

One of the merits of this programme is that it rekindles half-forgotten memories, or looks at them from a slightly different viewpoint. Also it adds to one's store of local lore—as when Eric described so vividly the butcher's business in John Street begun by his grandfather, and Ian spoke of the building of the local buses by Messrs Harvey along the waterfront near the big piers. A twenty-seater bus! But that was the only way to get to Kirkwall in the 1920s, other than walking; for you could count the number of local cars on your fingers.

Ian and Eric wondered about the piece of waste ground in Alfred Square—why had nobody ever built there? It is possible that there were houses and yards there. Quite a few houses must have been uprooted when the Northern Lighthouses established their pier and storehouses—at the end of last century, was it?

Unfortunately one of the tapes was missing, so I have yet to hear Eric and Ian on the Plainstones and Graham Place. I am looking forward to having that blank filled.

They spoke about the school near the top of Hellihole—one of the schools that flourished in Stromness prior to the Education Act of 1872, when education became compulsory. Wasn't the headmaster of that peedie school Samuel Hourston? In the 1930s there was still a competitive Samuel Hourston Bursary for senior pupils in Stromness Academy... Incidentally, how many small crofts must have been swallowed up to make way for the big school; and maybe too for some of the big houses at the back of the town?

I am glad that Ian and Eric paid tribute to the late George S. Robertson, Postmaster and Provost. In a hundred ways 'Doddie'

Robertson gave unstinting service to Stromness, for all of which he neither expected nor received any reward. But I hope that some day his work for the town will be adequately recorded. Late in life he took up art, and the best of his 'primitive' paintings are striking.

He wrote, too, a brief history of Stromness and of the golf course. The latter pamphlet won the unstinted praise of the Poet Laureate, John Betjeman. GSR's brief autobiography, though it should have been fascinating, seemed to lack the quality of the two earlier works.

Of necessity, I think, one dimension of early 20th-century Stromness life had to be merely touched on—the 'characters' in which the town was so rich. Whole series could be done on those remarkable townsfolk—and none better than Ian and Eric to do it—but this is a region where one must tread delicately and warily, for descendants are still alive, and some folk are quick to see offence where only affectionate remembrance was intended.

So, we ought to be grateful that those memories are in the archives. It may be possible—for each Stromnessian has his or her own cherished memories—to enlarge the series.

It is staggering, and dismaying, to think of how much of value has been lost over the generations and the centuries... But, to end with a cliché, it's never too late to begin.

Tales of the Black Craig

15.11.1990

I met an old school friend John Sinclair in Victoria Street yesterday when I was shopping, and as always we got talking about the old times. For some reason the Black Craig became the main subject.

In the year 1836 in the month of March, a Dundee trading vessel struck the Black Craig, in a storm, and all the crew but one were lost. This survivor, Charlie Johnston, managed to scramble into a kind of fissure, or cave, in the crag face. It is a long shallow cave, and in spring tides nothing but fish could live in it.

Somehow this sailor managed to find his way into the deepest driest part of the cave. He found that a small box, or barrel of herring had got washed into the cave too.

Very likely they were salt herring, and he might have been driven mad with thirst after a day or two of that diet; but it so happened that there was a constant drip of fresh water from the roof of the cave.

The storm went on for two or three days.

Eventually Charlie Johnston emerged from the cave and climbed up the sheer crag-face to the top.

How surprised they must have been, the people in the croft of Quoy-of-Don, when this poor castaway presented himself at their door!

The tradition is that Charlie Johnston was lost out of another ship two years later.

From then to the present, that cave has been known as Charlie's Hole.

* * *

When I was young, there was a piece of folklore that the Black Craig claimed a victim every seven years.

Nobody has gone 'afore the face' there in my life-time.

The last victim was a herdie-boy called Isaac Mowat, thirteen years old. He was said to be herding the cattle of Feolquoy farm, and he was in company with another boy. Peering over the cliff verge, they saw a nest on a ledge below with eggs in it. The boy Isaac Mowat, leaning over to get the eggs, lost his balance and fell a hundred feet onto the stony shore below.

Not the oldest Stromnessian, when I was a child, could remember Isaac Mowat; so his death must have happened in the mid 19th century probably.

In my childhood, there was always a certain dread about the Black Craig whenever we saw it from Outertown, and I think the dread was connected with the legend that someone or other was bound to tumble over the edge every seven years... It is undeniably impressive, a magnificent rampart fronting the Atlantic, rising sudden and dramatic from the long fertile shoreland.

Many a sailor must have been glad of the landmark of the Black Craig, after a long voyage. Otherwise, they did well to give it a wide berth.

Vinland: the Birth of a Novel

29.11.1990

It's strange, the way the imagination works—the 'creative imagination', if you want to sound pompous.

Some years ago, on an idle morning, I thought I might as well write a boys' story about an Orkney lad who is there when Leif Ericson discovers America, five hundred years before Columbus. (Of course, the Red Indians, streaming across the Bering Strait had 'discovered' it a few thousand years earlier still.)

But one problem rose—how to get this Orkney boy to Iceland and Greenland in the first place?

Nothing simpler—his father Sigmund Firemouth, so called because of his violent temper, is a merchant skipper, and he brusquely orders his twelve-year-old son to join the ship on a trip to Iceland.

There the boy, frightened of his father's violence, stows aboard a ship that is being got ready for a voyage further west than Greenland. The master of this vessel is Leif Ericson...

And there I got stuck, somehow—or else I decided that the short story, that I thought might be ten thousand words long, wasn't really worth going on with.

There the story—*Vinland*—lay in a cardboard folder, gathering dead spiders and cobwebs, for a long while.

Then, last spring (1990), there came another dry season for the writer. It happens, the imagination has its seasons. And I remembered the unfinished torso of the story of the young Orkney boy, westward bound. It was only a matter of writing a few thousand words more and so rounding out the tale.

One of the satisfying things about writing, and about all the arts, is that there comes a time in the course of creating that the imagination takes over completely from the will... I found, partly to my dismay but mostly to my joy, that the pen was fairly scurrying over the paper; images and events came crowding in so fast that the pen could hardly cope with them, and the manuscript pages grew and grew on the table in front of me... Most of the writing was about what Leif Ericson and his crew found on the coast of Labrador, or Newfoundland, or Maine, or wherever it was that the Norsemen landed...

There was their encounter with the Indians; then the return to Greenland. But the boy had somehow to be got back to Orkney, so the device of a merchant ship sailing to Norway was adopted.

Now was the time to introduce royalty, for the King of Norway is anxious to hear all about the mysterious place called Vinland in the far West, and the Orkney boy is sent to the palace to inform the King— he, the Orkney boy, being more articulate than his shipmates.

By this time the story was really getting out of hand—it was 20,000 words long at least—and still the horizon of narrative kept broadening.

Home to his mother's farm of Breckness in Stromness parish comes Ranald. A few years pass. He is soon caught up in the surge of young men from Iceland, Shetland, Caithness, the Hebrides and Orkney who sail with Sigurd, Earl of Orkney, to the terrible battle of Clontarf, fought near Dublin on Good Friday 1014...

About this time the writing process was interrupted by other factors than 'a dry spell', for a few months.

But now the *Vinland* story is in full flood again, and taking ever more intriguing and diverting turns (at least for the writer); and I know now that I have a full-scale novel on my hands... Day after day the pages, filled with writing, go fluttering from the pad onto the pile on the table.

There are worse ways of passing the time; worse ways of earning a living.

Return of the Light

20.12.1990

First comes the ever-deepening dark, the shrinking sun, the withering of all things.

Then there is the winter solstice, when it seems the sun is a poor ancient crippled king who can hardly drag himself through the sky.

Would it happen, one year, that the sun would die and turn into a grey cinder? Then of course all the children of the sun—men and animals and plants, would die too.

This wonderment and fear is very ancient. The mystery of the return of the light is more wonderful still.

Most people think still that the earliest Orcadians were dull and primitive, just managing to stay alive with hunting and fishing. Maes Howe is a supreme rebuttal of such a foolish notion. Besides being good builders, the creative imagination was vivid in those ancestors of ours. The splash of sunlight, at sunset on the solstice, on a wall of the burial chamber inside, is a supreme affirmation of the triumph of light over darkness.

It may be said that those 'primitive Orcadians' were far more sensitive than we are about the great cosmic circlings, and about the eclipses and rekindlings of the human spirit.

This sense of joy, that the sun would not die after all and leave us in a world of perpetual darkness and ice, was common all through the northern hemisphere. The Scandinavian peoples celebrated Yule in the darkest time of the year, and the Romans had their feasts of Saturnalia.

But, unlike the Maes Howe folk—the dwellers near the lochs of Stenness and Harray, where 'the capital' of Orkney was, it seems, in those days—later people waited for a day or two to be quite certain that the sun was on the way back. Then, when the fountain of light had broken the ice of winter, they lit their torches and brought out the wineskins and set the great platters on the feast-table. And there was music and dancing.

Nobody can know for certain when Christ was born. The great feast of Christmas is set in the darkest time of the year, just after the winter solstice. It is a symbolical holiday; how better than in midwinter to celebrate the birth of 'the light of the world', the Light behind the light, who in the beginning established the sun and set the stars on their courses?

So it has come to be—and it will endure in spite of the rampant commercialism that attends Christmas increasingly (and necessarily so, human nature being what it is).

May we all have a merry Christmas, and—as Tiny Tim said—'God bless us, every one!'

Flavour of the Week

31.1.1991

Today is Thursday—and Thursday always has a particular flavour in Stromness, probably because it is early-closing day (or 'half-day' as we used to call it). And then, on a Thursday, as children, we would see the old folk reading *The Orcadian* on the street or in window-seats.

In fact, every day of the week, when we were children, had its own unique flavour.

Monday, in the days before washing machines, was 'washing day', and that went on from morning to night, with tubs, hot fires and boilers, scrubbing-boards, and the all-pervading smell of wet linen and woollens... We disliked Mondays, both for being washing day and the resumption of the school week.

Tuesday was a kind of nondescript day, made memorable by the arrival of *The Wizard* in Rae's shop, price twopence.

On Wednesday, the town was full of farmers and their women folk. After the Mart, the farmers would stand about the pierhead smoking their pipes. There wasn't even a pub in Stromness in those days for the farmers to clinch a bargain over a glass of whisky. The apple-cheeked farm-wives went with their covered baskets from shop to shop.

Thursday I've already spoken about.

Friday was a day of delight. True, there was the prison of school to endure (spelling, long division, the dates of kings and battles, etc), but Friday afternoon brought freedom, a long weekend of perfect joy. The weekend rarely turned out to be unalloyed joy, but the expectation of it made Friday the best of days... Besides, *The Hotspur* with its school stories came out on Friday, and *The Hotspur* was the best of all the six or seven boys' magazines.

It depended on the time of year, of course, how a child spent Saturday. You usually had a penny to spend, and that involved endless calculation. If the weather was bad, you stayed indoors and read books, or played games like ludo. On long summer days you might wander over the hills behind the town, or row in a flattie from pier to pier along the harbour.

On Sunday, most families put on their Sabbath suits and went to one of the three Presbyterian kirks: in our case, Victoria Street, or the UP Kirk. Several times during the long sermon my mother would pass a rustling bag of sweeties along the pew... There were always home-made cakes for tea on Sunday afternoon, especially sponge-cakes with jam in them, or cream... But later—oh, misery!—doing the homework that good boys and girls did on a Friday or Saturday... The shades of the prison-house were beginning to impinge, coldly.

Such was a child's week in Stromness sixty years ago. Every day had a different smell and taste and touch of its own. We were happy in a different way from adult happiness, and we endured miseries that could not be communicated.

And Stromness was the only place we knew. I must have been eight or nine before my parents took my brother and me to Kirkwall, on the bus, for the first time.

House Interiors

14.2.1991

House interiors have changed a great deal in the last half-century. I expect they are much more comfortable now, with deeper chairs and couches to sit on. I seem to remember that a lot of houses had black 'horse-hair' sofas, that it would be hard to match for ugliness, both to look at and for texture.

Nearly every working-class house had a stove, or range—black, also, like the horse-hair sofas—but they gave out a good heat and there the soup, mince and tatties, and fish were cooked, and in the oven an occasional cake. This was the kitchen—no 'living-rooms' in those days. In the kitchen you sat and talked, read, ate, and entertained visitors. And often there was a bed in it.

There was a special room upstairs called the parlour, and it was used for special occasions only—christening and funeral get-togethers, I expect, and small family weddings.

One extraordinary thing is that Orkney is burgeoning with artists nowadays, whereas sixty years ago the only framed pictures seemed to be cuttings from magazines. In our parlour there was a coloured print of General Wolfe (I think) entering Quebec, and John Bunyan dreaming of some episodes from *The Pilgrim's Progress*.

I forgot to say that the mantelpiece in most kitchens had its pair of china dogs, and there was always a tea caddy, and miscellaneous ornaments. And a calendar hung just beside the mantelpiece; the old folk insisted on calendars with big figures.

Strangely, there were few straw-back chairs in Stromness. It was in farm-houses that you saw them.

Stranger still—seeing that Stromness had been 'dry' since the early twenties—only a few houses brewed beer. A permit was required for brewing.

Most houses were lit with paraffin lamps—a big one that stood on the sideboard; smaller ones for going to bed with. The paraffin lamp must have been an enormous improvement on the 'cruisie', which by the 1920s was a collector's item. Only the grander houses had gaslight. But the council houses that were beginning to be built had gaslight and 'gas-rings' for cooking on. Tenants had to keep by them a plentiful hoard of pennies to feed the meter.

Electricity only came to Stromness in 1947.

In many houses, there was an old granny sitting knitting and wearing spectacles, and giving out sweeties called 'Scotch mixture' with cloves in them.

And then, in the window-sill, there would be a jam-jar with bluebells or daffodils in it, or the marigolds or mayflowers that the bairns brought home from the West Shore in summer.

The South Orkneys

7.3.1991

Perhaps it was on TV one evening that 'the South Orkneys' were mentioned as lying away down there near Antarctica.

I remember that Shackleton and his explorers visited the South Orkneys and came to a little place called Stromness.

I suppose there can't be a Hoy or a Finstown or Rousay in the South Orkneys, but I try to imagine what this other Stromness is like.

Does it have a pierhead where 'fishmen lounge at noon'? Does it have two little islands called Holms in the harbour? And a sheltering hill like Brinkie's Brae?

Do these other Stromnessians have a favourite road that skirts the ocean for two miles and ends in a little kirkyard above the rocks? Do they have a bar or two where they drink some kind of Raven Ale or Highland Park?

It must be in our midwinter that they can scarcely sleep at night for the lingering sun. And when our Stromness gardens are full of roses and lupins, their bushes are top-heavy with snow and all the blossoms they see are the frost-flowers in the windows. Do they have names like Flett and Linklater and Louttit?

No doubt they have television, like every community on earth. But they must have stories and legends, of whalers and explorers, and of the albatrosses that 'sleep upon their wings', and of creatures half-fish and half-human.

Did a spaewife like Bessie Millie sit in her cold hovel, waiting for the skippers to come with their sixpences to buy a fair wind around Cape Horn?

The more I think about that southern Stromness, the more curious I become. Perhaps our Community Council ought to send a letter there to see if they would like to be in touch with us.

They might ship us some whale-meat in exchange for Orkney cheese and beef—for I doubt if they have cattle roaming their pastures.

They might want to visit us in Shopping Week, and if so they would invite some of us to take part in a frosty festival of theirs.

They might send some of their fur-clad children to sit in our classrooms.

I assume that English is their language. How different is the speech of the South Orkneys from the North Orkneys? We would have to attune our ears to a different kind of speech-music.

These are idle speculations. But I'm sure some Orcadians and Shetlanders must have sheltered in that southern Stromness. If so, it would be interesting to hear from them. (But they should write to *The Orcadian*, not me. I am overburdened with letters as it is.)

The Real Earl Hakon

25.4.1991

Today is April 18; and the body of the man who had lain on a stony field in an island in Orkney all the night of April 16–17 would have been buried at last—word having come from the one and only earl that his earlier order was to be countermanded, that the body of the murdered man was to lie where it had fallen, among the first spring flowers and the larksong, under the night stars.

So the people of Egilsay, the crofters and fishermen, would have buried the dead Earl Magnus somewhere near the church where he had spent his last night on earth, and heard Mass in the morning before walking out to his death on the stony moor.

Nearly all attempts to tell the story since then have portrayed the killer of Earl Magnus—his cousin Earl Hakon—as a black-hearted villain, and a low treacherous scoundrel (however high he might have stood in the social and political scale of the time).

But any fair-minded reading of the main source, *The Orkneyinga Saga*, shows Hakon to have been an accomplished ruler, and a good man according to the 'mores' of the age.

For, consider, both Hakon and Magnus were faced with an old intractable situation, the overlordship of the King of Norway. For generations Norway had cleverly contrived to have two (and sometimes three) earls in Orkney, who were bound in the nature of things to have differences with one another. In those days, eight or nine centuries ago, to 'have differences' meant that violence was the only kind of political debate conceivable at that time.

So, when the strife was over, the defeated earl lost no time in sailing over to Norway and seeking arbitration and redress from the King. And the King saw to it that his protégé was well equipped with arms and ships and men when he returned to Orkney to take up the quarrel once more.

So, with an earldom almost permanently divided, Norway could assert again and again his supreme overlordship of Orkney. The King knew well that a single strong earl in Orkney would be almost independent, and as strong a ruler as he was himself... That very situation had happened two generations before, when Earl Thorfinn 'the Mighty' ruled alone from Birsay, careless of any interference from the royal houses of Norway or Scotland... But Earl Thorfinn had had two sons, and when he died in old age the manipulation and the troubles in Orkney began again.

Earl Hakon Paulson cast a very clear political eye on the situation. He was a shrewd practitioner of *realpolitik*. As he saw it, the only cure for Orkney's troubles in the early 12th century was a single earl and a single earldom. His cousin, Earl Magnus Erlendson—who might (Hakon thought) have been happier as a monk or as a retired country laird studying philosophy in his garden—stood in the way. The solution was simple—get rid of the difficulty by a single stroke of the axe.

Treachery had to be resorted to, to bring the situation about—namely, the luring of Earl Magnus to Egilsay that Easter weekend of 1117 under the pretext of a peace conference.

* * *

What happened after the murder (or, as it came to be seen almost at once, the martyrdom) is plainly written then.

The so-called black-hearted murderer wept, telling the story that night in Holm to Thora, Magnus's mother.

He ruled for many years, a fair and just and much-loved earl. He returned from a pilgrimage to the holy places and built the round church in Orphir, which must have been a most beautiful place before the iconoclasts wrecked it.

He sanctioned the burial of Magnus in Orkney's first cathedral on the Brough of Birsay.

Peace fell—and the Orcadians were happy and secure in the single rule of Earl Hakon, the good governor. And another kind of peace fell and furled like a dove about the thresholds of Orkney; and the Orcadians spoke with wondering voices about Saint Magnus and the benefits that flowed continually from his death-wound.

Work-Place and Dining-Room

2.5.1991

Some weeks, so many letters come that it is difficult to stem the tide. You have more than a passing sympathy with King Canute.

In past years, I think I must have replied to every letter I got. But that's no longer possible, for I have to keep space and energy for the other kinds of writing I do... So nowadays I only write necessary letters, and of course to old friends (for they become very important as a person gets older).

But still, one day a week, at least, has to be set aside for answering letters—and often the answering spills over into a second day.

I got the gift of a triple-compartment letter-rack at Christmas, and all letters received end there. At the end of each month, the letters have to be taken out and divided into two stacks—one lot that can be got rid of, and another lot that must be kept. (And that sorting takes up another morning.)

Today, two-thirds of the way through April, the letter-rack is full to overflowing... There it sits on the writing table, that letter-rack, waiting (it seems) to scatter its contents all over the pens and notebooks, the paper-clips and the rubbers and the pencil-sharpeners.

It is by no means a professional-looking desk. It is, in fact, the kitchen table, where I have my breakfast and sometimes other meals. On that table, first thing in the morning, before 9am, it holds the pot of tea, the butter, the plate with toast, the marmalade pot and the honey jar. (What could ever be more delicious than the first cup of tea in the morning?)

Breakfast over, the dishes are pushed aside and the writing-paper brought out, and one pen out of a whole sheaf of pens selected.

What has to be done today? It might be a story, or a poem, or an article that some magazine has asked for. No sense in waiting for 'inspiration'—there is no such thing, there is only the exercise of such skill as the writer has learned by years of experience, and of trial and error and approximation to success.

It is quite possible to write a poem to order—I am doing one this week, for the 750th anniversary of the founding of St John's Kirk in Perth.

Then, after two or three hours' work in the morning, the hand falters a little and it's time for the writing desk to be transformed once more to the kitchen table, where the tomato-sauce bottle is set down and the mustard and the beetroot, and the sausages unlinked and the egg laid beside the tomato...

How lucky, to have the work-place and the dining-room in the same place!... Think of the 'yuppies' who have to commute miles to their offices in the city, and then have to go into some chop-house or other for their lunch.

There's nothing to break the tranquillity here but bird-song from the garden outside, and the wind passing, and occasionally a splatter of rain on the kitchen window.

And if I look outside, there is the lingering glory of the daffodils, and the fresh-dug earth of the tattie-planters.

The Sounds of 'Music'

9.5.1991

The chief difference about life in Orkney now and sixty years ago is that noise has intensified and deepened. The young generation seems to accept all the din and frenzy, as if it was quite natural. To us oldsters it sets the teeth on edge; it can be completely disorientating.

Go into a pub, and quite suddenly the interior is liable to be shattered with noise; someone has put coins in the juke-box. It can, till the record ends, be quite impossible to talk to your friend across the table. The din seems to work its way into the beer and spoil it. The music itself is often frightful and barbarous, as if we are trembling on the verge of a new Dark Age. You look around, to see if the other people in the bar are as shaken as yourself. Not at all—they accept it as a part of modern life.

As for me and some of my contemporaries, we throw back the dregs of the lager, and seek the peace outside. The noise of whitemaas and waves has been there since Stromness was a hamlet of fishing booths, and will still be there in the thirtieth century when a guide is showing tourists from Mars round the ruins...

We are not likely to forget the tearing up of the complete street three years ago and less, for the laying of drains, and the inferno of noise that accompanied it. The community accepted it with stoicism. (The original laying of drains a century ago would have been done silently, with pick and shovel; but I expect would have taken longer...)

One solitary experience of ten or twelve years ago impressed me. I was walking on a fine day round the West Shore when I became conscious of a loud cacophony approaching. It was a young person carrying a transistor. On that marvellously beautiful coast the air was hideously torn apart—it was almost like blasphemy. Perhaps the most astonishing thing about this incident is that the young person didn't even appear to be listening to the appalling din he was making. I tell this with a certain amount of shame, because I ought to have reproached him, and I didn't.

Quarrels, confrontations, use up too much mental energy. Yet now I feel it is a kind of cowardice to let such things pass without complaint—every mute surrender threatens more and more the natural sounds and silences that are so marvellously beautiful on the shores of Hoy Sound and in a hundred other Orkney places: indeed, worldwide.

There was, of course, the wireless in our young days, and young folk listened to the new popular music. There was Henry Hall and the BBC dance orchestra, and Joe Loss and his band, and Victor Sylvester, and many others. But their songs and lyrics, though often sentimental and frail as thistledown, at least didn't infest the whole of civilisation with the rantings of 'old chaos', which nobody can avoid entirely, nowadays.

Last night Scotland was playing football against San Marino (the lion rampant against a little Italian mouse) and didn't one of those dance tunes of sixty years ago flower unexpectedly on my lips, 'I dream of San Marino / 'Neath the blue Italian skies...' Many an evening we listened to it on our battery radio; and it was such a quiet piece of sentimentality that no pensioner could possibly have objected to it.

A Sad Story

30.5.1991

Stromness voted itself 'dry' in the early 20s and so all the pubs in Stromness—a sizeable number of them—had to put up their shutters.

There must have been a lot of ill-feeling in the town in those days. Farmers at the Mart on a Wednesday—fishermen mooring their boats after a hard day off the Kame or Black Craig—clerks and shop-workers wanting to wash the dust out of their throats...

I remember quite distinctly one story, out of hundreds.

An honest tradesman who lived at the South End sorely missed his pint at the end of the day.

One evening he thought he would walk to the Pomona Inn in Finstown for an ale or two. Also he carried a sack in his hand to bring a dozen or so bottles of beer home.

The road home was longer perhaps than the road to the Pomona, freighted with his sack of beer bottles. But maybe he walked the seven miles in a kind of dance, what with the beer he had drunk in the Pomona and the delightful prospect of a few thirstless evenings at home.

Being a peaceful man, he didn't want to upset the 'dry' burghers of Stromness by brazenly going through the street with his clanging load.

(I knew this man well. Many a time I've sat at his feet listening to his stories.)

He walked along the Back Road, hoping to descend to his house on the steep grassy slope beside the May Burn. There was only a couple of hundred yards to go; then he was home.

By this time he was a bit tired. He decided to sit on a wall. His journey was all but accomplished.

On the other side of the wall was a pile of granite stones.

Maybe he was too tired—maybe he went off into a brief snooze or dwam. Anyway, he came to himself with the sound of a great smashing of glass and burbling of liquor.

The sack of beer bottles he was carrying on his back had slipped out of his grasp and perished on the hard granite rocks.

What could any man do in such a situation?

My old friend had been through many hard times in his life. He had reached a kind of philosophic stance. Many a worse mischance had befallen him.

I suppose he just went home and put his kettle on for a pot of tea.

* * *

I suppose a book could be written about the civil war concerning drink that raged in Stromness at that time.

But all that the tumult and the shouting have left behind are a few stories.

Sea-Haar

6.6.1991

It comes creeping in from the North Sea all night, and we wake up to a morning when we can hardly see across the street for haar. The Holms are ghosts, Orphir has been wiped from the map. And 'Oh,' we complain to each other, 'what a poor day again'...

It was a bit like that yesterday morning.

I was sitting at the writing-table after breakfast, when there was a splash of gold in the kitchen. And when I looked through the kitchen window, the sky was all blue.

We old guys know that it is going to be a fine summer day.

The sea-haar is not a grey sinister enemy at all—it is a harbinger of light and warmth.

Long experience has taught us, over the years.

Take that astonishing summer of 1947, for example. 1947 is ancient prehistory to young Orcadians, but to us pensioners it was the most remarkable summer ever.

Every day from July to early September conformed, it seems in retrospect, to the same pattern.

We woke to a grey morning, with fog covering Stromness like a shroud. Then about 11am, there came a tear in the shroud, through which a patch of blue appeared. A wave sparkled in the harbour, and was suddenly molten gold. Great slashes and gaps of blue appeared everywhere in the sky. The fog took itself off, silently, and there it lay, a solid bank in the West.

And into the full sunlight came the folk of Orkney. And the few tourists that were around in those days must have thought they had come to the Hesperides, or the Isles of the Ever-Young.

I can't remember much other than the beautiful mysterious weather of that summer.

I know we went often to the West Shore and Warbeth. There weren't many cars in 1947. People organised bus tours to Birsay and South Ronaldsay (across 'the barriers' which were a thrilling novelty then). I remember immense drifts of wild cotton across in Orphir. Fishing boats came in with mackerel, which people were given at the pier for nothing; but the mackerel were eaten warily to begin with in the houses, for in those days it was a kind of 'taboo' fish. (Sea customs were hard to break then.)

And every evening we played putting on the famous Putting Green at Ness.

Maybe we would be stacking our putters away when there was a lick of grey over the sea, where the harbour of Hamnavoe becomes meshed with Hoy Sound. And where, suddenly, was Cava? It was blotted out. And there, along the Coolags and the Ward Hill of Hoy, a scarf of sea-haar had been flung, silently. Then suddenly the Holms were wiped from the map, and the dozen piers of Stromness were ghosts... Put your hand to a wall, going home: the stonework gave back the gathered heat of the day.

It was all mysterious and beautiful.

Memory has very likely deceived me in this, but every day of that distant summer seemed to be like that—an extraordinary ballet of sea-haar and sun.

Probably not everyone was pleased; because memory suggests that there was not a drop of rain from mid July till early September. The farmers wouldn't have liked that. Nor the town officials who kept an anxious eye on the level of the reservoir on the Loons.

This idyll might have gone on forever.

But one day in early September we were putting on the intricate green at Ness when a few drops of rain fell out of a black cloud. It was round about the time of the Lammas Market.

Ever since that day, forty-five years ago, the weather has been a broken mishmash of wind and rain and fleeting light.

The Craft of Verse-Writing

20.6.1991

I think it was the Roman poet Horace who told writers: 'Keep your piece nine years'—in other words, don't rush to your friends with the latest poem written in the white heat of inspiration and let them enjoy the lyric raptures, but put the thing away in a drawer and forget about it for a long time...

Then, when you open the drawer and discover the piece of paper and the words on it, it mightn't be so marvellous after all. It might, in fact, be pretty awful. The diamond might have changed to a cinder.

I had a similar experience the other day. Over the autumn and winter I had written a novel and was quite smug about it. However, yesterday I cast an eye over one particular section of it and discovered that it wouldn't do at all. It would have to be entirely rewritten. A daunting task, but a challenge too, and a relief to know that what had been poorly done might (with luck) be better done.

So I scribbled and scribbled away all of yesterday morning, trying to reverse the tide.

Was I glad of a glass of orange juice out of the fridge, after all that hard work!

* * *

There's a hidden bird, a blackbird or a thrush, that has taken to singing all day long, it seems, at Mayburn.

Its raptures and joys and trillings and carollings are so marvellous that we poets ought to be envious. Well, a few poets have tried to express their gratitude—Keats with his Nightingale, Shelley and Hopkins with their Lark poems, Hardy with his midwinter turn-of-the-century Thrush.

I get a fair number of verses sent to me through the post. Ah, that those verse-makers had the natural springs and well-heads and fountains of melody of that bird celebrating the midsummer through my window!

Alas, most verse-makers nowadays think that all they have to do is throw down their emotions in words on a piece of paper, chop the words into lines of different lengths, and there is a poem.

There, in 999 cases out of a thousand, is only a mess, a splash of the everlasting chaos.

'Keep your piece nine years'—never was better advice, sent to us from a great poet who lived 1,800 years ago.

But, even more important, years have to be spent learning the craft of verse-writing. The young person has to master such forms as the sonnet, heroic couplet, iambic pentameter, rondel, the Spenserian stanza and the Burns stanza, etc—even the limerick and the clerihew will help him or her in the craft they want to master. It is a hard discipline, but if one is sincere about it there is joy in the labour and the achievement.

There's no easy way to climb Parnassus.

There's that bird again, having his own private festival on some chimney or telephone line—only he does it purely, spontaneously, naturally.

And the experts tell us, he's only making these noises to defend his territory, not because he is happy in the summer days.

But I think, with Shelley and Hopkins, that he is singing out of purest joy.

Midsummer Sunset

4.7.1991

I think there may be more tourists than ever this year—it seems that way, even in June.

How bewildered they must be with our weather! For, one day you see them on the street, in waterproofs, under umbrellas, leaning into the relentless rain; and you feel sad for them and for Orkney.

By afternoon, the rainclouds have taken off, and there's the sun again, glittering out of the wet flagstones.

You can get three or four different kinds of weather in one day.

The solstice is on 21st June, but for some reason midsummer falls officially on the 24th (Johnsmas)... I suppose for the same reason that Christmas comes a few days after the winter solstice.

Anyway, midsummer 1991 gave us one of the loveliest evenings imaginable, driving home from a concert in the Phoenix... Leaving Kirkwall, the thud-thump of Runrig could be heard across two fields. The marvellous midsummer sunset was in the north-west, and the glow would not leave the sky all night. Now and then Donald Morrison's car topped a rise and then the sun on the horizon gave us a golden glance.

The farm-houses of St Ola, Firth, and Stenness seemed, in Edwin Muir's words, to be 'sunk in time', and they had the tranquillity and radiance and nearness of legendary dwellings. (I think Edwin Muir would have been enchanted by such an evening.)

And there, in the east, hung the almost full moon, like a paper Chinese lantern, frail because there was still too much sunlight to allow it full brilliance.

We topped the brae of Cairston and there lay the harbour of Hamnavoe, twilit and tranquil and brimming, with a sprinkling of lights here and there from the houses.

A few people moved about the pierhead like folk in a timeless trance.

Earlier that afternoon, I had been visited by a German radio journalist. He was proposing to walk west along the coast in the late evening. 'Be careful,' I told him, 'for the trows and fairies are out in force at midsummer and they might carry you off'... But I saw him next day; he had got safely to the Black Craig and back ... you're all right if you're not carrying a fiddle, I suppose.

But to return to that extraordinarily beautiful evening of the 24th. The hills and houses seemed very close, in the purity of the light. The old folk used to warn that such a rare clarity was a presage of rain. 'The hills are too close,' they would say. They generally knew what they were talking about, weatherwise.

Next morning Stromness was awash with rain. Orphir was veiled and shrouded with rain. Rain danced on the flagstones. There again went the tourists, singly and in throngs, buttoned up to the chin in oilskins. Could this be the same place that they had wandered through, enchanted, twelve hours before? And the gutters burbled and sang with rain, and the grass and rosebushes and tatties drank their fill.

Thankfully, John Gray gave us a lift to the Johnsmas Foy at the new Academy theatre in his car. So we didn't get wet. And this year's Foy was a specially delightful mixture of verse and music and narrative.

The Day of Freedom

11.7.1991

A few days ago the children were released from school. (I write 'released' as if school was a prison. I don't think it is a prison nowadays; at least it is less of a prison than it was in the 1930s.)

Then indeed we were like small prisoners being set free—the only misdemeanour being that one year, long ago, we had reached the age of five, and the law of the land dragged us relentlessly to those grim portals.

There came a certain relaxation in the school régime before the actual day of release.

There were the school sports one afternoon at the Market Green— in which Ian MacInnes and I won sixpence each some years on the trot for coming first in the three-legged race... Apart from that, my athletic abilities amounted to nothing.

And, some time in June, I think, we began to wear sandals or plimsolls to school instead of tackety shoes—a sign that winter was over with.

Little by little the school régime lightened. Instead of multiplication tables and spelling and geography we were allowed to read *The Orkney Book*. There was a great pile of those books in the classroom cupboard, and there they lay stacked most of the year, unread. Why, it is difficult to know, for *The Orkney Book* was designed to enlighten young Orcadians about their native islands. I expect the exigencies of the school curriculum allowed no room for a book that would have been so enriching to young minds... For a few brief summer hours we revelled in *The Orkney Book*.

So many copies there were in that classroom cupboard! Now a copy of *The Orkney Book* is a collector's item.

The day of freedom drew on, on golden feet.

And finally it was here! Our kind teacher, Miss Smith, went round the class and she laid a penny on each desk.

I expect ten-year-olds nowadays hardly know what a penny is. (They call it 'one pence', for one thing.) To them it is a contemptible thing; to us it was a coin to be treasured—it could buy a bag of caramels or half a dozen hooks to fish with or a poke of chips from Davidson's chip shop that has long been swept away, with other houses, to make way for Gray's Noust.

And then at 1pm Mr Wilson the janitor rang the bell that announced the start of the seven-week-long summer holiday.

Hundreds of children burst out of the school gates, cheering wildly.

Since the world began there had not been a day like it!

I don't know what happened that afternoon. Most of the boys, I'm sure, fled to the piers with their sillock lines.

Or they kicked empty tins along the street with the sheer exuberance of the time. Or they began to be a seven-weeks torment to their mothers (already harassed enough, poor women, with work and poverty and keeping up appearances).

Out of those first afternoons of freedom, I can remember only one. I went away, alone, into a quiet place where few folk came, and I sat down and revelled in pure unadulterated joy, secretly and silently.

Such moments come rarely in time, but they may be the stuff of poetry and—in Wordsworth's phrase—'intimations of immortality'.

Summer Is Here

18.7.1991

Suddenly the temperature goes up, after a longish cold spell.

The winter clothes begin to be a burden.

The tattie shaws push up. Another week, and we'll be having the first boiling.

That thrush sings and sings all day from a wall or a bush nearby.

The butter, from being a stone-hard cube, almost swims in its own yellow sea.

Tourists go here and there, wide-eyed. Children erupt everywhere, at close-end and pierhead.

Stromnessians look south but some want to go no further than Hoy. Boats dance in the dazzle of the harbour. Yachts lean into light breezes. There's a bloom of sea-haar on the horizon westward. It pokes a tentative finger among the folds of Hoy, or sets a wisp of fog on the sea.

I pause sometimes in the middle of writing and think of a glass of cold yellow lager, and of sitting in the balcony of a certain hostelry looking out over the sea towards the Scapa Flow islands and the Flotta flare.

The fuchsia bushes, dense-leaved, think of hanging out their bells.

What's this? There are coloured lights strung across Graham Place, and little triangular flags flutter in the breeze. Can it be that Shopping Week is upon us once more? Certainly Shopping Week is imminent. In every shop-window ladies are hard at work putting on the best display that ever was.

'Click-click-click,' go the cameras—German, Japanese, and American cameras—and Graham Place and Flaws's pier will be recorded another ten thousand times before the end of August. (And to think that, a century ago, the only depictment of Stromness was the Daniell print of 1814...)

Ice-cream and Coca-cola at the Pierhead. And plastic containers of chips and haggis or polony or fish for those who have no tables to sit at.

The tourists sit writing postcards to their folks in Preston or Pennsylvania or the Pyrenees—'Wish you were here' ... 'The Orcadians look just like other people'...

'Have just paid a visit to the little cot our great-grandparents lived in, up among the hills!'...

The street is getting more difficult for people on foot.

Increasingly you hear, 'Something will have to be done about this traffic'... 'A pedestrian precinct'... 'One-way traffic'... It's true, every time you walk along the street you have to inhale twenty lungfuls of exhaust fumes.

The wild white clover is in the ditches, with its sweet enchanting smell. And the meadowsweet and the irises are hastening towards us... A white butterfly drifts past the window.

Summer is here.

Little did I think when I started to write this column, that it would spin itself out to such inordinate length!... And still there are a hundred things that could be celebrated, such as the first Orkney tomatoes, and the ale that was brewed in March and is in its full maturity now.

Gavin Muir

25.7.1991

Gavin Muir, the only son of Edwin and Willa Muir, died a few weeks ago in Edinburgh.

Willa Muir describes vividly how Gavin in his childhood was knocked over in London by a lorry; and this accident resulted in severe deafness for the young boy.

The deafness was a particularly bad affliction in that Gavin was a gifted musician. He played the piano well in the great gilded drawing-room at Newbattle. But all thought of a professional career in music had to be abandoned.

He was also a brilliant mathematician, an honours graduate from St Andrews University. He liked—again at Newbattle Abbey when his father was Warden there—to work out complicated deductions. Long before we heard of computers, Gavin Muir had the mind of a benign computer.

It was at Newbattle in 1951–52 that the students and I got acquainted with Gavin, though (as far as I know) he had few intimate friends.

Gavin was at that time very radical in politics. When the newspapers were delivered to the crypt (our common-room) each morning, he was always there first of all, eagerly turning the pages, and saying aloud, 'Lies!' and 'Nonsense!' as he read the effusions of some right-wing journalist.

Gavin was too deaf to attend our student debates or attend lectures, but he often accompanied us up the steep road to the Justinlees bar at Eskbank, a mile away. There we drank beer merrily.

The only time that Edwin was really upset with me was one evening when Gavin and I returned slightly noisy with Eskbank ale, while a concert was in progress in the crypt.

Next morning we got our telling-off from Edwin and Willa. That stricture administered, they were all kindness and consideration again, 'as though it had never been'.

Most days the college would be brimming over for an hour or so with piano music—Beethoven and Mozart and Chopin. Gavin Muir was having his lyrical dance around the keyboard. His music enriched an already beautiful place.

In appearance, Gavin was tall and dark and slender. There was much more of the mother than the father in his face, and he had his mother's exuberant sense of humour, only curbed somewhat by his father's restraint.

The strange thing is that he had not inherited his parents' literary gifts. His favourite author while we were at Newbattle was an extreme socialist American novelist called Howard Fast.

Gavin visited Orkney once or twice with his parents (apart from lengthier visits in childhood).

I last spoke to him, possibly in Milne's Bar in Edinburgh, twenty years ago.

Already, then, he was becoming something of a recluse. It is not easy, when one is very deaf, to be an outgoing sociable person.

That childhood accident had dealt him a cruel blow.

Gavin's cousin in Glasgow, Mrs Ethel Ross, wrote last week to tell me the sad news.

Now may he rest in peace.

Town and Parish: the Beginnings

1.8.1991

What is the real name of our town? Stromness—though a good name—is not entirely satisfactory. There is always the possibility of confusion between town and parish.

Yet the little hamlet of fishing bothies under Brinkie's Brae must have had a distinctive name from earliest times. 'Shore-side' it seems to have been called, off and on. But a name like that is dull and uninteresting.

Hamnavoe—'the haven-bay'—it was called by the early Norse settlers. It is a pity that that name was dropped, it is so beautiful itself and so vivid.

There was a period in the 18th century, round about the time of Gow, when the growing village was called 'Kerston', after the district to the north-east, nowadays known as Cairston. Cairston was an important district once—not only was the Norse stronghold there that Sweyn Asleifson besieged, but Kirk and Manse were at Congesquoy, down by the shore.

But eventually the compromise name Stromness was arrived at, and it is here until there is a nuclear holocaust or the melting ice-caps bring the sea level above the roofs.

The best name of all—Hamnavoe—can only be used in fiction or in verse.

* * *

It is difficult to imagine what the first settlers must have been—but not entirely impossible.

Imagine a first Norse settlement at Breckness, say, or at Cairston.

There was bound to be faction and troubles, with such turbulent immigrants. And yet one man had to assert his will, so that the wheel of agriculture could be set in motion.

There might well be brawls at the ale-bench in the new farm-house, splashings of ale and blood, and violent language.

Then the farmer would be strict and stern! The troublemakers were given short notice to quit. Where could they go? About the only place where they could be safe from the tyranny of the farm was in the little haven-bay three miles away, tucked away so neatly between the granite hill and two little green islets.

There they pitched their rough tents, until they could get wooden huts built.

The land round about was too hard and obdurate for agriculture.

Therefore they had no alternative. They must become fishermen, or starve.

So their little fishing boats were built even before their huts and bothies.

And the farm folk at Breckness could see them fishing off the Kame of Hoy, or off the heel of Graemsay, or under the Black Craig.

And maybe, after a time, there was an exchange of fish for grain— and the two communities, town and parish, lived together in peace.

One of Those Days

8.8.1991

Some days everything you do seems to go wrong.

I was just listening for the first time to the new Highland Park tape when a singing voice got all jumbled, and the thin coil that releases the sound was in a hopeless tangle.

Earlier, at 7am, I was making breakfast toast when a blue-black reek rose from the toaster. It seems the toaster was adjusted to deal with *frozen* bread.

I cut open a plastic bag of lentils, and didn't lentils cascade and dance all over the kitchen table and floor.

I wrote a letter to a lady and then couldn't find her address.

'One of those days,' people say in a resigned kind of a way.

I haven't lit the fire yet—there *may* be problems there. It's a mild day—fog after early sun—the attempt will be made to light the fire after I've had my soup. It may well go out.

The broth is burbling away in its pot... May the dark sprites leave the soup alone, at least.

These days of small misfortunes certainly seem to happen—whether by chance or some temporary dulling of the faculties no one in recorded history can say, for sure.

Other small things have happened today which I'd better not mention here.

But not everything is withershins. After breakfast I glanced at a poem about Saint Magnus in Papa Stour, Shetland, that I had given up two years ago. Today, with a small adjustment here and there, I think this poem might come off!

Keep thinking of the good things.

Well, I went to bed this afternoon, as old men often do, and there was a play about Marie Lloyd the music hall lady just beginning on the radio. When I woke, after a good sleep, the play was just ending.

Nothing wrong with that.

Also, I managed to make a phone call that I've been too lazy and too shy to make for a fortnight... A bonus point, that, too.

I shouldn't maybe be writing this at all. A debt-collector or some similar sinister person might come knocking at the door in half an hour (though I have no bad debts that I know of).

Or the soup might scald my tongue.

Or a cinder might jump out of the fire and burn a hole in my carpet...

There's another summertime nuisance—a stupid bluebottle loose in the kitchen as I write. I open the window for it; it is too dim to do anything but blunder against the panes and sing crazy songs... Ten to one, at reading time tonight the same bluebottle will attack reading-lamp and book.

So the pattern of a day slowly declares itself—seemingly full of mis-chances but with good things counter-balancing all the time.

My friends Peter and Betty Grant left on this morning's *Ola*, after a three-weeks' stay. That was the biggest misfortune of all, and it's maybe their absence that's caused me to blunder into things... Steady on. The holiday has left forever a fragrant memory.

A Shadow on the Mind

22.8.1991

What a strange way to put it—you 'catch a cold', as if you'd been on the look-out for one and at last you've tracked it down.

Much truer to say, a cold catches you, and just as you least expect it, in high summer. And a summer cold, they say, is the worst to shake off.

This nasty cold bug must have been drifting around in the Show Park, Dounby, last Thursday afternoon—and on a lovely day too of sun and mild wind—because soon after Brian Murray and I got back to Stromness to enjoy a pint of lager in the balcony of the Braes Hotel, I got a little catch in the lungs and my nose was a dripping tap. Soon afterwards the cough began.

Then I knew that the cold had hooked me good and proper.

Next morning my voice was all roughed up as though it had been scoured with emery paper.

Also, I had woken in the dead hours of the night with red-hot barbed wire deep in the chest.

Strange, that you come through all the rigours of winter unscathed, and now, in the midst of the summer festivals, this cold sticks its hook in you.

Well, it could be worse, much worse. I can eat and sleep and move about the house, and speak in this strange husky voice.

Every cold seems to be different from every other cold. This cold puts a shadow on the mind. Nothing seems to make sense or have any meaning. You realise the full power of that great Old Testament poet—'vanity of vanities, all is vanity'...

Books and music are drained of all their magic. Also, a score of irascible years are suddenly added to the sum of your days—you are a doddering nonagenarian instead of a sprightly near-septuagenarian—and so bad-tempered about little things!

Thank goodness, in a way, there's work to be done, because it would be pure misery to hang around feeling sorry for yourself. There's paper and a pen and you can write; though that is an effort, like everything else.

What about a little detective story, in which the detective is a cat—Gypsy, of course—and the murder victim is a huge Alsatian dog called Augustus? (Augustus ought to have been a rottweiler, I suppose, or a pit bull terrier.) And so Gypsy with subtle feline skills as sure almost as Miss Marple's, sets out in search of the murderer.

That's one way of tholing the miseries of a summer cold. It takes the mind off on a brief hour-long holiday every morning, into the realms of fantasy.

Letter from Foresterhill

26.9.1991

Another beautiful morning in Aberdeen. So far, September has been a fine month. Two evenings ago, the overcast sky let loose torrents of rain, and there was thunder and lightning. However, the gardeners and farmers of Aberdeenshire must have been glad of the rain, for the ground is parched with a long drought.

There's nothing much to do in this ward but read—I've dipped into books by Rebecca West, Edmund Wilson, Robert McLellan, and this morning from the hospital library I borrowed J. G. Ballard's *Empire of the Sun*, a novel about a boy in Shanghai in the days following Pearl Harbor.

It's a bore reading all the time, and so far I've steadfastly refused to switch on the TV in the corner. As I don't take a newspaper either, I have no idea what's going on in the great world outside.

At the weekend, a kind auxiliary nurse brought me a pack of playing cards and I have played three games of patience, in all of which I failed.

But two days ago I received a shoal and a shower of mail re-addressed from Orkney, and some of those letters had to be answered quickly. So, yesterday morning was busy—the blue biro I bought from the hospital-shop trolley fairly scurried across page after page. It was when I bought stamps they told me that the price of posting a letter has gone up again from 22p to 24p.

One of my letters was from an editor asking for a few poems. I had thought I wasn't in the mood for writing verse, but it's strange how quickly the impulse responds to such a prompting. Before the afternoon was over I had written two pieces of verse, one quite good, the other doubtful. But that task, with six letters written in addition, was sufficient for one day, I thought.

But if it hadn't been for my old friend Peter and his car I would have felt very claustrophobic. We have been for drives on a few afternoons— through Ellon and on to the River Ythan, past wheat fields and barley fields to Banchory; to the harbour filled with oil-boats, and Matthew's Quay where the *St Rognvald* was lying; to Crathes and through Stonehaven on a bright Sunday afternoon where a lot of folk were sitting on the sea wall outside a tavern drinking lager in the sun. I have never felt so like a pint of ice-cold lager, for some of the medicines I take make the mouth and throat very dry.

And after those pleasant car journeys, how delightful to sit down and partake of Betty's delicious meals, and afterwards talk about books and people over coffee.

Just before 8pm Peter drives me back to Foresterhill.

Shut up in Vulcan's Smithy

17.10.1991

That must have been a very loud thunderstorm in the middle of the night last week—for it woke most of the Stromnessians I have spoken to, as well as myself.

It was like what a tremendous artillery barrage must be, or a ton of stones getting emptied on the roof. It takes a lot to waken me in the middle of the night!

A few seconds later, there was a vivid stroke of lightning, then the thunderous voice spoke again.

Soon after that, I went to sleep again.

Some people are terrified of thunder—it must be a dread that goes right back to the beginning of the animal creation. Dogs get very upset by thunder, and cats get uneasy (though they don't create such a row about it).

Other folk—like myself—don't worry about it unduly.

Thunder and lightning is, I'm told, a daily experience in some parts of the world. In Orkney it is rare.

It must be twelve years ago—in summer too, if I'm not mistaken, and in broad daylight—that the mother and father of thunderstorms broke over Orkney. That was the wildest dance of rain, thunder and lightning that I ever experienced, and I seem to remember that one or two Stromness houses were flooded with rain-water instead of the more common sea-water.

It was, that thunderstorm, as if we were shut up in Vulcan's smithy and the god was using the hills round about Stromness—Miffia, Brinkie's Brae, Ernefea, Kringlafiold—for his anvil; and the lightning was his forge with the bellows blowing it into sudden incandescence.

School children who had never seen lightning nor heard thunder were terrified at the cosmic goings-on that morning. It may be that a farmer here and there had been complaining of drought. If so, they had their hearts' desire of rain that spectacular morning.

Compared to that, our little storm a few nights back was only a few fire-crackers going off.

Even more rare in Orkney than thunderstorms (thank goodness) are earth tremors.

But I distinctly remember, when I was very young, the 'old folk' speaking about the earthquake that trembled under Outertown and upset some ornaments from some farmhouse dressers. (That must have been sometime in the late 20s.) But it was the merest under-earth shiver, not the rouse and rage deep in the bowels of the earth that tears the delicate skin on which we humans blissfully exist for the most part; and brings down hall and hovel. That hideous pell-mell should warn us how fragile is our tenure of earth.

Nor do we Orcadians live in dread of volcanoes.

In fact, Orkney is about as safe a place as anywhere to inhabit.

Seventy Today

24.10.1991

When I was ten years old, to be seventy seemed to be very very old. You could never imagine yourself living to such an age! There were plenty of old men in Stromness, retired people and shopkeepers and ex-sailors.

They seemed to have been there always, and always would be fixed in time.

And the very young children too—they would always be the same— they would never grow old. (For an extraordinarily lucid account of this sense of timelessness that young people have, read Edwin Muir's autobiography.)

But time goes on shuttling its thread through us. By the time I was twenty, I knew there were such things as birth and death. There was plenty of the latter, for it was the time of the Second World War, and contemporaries were being cut down, young men who had gone to school with me.

I thought, all things considered, it was a wonder that I had reached the age of thirty, in 1951. But that was one of the best years ever for me, being at Newbattle Abbey College and being very happy for a whole winter and spring.

The strange thing is, time gets more confused as you get older. Of 1961, I don't remember too much, except that I enjoyed two pints of beer a day (sometimes more) with delightful companions, and the only work I did was write the occasional story or poem—but that was so enjoyable it could hardly be called work.

About 1971, when I was fifty, I don't recall too much either, I had flit from the delightful neighbourhood of Well Park to a kind of watch-tower house at Mayburn Court, and I seemed to spend a lot of time (apart from writing stories and poems) brewing ale of considerable potency in a plastic bin. In wild wintry weather there was no need to trudge to the bars...

I spent some months writing a novel called *Greenvoe* in that year.

About 1981, I am a bit vaguer still. The writing had become a kind of drug; I would have found life meaningless if I didn't sit at my writing desk for three hours or so every morning. How pleasant, having only to commute to work by coming downstairs and shoving the butter, marmalade pot and teapot to one side. That's about all I can remember of 1981 except that I spent three pleasant weeks in the Piper Ward of the Balfour.

Today I've reached the very advanced age of seventy. Those very old greybeards with sticks, from my childhood, belonged to what Edwin Muir called the 'fable'. A boy of ten is a part of the fable too, but he cannot realise that time has him by the hand and is hurrying him on through the seven stages that Shakespeare wrote about. But so it is, and we have to make the best of the things that have been given us under the sun.

Menace from the May Burn

14.11.1991

A bewildering variety of weathers, now at the beginning of November.

October built up to a tremendous climax on Hallow-E'en. Orkney was lashed with gale and sheets of driven rain.

The little May Burn, that in summer is only the gentlest song, overgrown with grass and often invisible, now came down at the side of Faravel, a brimming quarrelsome stream. All that good water, coming flush from the hills behind the town, that once would have been made into 'Old Orkney', going to waste...

Then when November came in, the weather decided to behave in a more seemly fashion.

Sunday, 3 November, was a beautiful late autumn day, with clouds and sunbursts and rainbows—one of those days when young folk (and the young in heart) love to walk along the West Shore and test themselves against the bracing Atlantic winds.

I had two visitors that evening, and they shook the rain from themselves. Certainly, they had walked through a prolonged heavy shower. But intense rain like that doesn't last long, I reassured them, over tea and cake. The wind would soon blow the sky clear and let the stars through.

We had a pleasant evening, talking about books mostly beside the cheerful fire.

But through our conversation came the steady pulse of the rain outside—an even denser rhythm—and a rather unusual wash and surge (different from the sound of the flood tide against the piers).

This is a very slow-moving raincloud, we agreed.

It was only when I was seeing them off at the open door that we could see what the rain was doing.

There's a close beside Mayburn Court that we used to call Distillery Close (though now for some reason it is called Alfred Terrace). Distillery Close was a tumultuous raging river! It rushed down the steps onto the street and swerved past the Museum and washed against the piers below.

The little pastoral May Burn couldn't take all the weight of rainwater. It had burst its banks and sent this raging torrent down past the doors ... it was such a ferocious outpouring that some of the folk in Distillery Close, coming home, couldn't get into their houses!

It was awesome and a bit frightening, that cloudburst.

We South-Enders have only seen that phenomenon once before, a dozen years ago or thereby...

In the morning, the flood had dried up again.

The wind turned into the north and blew cold. There was a salting of snow on Orphir and Hoy. At the corners of some houses lay a little drifted hail and sleet.

Yet it was pleasant, yesterday afternoon, walking through Stromness under the blue-and-silver surge of sky.

Later, there were fireworks and squibs along the street, and (I'm told) a big bonfire at Ness.

A Precarious Verge

5.12.1991

They say, as you get older you don't need so much sleep.

Well, it varies a good bit. Sometimes I wake up about five on a dark November morning, and can't get to sleep again, and the time between then and getting up can be long enough.

Switch on the bedside radio, and the same news bulletins come over and over—not much fun in that...

But through the blue curtain the light begins to pale, and on one recent morning there was a rectangle of gold above my bed—and yesterday morning I saw the sun coming up over Houton.

Those clear sunrises have been rare this autumn. There was a week or more of the lamentation of wind and rain recently that didn't exactly uplift the mind.

* * *

A full moon last weekend, and going to Kirkwall on Sunday morning the Bush and the Loch of Stenness were mingling their brimming waters.

There's something about a full flood. In childhood, how delightful it was to watch the harbour water lapping the topmost stones of Clouston's pier ... and what more desolating than a really low ebb... Those moods of childhood can linger on into age.

But there might come a time when high tides are not friendly any more, but will wipe out low-lying Pacific Islands and cause permanent floods in coastal communities.

The radio announcer one morning said that an iceberg the size of Wales had broken off from Antarctica and was drifting north, disintegrating in the warmer currents but causing unforeseen difficulties to shipping in the area.

An iceberg the size of Wales!... You immediately think of global warming—for who has ever heard of such a thing before?

Our grandchildren are going to be faced with problems we have never given the slightest thought to.

We live on a precarious and delicately-balanced verge.

The latest Orkney Heritage newsletter has a brief article on the subject by Ian MacInnes. We ought to ponder it carefully.

But humanity has an ingrained carelessness about such inconvenient possibilities. 'Things have been all right so far, for centuries. Best not

317

to worry about such things. They may never happen...' We may still be thinking along those lines when the waves are lapping across Graham Place.

True: we oughtn't to *brood* about such an image. At the same time, let the image not lie idle at the back of our minds.

* * *

Brinkie's Brae and the Outertown ridge certainly protect Stromness.

It was calm at Mayburn yesterday, but as I walked up the higher steps at Faravel the wind began. It was a cold bracing wind, not unpleasant, and on the summit of the Quildon road it was blowing harder still.

But it was dry, and the sunlight seemed more precious as it dwindled into the last month before the solstice.

'The Quirks of Blazoning Pens'

12.12.1991

Ballpoint pens are a strange breed, in that each pen has its own 'personality'. Sometimes they go like a sweetie; sometimes they limp along, making faint marks on the paper, causing bad temper and even spelling errors.

But I suppose we ought to be glad of them—especially considering the first pens we had to use in schooldays.

We must have been seven or eight when the first pens were dished out to us, but they were only for special purposes, writing 'compositions' or doing 'copy-books'.

Then the solemn ritual was gone through of the filling of the ink wells, probably from a big jar of ink (I forget exactly). Then the fitting of the nibs into the pen-holders. Then the messy business of writing—school children (especially boys) were forever blotting and scratching out.

The copy-books, I'm sure, were meant to instil in us a good uniform style of writing. We had to copy the copperplate script printed on top of the page—always a proverb that was meant to instil wisdom into us as we toiled away at our inky splatterings and splotches—'A burnt child dreads the fire'... 'Too many cooks spoil the broth'... etc.

Fountain pens were already available, but the pedants and bureaucrats who worked the school system in St Andrew's House or elsewhere decreed that ordinary pen-nibs gave the writing more character and style... So, when somebody gave us a Platignum fountain pen, for Christmas or a birthday, we wore it with pride in the breast pocket of our jackets; it was a kind of status symbol.

'Platinum,' we were assured by the older boys, 'is far more valuable than gold.'... Innocents that we were, we assumed that the 'Platignum' pen had a platinum nib. We never questioned how, therefore, the 'Platignum' pen cost only one and six (or in the new money, seven and a half pence).

Those school pen-nibs too had personalities of their own. Some flowed smoothly enough, others scratched and spat out little gobbets of blue-black ink. If that happened, you had to summon up your courage and ask the teacher for a new nib—otherwise the page would be a frightful mess.

At last, when the task—composition or copy-book—was over, we laid a sheet of blotting paper over the wet ink. And we sighed, maybe, for the days in infant school when we wrote with slate pencils on slates. The well-brought-up boys and girls cleaned their slates with a damp cloth, but most of us ragamuffins spat on the slate and rubbed it dry with the sleeves of our jerseys.

We never paused to wonder at the word 'pen' or 'pencil'. It must derive from the feather or quill from the wing of a large bird like a goose, that people were still writing with last century in counting houses and offices all over the western world... Then, when the tip got worn or blunt, one sharpened it anew with a pen-knife.